Diversity and First Nations Issues in Canada

SECOND EDITION

John Roberts
Darion Boyington
Shahé S. Kazarian

emp

2012
Emond Montgomery Publications
Toronto, Canada

Emond Montgomery Publications Limited
60 Shaftesbury Avenue
Toronto ON M4T 1A3
http://www.emp.ca/highered

Printed in Canada.
Reprinted July 2014.

We acknowledge the financial support of the Government of Canada through the Canada Book Fund for our publishing activities.

Acquisitions editor: Bernard Sandler
Developmental editor: Sarah Gleadow
Developmental and copy editor: Jamie Bush
Production editor: Jim Lyons
Assistant production editors: Andrew Gordon and Cindy Fujimoto
Permissions editor: Maria DeCambra
Proofreader: Claudia Forgas
Typesetter: Tara Wells
Indexer: Paula Pike
Cover designer: Tara Wells
Cover image: Maxim Tupikov, iStockphoto.com

Library and Archives Canada Cataloguing in Publication

Roberts, John A., 1944-
    Diversity and First Nations issues in Canada / John Roberts, Darion Boyington, Shahé S. Kazarian. — 2nd ed.

Includes index.
ISBN 978-1-55239-490-8

    1. Police-community relations—Canada.   2. Multiculturalism—
Canada.   3. Native peoples—Canada.   4. Law enforcement—
Canada.   5. Police—Canada.   6. Discrimination—Canada.
I. Boyington, Darion   II. Kazarian, Shahe S., 1945-   III. Title.

HV8157.R63 2011   363.2'30971   C2011-907903-8

Contents

PART I   DIVERSITY ISSUES IN CANADA

PART II   FIRST NATIONS ISSUES IN CANADA

Preface

The second edition of *Diversity and First Nations Issues in Canada* has been extensively revised and updated. As the new census figures illustrate, Canada's over 31.2 million people compose a cultural, ethnic, and linguistic mosaic unlike any other in the world.

Diversity and First Nations Issues continues to support college and university courses that combine elements of diversity issues in law enforcement and First Nations issues. Part I of the text explores the basic concepts of diversity, multiculturalism, and human rights in a Canadian context. A portrait emerges of the nature and scope of Canadian diversity, and its many benefits to our society. The rights and freedoms enshrined in Canadian human rights legislation are discussed, and the role of police in upholding these is highlighted. Readers gain an understanding of cultural and religious diversity, and a greater awareness of topics including family violence, mental health issues, and developmental disabilities. Part I concludes with an in-depth examination of the efforts of Canadian police services both to diversify the face of policing itself and to increase the diversity competency of their officers. Throughout Part I, the focus remains on the relationship between law enforcement and the diverse communities they serve—specifically, perceptions of police in the community, the evolution of policing culture, and the benefits and challenges of diversity for policing, including the strategies and skills needed for policing with diversity competency. A greater awareness and understanding of diversity, and a focus on our many similarities rather than our differences, is critical to helping reduce conflict and misunderstanding.

The socio-economic issues facing First Nations people today are a legacy of colonization and forced assimilation. Part II of the text begins by contrasting pre-contact First Nations and European cultures, laying the foundation necessary for understanding their past and present interactions and relations. The treaty process in which Aboriginal people lost vast areas of their traditional lands is explored, setting the stage for a discussion of land claims, which are commonly misunderstood by many members of the Canadian public. An examination of the residential school system—a shameful period of Canadian history that many Canadians are only now beginning to understand, following a historic apology to survivors by the Canadian government—illustrates the historical attitude toward Aboriginal people and informs a discussion of the effects of Aboriginal people's long history of mistreatment in Canada, which are felt to this day. Even as they form the fastest-growing segment of the Canadian population, Aboriginal people continue to be overrepresented in the criminal justice system, and experience inequalities in education, income and labour market participation, and physical and mental heath and well-being. Although there have been some improvements in recent years—including changes within the justice system to address the unique needs of Aboriginal offenders—the situation remains critical. The future promises both new challenges and opportunities to overcome existing ones.

As always, we have received excellent professional guidance from the team at Emond Montgomery. To Bernard Sandler, Sarah Gleadow, Jamie Bush, and Jim Lyons—thanks again. To Paul Emond—it's always a pleasure.

John Roberts
Darion Boyington
Shahé Kazarian

November 2011

PART I

Diversity Issues in Canada

A Portrait of Canadian Diversity

THE CONCEPT OF MULTICULTURALISM

The term **multiculturalism** has different meanings and associations. It can suggest an ideal of cultural variety, and it can describe the actual state of a society—its condition of having a diverse population. Multiculturalism exists in many countries, including Australia, the United Kingdom, and the United States. In some of these places, it is a cause for celebration as well as a plain fact. Only in Canada, however, is multiculturalism both a national ideology and a state policy. Canada is the first nation to make a policy of multiculturalism part of its national constitution (Kazarian, Crichlow, & Bradford, 2007, p. 39).

THE CONCEPT OF DIVERSITY

Diversity refers, in a general sense, to the variety of human qualities among different people and groups (University of Maryland, 2000).

More specifically, it refers to the ethnic, social, or gender variety in a community of people. When we consider the diversity of a community, we look at its members in two aspects or dimensions: primary and secondary. *Primary* dimensions include a person's age, **ethnicity**, gender, physical abilities and qualities, race, and sexual orientation. *Secondary* dimensions include the person's educational background, geographic location, income, marital status, parental status, religious beliefs, and work experience. Secondary dimensions are less fixed than primary ones (Kazarian et al., 2007, p. 4).

FOUR STATE IDEOLOGIES

Host cultures—cultures that receive immigrants and refugees—tend to have one of four ideologies, or belief systems, regarding how to incorporate the new members of their society. These four ideologies are as follows: multiculturalism ideology, civic ideology, assimilation ideology, and ethnist ideology.

CHAPTER OBJECTIVES

After completing this chapter, you should be able to:

- Understand the concepts of multiculturalism and diversity.
- Discuss the four state ideologies of host countries.
- Define Canada's concept of multiculturalism.
- Understand Canadian society, immigration trends, and Canadian diversity.

---

multiculturalism
a policy relating to or designed for a combination of several distinct cultures

diversity
the variety of human qualities among different people and groups

ethnicity
the culture of origin with which an individual or group identifies within a multicultural context

Multiculturalism Ideology

multiculturalism ideology
ideology that recognizes and supports people of diversity in maintaining or promoting their diversity, providing that their practices do not clash with the laws of the nation

values
standards or principles; ideas about the worth or importance of certain qualities, especially those accepted by a particular group

The **multiculturalism ideology** supports people of diversity in maintaining or promoting their distinctive culture, provided that this culture does not clash with the criminal and civil laws of the nation. Four main principles are associated with the ideology of multiculturalism. First, people of diversity are expected to adopt the public **values** of the host nation: its democratic ideals, constitutional and human rights provisions, and civil and criminal codes. A second principle is that the private values of individual citizens are protected. Private values are the attitudes and beliefs that people hold in private life, shown in their relations with family and friends as well as in their wider social circle. A third principle of multiculturalism ideology is that the state recognizes multicultural values and protects them from interference by other people and by the state itself. The fourth principle is that the state should fund the ethnocultural activities of both its long-standing citizens and its newcomers, since both groups contribute to the state through taxation.

Civic Ideology

civic ideology
ideology that subscribes to multiculturalism ideology principles but does not support state funding to maintain and promote ethnocultural diversity

The second approach a society may take to the diversity of its citizens is the **civic ideology**. This ideology is the same as the multiculturalism one except that it doesn't support state funding for the promotion of ethnocultural diversity. Great Britain is an example of a state that supports civic ideology.

Assimilation Ideology

assimilation ideology
ideology that expects people of diversity to relinquish their culture and linguistic identity and adopt the culture of the host state

The **assimilation ideology** is a homogenization or "melting pot" ideology. According to this ideology, newcomers to a country should give up their cultural and linguistic identities and adopt the culture of the host state. In return, the state protects the private values of individual citizens while reserving the right to limit the expression of these values under certain circumstances. The United States supports assimilation ideology.

Ethnist Ideology

ethnist ideology
ideology that expects people of diversity to assimilate, but the state defines which groups should assimilate and thus which ones are not rightful members of the state

The **ethnist ideology** is similar to the assimilation ideology except that the state exerts more control over which groups are permitted to assimilate (Kazarian et al., 2007, p. 39). For example, the state may require that an immigrant be part of a certain ethnicity, religion, or race to be accepted as a citizen. Japan and Israel subscribe to ethnist ideology.

EXERCISE 1

1. Which of the four state ideologies does Canada practise? Give reasons for your answer.
2. For each of the following statements, indicate whether it represents a multiculturalism, civic, assimilation, or ethnist ideology, or a combination of more than one:
   a. Individuals from diverse countries should be encouraged to maintain their cultural heritages.

b. Canada is a better place because people of various ethnic backgrounds come to live here.

c. Canadians would be better off if all immigrants abandoned their cultural and linguistic identities.

d. The government should not support ethnic-language radio, television, or newspapers.

e. Canada should be selective about which immigrants it accepts.

f. Multiculturalism is Canada's main source of political, economic, and social wealth.

g. Immigrants should be forced to learn English or French.

h. Newcomers should combine the best of their heritage culture with the best of the host culture.

i. Multiculturalism is "mosaic madness."

j. The host state should recognize foreign professional credentials (for example, medical degrees) as equivalent to Canadian credentials.

CANADA AND THE CONCEPT OF MULTICULTURALISM

Canada has been defined by its dominant cultures. This occurred in three distinct historical stages:

1. Canada as a Colony of the British Empire

   a. An external authority in England exercised sovereignty.

   b. Canadians had limited democratic rights, and were governed by a political elite.

   c. The dominant cultures were English and French, although the British sought to assimilate the French.

2. Canada as an Independent "White Dominion" in the British Empire/ Commonwealth

   a. Sovereignty was increasingly exercised within the Dominion.

   b. Canadians had full democratic rights, and were governed by Parliament.

   c. The dominant culture was British, although immigrants began arriving to colonize the West.

   d. Commitment to the British Empire and a policy of assimilation still produced cultural uniformity in Canada (except in Quebec). Canadians were British subjects until 1947.

3. Canada as a Fully Sovereign and Independent Nation-State

   a. Canada became completely independent of British sovereignty (1931–1949).

   b. The divide between French and English was temporarily settled through constitutional reform.

   c. European immigration slowed while people from other parts of the world began to immigrate to Canada.

    d. The subsequent immigration boom caused a substantial demographic shift in the latter half of the 20th century.

    e. The assimilation of French Canadians and Aboriginal peoples was eventually replaced by the concept of multiculturalism.

EQUAL RIGHTS AND THE POLICY OF MULTICULTURALISM

Canada faces a difficulty when it comes to diversity issues. On the one hand, Canadians live in a rights-based culture; we assume that all citizens should be treated equally under civil law and that no one will receive any unearned benefits because of his or her identity. This is the rule of law upon which Canada was founded.

But there is tension between this assumption of equal rights and the principles of Canada's multiculturalism, which supports a cultural group's rights to retain its values and way of life within the wider sphere of Canadian society. The equal-rights culture focuses on the individual; multiculturalism focuses on the group.

Multiculturalism became a formal policy in Canada under Prime Minister Trudeau in 1971. The policy became law with the *Canadian Multiculturalism Act* of 1988. Further protections for minorities are enshrined in s. 15 of the *Canadian Charter of Rights and Freedoms* (1982). These formal policies and laws are meant to address the needs of new Canadians and disadvantaged groups. However, the government's need to interpret multiculturalism from an equal-rights point of view—that is, from the standpoint that everyone is fundamentally equal—has weakened the formal policy of multiculturalism as a tool for addressing inequalities and **discrimination** related to culture. How does it weaken it? For one thing, an assumption of general equality can blur our understanding of just how deeply disadvantaged an immigrant population can be. Further, the equal-rights perspective is sometimes unaccepting of cultural practices that do not meet Canadian standards of equal treatment for all individuals. At what point, for example, does the government discourage the traditional custom of a minority group in Canada—perhaps a custom related to gender—on the grounds that it violates the liberal ideal of equal rights?

Informal multiculturalism refers to the popular idea of multiculturalism held by people in a society where diversity exists. In Canada, informal multiculturalism accepts social diversity as a given and takes it for granted that the relative lack of success of people from disadvantaged groups is owing to the persistence of discriminatory and stereotypical attitudes rather than to the failings of particular formalized policies. According to this viewpoint, the persistence of discriminatory attitudes needs to be examined, as do the ways in which the imbalances of power between minority and majority populations work themselves out in daily life (Baxter, 2003).

discrimination
a process by which a person is deprived of equal access to privileges and opportunities available to others because of prejudice

EXERCISE 2

After examining the historical stages of Canada's cultural development, discussed above (that is, its evolution from colony to independent nation-state), can you explain how a multiculturalism policy came to emerge in the final stage?

CONCEPT OF THE HOST COMMUNITY

A **host community** is sometimes called the host culture or nation, the dominant culture or society, or the majority culture. A host community consists of people long established in a country, though the history of their **settlement patterns** may differ. Whether descended from English settlers, from First Nations people, or from more recent immigrants, the members of a host community determine the basic character and attitudes of the society.

Host communities are made up of groups of people who have the power and influence to change attitudes toward the less established communities in the society. These people set the tone for how the rest of society views and deals with the less powerful *other*. In Canada, for example, the host culture might begin to change its views about the rights of gay and lesbian communities and cease to view marriage as an exclusively heterosexual institution, with the result that, after a time, legislation is introduced allowing for gay and lesbian marriages. Host communities also determine immigration policies—that is, who is a desirable addition to the host culture and who is undesirable. Finally, by assimilating newcomers and expecting them to accept its established patterns, the host community influences the settlement and adaptation patterns of those it accepts as newcomers. And the influence doesn't only go one way. Majority host communities are influenced in turn by the minority groups they come in contact with.

host community
comprises groups of people who have the power and influence to shape attitudes toward the remaining groups in society

settlement patterns
the variety of ways people physically establish themselves in a country, whether born there or as immigrants

ACCULTURATION ORIENTATIONS OF HOST COMMUNITIES

Acculturation refers to the process by which one cultural group acquires from another group new cultural attributes that may eventually be absorbed into its own system. With immigrant groups, host communities adopt one or more of the following acculturation orientations (in other words, approaches to cultural adaptation):

- An **integrationist** host community encourages immigrants both to adopt important features of the host culture and to maintain aspects of their heritage culture.

- An **exclusionary** host community is intolerant of the wishes of immigrants or other cultures to maintain their heritage cultures. At the same time, it does not allow them wholly to adopt the host culture. Host community members are ambivalent about newcomers.

- An **assimilationist** host community demands that immigrants give up their cultural identity and adapt totally to the host culture. In other words, new ethnic communities are expected to participate in ethnocultural institutions that are not their own (Kallen, 2003). Over time, the host culture accepts as full-fledged citizens those who have been culturally absorbed.

- A **segregationist** host community distances itself from immigrants and their cultures. It allows them to maintain their heritage culture, but would prefer that they return to their countries of origin. Members of the host community believe that immigrants "can never be incorporated culturally or socially as rightful members of the host society" (Bourhis et al., 1997).

acculturation
process of change in the cultural patterns of an ethnic group as a result of contact with other ethnic groups

integrationist
supportive of immigrants' adopting features of the host culture while maintaining aspects of their heritage culture

exclusionary
intolerant of immigrants' heritage culture and of immigration in general

assimilationist
intolerant of immigrants' heritage culture, demanding that they relinquish the culture and adopt the host culture

segregationist
opposed to immigrants and other cultures, preferring that immigrants return to their countries of origin

ACCULTURATION ORIENTATIONS OF SETTLER GROUPS

Immigrants exhibit one of four modes of acculturation—marginalization, assimilation, separation, and integration—which together form the acronym MASI:

marginalization
simultaneous rejection of the culture of origin and the host culture

assimilation
absorption of groups of different cultures into the main culture

separation
individual rejection of the host culture and maintenance of the culture of origin

integration
embrace of the host culture of settlement and continued maintenance of culture of origin

- **Marginalization** occurs when people reject the host culture as well as their heritage culture, disenchanted with both.
- **Assimilation** involves giving up one's traditional culture in favour of the host culture.
- **Separation** occurs when an individual rejects the host culture and maintains his or her culture of origin.
- **Integration** occurs when immigrants at once embrace the host culture and maintain their culture of origin.

Integration is generally seen as the most desirable mode of cultural adaptation (Berry, 2006). Immigrants who adapt in this way show good levels of psychological adjustment and personal satisfaction. These are important considerations from an economic perspective and also from a law-and-order perspective; members of ethnic groups who are integrated are less likely to engage in disorderly or criminal activity. Because integrationists do not practise separation—do not isolate themselves from the host culture—their allegiance to their heritage culture does not lessen their commitment to the welfare of the host nation (Berry & Sam, 1997).

HISTORY OF IMMIGRATION AND DIVERSITY IN CANADA

Immigration is and always has been an important factor in Canadian society. The 2006 census reports that 1,109,980 people immigrated to Canada in the five-year period between 2001 and 2006, an average of about 200,000 people yearly. This process began several centuries ago, with the arrival of English and French explorers and settlers. At first contact between Aboriginal peoples and European peoples in Canada, there were 56 Aboriginal nations speaking more than 30 languages. The French and English colonized the eastern part of what is now Canada, and signed treaties with First Nations peoples acknowledging Aboriginal nationhood.

In 1867, the English and French languages were given constitutional status at Confederation. Bilingualism became the core of Canada's approach to diversity. From the late 1800s to the mid-1900s, Canada's immigration policy was based on supplying a labour pool for settlement and agriculture; after this, immigration policy was based on establishing a Canadian industrial base. Canada recognized the right of minorities to maintain their culture and traditions, with some exceptions, such as the Japanese during the Second World War.

In 1950, as a result of the Massey-Levesque Commission, which linked cultural diversity and Canadian identity, ethnocultural diversity gradually came to be understood as an essential ingredient in a distinct Canadian society. At that time, 92 percent of Canada's population growth was the result of birth rate. By 2001, immigration had outpaced the natural birth rate, and accounted for 53 percent of overall population growth.

The 1960 *Canadian Bill of Rights* outlawed discrimination by federal agencies on the grounds of race, national origin, colour, religion, and gender. This policy was reflected in the *Immigration Act* of 1960, which stated that immigrants were not to be refused entry into Canada on the grounds of race, national origin, colour, or country of origin. This Act resulted in more immigration from Southern Europe, from Africa, and from the West Indies.

The *Official Languages Act* of 1969 required the government to give equal status, rights, and privileges to both official languages in federal institutions. It further required that these institutions must serve Canadians in the official language of their choice.

The 1970s and 1980s saw substantial numbers of refugees admitted to this country. In some cases, this was a result of Canada's official multiculturalism policy, established in 1971, which provided for programs and services to help individuals from diverse cultures overcome barriers to their full participation in Canadian society.

The 1982 *Canadian Charter of Rights and Freedoms* granted parents who are members of an English or French linguistic minority in the communities where they live to have their children educated in the official language of their choice. Section 27 of the Charter stated that the courts were to interpret the constitution in a manner that would preserve and enhance the multicultural nature of Canada:

> 27. This Charter shall be interpreted in a manner consistent with the preservation and enhancement of the multicultural heritage of Canadians.

Jean Chrétien, as minister of justice, commented on the importance of the Charter in protecting the rights of a multicultural and ethnically diverse population (1982, p. v):

> In a free and democratic society, it is important that citizens know exactly what their rights and freedoms are, and where to turn for help and advice in the event that those freedoms are denied or those rights infringed. In a country like Canada—vast and diverse, with 11 governments, 2 official languages, and a variety of ethnic origins—the only way to provide equal protection for everyone is to enshrine those basic rights and freedoms in the Constitution.

The concept of diversity expanded from language, ethnicity, race, and religion to include gender, sexual orientation, ability (or disability), and age. The rights of diverse groups are enshrined in other Canadian legal responses to diversity, including the following federal legislation:

- the *Canadian Human Rights Act,*
- the *Employment Equity Act,* and
- the *Canadian Multiculturalism Act.*

Provinces have responded to diversity issues by passing similar legislation, including pay equity acts, and developing programs to promote diversity. On the international stage, Canada is signatory to, among others, the following agreements:

- the *Universal Declaration of Human Rights,* and
- the *International Covenant on Economic, Social and Cultural Rights.*

REFUGEE POLICIES

Article 1 of the 1951 United Nations *Protocol Relating to the Status of Refugees* (1983) defines a refugee as any person who

> owing to well-founded fear of being persecuted for reasons of race, religion, nationality, membership of a particular social group or political opinion, is outside the country of nationality and is unable or, owing to such fear, is unwilling to avail himself of the protection of that country; or who, not having a nationality and being outside the country of his former habitual residence as a result of such events, is unable or, owing to such fear, is unwilling to return to it.

Welcoming refugees should be seen not as an immigration issue, but as a human rights issue.

Canada has been home to refugees since before Confederation. The United Empire Loyalists, for example, flocked to Canada (along with many non-British subjects) during the American Revolution in 1776. Similarly, English Puritans found refuge in Canada in the 1600s after suffering religious persecution in their native country. Scots settled in Canada after the Highland Clearances of the 1600s, the Irish during the potato famine of the 1800s, Russians as a result of the Bolshevik Revolution, and Armenians after 1923. The origins of Canada's refugees continue to change. Refugees just after the Second World War were primarily from Eastern Europe. Nowadays, the majority come from places such as South Asia, Somalia, Cambodia, Vietnam, and Guatemala.

Canada's humanitarian tradition with respect to refugees continues to be strong. From 1995 to 2004, Canada welcomed more than 2.1 million immigrants, among them 265,685 refugees (12 percent of all immigrants) who were granted permanent residence (Canadian Council for Refugees, 2005). In 2010, Canada gave permanent residence to 24,000 refugees (Citizens for Public Justice, 2011).

refugee policy
humanitarian policy, based on the United Nations definition of a refugee, that assesses eligibility for entry to a country based on refugee status

Immigration and refugee policies need periodic renovation, and such changes have occurred in Canada. The 1976 Canadian *Immigration Act* introduced a **refugee policy** that formalized the country's approach to identifying and selecting refugees. The Act identified three routes to granting qualified refugees permission to resettle in Canada: overseas selection, special programs, and inland refugee-status determination. Amendments passed in 1995 to the *Immigration Act* have made it easier to deport a permanent resident with a serious criminal background.

In 1996, a review of Canada's refugee and immigration policy was initiated with the aim of making fundamental policy reforms and introducing new legislation. This resulted in the reintroduction of the *Immigration and Refugee Protection Act* of 2001. This Act and its accompanying regulations had the following aims:

- to be simpler, more modern, and more coherent than previous legislation;
- to respond effectively to Canada's global challenges of the 21st century;
- to ensure that Canada can preserve immigration as a source of diversity, richness, and openness to the world;
- to enhance Canada's advantage in the global competition for skilled workers;
- to maintain and enhance the country's strong humanitarian tradition;

- to deter migrant trafficking and to punish those who engage in this form of slavery; and

- to maintain confidence in the integrity of the immigration and refugee-protection program.

The main reason for the most recent changes to the country's refugee policy is to clear the backlog of refugee cases. On June 29, 2010, Bill C-11, the *Balanced Refugee Reform Act*, received royal assent. This Act affects the Immigration and Refugee Board of Canada (IRB) and is intended to improve Canada's asylum system, resettle more refugees from abroad, and make it easier for refugees to start their lives in Canada (Citizenship and Immigration Canada, 2011).

EXERCISE 3

Examine the following quotation. Do you feel that acceptance and respect for diverse cultures have to be legislated? Do you believe that, with increasing immigration, this respect and acceptance might not be given so readily by Canadians? Give reasons for your answer.

> Canada's approach to diversity is based on the belief that the common good is best served when everyone is accepted and respected for who they are, and that ultimately makes for a resilient, more harmonious and more creative society. (Canadian Heritage, 2001)

CANADA'S ABORIGINAL PEOPLES

As mentioned at the beginning of this chapter, there was a significant Aboriginal presence in Canada when the first Europeans arrived. Aboriginal cultures were greatly affected by contact with Europeans. From the first, Aboriginal nations were at a disadvantage. They faced social changes, new technologies, and imported diseases, as well as the Europeans' quest for new lands.

The French and the British were the main European influences in North America from the 1500s to the early 1900s. They competed for dominance by establishing settlements. Both sides courted First Nations peoples in their quest for trade and in their battles with each other over control of the continent. European settlement gradually pushed First Nations peoples off the land, and Aboriginals became dependent upon Europeans for their livelihood. Hunting skills disappeared, languages were lost, traditions were abolished. Aboriginals came to be seen as wards of the government, unable to take care of themselves. Missionaries moved in to "save" the lost Aboriginal souls, one result of which was the infamous residential school system in which many Aboriginal children were physically and sexually abused.

In the second half of the 20th century, oppressed peoples around the world challenged the remnants of colonialism and demanded equality. Some of these peoples proclaimed their independence and forged new nations. Others, such as the First Nations, Inuit, and Métis of Canada, demanded the right to sovereignty and self-determination within the framework of Canada (Roberts, 2006).

Attempts to address the needs of Canada's Aboriginal peoples began in 1973. This was when Aboriginal land rights, based on a group's traditional use and occupancy of a certain area of land, were first recognized. In 1982, the *Charter of Rights and Freedoms* recognized and affirmed the treaty rights of Aboriginal peoples to protect their cultures, traditions, and languages. In 1996, the Royal Commission on Aboriginal Peoples presented a comprehensive five-volume report to Parliament identifying the legal, political, social, economic, and cultural issues that need to be addressed to ensure the future survival of Canada's First Nations, Inuit, and Métis. Two years later, the government responded with a plan to work in partnership with Canada's Aboriginal peoples to improve their health, housing, and public safety; to strengthen their economic development; and to help them implement self-government. As of 2011, the government's plan is being carried out, but the limited scope of the plan and the wide-ranging needs of Aboriginal peoples make progress difficult.

Aboriginal peoples account for a significant portion of the Canadian population. The 2006 census revealed that 1,678,200 individuals in Canada reported Aboriginal ancestries, while descendants of the First Peoples of Canada represented 5.4 percent of the country's population (Statistics Canada, 2006a). Those claiming North American Indian ancestry numbered about 1.3 million people, making them the largest Aboriginal ancestry group. Another 409,100 individuals reported Métis ancestry, and 65,900 individuals reported Inuit ancestry.

Aboriginal cultures will be lost if modern governments do not help protect them by enabling Aboriginal peoples to continue their traditional ways of life on their ancestral lands. In both North America and Australia, hundreds of Aboriginal languages and cultural practices are either extinct or endangered. If the rights of Aboriginals to freely hunt, fish, or travel are not restored or maintained, their culture will disappear (University of Maryland, 2000).

EXERCISE 4

Conduct a research study into some of the problems facing Aboriginal peoples today. Use headings such as

a. loss of language
b. health issues
c. interaction with the justice system
d. education levels
e. unemployment
f. urban migration
g. land claims issues.

How is the government involved in addressing these issues, and how are Aboriginal peoples dealing with these issues apart from government initiatives?

IMMIGRATION TRENDS

This section examines immigration into Canada after the turn of the 21st century. Unless otherwise indicated, statistics are from Statistics Canada (2006c).

Ethnic Origins

Ethnic origin, as defined in the census, refers to the ethnic or cultural group to which an individual's ancestors belonged. The 1901 census recorded about 25 different ethnic groups in Canada. At that time, people of either Aboriginal, British, or French origins made up the majority of the ethnic groups reported.

The list of ethnic origins in 2006 includes much greater variety (see Table 1.1); more than 200 different ethnic origins were reported in Canada's 2006 census (Statistics Canada, 2006c). Among these were the groups associated with Canada's Aboriginal peoples and with the European groups—the English, French, Scottish, and Irish—that first settled in Canada. There were also groups associated with immigrants who came to Canada over the last century: Germans, Italians, Chinese, Ukrainians, Dutch, Polish, and East Indians, among others. Among newer groups reported in 2006 were Montserratians from the Caribbean, and Chadians, Gambians, and Zambians from Africa. Table 1.2 shows the most prevalent ethnic origins in Canada, and how these origins have changed over three generations. The statistics concerning the third generation reflect responses to the 2006 census.

By 2006, 11 Canadian groups with distinct ethnic origins had passed the 1 million mark. The largest group, just over 10 million people, reported their ethnic origin as Canadian, either alone or with other origins.

Visible Minorities

Visible minorities are legally recognized in Canada; they are one of four groups designated under the *Employment Equity Act.* (The other three such groups are women, Aboriginal people, and people with disabilities.) The 2006 census enumerated 5,068,100 individuals who identified themselves as members of the **visible minority** population (Statistics Canada, 2006b). They made up 16.2 percent of the total population of Canada (see Figure 1.1).

visible minority
individuals, other than Aboriginal peoples, who are non-Caucasian in race or non-white in colour

The visible minority population in Canada has grown steadily over the past 25 years. In 1981, the estimated 1.1 million people in this group represented 4.7 percent of Canada's total population. In 1991, 2.5 million people were members of a visible minority group, 9.4 percent of the population. This number increased to 3.2 million in 1996, which was 11.2 percent of the total population. By 2001, their numbers had reached an estimated 3,983,800—13.4 percent of the total population. Between 2001 and 2006, the rate of growth of the visible minority population was 27.2 percent, five times greater than the whole population's 5.4 percent rate of growth.

The 2006 census showed that three-quarters (75 percent) of the immigrants who arrived in Canada between 2001 and 2006 belonged to a visible minority group. If current trends continue, Canada's visible minority population will continue to grow more quickly than the rest of the population; by 2017, according to projections, visible minority groups could represent roughly one-fifth (20 percent) of Canada's total population.

The Distribution of Visible Minority Groups

South Asians—people from the southern part of Asia, including, among others, people from Bangladesh, East India, Pakistan, and Sri Lanka—became Canada's

Table 1.1   Ethnic Origins, 2006 Counts, for Canada, Provinces, and Territories

	Total responses	Single responses	Multiple responses
	number		
Total population	31,241,030	18,319,580	12, 921,445
Ethnic origin			
Canadian	10,066,290	5,748,725	4,317,570
English	6,570,015	1,367,125	5,202,890
French	4,941,210	1,230,535	3,710,675
Scottish	4,719,850	568,515	4,151,340
Irish	4,354,155	491,030	3,863,125
German	3,179,425	670,640	2,508,785
Italian	1,445,335	741,045	704,285
Chinese	1,346,510	1,135,365	211,145
North American Indian	1,253,615	512,150	741,470
Ukrainian	1,209,085	300,590	908,495
Dutch (Netherlands)	1,035,965	303,400	732,560
Polish	984,565	269,375	715,190
East Indian	962,665	780,175	182,495
Russian	500,600	98,245	402,355
Welsh	440,965	27,115	413,855
Filipino	436,190	321,390	114,800
Norwegian	432,515	44,790	387,725
Portuguese	410,850	262,230	148,625
Métis	409,065	77,295	331,770
Swedish	334,765	28,445	306,325
Spanish	325,730	67,475	258,225
American (USA)	316,350	28,785	287,565
Hungarian (Magyar)	315,510	88,685	226,820
Jewish	315,120	134,045	181,070
Greek	242,685	145,250	97,435
Jamaican	231,110	134,320	96,785
Danish	200,035	33,770	166,265
Austrian	194,225	27,060	167,195

Source: Statistics Canada, Census of Population, 2006. http://www40.statcan.gc.ca/l01/cst01/demo26a-eng.htm.

largest visible minority group in 2006, surpassing the Chinese for the first time (see Table 1.3).

The census listed 1,262,865 individuals who identified themselves as South Asian, an increase of 37.7 percent from the 917,100 individuals listed in 2001. They represented 24.9 percent of all visible minorities, or 4 percent of the total population of Canada. By comparison, between 2001 and 2006, the number of individuals in Canada who identified themselves as Chinese increased 18.2 percent, from 1,029,400 to 1,216,570. This group accounted for about 24 percent of the visible minority population and 3.9 percent of the total Canadian population. The number of people in Canada identifying themselves as Black rose 18.4 percent between 2001 and 2006, from 662,200 to 783,795, making them the third largest visible minority group. They accounted for 15.5 percent of the visible minority population and 2.5 percent of the total Canadian population in 2006 (Statistics Canada, 2006c).

Table 1.2   Top 10 Ethnic Origins[1] by Generational Status for People Aged 15 Years and Over, Canada, 2006

First generation			Second generation			Third generation or more		
Ethnic origin	*number*	*%*	*Ethnic origin*	*number*	*%*	*Ethnic origin*	*number*	*%*
Chinese	916,845	15.0	English	1,035,145	25.8	Canadian	7,236,370	46.6
East Indian	612,460	10.0	Scottish	635,600	15.9	English	3,794,250	24.4
English	547,865	8.9	Canadian	613,445	15.3	French	3,530,505	22.7
Italian	366,205	6.0	German	524,645	13.1	Scottish	2,865,800	18.4
German	352,805	5.8	Irish	496,990	12.4	Irish	2,755,420	17.7
Filipino	288,515	4.7	Italian	439,275	11.0	German	1,604,225	10.3
Scottish	271,545	4.4	French	284,900	7.1	North American Indian	813,405	5.2
Irish	230,975	3.8	Dutch (Netherlands)	253,325	6.3			
Polish	213,715	3.5	Ukrainian	212,860	5.3	Ukrainian	642,955	4.1
Portuguese	195,480	3.2	Polish	203,725	5.1	Dutch (Netherlands)	376,555	2.4
						Polish	364,980	2.3

Note:

1. Table shows total responses. Because some respondents reported more than one ethnic origin, the sum of the total responses is greater than the total population, or 100%.

Source: Statistics Canada, Census of Population, 2006. http://www12.statcan.ca/census-recensement/2006/as-sa/97-562/table/t1-eng.cfm.

EXERCISE 5

Research one of the predominant visible minority groups in Canada (South Asians, Chinese, or Blacks) and list reasons why the group may have immigrated to Canada. Use the headings

- social conditions in country of origin
- economic conditions in country of origin
- religious freedom concerns
- employment opportunity concerns
- educational opportunity concerns
- health concerns.

Discuss ways in which immigration to Canada may have either relieved or failed to relieve some of these conditions or concerns.

Metropolitan Areas and Visible Minority Groups

According to the 2006 census, 95.9 percent of visible minority groups resided in Canada's metropolitan areas, compared with 68.1 percent of the country's total population that lived in these areas. In 2006, at least 100,000 visible minority persons lived in each of Toronto, Vancouver, Montreal, Calgary, Ottawa-Gatineau, Edmonton, and Winnipeg. Six in ten visible minority individuals resided in either Toronto (42.9 percent of the population) or Vancouver (41.7 percent of the population) (Statistics Canada, 2006c).

As in 2001, Toronto in 2006 had the highest share of visible minority residents of all the metropolitan areas of Canada (see Table 1.4). This was because a large share of visible minority immigrants settled there between 2001 and 2006. During

Figure 1.1   Number and Share of Visible Minority Persons in Canada, 1981–2006

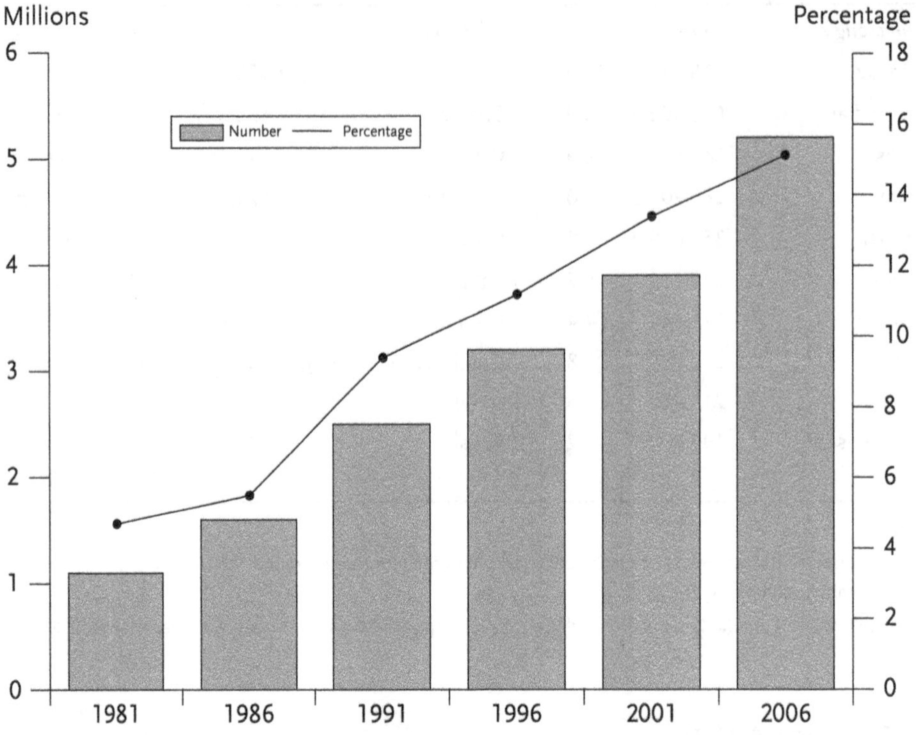

Source: Statistics Canada, censuses of population, 1981–2006. http://www12.statcan.ca/census-recensement/2006/as-sa/97-562/figures/c1-eng.cfm.

this period, Toronto took in 40.4 percent of all newcomers to Canada; 81.9 percent of these newcomers belonged to a visible minority group. The two largest visible minority groups in Toronto in 2006 were South Asians (684,100) and Chinese (486,300).

Other Trends Among Immigrant Groups

Some notable trends among newcomers to this country, according to Statistics Canada (2006c), include the following:

• As of 2006, the number of immigrants who mostly use the English language at home reached 49.9 percent of the total immigrant population aged 17 and over. This compares with 66.4 percent of the total number of people in Canada who claim that English is the language they most often use at home. Of the unofficial languages, the Chinese languages (635,680) and Punjabi (199,760) are the ones most commonly used as a first language at home by immigrants aged 17 and over (see Table 1.5).

• The incidence of people reporting multiple ethnic ancestries continued to rise in 2006. An estimated 41.4 percent of the population reported more than one ethnic origin, compared with 38.2 percent in 2001 and 35.8 percent in 1996.

Table 1.3   Visible Minority Groups, 2006 Counts, for Canada, Provinces, and Territories—20 Percent Sample Data

Geographic name	Total population by visible minority groups	Total visible minority population[1]	South Asian[2]	Chinese	Black	Filipino	Latin American	Southeast Asian[3]
Canada	31,241,030	5,068,090	1,262,865	1,216,570	783,795	410,695	304,245	239,935
Newfoundland and Labrador	500,605	5,720	1,590	1,325	905	305	480	120
Prince Edward Island	134,205	1,830	130	250	640	30	215	30
Nova Scotia	903,090	37,680	3,810	4,300	19,230	700	955	815
New Brunswick	719,650	13,345	1,960	2,450	4,455	530	720	440
Quebec	7,435,905	654,355	72,845	79,830	188,070	24,200	89,505	50,455
Ontario	12,028,895	2,745,205	794,170	576,980	473,765	203,220	147,135	110,045
Manitoba	1,133,510	109,095	16,560	13,705	15,660	37,790	6,275	5,665
Saskatchewan	953,845	33,900	5,130	9,505	5,090	3,770	2,520	2,555
Alberta	3,256,355	454,200	103,885	120,275	47,075	51,090	27,265	28,605
British Columbia	4,074,385	1,008,855	262,290	407,225	28,315	88,080	28,960	40,690
Yukon Territory	30,195	1,220	195	325	125	210	95	145
Northwest Territories	41,060	2,270	210	320	375	690	85	355
Nunavut	29,325	420	80	80	100	75	25	10

Notes:

1. The *Employment Equity Act* defines visible minorities as "persons; other than Aboriginal peoples; who are non-Caucasian in race or non-white in colour."
2. For example, "East Indian," "Pakistani," "Sri Lankan," etc.
3. For example, "Vietnamese, "Cambodian," "Malaysian," "Laotian," etc.

Source: Statistics Canada, Census of Population, 2006. http://www12.statcan.ca/census-recensement/2006/dp-pd/hlt/97-562/pages/page.cfm?Lang=E&Geo=PR&Code=01&Table=1&Data=Count&StartRec=1&Sort=2&Display=Page.

- Canada's visible minority population is ethnoculturally diverse (in other words, many of its members represent a blend of ethnic and cultural backgrounds), more so in some groups than in others.

- In 2006, over one-half (52 percent) of Black visible minority people reported Caribbean origins, with another 42.4 percent reporting African origins. Members of Black visible minority groups also reported British Isles origins (11.6 percent), Canadian origin (10.9 percent), and French origin (4.1 percent).

- Most members of South Asian visible minority groups reported backgrounds from the Indian subcontinent: East Indian origin, sometimes in combination with other origins (69.0 percent); Pakistani (9.3 percent); Sri Lankan (7.8 percent); Punjabi (4.1 percent); Tamil (2.7 percent); and Bangladeshi (1.8 percent).

- The most frequently reported origin among Latin American visible minorities was Spanish. Among the Arab visible minorities, it was Lebanese. It was Iranian among the West Asians, and Vietnamese among the Southeast Asians.

Table 1.4   Count, Percentage Distribution, and Relative Ratio of Visible Minority Population, by Census Metropolitan Areas, 2006

Census metropolitan areas	Total population	% of total population	Visible minority population	% of visible minority population	Relative ratio[1]
Canada	31,241,030	100.0	5,068,090	100.0	?
Toronto	5,072,075	16.2	2,174,065	42.9	2.6
Vancouver	2,097,965	6.7	875,300	17.3	2.6
Montréal	3,588,520	11.5	590,375	11.6	1.0
Calgary	1,070,295	3.4	237,890	4.7	1.4
Ottawa–Gatineau	1,117,120	3.6	179,295	3.5	1.0
Ottawa–Gatineau (Ont. part)	835,475	2.7	162,405	3.2	1.2
Ottawa–Gatineau (Que. part)	281,650	0.9	16,890	0.3	0.4
Edmonton	1,024,825	3.3	175,295	3.5	1.1
Winnipeg	686,035	2.2	102,940	2.0	0.9
Hamilton	683,445	2.2	84,295	1.7	0.8
Kitchener	446,495	1.4	61,455	1.2	0.8
Windsor	320,730	1.0	51,200	1.0	1.0
London	452,575	1.4	50,300	1.0	0.7
Abbotsford	156,645	0.5	35,715	0.7	1.4
Victoria	325,060	1.0	33,870	0.7	0.6
Oshawa	328,065	1.1	33,700	0.7	0.6
Halifax	369,455	1.2	27,645	0.5	0.5
St. Catharines–Niagara	385,035	1.2	25,470	0.5	0.4
Québec	704,180	2.3	16,355	0.3	0.1
Guelph	126,085	0.4	16,025	0.3	0.8
Saskatoon	230,850	0.7	14,865	0.3	0.4
Regina	192,435	0.6	12,605	0.2	0.4
Barrie	175,335	0.6	10,130	0.2	0.4
Kingston	148,475	0.5	8,600	0.2	0.4
Kelowna	160,565	0.5	8,320	0.2	0.3
Sherbrooke	183,635	0.6	7,000	0.1	0.2
Brantford	122,825	0.4	6,715	0.1	0.3
Saint John	120,875	0.4	3,805	0.1	0.2
St. John's	179,270	0.6	3,460	0.1	0.1
Greater Sudbury	156,395	0.5	3,280	0.1	0.1
Thunder Bay	121,050	0.4	3,275	0.1	0.2
Peterborough	115,140	0.4	3,095	0.1	0.2
Moncton	124,055	0.4	2,425	0.0	0.1
Trois-Rivières	138,555	0.4	2,270	0.0	0.1
Saguenay	149,600	0.5	1,280	0.0	0.1

Notes:

? not applicable.

1. The relative ratio shows whether the share of visible minority population in a given location is higher than the share of the total population in the same location. For example, Montréal has a ratio of 1.0, which means that Montréal's share of visible minorities in Canada (11.6%) is roughly the same as Montréal's share of the total population of Canada (11.5%).

Source: Statistics Canada, Census of Population, 2006. http://www12.statcan.ca/census-recensement/2006/as-sa/97-562/table/t2-eng.cfm.

Immigration and Diversity

There has been a fundamental transformation in Canadian immigration since 1961. The "Old Canada" is still present—a country that resists multiculturalism; is predominantly rural, conservative, and white; and opposes social change. But this dated version of our country is no longer the main one, and it is under pressure from diverse ethnicities. This pressure will have a profound effect on, among other things, the ways people communicate and on the ways public services will be delivered. As we become aware of cultural barriers to communication and the need to communicate on a global scale, we will see the need to incorporate the languages of diverse cultures into the public sphere. This will lead, for example, to a requirement that public service and business workers be bi- or even trilingual.

Before 1961, the Canadian government deliberately sought to retain the British nature of Canadian society. Canadian culture was bound by a fairly uniform code of moral attitudes and manners. Profound differences of opinion or culture were not readily tolerated. The general cultural emphasis was on work, the accumulation of wealth, the written word, codified laws and regulations, and punctuality.

Since 1961, immigration has produced a society where social customs and manners are more diverse, dynamic, and fluid. These changes pose a challenge to Canadian civil authorities. How will someone from a small African community be integrated into Canadian culture? How can we expect that person to understand something as complicated as Canada's *Criminal Code*? Most people who have been in Canada for more than three generations take for granted their understanding of what is socially acceptable, legal or illegal, or simply right and wrong; they have been raised within this cultural context. Such people also tend to assume that the predominant customs and laws in this country are somehow natural or superior to others. These assumptions are now being challenged, and the question of national identity—what is a Canadian?—remains open.

One of the challenges facing newcomers to this country is poverty. This condition is widespread among immigrant groups, and it is a problem not only for them but for our society as a whole. The children of immigrants and visible minorities are twice as likely to live in poverty as other Canadian children. Almost one in two recent immigrant children lives in poverty (Brown, 2005). As Laurel Rothman (2005) has said,

> Here in one of the wealthiest countries in the world, with the lowest unemployment rate in 30 years, it seems an irony that so many [immigrant] children still live in poverty. All of these groups are growing ... [O]ur national policy is to increase the number of immigrants ... but at the most basic levels of food and housing and income, these groups are being marginalized.

One of the many reasons for this poverty is that male immigrants face barriers to good jobs. Earnings of full-time male workers who recently immigrated to this country fell significantly in the period 1980–2006, while earnings of Canadian-born men rose slightly. Discrimination still influences hiring, despite the laws against it. Our society resists recognizing the professional credentials of immigrants, despite the shortage of qualified people in certain areas of our labour force, such as doctors in Ontario or skilled workers across the country. The low wages earned by

Table 1.5   Language Spoken Most Often at Home by Immigrant Status and Broad Age Groups, 2006 Counts, for Canada, Provinces, and Territories—20 Percent Sample Data

Language spoken most often at home	Total population[1]			Non-immigrant population[2]			Immigrant population[3]		
	Total	Age 0 to 16	Age 17 and over	Total	Age 0 to 16	Age 17 and over	Total	Age 0 to 16	Age 17 and over
Total	31,241,030	6,468,110	24,772,920	24,788,725	5,990,220	18,798,500	6,186,950	436,940	5,750,005
Single responses	30,665,030	6,326,995	24,338,030	24,572,740	5,885,700	18,687,040	5,839,045	402,265	5,436,780
English	20,584,775	4,424,335	16,160,440	17,593,575	4,237,700	13,355,875	2,880,090	169,735	2,710,355
French	6,608,120	1,280,200	5,327,920	6,290,910	1,240,560	5,050,355	297,570	36,980	260,590
Non-official languages	3,472,130	622,460	2,849,670	688,250	407,440	280,810	2,661,380	195,550	2,465,835
Chinese languages[4]	796,145	109,985	686,160	92,375	66,940	25,435	677,405	41,725	635,680
Panjabi (Punjabi)	278,500	61,455	217,045	67,215	53,340	13,875	207,545	7,785	199,760
Spanish	209,955	46,805	163,150	38,785	25,910	12,870	153,055	17,335	135,715
Italian	170,330	4,385	165,940	21,040	3,885	17,155	148,110	435	147,675
Arabic	144,745	36,305	108,440	28,375	22,800	5,580	109,690	12,095	97,600
Aboriginal languages[5]	129,340	44,760	84,580	129,120	44,735	84,385	185	20	170
German	128,345	37,330	91,015	71,010	29,455	41,555	54,185	7,030	47,155
Tagalog (Pilipino, Filipino)	119,340	12,415	106,925	6,810	4,585	2,225	107,770	7,620	100,145
Vietnamese	111,440	21,180	90,260	24,225	19,070	5,155	85,850	2,005	83,850
Portuguese	103,870	7,825	96,045	15,220	6,125	9,090	85,940	1,355	84,585
Urdu	102,805	31,845	70,960	18,925	15,990	2,935	80,910	15,270	65,645
Polish	101,570	12,305	89,260	15,905	10,545	5,355	84,825	1,695	83,130
Korean	101,495	20,465	81,030	7,005	4,675	2,325	77,600	10,385	67,215
Persian (Farsi)	97,220	19,775	77,440	10,275	8,970	1,300	83,980	10,395	73,585
Russian	93,805	16,195	77,610	8,110	6,060	2,055	82,720	9,705	73,020
Tamil	92,680	21,035	71,640	17,660	16,425	1,230	72,475	4,255	68,220
Other languages[6]	690,510	118,375	572,105	116,180	67,900	48,240	549,090	46,450	502,645
Multiple responses	576,005	141,115	434,890	215,985	104,520	111,460	347,905	34,680	313,225
English and French	94,060	23,780	70,275	79,025	22,240	56,785	14,110	1,310	12,795
English and non-official language	406,455	96,725	309,730	114,915	68,370	46,545	282,080	26,995	255,085
French and non-official language	58,890	16,055	42,825	15,185	10,395	4,790	42,270	5,370	36,905
English, French and non-official language	16,600	4,545	12,055	6,855	3,515	3,340	9,445	1,010	8,435

Notes:

1. The total population count includes the non-immigrant population, the immigrant population and the non-permanent resident population. The non-permanent resident population is not shown separately.

2. Non-immigrants are persons who are Canadian citizens by birth. Although most Canadian citizens by birth were born in Canada, a small number were born outside Canada to Canadian parents.

3. Immigrants are persons who are, or have ever been, landed immigrants in Canada. A landed immigrant is a person who has been granted the right to live in Canada permanently by immigration authorities. Some immigrants have resided in Canada for a number of years, while others are more recent arrivals. Most immigrants are born outside Canada, but a small number were born in Canada. Includes immigrants who landed in Canada prior to Census Day, May 16, 2006.

4. All Chinese languages are grouped together. For a detailed breakdown of Chinese languages, see Figure 9F in the 2006 Census Dictionary. For a full list of languages collected in the census, see Appendix G in the 2006 Census Dictionary.

5. All Aboriginal languages are grouped together. For a detailed breakdown of Aboriginal languages, see Figure 9A in the 2006 Census Dictionary. For a full list of languages collected in the census, see Appendix G in the 2006 Census Dictionary.

6. This is a subtotal of all languages collected by the census that are not displayed separately. For a full list of languages collected in the census, see Appendix G in the 2006 Census Dictionary.

Source: Statistics Canada Census of Population, 2006. http://www12.statcan.ca/census-recensement/2006/dp-pd/hlt/97-557/T405-eng.cfm?Lang=E&T=405&GH=4&GF=1&G5=0&SC=1&SR=1&S=8&O=A&D1=1.

immigrants put a strain on our social services. Some immigrants are returning to their homelands because they can't make a living here.

EXERCISE 6

Two problems facing immigrants—poverty and lack of acceptable credentials—are mentioned in the previous paragraph. List some of the other problems faced by immigrants, and give examples of each.

DEVELOPING A CANADIAN IDENTITY

Demographic trends indicate that more and more people in this country are identifying themselves as Canadian. In the 2006 census, the most frequently reported ethnicities among third-generation immigrants over 15 years of age were as follows (see Table 1.2, above).

- Canadian (7.2 million),
- English (3.7 million),
- French (3.5 million),
- Scottish (2.8 million),
- Irish (2.7 million),
- German (1.6 million).

These numbers tell us that, in 2006, over 40 percent of the population identified themselves as Canadian. This fact might suggest the possibility of identifying a Canadian identity. However, a study done by Rudolf Kalin and John W. Berry (2000) suggests that the majority of those who identify themselves as Canadian are members of the Charter groups—in other words, descendants of English and French settlers. Slightly fewer than one-half of people from other ethnic heritages chose to identify themselves as Canadian.

It is likely that as successive generations of immigrant families live in Canada, their members will lean more toward identifying themselves as Canadian. But this will be a gradual process. According to Statistics Canada (2006c), immigrants were more likely than people born in Canada to report a strong sense of belonging to their ethnic or cultural group, and immigrants who had recently arrived indicated that their ethnic or cultural ancestry was important to them. This allegiance is reflected in the fact that there are more than 250 ethnic newspapers and magazines produced in the Toronto area alone. The mission of these media is to inform, to build community, and, as time goes on, to pass their cultural legacy on to the next generation.

Statistics show that the first generation of immigrants has the strongest sense of belonging to an **ethnic group**, with this sense of ethnicity declining considerably by the third generation (see Table 1.2, above). Identification with Canada increases with time in Canada, as does participation in non-ethnic organizations. Multiculturalism and cultural diversity seem to be working for Canada. It seems likely that, in time, a true Canadian identity will emerge—an identity that, instead of simply assimilating the country's new members into a uniform culture, will register their

ethnic group
group of individuals with a shared sense of peoplehood based on presumed shared socio-cultural experiences and/or similar characteristics

diverse values as contributions to Canadian society. And these new members, in turn, will come to see themselves as Canadian.

The search for a Canadian identity is probably premature right now. But when this identity does emerge, it will be characterized by openness, tolerance, multiculturalism, and diversity. This identity won't define itself negatively, against the melting-pot identity of the United States ("Our identity is that we're not like them"). It will be a positive identity of different textures and contours, expressing a society where people of all origins and ethnicities will be free to maintain their cultures and traditional faiths and customs. There is still a way to go, but it's happening.

EXERCISE 7

How would you define the Canadian identity? What is a Canadian? How does a Canadian differ from a citizen of any other country in the world? How do Canadians differ from Americans? Be specific in your answers, and give concrete examples.

CHAPTER SUMMARY

Canada is a diverse, multicultural country that encourages all groups to retain their cultures and cultural practices. The process of embracing diversity has been lengthy; beginning in colonial times, it has now reached the stage where Canada accepts more than 200,000 immigrants yearly. South Asians are now the most numerous immigrants. South Asians, Chinese, and Blacks are the largest visible minority populations. This trend has many implications for the development of a Canadian identity.

KEY TERMS

acculturation
assimilation
assimilation ideology
assimilationist
civic ideology
discrimination
diversity
ethnic group
ethnicity
ethnist ideology
exclusionary
host community

integration
integrationist
marginalization
multiculturalism
multiculturalism ideology
refugee policy
segregationist
separation
settlement patterns
values
visible minority

REFERENCES

Balanced Refugee Reform Act. (2010). SC 2010, c. 8.

Baxter, P. (2003). *A portrait of Canadian diversity.* Unpublished manuscript. Barrie, ON: Georgian College.

Berry, J.W. (2006). Acculturation: A conceptual overview. In M.H. Bornstein & L.R. Cote (Eds.), *Acculturation and parent-child relationships: Measurement and development* (pp. 13–30). Mahwah, NJ: Lawrence Erlbaum Associates.

Berry, J.W., & Sam, D. (1997). Acculturation and adaptation. In J.W. Berry, M.H. Segal, & C. Kagitcibasi (Eds.), *Handbook of cross-cultural psychology: Social behavior and applications.* Vol. 3 (pp. 291–326). Needham Heights, MA: Allyn and Bacon.

Bourhis, R.Y., Moise, L.C., Perreault, S., & Senecal, S. (1997). Towards an interactive acculturation model: A social psychological perspective. *International Journal of Psychology, 32,* 369–386.

Brown, L. (2005, November 24). Native, minority kids twice as likely to be poor. *The Hamilton Spectator,* p. A11.

Canadian Charter of Rights and Freedoms. (1982). Part I of the *Constitution Act, 1982,* RSC 1985, app. II, no. 44.

Canadian Council for Refugees. (March 2005). An overview of Canada's refugee policy. http://ccrweb.ca.

Canadian Heritage. (2001). Canadian diversity: Respecting our differences. http://www.pch.gc.ca/pgm/ai-ia/rir-iro/gbll/divers/index-eng.cfm.

Canadian Multiculturalism Act. (1985). RSC 1985, c. 24 (4th Supp.).

Chrétien, J. (1982). *Canadian Charter of Rights and Freedoms: A guide for Canadians.* Ottawa: Supply and Services.

Citizens for Public Justice. (2011, April 14). Election 2011 Canadian refugee policy: Looking back, looking forward. http://www.cpj.ca/en/election-2011-canadian-refugee-policy-looking-back-looking-forward.

Citizenship and Immigration Canada. (2011). Balanced refugee reform. http://www.cic.gc.ca/english/refugees/reform.asp.

Immigration and Refugee Protection Act. (2001). SC 2001, c. 27.

Kalin, R., & Berry, J.W. (2000). Ethnic and self-identity in Canada: Analyses of 1974 and 1991 national surveys. In M.A. Kalbach & W.E. Kalbach (Eds.), *Perspectives on ethnicity in Canada* (pp. 88–110). Toronto: Harcourt Brace.

Kallen, E. (2003). *Ethnicity and human rights in Canada: A human rights perspective on race, ethnicity, racism and systemic inequality.* New York: Oxford University Press.

Kazarian, S., Crichlow, W., & Bradford, S. (2007). *Diversity issues in law enforcement* (3rd ed.). Toronto: Emond Montgomery.

Roberts, J. (2006). *First Nations, Inuit, and Métis peoples: Exploring their past, present, and future.* Toronto: Emond Montgomery.

Rothman, L. (2005). Report card on child poverty in Canada by the coalition Campaign 2000. http://www.campaign2000.ca.

Statistics Canada. (2001). *2001 census: Analysis series.* Canada's ethnocultural portrait: The changing mosaic. http://www.statcan.ca/bsolc/english/bsolc?catno=96F0030X2001008.

Statistics Canada. (2006a). 2006 census: Aboriginal peoples in Canada in 2006: Inuit, Métis and First Naitons, 2006 census. http://www12.statcan.ca/census-recensement/2006/as-sa/97-558/p2-eng.cfm.

Statistics Canada. (2006b). 2006 census release topics. http://www12.statcan.ca/census-recensement/2006/rt-td/index-eng.cfm.

Statistics Canada. (2006c). Canada's ethnocultural mosaic, 2006 census: Findings. http://www12.statcan.ca/census-recensement/2006/as-sa/97-562/index-eng.cfm.

United Nations. (1983). *Convention and protocol relating to the status of refugees: Final act of the United Nations Conference of Plenipotentiaries on the Status of Refugees and Stateless Persons and the text of the 1951 Convention Relating to Refugees. Resolution 2198 adopted by the General Assembly and the text of the 1967 Protocol Relating to the Status of Refugees.* New York: United Nations.

University of Maryland. (2000). Diversity database. http://www.umd.edu/diversity.

REVIEW QUESTIONS

TRUE OR FALSE?

_____ 1. The term *multiculturalism* can suggest an ideal of cultural diversity.

_____ 2. The term *ethnicity* refers to the ideologies of host cultures.

_____ 3. Ethnist ideology is a "melting pot" ideology that accepts all immigrants indiscriminately.

_____ 4. There is tension between Canada's assumption that all citizens should be treated equally under the law and its principles of multiculturalism.

_____ 5. Multiculturalism became a formal policy in Canada under Prime Minister Trudeau in 1971.

_____ 6. A host community is made up of groups of people who have the power and influence to change attitudes toward the less established communities in the society.

_____ 7. "Assimilation" refers to an immigrant's rejection of his or her culture in favour of absorption into the main culture.

_____ 8. Aboriginal peoples were not recognized under the 1982 *Canadian Charter of Rights and Freedoms.*

_____ 9. As of 2006, the three largest visible minorities in Canada were South Asians, Chinese, and Aboriginals.

_____ 10. More visible minority people live in Toronto than in any other city in Canada.

MULTIPLE CHOICE

1. *Diversity* refers to
   - (a) country of origin
   - (b) the variety of human qualities among different people and groups
   - (c) a national ideology of a country or state
   - (d) the prevailing attitude of the host country

2. Ethnist ideology is an ideology in which the state
   - (a) defines which groups are permitted to assimilate
   - (b) promotes a "melting pot" approach to assimilation
   - (c) promotes a "homogeneous" approach to assimilation
   - (d) creates funding for new Canadians

3. The *Multiculturalism Act* of 1988 was inaugurated to
   - (a) deny to new Canadians the rights that are held by other Canadians
   - (b) define the number of immigrants who could arrive in Canada
   - (c) address the needs of new Canadians and disadvantaged groups
   - (d) declare the dominant culture of Canada to be British

4. A host community consists of people who
   - (a) determine the basic character and attitudes of the society
   - (b) have a friendly attitude to all immigrants
   - (c) come from English and French cultures
   - (d) have a variety of marriage institutions

5. Marginalization occurs when
   - (a) the cultural patterns of an ethnic group change
   - (b) the host community rejects the immigrants' heritage culture
   - (c) an immigrant rejects the host culture as well as his or her heritage culture
   - (d) a visible minority immigrant group moves close to the host country's border

6. Canada has been home to refugees since
   - (a) 1967
   - (b) the Second World War
   - (c) the latest census
   - (d) before Confederation

7. From the 1500s to the early 1900s, the main European influences in North America were
   - (a) the Vikings and Norsemen
   - (b) priests and missionaries
   - (c) Spain and Portugal
   - (d) the English and French

8. Visible minorities are persons other than Aboriginals who are

    (a) Caucasian in race or non-white in colour

    (b) Non-Caucasian in race or non-white in colour

    (c) Caucasian in race or white in colour

    (d) Non-Caucasian in race or white in colour

9. Between 2001 and 2006, 75 percent of the immigrants who arrived in Canada were

    (a) members of a visible minority group

    (b) South Asian

    (c) from Jamaica and/or Trinidad

    (d) European and Asian

10. Most new Canadians come from

    (a) South Asia

    (b) the Philippines

    (c) China

    (d) Pakistan

FILL IN THE BLANKS

1. Canada is the first nation to make a policy of _____ part of its national constitution.

2. The assimilation ideology is a homogenization or _____ ideology.

3. When Canada was a colony of the British Empire, Canadians had limited _____ _____ and were governed by a political elite.

4. Discrimination is the process by which a person is _____ of equal access to privileges and opportunities available to others.

5. Acculturation is the process of change in the _____ patterns of an ethnic group as a result of contact with other ethnic groups.

6. The four designated groups under the *Employment Equity Act* are women, people with disabilities, _____, and visible minorities.

7. The South Asians, Chinese, and Blacks were the three largest _____ groups in 2006.

8. Immigrants to Canada are increasingly from _____.

9. Before 1961, the Canadian government deliberately sought to retain the _____ nature of Canadian society.

10. The children of immigrants and visible minorities are twice as likely to live in _____ as other Canadian children.

Human Rights and Freedoms

2

INTRODUCTION

The evolution of civil rights has influenced human conditions around the world, inspiring nations and improving their peoples' quality of life. This chapter discusses human rights and freedoms, for four main reasons. First, they reflect the collective conscience of nations. Second, they provide the international community with basic standards of equality and fairness. Third, law enforcement agencies need to understand human rights and freedoms to fulfill their mandate. Fourth, the current tension between two very different ideals of law enforcement—democratic community policing as opposed to the dictatorship policing that has evolved in response to terrorist threats in Western countries—centres on questions about human rights and freedoms.

INTERNATIONAL HUMAN RIGHTS AND FREEDOMS

The general idea of human rights—that is, the idea of basic claims or privileges to which all humans are entitled—originated with the ancient Greeks and Romans. Today's notion of human rights was strongly influenced by England's 1215 *Magna Carta*, or Great Charter, which was a response to the misuse of power by the monarchy and royal officials in medieval England. This document addressed, among other injustices, the unfair taxes imposed on the people and the people's inability to gain a fair hearing for their complaints. The *Magna Carta* informed many future attempts to establish human rights and freedoms, including the United States Declaration of Independence (1776) and the French Declaration of the Rights of Man and of the Citizen (1789). The ideals of liberty and equality are at the core of these documents, most of which affirm, for example, a person's right to pursue happiness, to own property, to enjoy free speech, and not to be imprisoned arbitrarily.

In 1946, the General Assembly of the United Nations established the Commission on Human Rights. Two years later, the Office of the United Nations High Commissioner for Human Rights (1948) set down the *Universal Declaration of*

Human Rights. The 30 articles of this document recognize the equality and dignity of all people, and grant people certain inalienable human rights, including the right to freedom, security, personal expression, an adequate standard of living, and education. The UN Human Rights Council replaced the UN Commission on Human Rights in 2006, with a mandate to uphold the highest standards in the promotion and protection of human rights. The council includes members from 47 states—13 each from African and Asian states, six from Eastern European states, eight from Latin American and Caribbean states, and seven from Western European and other states (including Canada)—and its purpose is to address human rights violations around the world and make recommendations on them. In June 2011, for example, the council established an independent expert to investigate the situation of human rights in Côte D'Ivoire, the former African country of Ivory Coast, and it initiated a study of discriminatory laws and practices around the world.

EXERCISE 1

Before beginning this section, read the eight statements below. Indicate whether you agree or disagree with each statement, and give reasons for your view. Do you believe that Canadian human rights legislation would address each of these situations? As you go through this chapter, come back to these statements and indicate which act, code, right, or policy in Canada might address each situation.

1. As a society, we should recognize only marriages involving opposite-sex couples.
2. If women want to breastfeed their infants, they should do so in the privacy of their homes, not in public.
3. A Christian country should require that all public school students say the Lord's Prayer each morning before class.
4. Gay or lesbian couples should not have the same rights as heterosexual married couples.
5. Human rights and freedoms provisions enable criminals to get away with murder.
6. Muslim women should have the right to wear a *niqab* (face veil) while testifying in court.
7. Employers should have the right to give drug tests to all potential employees.
8. The law should protect police officers better, so that they can do their jobs without constant fear of reprisal.

HUMAN RIGHTS IN CANADA: FEDERAL

Canadian Human Rights Act
the federal statute that prohibits discrimination based on race, national or ethnic origin, colour, age, sex, marital status, family status, disability, sexual orientation, or conviction for an offence for which a pardon has been granted

Human rights legislation in Canada started 250 years ago. The *Royal Proclamation of 1763* gave provincial legislatures in Canada the right to pass laws in relation to property and civil rights and to local private matters. The Proclamation was followed by the *British North America Act* (now called the *Constitution Act, 1867*), which gave the provinces power over property and civil rights and gave the federal government power over divorce and marriage. The *Canadian Bill of Rights* was introduced in 1960 to protect individual rights and freedoms. In 1977, the federal government passed the **Canadian Human Rights Act**.

Canadian Human Rights Act

The term **discrimination** means harassing someone or treating someone unfavourably based on prejudice. Examples of discrimination could include the following:

- refusing to hire someone because of his or her age;
- denying a promotion to a female employee;
- having an office that is not accessible to people in wheelchairs;
- using racist language in the workplace;
- requiring job applicants to have work experience in Canada;
- refusing to hire a person who for religious reasons cannot work on certain days, even though this person's absences would not cause the employer undue hardship; and
- paying employees in female-dominated jobs less than those in male-dominated jobs of equal value.

discrimination
a process by which a person is deprived of equal access to privileges and opportunities available to others because of prejudice

The *Canadian Human Rights Act*, which the federal government passed in 1977, prohibits discrimination based on a person's race, national or ethnic origin, colour, religion, age, sex, sexual orientation, marital status, family status, disability, or pardoned conviction (that is, a conviction for which a pardon has been granted). The Act was amended in 1996 to include sexual orientation (not included in the original 1977 Act) as a prohibited ground of discrimination and underwent, in 2000, a comprehensive review by the *Canadian Human Rights Act* Review Panel.

The Act is administered by the **Canadian Human Rights Commission**, a government agency with the mandate to investigate human rights complaints against federally-regulated employers and to develop policies and address issues related to discrimination. In s. 40(1), the Act stipulates that "any individual or group of individuals having reasonable grounds for believing that a person is engaging or has engaged in a discriminatory practice may file with the [Canadian Human Rights] Commission a complaint in a form acceptable to the Commission." The Commission—which is also empowered, under the *Employment Equity Act*, to ensure that employers within federal jurisdiction provide equal opportunity for women, Aboriginal peoples, the disabled, and visible minorities—has developed policies on many matters, among them the following:

Canadian Human Rights Commission
the federal body responsible for investigating and adjudicating complaints concerning violations of the *Canadian Human Rights Act*

- harassment in the workplace;
- drug testing in the workplace;
- the employment rights of those with HIV/AIDS;
- pregnancy and human rights in the workplace;
- accommodating people with environmental sensitivities; and
- mental health issues in the workplace.

The *Canadian Human Rights Act* is constantly in flux, subject to continual amendments. In 2010, for example, the Act was amended to prohibit discrimination on the basis of gender identity or expression. Two years before, in 2008, s. 67 of the Act was repealed, an important human rights development for Aboriginal peoples in Canada. Section 67 had had the effect of exempting the *Indian Act* (an old piece of legislation, first enacted in 1876) from the provisions of the *Human Rights Act*. What this meant, practically speaking, was that any actions taken and decisions made by Aboriginal leaders or the federal government under the *Indian Act*—decisions and actions that affected Aboriginal people living or working on reserves—were not subject to the protections of the *Human Rights Act*. In other words, Aboriginal peoples on reserves were unable to file discrimination-related complaints with the Canadian Human Rights Commission if those complaints arose from actions taken under the *Indian Act*. With the amendment, Aboriginal peoples have full access to the human rights complaint-resolution mechanism available to other Canadians.

Canadian Charter of Rights and Freedoms

Canadian Charter of Rights and Freedoms
the part of the Canadian Constitution that protects the rights and freedoms that are deemed essential to maintaining a free and democratic society and a united country

The **Canadian Charter of Rights and Freedoms** was introduced in the *Constitution Act, 1982*; it forms the first part of the Act. The Charter sets out *minimum* rights for Canadian citizens. These ten basic rights and freedoms, which apply to all governments (federal, provincial, and territorial), are summarized in Table 2.1.

Guarantee of Rights and Freedoms, and Fundamental Freedoms

fundamental freedoms
freedom of conscience and religion; freedom of thought, belief, opinion, and expression, including freedom of the press and other media of communication; freedom of peaceful assembly; and freedom of association

Section 1 of the Charter guarantees certain rights and freedoms to all Canadians subject to reasonable and legal limits, and s. 2 lists the **fundamental freedoms**. The Charter guarantees freedom of speech, and freedom of the press and other media. The following measures, for example, which were once considered legally acceptable, are contrary to the spirit of the Charter:

1. requiring newspapers to reveal their sources of news;
2. banning the propagation of certain political ideologies by closing down any premises used for that purpose;
3. prohibiting the distribution of any book, pamphlet, or tract without permission of a chief of police; and
4. restricting a religious group's right to free expression and religious practice.

Finally, the Charter ensures Canadians' right to gather in peaceful groups and—a similar protection—their freedom of association, which is their individual right to come together with other people and collectively express, promote, pursue, and defend common interests. These freedoms are not absolute. For example, freedom of speech is subject to laws governing libel and slander, in recognition of the fact that speech is capable of harming people. We can see the need for such a restriction when we consider such things as hate literature.

Democratic Rights

democratic rights
rights to vote and to run in an election and the assurance that no government has the right to continue to hold power indefinitely without seeking a new mandate from the electorate

In addition to enshrining certain fundamental freedoms, the Charter gives all Canadian citizens **democratic rights** to vote or run in an election (s. 3), as well as the assurance that no government has the right to continue to hold power indefinitely without seeking a new mandate from the electorate (s. 4). It should be noted that

Table 2.1   Basic Rights and Freedoms Enshrined in the Canadian Charter of Rights and Freedoms

1. Guarantee of rights and freedoms
2. Fundamental freedoms
3. Democratic rights
4. Mobility rights
5. Legal rights
6. Equality rights
7. Official languages of Canada
8. Minority language educational rights
9. Enforcement
10. General

Source: *Canadian Charter of Rights and Freedoms*, part I of the *Constitution Act, 1982*, RSC 1985, app. II, no. 44.

s. 46 of the Ontario *Police Services Act* restricts police officers' right to run for office: "No municipal police officer shall engage in political activity, except as the regulations permit." The regulations under the Act state that a serving police officer may run for office only if granted a leave of absence (O. Reg. 89/98, s. 1).

Mobility Rights

Section 6 of the Charter grants **mobility rights** to Canadian citizens and permanent residents. This guarantees their freedom to enter, remain in, or leave the country, as well as to live and seek employment anywhere in Canada. Provinces reserve the right to set residence requirements for certain social and welfare benefits, and to establish employment standards applicable to both newcomers and long-time residents.

mobility rights
the freedom to enter, remain in, or leave the country, and to live and seek employment anywhere in Canada

---

GUARANTEE OF RIGHTS AND FREEDOMS

1. The *Canadian Charter of Rights and Freedoms* guarantees the rights and freedoms set out in it subject only to such reasonable limits prescribed by law as can be demonstrably justified in a free and democratic society.

FUNDAMENTAL FREEDOMS

2. Everyone has the following fundamental freedoms:
    (a) freedom of conscience and religion;
    (b) freedom of thought, belief, opinion and expression, including freedom of the press and other media of communication;
    (c) freedom of peaceful assembly; and
    (d) freedom of association.

Source: *Canadian Charter of Rights and Freedoms*, part I of the *Constitution Act, 1982*, RSC 1985, app. II, no. 44.

Legal Rights

legal rights
the basic legal protections granted to all Canadian citizens in their dealings with the state and justice system

The **legal rights** section of the Charter (ss. 7–14), known as the lawyers' section, provides basic legal protection for Canadian citizens in their dealings with the state and its justice system (see the box on page 33). More specifically, Canadian citizens' right to life, liberty, and security entails a prohibition against unreasonable search or seizure by the police as well as against police officers' execution of these functions in an unreasonable manner—for example, with unnecessary force. These legal rights also prohibit a person's being detained or held arbitrarily. This means that a police officer has to show reasonable cause for detaining an individual.

The legal rights concerning arrest and detention protect Canadian citizens from arbitrary or unlawful actions by law enforcement agencies. When being held or arrested by any authority, people have the following rights:

1. to be informed of the reasons for their being taken into custody;
2. to be instructed of their right to contact and consult a lawyer without delay;
3. to have a court determine quickly whether the detention is lawful.

Finally, the legal rights set out in the Charter prohibit subjecting any individual to cruel and unusual treatment or punishment.

Equality Rights

equality rights
the rights of all Canadians, regardless of race, national or ethnic origin, colour, religion, sex, age, or mental or physical disability, to be equal before the law and to enjoy equal protection and benefit of the law

Section 15 of the Charter, **equality rights**, establishes that all Canadians, regardless of their race, national or ethnic origin, colour, religion, sex, age, or mental or physical disability, are equal before the law and are to enjoy equal protection and benefit of the law (see the box on page 33). (Sexual orientation is not specifically mentioned in this section, but a Supreme Court ruling in 1995 made sexual orientation a prohibited ground of discrimination.) In reality, equality rights are difficult to enforce in a legal context, since some citizens are less able than others to pay for a legal defence. For example, a defence against an impaired driving charge can easily cost $10,000, which many people cannot afford. And if a citizen elects to avoid a costly defence by acting as his own counsel, his lack of legal expertise undermines equality rights another way; he is less likely to win his case than professional counsel would be.

EXERCISE 2

What are the implications of human rights and freedoms to the following duties of law enforcement officials?

1. preserving the peace
2. preventing crimes and other offences, and providing assistance and encouragement to other persons in the prevention of crimes and other offences
3. assisting victims of crime
4. apprehending criminals, other offenders, and others who may lawfully be taken into custody
5. laying charges, prosecuting, and participating in prosecution
6. executing warrants and performing related duties
7. performing the lawful duties assigned by their superiors
8. completing prescribed training

LEGAL RIGHTS

7. Everyone has the right to life, liberty and security of the person and the right not to be deprived thereof except in accordance with the principles of fundamental justice.

8. Everyone has the right to be secure against unreasonable search or seizure.

9. Everyone has the right not to be arbitrarily detained or imprisoned.

10. Everyone has the right on arrest or detention
    (a) to be informed promptly of the reasons therefore;
    (b) to retain and instruct counsel without delay and to be informed of that right; and
    (c) to have the validity of the detention determined by way of habeas corpus and to be released if the detention is not lawful.

11. Any person charged with an offence has the right
    (a) to be informed without unreasonable delay of the specific offence;
    (b) to be tried within a reasonable time; ...
    (d) to be presumed innocent until proven guilty ... ;

12. Everyone has the right not to be subjected to any cruel and unusual treatment or punishment.

13. A witness who testifies in any proceedings has the right not to have any incriminating evidence so given used to incriminate that witness in any other proceedings, except in a prosecution for perjury or for the giving of contradictory evidence.

14. A party or witness in any proceedings who does not understand or speak the language in which the proceedings are conducted or who is deaf has the right to the assistance of an interpreter.

Source: *Canadian Charter of Rights and Freedoms*, part I of the *Constitution Act, 1982*, RSC 1985, app. II, no. 44.

EQUALITY RIGHTS

15(1) Every individual is equal before and under the law and has the right to the equal protection and equal benefit of the law without discrimination and, in particular, without discrimination based on race, national or ethnic origin, colour, religion, sex, age, or mental or physical disability.

(2) Subsection (1) does not preclude any law, program or activity that has as its object the amelioration of conditions of disadvantaged individuals or groups including those that are disadvantaged because of race, national or ethnic origin, colour, religion, sex, age or mental or physical disability.

Source: *Canadian Charter of Rights and Freedoms*, part I of the *Constitution Act, 1982*, RSC 1985, app. II, no. 44.

official languages
English and French, as confirmed by the Charter, which guarantees that the federal government will serve members of the public in the official language of their choice

Official Languages of Canada

Sections 16 to 22 of the Charter confirm that English and French are Canada's two **official languages** but do not require any member of the public to become bilingual (see the box below). Rather, these sections give people the right to communicate with the federal government in either language, to receive federal government services in the official language of their choice, and to use either language in Parliament or in all courts of law that are under federal jurisdiction.

OFFICIAL LANGUAGES OF CANADA

16(1)   English and French are the official languages of Canada and have equality of status and equal rights and privileges as to their use in all institutions of the Parliament and government of Canada.

(2)   English and French are the official languages of New Brunswick and have equality of status and equal rights and privileges as to their use in all institutions of the legislature and government of New Brunswick. ...

17(1)   Everyone has the right to use English or French in any debates and other proceedings of Parliament.

(2)   Everyone has the right to use English or French in any debates and other proceedings of the legislature of New Brunswick.

18(1)   The statutes, records and journals of Parliament shall be printed and published in English and French and both language versions are equally authoritative.

(2)   The statutes, records and journals of the legislature of New Brunswick shall be printed and published in English and French and both language versions are equally authoritative.

19(1)   Either English or French may be used by any person in, or in any pleading in or process issuing from, any court established by Parliament.

(2)   Either English or French may be used by any person in, or in any pleading in or process issuing from, any court of New Brunswick.

20(1)   Any member of the public in Canada has the right to communicate with, and to receive available services from, any head or central office of an institution of the Parliament or government of Canada in English or French, and has the same right with respect to any other office of any such institution where

(a)   there is a significant demand for communication with and services from that office in such language; or

(b)   due to the nature of the office, it is reasonable that communications with and services from that office be available in both English and French.

(2)   Any member of the public in New Brunswick has the right to communicate with, and to receive available services from, any office of an institution of the legislature or government of New Brunswick in English or French.

21.   Nothing in sections 16 to 20 abrogates or derogates from any right, privilege or obligation with respect to the English and French languages, or either of them, that exists or is continued by virtue of any other provision of the Constitution of Canada.

22.   Nothing in sections 16 to 20 abrogates or derogates from any legal or customary right or privilege acquired or enjoyed either before or after the coming into force of this Charter with respect to any language that is not English or French.

Source: *Canadian Charter of Rights and Freedoms*, part I of the *Constitution Act, 1982*, RSC 1985, app. II, no. 44.

Minority Language Educational Rights

Section 23 of the Charter uses three main criteria to determine which Canadian citizens of the English- and French-speaking minorities in each province are entitled to have their children educated in their own language (see the box on page 36). The first criterion is *mother tongue*. The Charter stipulates that individuals whose first learned and still understood language is French and who live in a mainly English-speaking province have the constitutional right to have their children educated in French; those whose mother tongue is English and who live in a mainly French-speaking province have the right to have their children educated in English. The second criterion is the *language in which the parents were educated in Canada*. The Charter stipulates that individuals who were educated in one of the official languages—whether English or French—and live in a province where that language is in the linguistic minority have the right to send their children to a school that uses that minority language.

The third criterion relates to the *language in which other children in the family are receiving or have received their education*. The Charter protects the right of children whose siblings have received primary or secondary school instruction in either official language to be educated in the same language. In a separate section (s. 29), the Charter guarantees the establishment and operation of religious schools and provides them immunity from other provisions. Thus, the Charter ensures that neither the provision concerning freedom of conscience and religion nor the equality rights provision can override existing constitutional rights with respect to the establishment and state financing of religious schools.

Enforcement

Section 24 allows a person or group whose rights have been denied or infringed upon by law or by action taken by the state to apply to a court for a remedy (see the box on page 36). An example of a potential infringement would be a case where police have broken into and searched a person's premises and discovered incriminating evidence. In the subsequent trial, the courts could exclude the evidence if it is established that a right under the Charter was infringed and that the admission of the evidence would bring the administration of justice into disrepute.

General Rights of Aboriginal Peoples, Multiculturalism, and the Rights of Women

The rights of Canada's Aboriginal peoples (Indian, Inuit, and Métis), the protection of Canada's multicultural character, and the rights of women are addressed in ss. 25, 27, and 28 of the Charter, respectively (see the box on page 36).

Section 25 recognizes and affirms **Aboriginal peoples' rights** to preserve their culture, identity, customs, traditions, and languages, and any special rights that they have currently or rights that they may acquire in the future. (Section 35 of the Constitution recognizes and affirms existing Aboriginal and treaty rights. This section also ensures that any new benefits that Aboriginal peoples may gain from a settlement of land claims would not conflict with the general equality rights as set out in the Charter.)

Section 27 is a unique provision within the Charter in that it enshrines the multicultural character of Canadian society—that is, the maintenance and enhancement of Canada's **multicultural heritage**.

Aboriginal peoples' rights
the rights of Canada's Aboriginal peoples to preserve their culture, identity, customs, traditions, and languages, and to maintain any special rights that they have currently or may acquire in the future

multicultural heritage
the unique and constitutionally enshrined character of Canadian society

MINORITY LANGUAGE EDUCATIONAL RIGHTS

23(1) Citizens of Canada
(a) whose first language learned and still understood is that of the English or French linguistic minority population of the province in which they reside, or
(b) who have received their primary school instruction in Canada in English or French and reside in a province where the language in which they received that instruction is the language of the English or French linguistic minority population of the province,
have the right to have their children receive primary and secondary school instruction in that language in that province.
(2) Citizens of Canada of whom any child has received or is receiving primary or secondary school instruction in English or French in Canada, have the right to have all their children receive primary and secondary school instruction in the same language.

Source: *Canadian Charter of Rights and Freedoms*, part I of the *Constitution Act, 1982*, RSC 1985, app. II, no. 44.

ENFORCEMENT

24(1) Anyone whose rights or freedoms, as guaranteed by this Charter, have been infringed or denied may apply to a court of competent jurisdiction to obtain such remedy as the court considers appropriate and just in the circumstances.
(2) Where, in proceedings under subsection (1), a court concludes that evidence was obtained in a manner that infringed or denied any rights or freedoms guaranteed by this Charter, the evidence shall be excluded if it is established that, having regard to all the circumstances, the admission of it in the proceedings would bring the administration of justice into disrepute.

Source: *Canadian Charter of Rights and Freedoms*, part I of the *Constitution Act, 1982*, RSC 1985, app. II, no. 44.

GENERAL

25. The guarantee in this Charter of certain rights and freedoms shall not be construed so as to abrogate or derogate from any aboriginal, treaty or other rights or freedoms that pertain to the aboriginal peoples of Canada including
(a) any rights or freedoms that have been recognized by the Royal Proclamation of October 7, 1763; and
(b) any rights or freedoms that now exist by way of land claims agreements or may be so acquired. ...
27. This Charter shall be interpreted in a manner consistent with the preservation and enhancement of the multicultural heritage of Canadians.
28. Notwithstanding anything in this Charter, the rights and freedoms referred to in it are guaranteed equally to male and female persons.

Source: *Canadian Charter of Rights and Freedoms*, part I of the *Constitution Act, 1982*, RSC 1985, app. II, no. 44.

Finally, s. 28 ensures that all rights in the Charter are guaranteed equally to both sexes. Including this provision in the Charter ensures that these equality rights cannot be overridden by a provincial legislature or by Parliament.

Disputes Over Multiculturalism

Federal human rights legislation has had its critics and its controversies in Canada. Reconciling the cultural practices of immigrant communities with the mainstream values of Canadian liberal democracy is not always simple or straightforward. In the past few decades, the debate between multicultural religious accommodation and the secular "one law for all" approach has played itself out over and over around such issues as the right of Sikh police officers to wear turbans, the right of Sikh students to wear the ceremonial dagger known as the *kirpan* in schools, and the right of Jews to build temporary *succahs*, or huts, on balconies.

In 2003, a debate ignited in Ontario surrounding religiously based arbitration. The 1991 passage of the *Arbitration Act* made it possible for private parties to designate a religious arbitrator to resolve civil disputes; the arbitrator's decision would be considered legally binding, and the parties would have the right to appeal any decision that was not in accordance with Canadian law to a Canadian court. Since then, various groups have set up arbitration boards that render decisions based on religious principles.

In 2003, the Islamic Institute of Civil Justice announced that it would start offering family arbitration founded on Sharia law. A major public firestorm erupted that pitted the values of religious freedom and multicultural accommodation against perceived threats to gender equality and the primacy of secular law.

In the debate, some charged that multiculturalism was eroding women's rights and argued that allowing religious courts to function would impede the integration of cultures into Canadian society; others worried that banning religious arbitration would simply drive the practice underground and deny community members the protection of the law. The debate ended in 2005, when Ontario Premier Dalton McGuinty announced that the *Arbitration Act* would be amended to end faith-based arbitration in family law matters, and to mandate that Canadian law be followed in the resolution of such disputes.

An ongoing topic of debate in this country, as well as in Britain and France, is the *niqab*, or face veil, worn by Muslim women. In 2009, a judge ordered a Toronto woman to testify without her *niqab* at a sexual assault trial (Muslim Matters, 2009). This raised the question, more publicly, of whether Muslim women should be allowed to appear as witnesses wearing a veil that covers everything but their eyes. The conflict here is between the right of a defendant to face an accuser in open court and the right of a Canadian to religious freedom. In October 2010, the Ontario Court of Appeal ruled that a Muslim woman is allowed to wear her *niqab* while testifying in court so long as her doing so doesn't compromise the fairness of the trial. Further complicating this issue is that, according to a majority of Muslim scholars, a Muslim woman is not obliged to wear the *niqab*; it is a personal choice (On Islam, 2010). In March 2011, the woman in the case appealed the matter to the Supreme Court of Canada (Canadian Press, 2011).

As of 2011, Bill 94 is being debated in Quebec's Parliament. This bill would effectively deny government services (such as child care, health care, and education) to women who wear the *niqab*. At the same time, a Conservative MP introduced Bill C-623 into the Canadian Parliament. This Bill would deny the right to vote to any woman wearing a burka, despite the fact that procedures are already in place to ensure that these women's identities are confirmed in private (Senra, 2011).

Visible Minority Canadians in the Labour Market

Canada's increasingly diverse society has a number of problems to address. One problem concerns inequities in the Canadian labour market. These were featured in a recent report, *Canada's Colour Coded Labour Market* (Block & Galabuzi, 2011). This report compares work and income trends among visible minority members of the Canadian population and the rest of the population (Myrie, 2011). Among the report's findings are the following:

- Immigrants from visible minority groups earn only 81 percent of what white immigrants earn.
- Earnings by male immigrants from visible minorities were 68.7 percent of white males' earnings.
- Canadian-born visible minority individuals earn less than other Canadian-born individuals with the same level of education.
- Visible minority women make 56.5 cents for every dollar white males earn, while visible minority males earn 75.6 cents.
- Canadian-born visible minority men earn 18 percent less than Canadian-born white men.

Despite our society's apparent adherence to the *Canadian Human Rights Act* and the *Canadian Charter of Rights and Freedoms*, the economic situation of many immigrants suggests that racism and discrimination are still factors in our society.

EXERCISE 3

1. You apprehend a citizen with limited English and French. You do not speak her language yourself, but as an officer it is your duty to inform her of her right to know why she's being taken into custody, of her right to contact and consult a lawyer forthwith to obtain legal advice, and of her right to have a court determine quickly whether her detention is lawful.
   a. What human rights and freedoms provisions would guide your decision in handling this case?
   b. What action would you take in this situation?
2. You take a Sikh man into custody. From your course on diversity issues in policing, you remember that a Sikh religious practice entails carrying a *kirpan* (ceremonial dagger).
   a. What human rights and freedoms provisions would guide your decisions in dealing with this man and his *kirpan*?
   b. What action would you take in this situation?

HUMAN RIGHTS IN ONTARIO

Human Rights Code

At the time that the *Canadian Bill of Rights* was enacted, the provinces developed their own human rights codes. Due to space limitations, this section focuses on a single one of these provincial codes: the **Ontario *Human Rights Code***, which was enacted in 1962.

In its preamble, the Ontario *Human Rights Code* recognizes that "the inherent dignity and the equal and inalienable rights of all members of the human family is the foundation of freedom, justice and peace in the world and is in accord with the *Universal Declaration of Human Rights* as proclaimed by the United Nations." Part I of the Code, which deals with **freedom from discrimination**, is provided on pages 40–41.

Part III of the Code concerns the **Ontario Human Rights Commission** and describes its mandate: to promote, protect, and advance human rights in Ontario. The Commission once had the task of hearing complaints, but—since 2008, when the *Human Rights Code Amendment Act* (Bill 107) was passed—now focuses on human rights issues of broad public interest and cases of systemic discrimination. The Commission is also responsible for developing new partnerships with communities, individuals, and the government to ensure that human rights are protected in Ontario.

Part IV of the Code outlines the complaint process. As of 2008, individuals who believe their rights have been infringed under the Code can file a complaint with the Human Rights Tribunal of Ontario. A person has the right to file a complaint up to one year after the date the discrimination occurred. The Tribunal has procedures in place to ensure that claims of discrimination are

- addressed in a timely manner,
- resolved fairly, and
- based on the facts and the law.

Bill 107 also created the Human Rights Legal Support Centre. The centre offers legal services to individuals in Ontario who believe they have experienced discrimination.

Human Rights Commission Policies and Initiatives

The Ontario Human Rights Commission has issued a number of policies to clarify or complement the Code, some of which are described below. In advancing its various policies, the Commission makes reference to harassment, to a poisoned environment, and to constructive discrimination. As defined in the Code (part II, s. 10(1)(e), **harassment** is a "course of vexatious comment or conduct that is known or ought reasonably to be known to be unwelcome." A poisoned environment is one in which a person or a group of people are treated differently for reasons related to prohibitory grounds, such as gender, race, and sexual orientation.

According to the Code (part II, s. 11(1)), **constructive discrimination** refers to "a requirement, qualification or factor ... that is not discrimination on a prohibited ground but that results in the exclusion, restriction or preference of a group of

Ontario *Human Rights Code*
the Ontario statute that protects the dignity and worth of every person and provides for equal rights and opportunities without discrimination that is contrary to law

freedom from discrimination
the standard set out in part I of the Ontario *Human Rights Code*, granting freedom from discrimination with respect to services, goods, facilities, accommodation, contracts, employment, and vocational associations, and freedom from sexual solicitation in the workplace and by those in a position of power

Ontario Human Rights Commission
the provincial body responsible for investigating and adjudicating complaints about violations of the Ontario *Human Rights Code*

harassment
unwelcome comments or conduct toward another person

constructive discrimination
a kind of discrimination that may not be obviously discriminatory and may seem based on a reasonable criterion, but that effectively excludes, restricts, or favours some people contrary to human rights laws

persons who are identified by a prohibited ground of discrimination." In other words, constructive discrimination refers to policies or practices that may not be obviously discriminatory but that have a discriminatory effect on a group protected under the Code. For example, an employer that requires all employees to work on Saturdays would be practising constructive discrimination against an employee who, for religious reasons, is unable to work on that day. But the notion of constructive discrimination comes with a significant restriction; the Code provides that constructive discrimination does not apply in a case where accommodating the employee's special needs would cause the employer undue hardship—for example, if the employee's religion prevented him from working on Saturdays, but the employer's business was only open on weekends.

Ontario Human Rights Code

PART I: FREEDOM FROM DISCRIMINATION

Services

1. Every person has a right to equal treatment with respect to services, goods and facilities, without discrimination because of race, ancestry, place of origin, colour, ethnic origin, citizenship, creed, sex, sexual orientation, age, marital status, family status or disability.

Accommodation

2(1) Every person has a right to equal treatment with respect to occupancy of accommodation, without discrimination because of race, ancestry, place of origin, colour, ethnic origin, citizenship, creed, sex, sexual orientation, age, marital status, family status, disability or the receipt of public assistance.

Harassment in accommodation

(2) Every person who occupies accommodation has a right to freedom from harassment by the landlord or agent of the landlord or by an occupant of the same building because of race, ancestry, place of origin, colour, ethnic origin, citizenship, creed, age, marital status, family status, disability or the receipt of public assistance.

Contracts

3. Every person having legal capacity has a right to contract on equal terms without discrimination because of race, ancestry, place of origin, colour, ethnic origin, citizenship, creed, sex, sexual orientation, age, marital status, family status or disability.

Accommodation of person under eighteen

4(1) Every sixteen or seventeen year old person who has withdrawn from parental control has a right to equal treatment with respect to occupancy of and contracting for accommodation without discrimination because the person is less than eighteen years old.

Idem

(2) A contract for accommodation entered into by a sixteen or seventeen year old person who has withdrawn from parental control is enforceable against that person as if the person were eighteen years old.

Employment

5(1) Every person has a right to equal treatment with respect to employment without discrimination because of race, ancestry, place of origin, colour, ethnic origin, citizenship, creed, sex, sexual orientation, age, record of offences, marital status, family status or disability.

Harassment in employment

(2) Every person who is an employee has a right to freedom from harassment in the workplace by the employer or agent of the employer or by another employee because of race, ancestry, place of origin, colour, ethnic origin, citizenship, creed, age, record of offence, marital status, family status or disability.

Vocational associations

6. Every person has a right to equal treatment with respect to membership in any trade union, trade or occupational association or self-governing profession without discrimination because of race, ancestry, place of origin, colour, ethnic origin, citizenship, creed, sex, sexual orientation, age, marital status, family status or disability.

SEXUAL HARASSMENT

Harassment because of sex in accommodation

7(1) Every person who occupies accommodation has a right to freedom from harassment because of sex by the landlord or agent of the landlord or by an occupant of the same building.

Harassment because of sex in workplaces

(2) Every person who is an employee has a right to freedom from harassment in the workplace because of sex by his or her employer or agent of the employer or by another employee.

Sexual solicitation by a person in position to confer benefit, etc.

(3) Every person has a right to be free from,

(a) a sexual solicitation or advance made by a person in a position to confer, grant or deny a benefit or advancement to the person where the person making the solicitation or advance knows or ought reasonably to know that it is unwelcome; or

(b) a reprisal or a threat of reprisal for the rejection of a sexual solicitation or advance where the reprisal is made or threatened by a person in a position to confer, grant or deny a benefit or advancement to the person.

Reprisals

8. Every person has a right to claim and enforce his or her rights under this Act, to institute and participate in proceedings under this Act and to refuse to infringe a right of another person under this Act, without reprisal or threat of reprisal for so doing.

Infringement prohibited

9. No person shall infringe or do, directly or indirectly, anything that infringes a right under this Part.

Source: Ontario *Human Rights Code*, RSO 1990, c. H.19, as amended.

A requirement, qualification, or factor is not discriminatory if it can be established that it is reasonable and bona fide (in good faith) in the circumstances. In the context of hiring, for example, two conditions are required to establish bona fide: first, it must be demonstrated that there is an objective relationship between the selection criteria and the job in question; second, it must be shown that the standards required for the job are imposed in good faith.

The Ontario Human Rights Commission periodically publishes human rights policies, including the following recent ones:

- Policy on preventing sexual and gender-based harassment (March 8, 2011)
- Policy on human rights and rental housing (July 21, 2009)
- Policy on discrimination because of pregnancy and breastfeeding (April 1, 2009)
- Guidelines on developing human rights policies and procedures (March 14, 2008)
- Policy on discrimination because of family status (April 3, 2007)

The following sections describe some other Ontario Human Rights Commission policies.

Policy on Discrimination and Harassment Because of Sexual Orientation

sexual orientation
a person's settled sexual preference, whether heterosexual, gay or lesbian, or bisexual

The Ontario *Human Rights Code* prohibits discrimination on the grounds of sexual orientation and same-sex partnership status. The Code defines **sexual orientation** as "more than simply a 'status' that an individual possesses; it is an immutable personal characteristic that forms part of an individual's core identity. Sexual orientation encompasses the range of human sexuality from gay and lesbian to bisexual and heterosexual orientations" (OHRC, 2000b).

The Code's current view of "spouse" and "partnership" can be traced to May 20, 1999, when the Supreme Court of Canada found the "opposite sex" definition of "spouse" in part III of Ontario's *Family Law Act* to be unconstitutional. In response to this decision, Ontario introduced Bill 5 (1999), which amended the *Family Law Act* so that its provisions concerning support obligations applied to same-sex partners. Bill 5 also amended the Ontario *Human Rights Code* by defining the term "marital status" to include "same-sex partnership status" and the term "spouse" to include "same-sex partner." "Same-sex partner" is further defined to mean the individual with whom a person of the same sex is living in a conjugal relationship outside marriage. Similarly, "same-sex partnership status" is defined to mean the status of living with an individual of the same sex in a conjugal relationship outside marriage. Further amendments to the Code, in 2005, sought to improve understanding of discrimination experienced by lesbian, gay, and bisexual individuals, and to assist organizational development of harassment-free environments.

Policy on Discrimination and Harassment Because of Gender Identity

In this policy (OHRC, 2000a), sex under the Ontario *Human Rights Code* is interpreted to include **gender identity**. Gender identity is not the same as sexual orientation; it applies to people—almost exclusively transgenderists and transsexuals—who undertake to change their birth-assigned gender in some way. Gender identity involves self-image, physical and biological appearance, behaviour, and gender-related conduct. The term "transgendered" refers to "people who are not comfortable with or who reject, in whole or in part, their birth-assigned gender identities" (OHRC, 2000a). Transgendered people include transsexuals, cross-dressers, and intersexed individuals.

gender identity
a term that applies to people, mostly transgenderists and transsexuals, whose self-perception is in some way at variance with their birth-assigned gender; involves self-image, physical and biological appearance, behaviour, and gender-related conduct

Policy on Sexual Harassment and Inappropriate Gender-Related Comments and Conduct

This policy (OHRC, 1996b) supports a person's fundamental right to freedom from sexual harassment and from other forms of unequal treatment expressed through demeaning comments and actions based on gender. The policy clearly distinguishes between, on the one hand, accepted social interaction or consensual relations and, on the other hand, behaviour that is known or ought reasonably to be known to be unwelcome. Also, the policy provides a framework for educational initiatives (for example, the development of training materials and anti-harassment policies) by employers and others.

There are two views of *sexual harassment*. Narrowly speaking, sexual harassment is an objectionable comment or conduct of a sexual nature. Broadly speaking, sexual harassment is not necessarily overtly sexual in nature; it may simply be conduct that is related to the recipient's gender and that demeans that person or causes him or her personal humiliation or embarrassment. Most cases of sexual harassment involve men harassing women. But women sometimes harass men, and sexual harassment between members of the same sex has been known to occur.

A person can be guilty of sexual harassment or discrimination without making explicit reference to gender or sex. Sexual discrimination may involve harassing comments or conduct whose gender basis is unspoken. Specific examples of sexual harassment and inappropriate gender-related comments and conduct include the following (OHRC, 1996b, s. 6):

1. gender-related comments about an individual's physical characteristics or mannerisms;
2. unwelcome physical contact;
3. suggestive or offensive remarks or innuendoes about members of a specific gender;
4. propositions of physical intimacy;
5. gender-related verbal abuse, threats, or taunting;
6. leering or inappropriate staring;
7. bragging about sexual prowess;
8. demands for dates or sexual favours;

9. offensive jokes or comments of a sexual nature about an employee, client, or tenant;

10. display of sexually offensive pictures, graffiti, or other materials;

11. questions or discussions about sexual activities;

12. paternalism based on gender which a person feels undermines his or her self-respect or position of responsibility;

13. rough and vulgar humour or language related to gender.

The Ontario *Human Rights Code* policy regarding sexual harassment is consistent with the laws in several countries on workplace discrimination and harassment. A harassment-free work environment is one without a hostile or abusive atmosphere—one in which an employee is not subjected to offensive remarks or behaviour or to intimidating, hostile, or humiliating working conditions.

Policy on Racial Slurs and Harassment and Racial Jokes

This policy (OHRC, 1996a) endorses the right of every individual to live and work in an environment that is free from race-related, demeaning comments and actions. The policy defines as discriminatory acts or expressions that are manifested through slurs, jokes, or behaviour intended to demean a person because of his or her race. *Racial harassment* involves offensive, humiliating, derogatory, or hostile acts or expressions that are racially based. A comment or conduct need not be explicitly racial in order to constitute racial harassment. The term "race" in the policy refers to all of the race-related grounds (that is, race, ancestry, colour, and ethnic origin) and to citizenship, place of origin, and creed.

EXERCISE 4

1. What are the implications of sexual harassment for the harasser?
2. What are the implications of sexual harassment for the victim?
3. How can sexual harassment be prevented?
4. How can harassment on the Internet be prevented? Is online harassment of people based on age, gender, sexual orientation, and so on, protected through human rights legislation? What about the right to freedom of speech?

Policy and Guidelines on Racism and Racial Discrimination

This policy (OHRC, 2006) updates and significantly expands on the existing policy (described above) on racial slurs and harassment and racial jokes. The policy now addresses a number of considerations related to racism, including racial profiling and employment-related discrimination. The policy also stresses the importance of developing an organizational culture that respects human rights and prevents racial discrimination.

This policy has had an impact on law enforcement. Numerous law enforcement agencies have been developing projects and offering education aimed at preventing racism and discrimination in policing, including the employment practices in policing. In 2011, the Windsor (Ontario) Police Service, Windsor Police Services Board, Ontario Police College, and the Ontario Human Rights Commission announced a major initiative to address policing and human rights issues.

HUMAN RIGHTS AND FREEDOMS: POLICE ABILITIES, KNOWLEDGE, AND SKILLS

The importance of human rights and freedoms to the quality of people's lives is increasingly recognized. Many countries are actively involved in upholding these rights for their citizens, and law enforcement plays a significant role in such initiatives. In recent years, however—in particular, following the 9/11 terrorist attacks on the United States—many Western governments, including Canada's, have become increasingly focused on national and international security concerns. This has created tensions between two police responsibilities: the duty to ensure civil order and the duty to ensure that civil liberties are upheld.

Police services operate in contexts of international, national, and provincial human rights provisions that enshrine basic individual and collective rights and freedoms at social and institutional levels. These provisions provide a society with a "collective conscience," so that it can protect the ideals of democratic citizenship and social justice. The human rights and freedoms acts, codes, and policies are more than just abstract principles and goals; their purpose is to transform a society plagued by human rights violations into one that treasures and preserves equal treatment and protection under the law.

At the international level, the United Nations Centre for Human Rights has developed international human rights standards specific to law enforcement. The standards address policing ethics and legal conduct, policing in democracies, non-discrimination in law enforcement, police investigations, arrest, detention, the use of force and firearms, civil disorder, states of emergency, armed conflict, protection of juveniles, community policing, and police violations of human rights, as well as the rights of women, refugees, non-nationals, victims, police command, and management.

Police legislation in Canada is consistent with international standards and with federal and provincial laws regarding human rights and freedoms. In its declaration of principles, the **Ontario *Police Services Act*** stipulates that police services shall be provided at the provincial level in accordance with the safeguards that guarantee the fundamental rights enshrined in the *Canadian Charter of Rights and Freedoms* and the Ontario *Human Rights Code* (principle 2). A police culture in which all police officers uphold the letter and the spirit of human rights laws and foster a climate of justice, respect, acceptance, and harmonious coexistence is key to maintaining both the integrity of the profession and a positive relationship with the general public.

However, the focus of law enforcement on counterterrorism and national security represents a challenge to policing that seeks to balance civil liberty and civil order; law enforcement must negotiate two conflicting approaches to policing. On the one hand, democratic community policing honours equally the imperatives of law and order and of due process; on the other hand, democratic dictatorship policing emphasizes law and order more than it does civil liberties. In practical terms, law

Ontario *Police Services Act*
a statute requiring that the police services provided throughout Ontario will reflect the safeguards enshrined in the *Canadian Charter of Rights and Freedoms* and the Ontario *Human Rights Code*

enforcement agents must at once honour human rights standards, respect the civil rights of citizens, and establish a trusting relationship with the communities they serve and protect. At the same time, they must do whatever is necessary to prevent threats to individual and collective rights and freedoms, and to national security.

EXERCISE 5

THE G20 TORONTO PROTESTS

A striking example of how the imperative of law and order can come into conflict with civil liberties is the G20 summit, held in downtown Toronto over two days in June 2010. This event occasioned a multi-million dollar security operation, mass demonstrations, and rioting. Clashes between members of the public and the police were highly publicized, and resulted in a slew of investigations and public inquiries. In all, more than 1,100 people were arrested—the largest mass arrest in Canadian history—though the majority were never charged. Ombudsman André Marin called the events "the most massive compromise of civil liberties in Canadian history" (CBC News, 2010).

In the aftermath of the summit, various groups cited the alarming number of illegal arrests, detentions, and incidents of police brutality, including the use of excessive force by some police in making arrests. The highly publicized example of Adam Nobody, tackled and punched repeatedly by officers, is perhaps the best-known case in point; the main officer involved, and another officer involved in another incident, have both been charged with criminal offences. Many individuals were detained for hours and then released without any charges being laid; others were packed into paddy wagons and dropped off outside city limits or taken to the G20 temporary jail.

Following the summit, the Canadian Civil Liberties Association (CCLA) called for a joint federal–provincial public inquiry to determine responsibility for the violations of fundamental rights and freedoms, including the following:

- the violent dispersal of protesters gathered in the designated "free speech zone" at Queen's Park, in the course of which tear gas and rubber bullets were used;

- mass detentions and arrests, and delays or failure to provide medical care to those arrested;

- an incident in which a group of protesters who had arrived from Quebec were awoken at a University of Toronto residence building and arrested en masse; and

- a prolonged mass detention in which police used, for the first time in the city's history, a controversial tactic known as "kettling"—the corralling of people by large cordons of police officers—to indiscriminately confine about 300 protestors and innocent bystanders for hours in torrential rain.

Throughout the summit, Toronto Police Chief Bill Blair emphasized the police responsibility to maintain security. He stressed that the police were working hard "to maintain order and restore the rule of law" and advised members of the public to leave areas when asked to do so if they did not wish to be involved with police. However, according to the chair of the police services board, the summit "stained the credibility of the Toronto Police"

(Kennedy, 2011, P. A1). In light of the G20 controversy, the CCLA has called for changes to police practices and training in situations where public order is concerned. This organization has emphasized the role that policing is supposed to play in facilitating the right to peaceful protests (CBC News, 2011). The CCLA cited incidents of police officers' removing their badges and telling protesters that martial law had been declared, and that they no longer had any rights and could be held as long as necessary.

One year after the summit, the *Toronto Star* interviewed 43 of the people who had been kettled—a technique that, at the time of writing, the police have decided never to use again—to find out how the experience changed them (Yang & Kennedy, 2011, IN3). For many, the experience sparked political activism, and nearly all reported that they now distrust police and have become reluctant to report minor incidents, to cooperate with investigations, or even to ask officers for directions.

An important element in any analysis of the G20 summit is Ontario Regulation 233/10, passed by the Ontario government without debate. This regulation brought parts of the area within the G20 security fence under the authority of the *Public Works Protection Act* (PWPA), a statute passed in 1939 to protect infrastructure works from Nazis during the war. Initially, the public was told that the regulation gave officers authority to demand identification and to detain anyone within five metres of the fence. In fact, there was no five-metre rule. But even after this misconception was corrected, searches and arrests continued to occur "well beyond the security zone" (CBC News, 2010).

The Toronto Police Services Board, Ontario's Office of the Independent Police Review Director, and the Ontario ombudsman have reviewed the events of the summit and the controversy surrounding Regulation 233/10. The government has been criticized for the way it passed the regulation and for not clarifying precisely how it would affect civilians. The ombudsman's report recommends that, in the future, the government provide the public with better information whenever police powers are temporarily expanded. At the time of writing, the province is preparing to begin the process of repealing the PWPA.

1. In extraordinary circumstances such as the G20, are the aims of maintaining civil order and upholding civil rights incompatible? How well do you think a balance was struck in the case of the G20?
2. In your opinion, who is responsible for the compromise of civil liberties at the G20? Do you think anything could have been done differently? If so, what?

EXERCISE 6

The vast majority of police officers protect the rights and freedoms of citizens. In rare cases, police abuse their authority. Three types of police abuse of authority have been identified (Freeman, 1996):

- *Physical abuse/excessive force.* This involves the use of more force than is necessary to carry out an arrest or search, or the "wanton use of any degree of physical force against another by the police officer under the colour of the officer's authority."

- *Verbal/psychological abuse.* "Relying on authority inherently vested in them based on their office, police verbally assail, ridicule, harass, and/or place persons who are under the actual or constructive dominion of the officer in a situation where the individual's esteem and/or self-image is threatened and/or diminished; threat of physical harm under the supposition that a threat is psychologically coercive and instils fear in the average person."
- *Violation of civil rights.* This includes "any violation of a person's constitutional rights, federally protected rights, and provincially protected rights even though the person may not suffer any apparent physical or psychological damage in the purest sense."

Read each description of a police action below, and indicate, using one of the following three acronyms, the nature of the abuse: PA if it is physical abuse/excessive force, VPA if it is verbal/psychological abuse, or VCR if it is a violation of civil rights.

- a. stopping a car without justifiable reason
- b. punching a citizen
- c. kicking a suspect
- d. spraying mace
- e. hitting a citizen with a flashlight
- f. using deadly force
- g. hitting a citizen with a baton
- h. overtightening handcuffs
- i. "bumping" a citizen's head as he or she is entering a police car
- j. holding someone incommunicado during interrogation
- k. conducting a search without a justifiable reason
- l. calling a citizen derogatory names
- m. not allowing a person held for interrogation to consult an attorney
- n. imposing a police-dominated atmosphere during interrogation
- o. sexually harassing a female suspect in custody
- p. not taking someone into custody because of his or her race
- q. booking a lesbian or gay person because of the person's sexual orientation
- r. taking someone into custody without legal grounds
- s. harassing a citizen because of the colour of his or her skin

EXERCISE 7

THE MAHER ARAR CASE

Identify and explain what you see as human rights violations in the following case study.

Maher Arar is a Canadian software engineer. CBC News (2007) has reported that on September 26, 2002, during a stopover in New York en route from Tunis to Montreal, Arar was detained by American authorities who may have been acting upon false and misleading information supplied by the Royal Canadian Mounted Police (RCMP). Despite carrying a Canadian passport, Arar was deported to Syria, held in solitary confinement in a Syrian prison where he was regularly tortured for over a year, and eventually released and returned to Canada in October 2003.

Arar's case reached new heights of controversy when an Ottawa journalist wrote an article on November 8, 2003, containing information leaked to her from an unknown security source, possibly within the RCMP. This information suggested that Arar was a trained member of an al Qaeda terrorist cell. The RCMP raided the journalist's house while investigating the leak. The raid was widely denounced and led to a public inquiry.

The episode strained Canada–US relations and led to a public inquiry in Canada, which cleared Arar and was sharply critical of the RCMP, other Canadian government departments, and the United States over its treatment of Arar. The United States did not participate in the inquiry, but maintained that Arar's removal to Syria was legal. Human rights groups dispute this. The Canadian government paid Arar $10.5 million in compensation for its part in his ordeal.

There are questions concerning the role of various government officials in the Arar case. RCMP Commissioner Giuliano Zaccardelli resigned in December 2006 over contradictions in his testimony to the House of Commons Committee on Public Safety and National Security with respect to what he knew at the time and what he told government ministers. Arar himself appealed to the United States Supreme Court, where he attempted to hold American officials accountable for labelling him an al Qaeda suspect and deporting him to Syria. In 2010, the Supreme Court declined to hear the appeal due to national security considerations.

Source: http://www.cbc.ca/news/background/arar.

EXERCISE 8

A police service allows a Sikh officer to wear his turban on duty, and allows Aboriginal officers to continue their practice of wearing braids down to their armpits (a traditional way for Aboriginals to connect, symbolically, with Mother Earth).

a. Is the police service justified in its decision? Explain.
b. Do you consider that allowing these traditional cultural practices within a police service represents the weakening of an official institution? Why or why not?
c. Do you consider the police service's acceptance of these practices as kowtowing to the whims of human rights activists?
d. Do you think these decisions might lead nudists to challenge the dress-code policy in certain institutions?
e. Can you think of other possible practices or events that some people might consider encroachments on the symbols of national institutions? Justify your choices.
f. What influence, if any, should human rights and freedoms provisions, especially those related to diversity, have on the decisions of a police service regarding its members? In what other areas of Canadian society might human rights and freedoms codes lead to challenges? (Consider, for example, a woman's right to go topless in public.)

CHAPTER SUMMARY

Human rights laws and policies enshrine basic rights and freedoms. With the institutions that administer them, they protect both citizens and social justice. They support equality and respect for all citizens, regardless of their culture, race, religion, gender, age, sexual orientation, gender identity, socio-economic status, or physical or mental ability. The response of governments to the 9/11 terrorist attacks has increased the tension between the imperatives of national security and law and order, on the one hand, and of civil liberties on the other.

THE GREAT DEBATE

Post-9/11 events involving law enforcement brought the debate concerning civil liberty versus national security to a head. Have one group take the position that individual rights should take precedence over national security. Have the second group take the position that national security should take precedence over civil liberty. Include in the debate specific situations, real or hypothetical, in which police must strike a balance between individuals' rights and the need for law and order.

KEY TERMS

Aboriginal peoples' rights
Canadian Charter of Rights and Freedoms
Canadian Human Rights Act
Canadian Human Rights Commission
constructive discrimination
democratic rights
discrimination
equality rights
freedom from discrimination
fundamental freedoms

gender identity
harassment
legal rights
mobility rights
multicultural heritage
official languages
Ontario *Human Rights Code*
Ontario Human Rights Commission
Ontario *Police Services Act*
sexual orientation

REFERENCES

Block, S., & Galabuzi, G.-E. (2011). *Canada's colour coded labour market: The gap for racialized workers.* Ottawa: Canadian Centre for Policy Alternatives. http://www.policyalternatives.ca/sites/default/files/uploads/publications/National%20Office/2011/03/Colour%20Coded%20Labour%20Market.pdf.

Canadian Bill of Rights. SC 1960, c. 44.

Canadian Charter of Rights and Freedoms. (1982). Part I of the *Constitution Act, 1982*, RSC 1985, app. II, no. 44.

Canadian Human Rights Act. (2008). RSC 2008, c. 30, as amended.

Canadian Human Rights Act Review Panel. (2000). Promoting equality: A new vision. http://dsp-psd.pwgsc.gc.ca/Collection/J2-168-2000E.pdf.

Canadian Press. (2011, March 17). Supreme Court to decide whether woman can wear niqab when testifying. *The Hamilton Spectator.* http://www.thespec.com/news/canada/article/503381--supreme-court-to-decide-whether-woman-can-wear-niqab-when-testifying.

CBC News. (2007, January 26). Maher Arar. *CBC.ca.* http://www.cbc.ca/news/background/arar/.

CBC News. (2010, December 7). G20 police rule slammed by ombudsman. *CBC.ca.* http://www.cbc.ca/news/canada/toronto/story/2010/12/07/ombudsman-g20-security-rule-report856.html.

CBC News. (2011, February 28). G20 "rights violations" require public inquiry: report. *CBC.ca.* http://www.cbc.ca/news/politics/story/2011/02/28/g20-report-inquiry-toronto.html.

Constitution Act, 1982. (1982). RSC 1985, app. II, no. 44.

Family Law Act. (1990). RSO 1990, c. F.3, as amended.

Freeman, A.P. (1996). Unscheduled departures: The circumvention of just sentencing for police brutality. *Hastings Law Journal, 47,* 677.

Human Rights Code. (1990). RSO 1990, c. H.19, as amended.

Kennedy, B. (2011, June 25). New poll finds "monumental shift" in public perception of Toronto police because of G20 actions. *The Toronto Star,* p. A1.

Muslim Matters. (2009, February 3). Canadian judge orders witness to remove niqaab. http://muslimmatters.org/?s=Canadian+Judge+orders+witness+to+remove++niqaab&x=5&y=7.

Myrie, E. (2011, March 24). Oh, Canada: Diverse but not inclusive. *The Hamilton Spectator,* p. A13.

Office of the United Nations High Commissioner for Human Rights. (1948). *Universal declaration of human rights.* http://www.un.org/en/documents/udhr/.

On Islam. (2010, October 14). Niqab "compromise" urged in Canada court. http://www.onislam.net/english/news/americas/449364.

Ontario Human Rights Commission (OHRC). (1996a, June 19). Policy on racial slurs and harassment and racial jokes. http://www.ohrc.on.ca/en/resources/publications.

Ontario Human Rights Commission (OHRC). (1996b, September 10). Policy on sexual harassment and inappropriate gender-related comments and conduct. http://www.ohrc.on.ca/en/resources/publications.

Ontario Human Rights Commission (OHRC). (2000a, March 30). Policy on discrimination and harassment because of gender identity. http://www.ohrc.on.ca/en/resources/publications.

Ontario Human Rights Commission (OHRC). (2000b, January 11). Policy on discrimination and harassment because of sexual orientation. http://www.ohrc.on.ca/en/resources/publications.

Ontario Human Rights Commission (OHRC). (2006). Policy and guidelines on racism and racial discrimination. http://www.ohrc.on.ca/en/resources/Policies/RacismPolicy.

Police Services Act. (1990). RSO 1990, c. P.15, as amended.

Public Works Protection Act. (1990). RSO 1990, c. P.55.

Senra, P. (2011, March 25). West shows its contradictions. *The Hamilton Spectator*, p. A15.

Yang, J., & Kennedy, B. (2011, June 25). Inside the G20 kettle. *The Toronto Star*, pp. IN1, IN3.

REVIEW QUESTIONS

TRUE OR FALSE?

_____ 1. Human rights reflect the collective conscience of nations.

_____ 2. The *Canadian Human Rights Act* of 1977 prohibited discrimination based on sexual orientation.

_____ 3. The *Canadian Charter of Rights and Freedoms* applies only to the federal government.

_____ 4. Upholding freedom of speech as a basic human right means that laws against libel and slander are unnecessary.

_____ 5. A serving police officer may run for political office only if granted a leave of absence.

_____ 6. Legal rights on arrest and detention don't protect Canadian citizens from arbitrary or unlawful actions by law enforcement agencies.

_____ 7. The *Canadian Charter of Rights and Freedoms* states that every Canadian citizen must be able to speak either English or French.

_____ 8. Harassment involves unwelcome comments or conduct toward another person.

_____ 9. Police legislation in Canada is consistent with international standards and federal and provincial laws covering human rights and freedoms.

_____ 10. Democratic community policing honours equally the imperatives of law and order and of due process.

MULTIPLE CHOICE

1. Understanding human rights and freedoms enables police to
   (a) create tensions within the community
   (b) measure the way that police treat non-diverse communities
   (c) fulfill their mandate
   (d) deal with the international community

2. Many attempts to establish human rights and freedoms have been informed by
   (a) England's industrial age
   (b) Winston Churchill
   (c) the *Magna Carta*
   (d) Queen Victoria

3. The legal rights section under the *Canadian Charter of Rights and Freedoms* is also known as the
   (a) police section
   (b) justice section
   (c) lawyers' section
   (d) *Criminal Code* section

4. "Equality rights" mean that every person is
   (a) protected from excessive legal fees
   (b) unable to get a lawyer if he or she has no money
   (c) equal before and under the law
   (d) equal except where the person has a physical disability

5. Police breaking into a person's residence and discovering incriminating evidence
   (a) does not violate a person's legal rights
   (b) always violates a person's legal rights
   (c) may be deemed to violate a person's legal rights, in which case the evidence will be inadmissible in court
   (d) is not covered under the *Canadian Charter of Rights and Freedoms*

6. A person can be guilty of sexual harassment or discrimination
   (a) only if the event occurs in the workplace
   (b) only if physical contact is made between two people
   (c) only if a specific reference to gender or sex is made
   (d) without making specific references to gender or sex

7. The violation of a person's civil rights by police can occur
   (a) only if the person suffers psychological or physical harm
   (b) even if the person does not suffer psychological or physical harm
   (c) if a person is known to have suffered psychological or physical harm previously
   (d) even if the police officer was justified in using physical force

8. A police officer who calls a citizen a derogatory name has committed
   (a) physical abuse
   (b) paternal abuse
   (c) verbal/psychological abuse
   (d) excessive force

9. Counterterrorist efforts since 9/11 have caused
   (a) a deterioration of police powers
   (b) a deterioration of civil liberties
   (c) tension between civil liberties and police powers
   (d) an increase in complaints against police

10. Democratic community policing
   (a) favours individual rights over law and order
   (b) denies due process to people
   (c) honours equally the imperatives of law and order and of due process
   (d) makes allowances for people from other countries

FILL IN THE BLANKS

1. The *Royal Proclamation* of 1763 gave provincial legislatures in Canada the right to pass laws in relation to property and _____ _____.

2. Any person in Canada who believes he or she has been discriminated against can file a complaint with the _____ _____ _____ _____.

3. The *Charter of Rights and Freedoms* guarantees rights and freedoms to all Canadians subject to reasonable and _____ limits.

4. A Supreme Court ruling in 1995 made _____ _____ a prohibited ground of discrimination.

5. The right to vote in an election is an example of a _____ right.

6. Individuals who believe their rights have been infringed under the Ontario *Human Rights Code* can file a complaint with the _____ _____ _____ _____.

7. _____ _____ refers to policies or practices that may not be obviously discriminatory but that have a discriminatory effect on a group protected under the Ontario *Human Rights Code*.

8. Verbal/psychological abuse is deemed to occur where a person under the dominion of a police officer receives a threat of physical harm that would instill fear in the _____ person.

9. Overtightening handcuffs is an example of _____ abuse.

10. Having national security as a priority is a challenge to policing that tries to balance civil liberty and civil _____.

Cultural Diversity

3

INTRODUCTION

Canada's over 31.2 million inhabitants compose a cultural, ethnic, and linguistic mosaic not found anywhere else on earth. According to the 2006 census, 6,186,950 individuals in this country were born outside Canada (Statistics Canada, 2007b). Most of these immigrants were attracted here by Canada's quality of life and its reputation for being peaceful, open, and welcoming toward people from different cultures.

The diversity of Canada—geographic, political, and ethnocultural—is a challenge for Canadian police. Canada is a federation of 10 provinces and 3 northern territories, with over three-quarters of the country's population living in urban areas (Sustainability Reporting Program, 2006). The different geographic regions of Canada pose varied problems with respect to distance, population, climate, and political jurisdiction. On the political side, some communities are served by federal services, some by regional services, and others by city services, with different laws and bylaws applying accordingly. In the cities, boundaries between regions and, in some cases, dense populations offer their own unique challenges. Nowadays, police have to contribute to international strategies against terrorism while continuing to combat crime and protect civil order domestically. In the course of these varied tasks, police encounter many different types of people from all walks of life.

Accounts of Canada's diverse population usually neglect the complex background of each cultural group and fail to consider the similarities and differences between the various groups. This is regrettable, because a better understanding of one another's cultures would improve social relations between Canadians, which might strengthen our national identity. And this, in turn, could enhance security and lawful conduct. This chapter focuses on the primary ethnocultural communities in Canada, and touches on some of the challenges associated with policing in the post-9/11 world.

CHAPTER OBJECTIVES

After completing this chapter, you should be able to:

- Explain the concepts of culture, race, ethnicity, and minority.
- Understand the concepts of prejudice and stereotyping.
- Understand the cultural values, beliefs, and practices of various ethnocultural communities in Canada, as well as their historical background in this country.
- Refine your understanding of specific cultures in the context of the post-9/11 environment.

EXERCISE 1

1. How could focusing on cultural differences rather than similarities affect the practice of law enforcement?
2. How would you go about involving police and the community in a joint effort to develop policing approaches that are responsive to ethnic and racial groups?

CONCEPTS OF CULTURE, ETHNICITY, RACE, AND MINORITY

There is a great deal of confusion over the terms *culture, ethnicity, race,* and *visible minority* (Kazarian & Evans, 1998). For example, the English and the French are sometimes called Canada's "two founding races" despite the fact that both cultural groups belong to the Caucasian race.

Culture

The term *culture,* in a narrow sense, means "folk tradition." The anthropological term for culture in this sense is *ethnoculture* (Kallen, 2003). This notion of culture refers to the distinctive ways of viewing and doing things shared by members of a particular ethnic community—practices they transmit to one another and to the next generation through a process of "enculturation." In a slightly broader sense, **culture** refers to the patterns of behaviour and behavioural consequences that are shared and transmitted among the members of a particular society (Linton, 1945). Triandis (1995, p. 36) refers to culture as "the man-made part of the environment" and describes it as having two aspects: the objective (for example, roads and bridges) and the subjective (beliefs, attitudes, norms, roles, and values). A person's culture shapes his or her unique world view, influencing how that person thinks, feels, acts, communicates, and interprets his or her environment. Culture is inherited—an accident of birth—but it is also a learned phenomenon; it is acquired, for the most part, through the ordinary process of growing up and participating in the daily life of a particular ethnic community (Kallen, 2003).

> **culture**
> the patterns of behaviour and behavioural consequences that are shared and transmitted among members of a particular society

Ethnicity

The term **ethnicity** (also known as *ethnic identity*) refers to the cultural origin (for example, British or Armenian) with which a person or group identifies *within a multicultural context,* such as Canada. Self-identification is the essence of ethnicity; a Canadian man of Armenian descent is legally a citizen of this country, but might (or might not) define himself, ethnically, as an Armenian Canadian. Ethnicity can be mostly symbolic, involving an attachment to and pride in one's cultural origin; or it can be behavioural, comprehensively expressed through participation in cultural behaviours and activities and the active wish to pass them on to one's children.

> **ethnicity**
> the culture of origin with which an individual or group identifies within a multicultural context

Census Canada defines ethnic origin as "the ethnic or cultural group(s) to which an individual's ancestors belonged" (Statistics Canada, 2006d). But there is a difference between "ethnic group" and "cultural group." Again, *ethnicity* implies self-identification. A person who is part of an "ethnic group" is one who sees himself as part of that group, who identifies with its culture. A person who belongs to a "cultural group" has a particular cultural heritage but may not identify with it. For example, a woman may be a member of the Estonian cultural group but choose to identify herself as Canadian. A person does not choose the cultural group to which he or she belongs; it is inherited. A person's ethnicity, on the other hand, depends on his or her identifying with a particular cultural group. An interesting feature of today's society—an effect of globalization and intermarriage among ethnic groups—is that many individuals have multiple ethnic ancestries and identities.

Race

The word *race* first appeared in the English language about CE 1500. It comes from the French word *race*, which has equivalents in Italian (*razza*) and in Spanish (*raza*). Beyond this, the origin of the word is obscure (Kallen, 2003). It was not until the 18th century that the term *race* was used to indicate major divisions of humankind, classified according to certain common physical characteristics such as skin colour (Kallen, 2003). Categorizing people by race is essentially a way of identifying them according to the ancestry or origin indicated by their physical characteristics. In the end, race is not an absolute marker of identity but a social concept, nowadays often rejected as a means of classifying people.

Originally, **race** referred both to biological characteristics (as in "white race," "black race," "yellow race," or "red race") and to cultural traits and values (as in "peasant race") (Berry & Laponce, 1994). The term is increasingly used in reference to such group markers as language, national origin, ethnicity, culture, and religion. In fact, the meaning of *race* has become so broad and loose that it has lost its value as a defining term. Social scientists and others use the term strictly in reference to physical or biological features.

race
a classification based on ancestry or origin as indicated by physical characteristics

Minority

For the purposes of this text, a minority (or subordinate) group within a society is one that has less social status than the majority group; its members wield less political and economic and/or social power than the majority (Kallen, 2003). For example, Blacks in South Africa are the numerical majority insofar as they constitute most of the country's population, but we would classify them as a minority in that country because they hold relatively little power politically, economically, and socially. The term *minority* is not and should not be used merely as a racial classification, to refer to those who are not white. In other words, any racial group in any society can hold the majority power and be considered the "majority group."

In short, the term *minority* applies to groups within a society that have less social, political, and economic power than the majority or host group. The minority group may also differ from the majority on the basis of race, religion, political affiliation, nationality, culture, or some other characteristics. But lack of power is their main defining feature. In Canada, a **visible minority** is a group of people, other than Aboriginal peoples, who are non-Caucasian in race or non-white in colour (*Employment Equity Act*, 1995), and the term is mainly used in the context of employment; visible minorities are one of the four groups—along with women, Aboriginal peoples, and people with disabilities—designated under the *Employment Equity Act* as beneficiaries of employment equity.

visible minority
individuals, other than Aboriginal peoples, who are non-Caucasian in race or non-white in colour

Visible minorities are a growing presence in Canada. By 2001, our visible minority population had reached 4 million people. In 2003, the Canadian Council on Social Development reported that almost 60 percent of visible minority immigrants to Canada in the past 10 years had come from Asia, with 20 percent from the Caribbean, Central and South America, and Africa. Visible minority groups account for 37 percent of the populations of both Toronto and Vancouver, the largest group being Asian. Hamilton, Ontario has a nearly 25 percent visible minority population, while Windsor, Ontario is at 22 percent. Close to 94 percent of Canada's visible minority immigrants have settled in urban areas (Canadian Council on Social Development, 2003).

By 2006, the census recorded 5,068,100 visible minority individuals in Canada, which is 16.2 percent of the total Canadian population. With respect to the provinces, Statistics Canada reports that Ontario was home to 2,745,200 visible minorities in 2006, a number that accounts for more than half of Canada's total visible minority population. British Columbia had the second largest share. Most visible minorities in Ontario live in major urban centres, with Toronto—including Mississauga, Brampton, Markham, Richmond Hill, and Vaughan—hosting the largest number (2,174,100) (Statistics Canada, 2006c).

EXERCISE 2

Newcomers to Canada, who are often especially vulnerable to crime, may fear police because they have experienced police corruption and brutality in their countries of origin. What are some things that police services could do to encourage these newcomers to cooperate with police when serious crimes occur in their neighbourhoods?

CULTURAL BELIEFS AND PRACTICES: CORE DIMENSIONS

There are 10,000 cultures and 6,170 distinct languages in the world (Moynihan, 1993; Triandis, 1995). It would be impossible to study all cultures in detail, but we can familiarize ourselves with the key characteristics of some of them—what we might consider their "personalities," and what psychologists call their *dimensions*. Several such dimensions or "personalities" of cultures have been identified, and we describe them below. Note that these dimensions are continuums, not categories; in other words, cultures are seen not as being entirely one thing or the other but as having more of some characteristics than others. A "dimensional" approach to cultures and cultural beliefs and practices allows us to see them in relation to one another, and works against the tendency to stereotype people, cultures, or cultural beliefs and practices.

- **Achievement Versus Relationship Culture**
  In achievement cultures, people primarily live to work, whereas in relationship cultures they work to live. Individuals from achievement cultures tend to focus on work and on getting the job done. Individuals from relationship cultures emphasize leisure and fun, the separation of work life from private life, close family ties, and nurturing social relations.

- **Tight Versus Loose Culture**

  Tight cultures impose clear-cut societal norms. Such cultures have only minimal tolerance for people who deviate from established norms and expectations. Predictability, certainty, and security are dominant values in tight cultures. Unlike individuals from loose cultures, which are less concerned about rules and conformity, individuals from tight cultures tend to be more anxious, insecure, and fearful of the consequences of violating the norms.

- **Low-Context Versus High-Context Culture**

  Cultures can also be described in terms of communication style. In low-context cultures, words are extremely important because they convey most of the message being sent. Low-context cultures include the host cultures of Canada, Britain, France, Germany, the United States, and most Scandinavian countries. In these countries, police officers use direct and logical language, usually without emotion, and they expect their words alone to convey their message. Low-context cultures are also time-oriented— that is, schedules are an important part of completing tasks.

  In high-context cultures, by contrast, words without emotion and context have very little meaning; words convey only part of the message being sent. Here, the spoken message needs to be understood in the context of the larger communication or social interaction. People from high-context cultures prefer to get to know strangers before developing a work relationship with them. Having long personal conversations prior to reaching agreements or to carrying out instructions is common in these cultures, to the annoyance of individuals from low-context cultures. Individuals from high-context cultures are also task-oriented—completing a task is more important to them than the schedule. Lateness or missing appointments may be less problematic in high-context cultures than it is in low-context ones. High-context cultures include Aboriginal cultures and African, Caribbean, Asian, and Latin American cultures.

- **Collectivism Versus Individualism**

  Cultures can also be viewed in terms of being *collectivist* ("we"-oriented) as opposed to *individualist* ("me"-oriented). Collectivist cultures are characterized by hierarchical structures and by identification with, loyalty to, and dependence on in-groups. The self-concepts of individuals from these cultures tend to depend on the in-groups rather than on distinct identities. The interdependence of the individual and the group is a critical feature of collectivist cultures, in which people value immediate and extended family (sometimes including ancestors), family honour, security, hierarchical relationships, obedience, conformity, group decisions, group "face," and group harmony. People from these cultures are likely to downplay their own goals and remain loyal to group goals. They believe that parents have an obligation to care for their children, and that children have an obligation to care for their aging parents. In collectivist cultures, elderly parents are expected to live with their children and command their respect.

  People from individualist cultures are likely to pursue personal goals and, when faced with a conflict between the group's goals and their own,

Table 3.1   Differences Between Individualist and Collectivist Cultures

Individualism	Collectivism
Pursuit of one's own goals	Loyalty to one's group
Nuclear family structure	Extended family structure
Self-reliant	Group-reliant
Time and energy invested for personal gain	Time and energy invested for group gain
Receptive to career changes	Relatively unreceptive to career changes
Relatively little sharing of material/non-material resources	Sharing of material/non-material resources
Emphasis on competition	Emphasis on cooperation
Relatively non-conformist	Conformist
Mistrust of authority	Respectful of status and authority

are likely to follow the latter. They tend to value independence, self-reliance, and competition over cooperation. They may also mistrust authority. Table 3.1 summarizes the differences between individualist and collectivist cultures.

Relative to European peoples, Aboriginal, African, Asian, and Latin-American peoples are collectivist, given their relative de-emphasis on the welfare of the individual in favour of the welfare of the community. Canada has been a collectivist country in the sense that it has "recognized collectivities as fundamental units and emphasized group rights over those of individual citizens" (Lock, 1990, p. 239). As Lock describes, "Whereas in America 'life, liberty, and the pursuit of happiness' were enshrined as fundamental ideals, in Canada 'peace, order, and good government' were laid down as overarching goals" (1990, p. 239).

It is important to note that collectivist individuals may be found in individualist cultures, and individualist individuals may be found in collectivist cultures. Individuals may also embrace individualism and collectivism at the same time.

STEREOTYPES AND PREJUDICES

stereotype
conventional, formulaic, and usually oversimplified conceptions that falsify reality through over-generalization and strip their subjects of individuality

Historically and, in some cases, to this day, stereotypes and prejudice have attached themselves to certain races, ethnicities, and minorities. A **stereotype** is a standardized, usually oversimplified conception of something, whether a person, group, event, or issue. Stereotypes falsify reality through over-generalization and strip their subjects of individuality. To say, for example, that all English people love tea and soccer is to affirm a stereotype, albeit a relatively harmless one. An example of a more harmful stereotype is that of the "drunken Indian," which continues to be a powerful one in mainstream society. Many believe that Aboriginal people "can't handle their liquor" or that "once they start drinking, they can't stop," or that, for biological reasons, Aboriginal people are, as a race, more susceptible than others to alcoholism and alcohol abuse. However, none of these stereotypes has any scientific basis. Many have suggested that alcohol abuse among Aboriginals should be viewed as a consequence of social, psychological, and economic disadvantages, not as a cause of these factors (Moynes, 1999).

A **prejudice** is an adverse judgment or opinion formed with little or no knowledge or experience or examination of the facts; a predetermined preference, idea, or bias. To be prejudiced is to hold unreasonable preconceived judgments or convictions about something. Prejudice can involve the irrational suspicion or hatred of a particular group, race, or religion. Prejudices cause people to judge prematurely and irrationally. When strongly held, they can be contagious, encouraging other people to succumb to them and become biased against someone or something. Prejudices affect their targets detrimentally, often forming the foundations of, among other things, racist and sexist attitudes.

Police in Canada need to ensure that stereotypes and secret prejudices do not influence their interactions with people in our diverse communities. In preparation for encountering different cultures and ethnicities, police officers should do the following: avoid being judgmental; increase their understanding of different cultures; understand that people of diversity are neither all saints nor all villains; recognize that they can learn a lot from people of diversity; and focus on similarities among people as much as on differences (Kazarian, Crichlow, & Bradford, 2007, p. 148).

prejudice
an adverse judgment or opinion formed beforehand with little or no knowledge or experience or examination of the facts; a predetermined preference, idea, or bias

EXERCISE 3

1. Consider a few of the stereotypes that you have encountered with respect to people of diversity. What effects do you think stereotypes have on the people who are subjected to them and on society generally?
2. What effects do you think stereotypes and prejudice have on law enforcement?

CULTURAL BELIEFS AND PRACTICES: SPECIFIC CULTURAL GROUPS

Canada is a multicultural and multi-ethnic society comprising more than 200 ethnic groups. The nation's minority cultural groups can be divided into three major categories, as follows: Aboriginal peoples, non-visible ethnic minority peoples, and visible minority ethnic peoples. The following sections will discuss the three major cultural groups and the major subgroups in each. Space limitations prevent us from discussing the many smaller groups. (A single chapter simply cannot begin to cover the international world within Canada.)

The 2006 census revealed changes in the numbers concerning ethnic origins in Canada. In the case of people who have been in Canada for three generations or more, the ethnic origins that have historically been most numerous—Canadian, English, French, Scottish and Irish—continue to be most numerous. In the case of first-generation immigrants, Chinese and East Indian are now the most common ethnic origins, with English now ranking third (see Table 1.2 in Chapter 1).

Aboriginal Peoples

Aboriginal peoples make up almost 4 percent of the population in Canada. This minority community, 54 percent of whom live in Canada's cities, is growing almost twice as fast as the rest of the country's population (see Table 3.2). In 2006, the

Table 3.2   Size and Growth of the Population by Aboriginal Identity, Canada, 1996 and 2006

Aboriginal identity	2006	Percentage change from 1996 to 2006[1]
Total population	31,241,030	9
Aboriginal identity population	1,172,790	45
First Nations People[2]	698,025	29
Métis[2]	389,875	91
Inuit[2]	50,485	26
Multiple and other Aboriginal responses[3]	34,500	34
Non-Aboriginal Population	30,068,240	8

Notes:

1. Data have been adjusted to account for incompletely enumerated reserves in 1996 and 2006.
2. Includes persons who reported a North American Indian, Métis or Inuit identity only.
3. Includes persons who reported more than one Aboriginal identity group (North American Indian, Métis or Inuit) and those who reported being a Registered Indian and/or Band member without reporting an Aboriginal identity.

Source: Statistics Canada, censuses of population, 1996 and 2006. http://www12.statcan.ca/census-recensement/2006/as-sa/97-558/table/t1-eng.cfm.

number of Canadians who reported themselves as being Aboriginal (First Nations, Métis, or Inuit) reached 1,172,790, an increase of 45 percent over the last decade (Statistics Canada, 2006a).

At the time of first European contact, more than 56 Aboriginal nations existed in Canada, speaking more than 36 languages (Canadian Heritage, 2004). These numbers have radically diminished. Infringements on the human rights of Aboriginal peoples began with the first European contact and have been continual through our country's history. The effects of this historical mistreatment are evident in the higher rates of poverty, poorer health, higher death and suicide rates, and far greater unemployment compared with other Canadians, as discussed in Chapter 10.

Attempts to address the needs of Canada's Aboriginal peoples began in 1973. This was when the Supreme Court of Canada first recognized Aboriginal land rights, which were based on an Aboriginal group's traditional use and occupancy of a certain area of land. In 1982, the *Canadian Charter of Rights and Freedoms* recognized and affirmed the treaty rights of Aboriginal peoples to protect their cultures, customs, traditions, and languages. In 1996, the Royal Commission on Aboriginal Peoples presented a comprehensive five-volume report to the Parliament of Canada identifying the legal, political, social, economic, and cultural issues that need to be addressed to ensure the future survival of Canada's First Nations, Inuit, and Métis peoples. One year later, the federal government responded with *Gathering Strength: Canada's Aboriginal Action Plan*, a proposal to work in partnership with Canada's Aboriginal peoples to improve health, housing, and public safety, strengthen economic development, and assist with the implementation of self-government (Canadian Heritage, 2004).

In 2008, the federal government issued a *Statement of Apology* to survivors of the residential schools and established the Truth and Reconciliation Commission to deal with the devastation wrought by that episode. The Commission held its first national event in Winnipeg in 2010. As of March 2010, the government has made a total of $5 billion in Common Experience Payments. These payments are part of the Indian Residential Schools Settlement Agreement, and are one way in which the government has sought to acknowledge and compensate residential-school survivors for the harm they suffered.

The history of Aboriginal peoples in Canada, as well as the federal–Aboriginal relationship, is discussed in detail in the second part of this book.

The Culture of Aboriginal Peoples

Underlying Aboriginal ethics, values, and rules of behaviour is a traditional need to promote social harmony within the community and thereby ensure the community's survival in harsh natural environments. Aboriginal culture has a collectivist orientation; it values group harmony over individual success. Aboriginal peoples have always cultivated a cooperative social climate, encouraging the members of an extended family, clan, band, or tribe to adopt patterns of behaviour that involve the suppression of conflict (Brant, 1990). Aboriginal ethics or principles of behaviour, which still apply today, are listed in Table 3.3.

Aboriginal peoples believe that *non-interference* helps promote positive relations between people. Teaching in Aboriginal culture is done by modelling—that is, by example—rather than by commanding or dictating. In adult–child relationships, this policy of non-interference takes the form of permissiveness. Brant (1990, p. 535) describes how this approach might be expressed in an Aboriginal family:

> A Native child may be allowed at the age of six, for example, to make the decision on whether or not he goes to school even though he is required to do so by law.

Table 3.3   Aboriginal Ethics of Behaviour

Non-interference	Physical, verbal, and psychological coercion are avoided, as is exertion of pressure by means of advising, instructing, coercing, or persuading.
Non-competitiveness	Rivalry is averted and social embarrassment of individuals is prevented.
Emotional restraint	Both positive (joy and enthusiasm) and negative (anger and hostility) emotions are suppressed.
Sharing	Generosity is encouraged while hoarding material goods is discouraged.
Concept of time	There is a belief in "doing things when the time is right."
Attitude toward gratitude and approval	Gratitude and approval are rarely shown, verbalized, or expected.
Principle of teaching by modelling	To learn, one is *shown* how rather than *told* how. Actions convey useful and practical information.

Source: Brant (1990, p. 536).

The child may be allowed to decide whether or not he will do his homework, have his assignment done on time, and even visit the dentist. Native parents will be reluctant to force the child into doing anything he does not choose to do.

Non-competitiveness is another principle of Aboriginal peoples' behaviour that enables them to avoid conflict between groups and between individuals. It is a policy in keeping with their collectivist orientation—their emphasis on group harmony over individual success.

Aboriginal cultures value *emotional restraint* because it promotes self-control and discourages the expression of strong, violent feelings, which often lead to conflict. But this social principle comes at a paradoxical price. Suppressing emotions may create a need for alcohol as an outlet, and alcohol abuse often leads its users back to violence. Alcohol-related domestic violence and violence within the community are serious issues for Aboriginal peoples living on reserves.

Sharing is an important part of Aboriginal collectivist cultures. In addition to its historical value as a survival tactic, sharing helps to suppress conflict by minimizing the likelihood of greed, envy, arrogance, and pride within the community. It also contributes to equality and democracy. Striving for individual gain—for prosperity and success and other assets, such as a superior education—is inconsistent with the ethic of sharing. Aboriginal society tends to be disapproving of individual ambition. This disapproval has been a factor in the skimming of Aboriginal society, a process by which young, talented Aboriginal people or those with a post-secondary education leave the reserve to live in non-Aboriginal society and marry non-Aboriginals (Brant, 1990).

The *concept of time* in contemporary Aboriginal life is also connected to Aboriginal peoples' emphasis on harmonious relationships (Brant, 1990). They tend to be less perturbed by delay or impressed by punctuality than are people from more individualistic cultures, in which personal success depends on meeting deadlines and anxious time-management. Aboriginal people are unlikely to be inconvenienced or annoyed by delays in starting scheduled meetings or social functions.

In Aboriginal cultures, excellence is expected at all times. A negative consequence of this core value is performance anxiety. Aboriginal people may avoid taking risks for fear of making mistakes or subjecting themselves to public scrutiny. At the same time, Aboriginal people do not expect or welcome praise or rewards when they achieve excellence. Being good is expected of everyone. Praise of the individual is likely to be seen as deceitful or, in group contexts, as embarrassing, because it does not credit the whole group. Praise that is not shared with peers is seen as damaging to peer relationships. By a similar principle, gratitude and approval are rarely expressed in Aboriginal culture. Both are considered superfluous because doing something for someone else is thought to carry its own intrinsic reward.

The ethical principles described above can bring Aboriginal people into conflict with mainstream cultural values. For instance, the Aboriginal emphasis on the collective rather than the individual can create an impression of uncompetitiveness that doesn't sit well with the contemporary business world. Mainstream culture expects people to be competitive, and labels them "lazy" or "indifferent" if they behave otherwise.

EXERCISE 4

For each of the following principles of Aboriginal ethics, think of situations where the principle might be in conflict with "mainstream" North American ethics:

- Non-interference
- Non-competitiveness
- Emotional restraint
- Sharing
- Concept of time
- Attitude toward gratitude and approval
- Principle of teaching by modelling

Non-Visible Ethnic Minority Peoples

Non-visible ethnic minority groups in Canada include the two founding peoples of Canada—that is, the English and the French—and a host of other cultural groups from Europe, including Germans, Italians, the Dutch, Australians, and New Zealanders. As we saw in Chapter 1 (see Table 1.2), English, French, Scottish, and Irish are the most frequently reported non-visible ethnic minority groups in Canada for third-generation or more Canadians.

While there are differences among the English, Scottish, Irish, and Welsh cultures, they have certain values in common. Traditionally, they have been individualistic, emphasizing work ethic, self-reliance, emotional reserve, the nuclear family structure, privacy, and democracy. Self-reliance and work ethic are connected; a reluctance to express affection is common, as is respect for personal privacy and an unwillingness to disclose personal concerns or difficulties to others. This unwillingness stems from the belief that personal problems reflect personal failures, which are best met with greater individual effort.

People of French heritage are likely to value their language and its preservation, their French culture and its distinctiveness, their families, and, in some cases, their religion.

Visible Minority Populations

As stated above, the term *visible minority* refers to whether a person belongs to a visible minority group as defined by the *Employment Equity Act*. This includes "persons, other than Aboriginal peoples, who are non-Caucasian in race or non-white in colour." There is significant variation among Canada's visible minority populations in terms of origin, linguistic characteristics, and religious affiliation. In Canada, the visible minority population consists primarily of South Asian, Chinese, Black, Arab, West Asian, Filipino, Southeast Asian, Latin American, Japanese, and Korean peoples.

Visible minority groups in Canada are, first of all, statistically significant, constituting 16.2 percent of the entire population (Statistics Canada, 2006b). Over 5 million individuals who identify themselves as visible minorities have made Canada their home. Their population in Canada increased, between 2001 and 2006, five times faster than the country's general population. In 1981, 1 in 20 Canadians was a visible minority; in 2001, it was 1 in 7; in 2006, it was nearly 1 in 6 (Statistics

Canada, 2006b). By 2017, about 20 percent of the Canadian population could be a member of a visible minority group (Bélanger & Malenfant, 2005, p. 19).

Today, the three largest visible minority groups in Canada are South Asians, Chinese, and Blacks, in that order; collectively, these three groups constitute two-thirds of the visible minority population in Canada. The following sections discuss these three groups, as well as Arabs. Space considerations preclude a detailed discussion of other visible minorities.

EXERCISE 5

Law enforcement officials want to be respected for their abilities and professionalism, not for their cultural backgrounds. What moral dilemmas could law enforcement officials from a particular culture (for example, English, Asian, or Black culture) encounter in dealing with the following:

- co-workers or suspects from the same culture, and
- co-workers or suspects from other cultures?

South Asians

South Asians include anyone whose ancestry can be traced, directly or indirectly, to the Indian subcontinent, a complex miscellany of states and ethnic groups (Tran, Kaddatz, & Allard, 2005, p. 21). Hence the term *South Asian* encompasses a great variety of ethnic backgrounds, including, among various others, Bangladeshi, Bengali, East Indian, Goan, Pakistani, Sikh, Sri Lankan, and Tamil. It also includes people who, though born in Canada or elsewhere—for example, the Caribbean or Great Britain—identify themselves as belonging to one of the ethnic groups that make up the population of South Asia. In short, *South Asian* is an umbrella term equivalent to *North American*, more a convenience for Canadian statisticians than an ethnicity that someone from the region would actually claim.

The first South Asian immigrants to Canada were Sikhs, whom white society viewed, though they were relatively few in number (5,000 in 1908), with the same animosity as it did Blacks, Chinese, and Japanese. The presence of Sikhs in British Columbia at the turn of the century prompted talk of a "Hindu invasion" in the popular press (despite the fact that the Sikh religion, known as Sikhism, is in fact opposed to Hinduism). As the First World War approached, white Canadians became even more obsessed with racial purity. The following screed, quoted in Henry and Tator (2005, p. 71), is typical of the period:

> To prepare ourselves for the irrepressible conflict, Canada must remain a White Man's country. On this western frontier of the Empire will be the forefront of the coming struggle … . Therefore we ought to maintain this Country for the Anglo-Saxon and those races which are able to assimilate themselves to them. If this is done, we believe that history will repeat itself and the supremacy of our race will continue.

The prevalence of such white supremacism in the province led British Columbia to pass laws barring South Asians from participating in elections, even though they were British citizens. Most people of Asian descent of any kind, whether British citizens or not, were denied voting rights in Canada. This disenfranchisement had a negative economic impact on Asian Canadians. Excluded from voters' lists, they could neither bid on government contracts nor enter professions such as law, education, or medicine. South Asians did not get the franchise until the late 1940s (Baxter, 2003).

Despite the wide variety of their national and ethnic origins, South Asians have certain cultural values in common. Compared with other visible minority groups in Canada, they are remarkable for having strong ties not only to family and community but also to their linguistic, religious, and ethnic origins, as well as to Canada and its ideals (Tran, Kaddatz, & Allard, 2005, p. 22).

It is not surprising, given South Asians' varied origins, that linguistic diversity is a conspicuous feature of their culture in Canada. The linguistic collective of the Indian subcontinent includes more than 75 languages, of which Punjabi, English, and Tamil are the three most common (Tran et al., 2005, p. 22). Their traditional languages are important to South Asians. Compared with other visible minority cultures (the Chinese, for example), they are considerably more concerned about maintaining their mother tongues and passing them on to their children.

South Asians are also diverse in their religious beliefs. Sikhism, Hinduism, Islam, and Christianity are the religions most often practised in the South Asian community, with each ethnic subgroup adhering strongly to its particular faith. Of all visible minority groups in Canada, South Asians are the most likely to say that their religion is important to them, and the most likely to have participated in a religious activity within the past year (Tran et al., 2005, p. 23). This commitment to religion is not only evident in newcomers; it is maintained by second-generation South Asians, too.

South Asians maintain close ties both with their countries of origin and with their ethnocultural communities in Canada. This community closeness has a historical basis; it is partly a consequence of the harsh conditions and prejudice that South Asians faced on arriving in Canada a century ago, when community ties and support were crucial to their survival. More than other visible minority groups, South Asians tend both to work and to socialize with members of their own ethnic group. Many South Asians in Canada have co-workers with the same ancestral origins, and South Asians are the least likely of all visible minority groups to marry outside their own communities (Tran et al., 2005, p. 22).

A strong sense of family obligation and belonging is common among South Asians, who, like the Chinese and other visible minority groups, are more likely to live in multi-generational households made up of parents, children, spouses, and other relatives. Fewer than 1 in 10 South Asian seniors in Canada lives alone, compared with the 3 in 10 seniors in the general population who do so.

In keeping with their generally retentive attitude to origins, South Asians set much store by their cultural customs and traditions—for example, celebrations, food, and clothing—and they believe in the importance of maintaining them. Time does little to alter this attitude; second-generation South Asians feel as strongly about retaining their original culture as more recent arrivals do (Tran et al., 2005, p. 23).

An interesting characteristic of South Asians in Canada is that despite strong and persistent allegiance to their original cultures, they are also very patriotic where Canada is concerned. Of all visible minority groups in Canada, South Asians feel the strongest about being Canadian and about belonging to Canada, and are the most likely to vote. They are also more likely than other Canadians to feel an allegiance to their province and to the cities and towns where they live. For South Asians, pride in and awareness of ethnic origin does not lead to insularity; they are very active in the civic life of this country.

Chinese

The Chinese in Canada, though varied in their languages, countries of birth, and religious affiliations, are strongly linked by a single ethnicity, all identifying themselves as Chinese.

Chinese immigration to Canada has occurred in three distinct waves over the past 150 years. The first immigrants settled in British Columbia in 1860, drawn north from California, where they had gone in search of gold, by news of gold in the Fraser River area. When the Fraser River gold rush ended, many of the Chinese prospectors stayed on in Western Canada and moved into other kinds of labour—domestic service, farming, and, eventually, railway building (Chui, Tran, & Flanders, 2005, p. 24).

The next wave of immigration came two decades later, when Chinese workers, known as "coolies," were brought in as part of the manual labour force to build the Canada Pacific Railway (1881–1885). This was a vast, dangerous undertaking that brought the Chinese work-gangs much hardship and scandalously low pay; they were exploited, then released without prospects once the railway was finished. (In 2006, the government of Canada issued Chinese Canadians a formal apology for their treatment during and after the building of the CPR.)

A long spell of official discrimination against Chinese people followed, beginning with the 1885 *Act to Restrict and Regulate Chinese Immigration*. This Act introduced a "head tax" of $50 (later increased to $500), required of any person of Chinese origin seeking to enter Canada. The *Chinese Immigration Act* (1923) followed, denying Chinese residents of Canada the right to vote, obtain citizenship, or work in certain occupations. This legislation effectively put an end to Chinese immigration until the 1940s, when the Act was repealed (Chui et al., 2005, p. 25).

The next wave of Chinese immigration had its beginnings in the late 1960s, when Canada's immigration policy changed; national origin was removed as a selection criterion and replaced by a concern for skills and education. By the mid-1980s, Chinese immigration had gained momentum, and this continued for the next two decades, with an average of 35,400 immigrants arriving in Canada annually between 1981 and 2001 (Chui et al., 2005, p. 25). By the beginning of the 21st century, the Chinese formed the largest visible minority group in Canada. Approximately two-thirds of recent Chinese immigrants have come from the People's Republic of China. Most of the remainder come from Hong Kong, and a smaller proportion from Taiwan. The socio-economic profile of these latter-day Chinese immigrants, most of them wealthy, educated urbanites, differs significantly from that of earlier Chinese immigrants, who were manual labourers with few resources. Most Chinese immigrants of the new wave have chosen to live in big urban centres, such as Vancouver or Toronto (Chui et al., 2005, p. 27).

The Chinese language, which after English and French is the third most common mother tongue in Canada, is composed of different dialects. These vary according to the speaker's region of origin, though all are based on the same written language of Chinese characters. The two most common dialects are Cantonese and Mandarin (Chui et al., 2005, p. 32).

Religion is not an important factor in the lives of many Chinese, more than half of whom have no religious affiliations. This number is higher for those with roots in the People's Republic of China, but still significant among those from Hong Kong and Taiwan. The religions most common among Chinese who do claim religious affiliations are Buddhism and Christianity (Roman Catholicism and Protestantism) (Chui et al., 2005, p. 32).

The Chinese in Canada today perceive themselves as hard-working, industrious people, and the employment statistics bear this out. During the past 20 years, Chinese immigration has accounted for a significant percentage of the growth in the Canadian labour market. Gravitating toward white-collar occupations, many Chinese have found employment in the business and administrative spheres and in the natural and applied sciences. They are a family-centred community—the main reason given by Chinese immigrants for choosing to live in the urban centres of Toronto and Vancouver was that they had family living there already. Like the South Asians, Chinese individuals are more likely than those in the general population to live in a family household, often with several generations living under one roof. Respect for the elderly and responsibility for aging parents are traditional in Chinese culture, and their elderly, as with seniors in the South Asian community, are much less likely than those in the general population to live alone (Chui et al., 2005, p. 32).

Blacks

According to the 2006 census, a total of 783,795 people in Canada identified themselves as Black (Statistics Canada, 2006e). Blacks have a long and tragic history of colonization and slavery in North America. In the United States, a small number of Africans brought from England to work as farm labourers early in the 17th century had grown, by the 19th century, to a slave population in the millions.

One of the great myths of Canadian society is that it has never had slavery; in fact, slavery was practised in Canada from the beginning of the 17th century. It was legalized in 1709 and continued until the abolition of slavery throughout the British Empire in 1834. The passage of the *Fugitive Slave Act* in the United States in 1850 greatly increased the number of Blacks coming to Canada; it required that all runaway slaves—even those who had escaped to non-slaveholding areas of the United States—be returned to their masters. But these Black refugees were unwelcome in Canada; they were subjected to racial prejudice and ridicule both personally and in the press, and were seen as responsible for a disproportionate amount of crime.

Historically, the Canadian government has consistently resisted the immigration of Blacks. In the early 1900s, when the government was attempting to lure experienced farmers from the United States, the Immigration Branch informed its American agents that Blacks should not be among those encouraged to come to Canada. The government often rejected Blacks on medical or other non-racial grounds, so as not to be accused of overt racism (Baxter, 2003).

The history of racism in Canada toward people of African descent should not be understated. In 1903, J.S. Woodsworth, the founder of the CCF political party, expressed an antipathy toward Blacks that is startling though perhaps typical of the time; he asserted that the "very qualities of intelligence and manliness which are the essentials for citizens in a democracy were systematically expunged from the Negro race" (Henry & Tator, 2005, p. 66). Following are some other examples of racism from Canada's past:

- 1785: Sheriffs in Saint John, New Brunswick, were instructed to deny Blacks the right to vote.
- 1795: Blacks in Saint John were denied fishing rights.
- 1830s: Some churches in Canada consigned Black worshippers to back galleries.
- 1850s: Blacks were denied admission to hotels in Ontario cities such as Chatham, Hamilton, and Windsor.
- 1850: The *Separate School Act* enabled whites to relegate Blacks to all-Black schools with exclusively Black teachers. This practice continued up to the 1960s.
- 1920s: The Ku Klux Klan grew to the point of having 119 chapters throughout Canada.
- 1924: The City Commissioner of Edmonton banned all Blacks from public parks and swimming pools.
- 1918–1939: McGill University had racial segregation regulations that were maintained until well after the Second World War.
- 1954: A teacher was dismissed from a teaching position in Victoria, British Columbia, merely for being married to a Jamaican woman.

As can be seen from the timetable above, discrimination against Blacks continued long after the abolition of slavery in 1834. All provinces with significant Black populations had segregation laws on the books for most of the 20th century. In Ontario, school segregation continued to be legal until 1964, while residential segregation was imposed through restrictions on deeds and leases. When a Black person applied for an apartment, for example, he or she would be untruthfully told that it was already taken.

Although African Canadians have been resilient in the face of slavery, segregation, and racist theories and practice, their battle against discrimination is ongoing. In Canada, Blacks continue to face particularly harsh obstacles to success. Census data continues to show that they suffer more unemployment than do those in the general adult population, and that they have lower incomes (Milan & Tran, 2004, p. 7). They are also more likely to feel discriminated against on the basis of their ethnicity, culture, race, skin colour, language, accent, or religion. After Aboriginal peoples, they are the most stigmatized of all visible minorities in Canada, and this has cost them heavily in terms of economic success and in their relationships with the justice system (Baxter, 2003).

Arab Peoples

The fastest-growing visible minority group in Canada, after the South Asians, are people of Arab heritage. The first Arabs arrived in Canada over 100 years ago, in the late 19th century, most of them emigrating from a small region of Syria. The majority went to Montreal, where they worked as unskilled labourers and, very often, as pedlars, an occupation that eventually led to their dispersion throughout Canada and to their establishing themselves as settled merchants and wholesalers (Multicultural Canada, n.d.). The second wave of Arab immigration began a century later, after 1961, when Canada's immigration policy changed, and the country became more receptive toward non-European ethnic groups. Arab immigration to Canada has accelerated since then, and between now and 2017 the Arab community is expected to have among the highest growth rates of any ethnic minority group in Canada (Bélanger & Malenfant, 2005, p. 20).

Originally denoted "Syrians and Turks," Arab immigrants are now identified, for immigration purposes, according to their countries of birth, which are very diverse. The majority of Arabs living in Canada are Lebanese, Syrian, Egyptian, Chaldean/Iraqi, and Palestinian/Jordanian, and more than half of all Arab Canadians were born outside the country. Arabs, like Chinese people, tend to be very conscious of sharing a common ethnocultural origin that transcends variations in original citizenship, dialect, and political affiliation (Multicultural Canada, n.d.).

There are various dialects of spoken Arabic, with significant regional differences in vocabulary and accent. The written Arabic language, however, is the same everywhere, used and recognized throughout the Arab world. It is a significant factor in Arab ethnicity—in their strong sense of belonging to a single ethnocultural group.

Religion is more important to Arab Canadians than it is to people in the general population; in 2001—the last time Statistics Canada recorded data concerning religion—Arabs were found much more likely than those in the general population to report a religious affiliation. Early Arab immigrants to Canada were Christian, but since 1961 the majority have been Muslim. In 2001, Arabs in Canada were divided almost equally between Christianity and Islam. The immigration trends of the last ten years suggest that Islam is by now the leading religion of Arab Canadians. But it is worth reminding ourselves that the Muslim community in Canada is not entirely composed of Arabs. At last count, there were approximately 580,000 Muslims in Canada (Statistics Canada, 2001); the 2006 census identified 265,500 Canadians of Arab origin (Statistics Canada, 2006e).

Arabs in Canada lay great emphasis on education and are very well educated compared not only with other visible minority groups but with the general population. Young Arab Canadians are more likely to be in school than most young Canadians are, and much more likely to have university degrees or post-graduate degrees. In 2001, 10 percent of Arab Canadians had either a master's degree or a doctorate, compared with 5 percent of people in the general population (Statistics Canada, 2007a). Concerned about academic accomplishment, Arabs are also very conscious of their cultural heritage and proud of their many intellectual contributions to Western civilization in language, mathematics, and science (Multicultural Canada, n.d.).

The family is a central institution for Arab Canadians, who are less likely than other Canadians to live alone and more likely to be married (Statistics Canada, 2007a). They hold marriage, childbearing, and childrearing in high regard, and prefer to marry within their own local community (Multicultural Canada, n.d.). Kinship ties are strong, with family obligation extending beyond the immediate nuclear family of husband, wife, and children. In the Arab community, as in the

South Asian and Chinese communities, seniors are less likely to live alone than are seniors in the general population (Statistics Canada, 2007a). Unmarried daughters continue to live with their parents, regardless of age.

In Arab culture, the concepts of honour and shame are very important, and family members are interdependent in matters of reputation. For example, a woman's losing her virginity before marriage brings shame and dishonour to her family, as do certain medical conditions, such as mental illness. In Arab culture, such events and conditions may be concealed because of the shame they bring to the family and because of the damage they may do to the marriage opportunities of other family members.

Discrimination has been a concern in the Arab Canadian community for decades, with the media at times presenting a simplistic and stereotypical image of Arab culture. Statistics confirm that the incomes of Arab people do not reflect their levels of academic accomplishment (Statistics Canada, 2007a). Since 9/11, this discrimination has intensified and manifested itself in new contexts, due to factors that include heightened security concerns, simplistic media coverage, and Islamophobia. Many Arabs feel demonized, unfairly linked to terrorism by virtue of ethnic or religious association. Despite this sense of being discriminated against, many Canadians of Arab origin, like South Asians, feel a strong sense of belonging to Canada and are active in Canadian society. A large proportion of Arabs, compared with other visible minority groups, vote in elections and participate in community associations (Statistics Canada, 2007a).

EXERCISE 6

Consider how the following factors may influence your reactions to individuals from various ethnocultural groups:

1. your upbringing
2. media portrayal of specific religions
3. police culture
4. past personal experiences
5. a person's appearance
6. a person's skin colour

CULTURAL DIVERSITY: POLICE ABILITIES, KNOWLEDGE, AND SKILLS

Culture, race, and ethnicity influence individual values, practices, and codes of conduct. Diverse values and customs enrich a country's quality of life, but they may also be a source of conflict, misunderstanding, and violence.

Ethnocultural groups and their community leaders have certain responsibilities:

- to respect others' rights and freedoms;
- to live peacefully with diversity;
- to recognize that there is one secular law for all;
- to obey the law of the land; and
- to protect the civil order of the nation.

Conflict and misunderstanding are more likely where certain ethnocultural groups consider themselves superior and others inferior, or where different laws apply to different groups. All of these groups, as well as the police, need to respect diversity and to uphold a core value called **diversity equity**, according to which no ethnocultural group is superior or inferior to any other.

Police must resist simplistic perceptions of ethnocultural groups. In Western countries, the post-9/11 demonization of Arab communities showed how these distortions can occur. Some people equated "Arab" and "Muslim Arab" with "terrorist," on the grounds that some Arab communities and their leaders failed to condemn terrorism absolutely after 9/11 or were slow to do so, or, as in a few cases, reacted jubilantly to news of the tragedy. Police need to remember that very few Arabs are fundamentalists, extremists, radicals, fascists, or terrorists, and that terrorists are likely to defy demographic, racial, or ethnic profiles. They may emerge from any demographic category—male or female, young or old, immigrant or citizen—and from any ethnocultural group or nationality, whether African, Asian, European, Hispanic, or Middle Eastern.

Colour-blind and democratic law enforcement is needed to protect civil order and curb terrorist threats. All those who pose a real terrorist threat, whatever their race, ethnicity, or religion, must be subject to democratic policing measures, including screening, scrutiny, surveillance, and criminal prosecution. Of course, targeting the terrorist danger itself can only do so much; it combats the outward expression of the problem while ignoring its underlying causes. Sound, mutually respectful relations between police and community, marked by trust and open communication, are key counterterrorism measures.

Police should be neither complacent nor overzealous. Protection of civil order is critical. Ethnocultural groups and their leaders must understand the responsibilities police have in Canada and the practices they are obliged to follow. And police must offer these groups the reassurance of a democratic approach to policing. By declining to identify terrorism with a particular ethnic group and by maintaining diversity equity in the law enforcement psyche, police recognize all people's humanity and thereby promote the humanity of policing. This creates a climate of mutual trust and, ultimately, a safer, more secure Canada.

diversity equity
a value according to which there are no superior or inferior cultural groups

CHAPTER SUMMARY

It is important to remember that most ethnocultural categories—South Asians, for example—include a variety of cultures and ethnic origins, and that within the various subcategories are individuals with highly personal beliefs and attitudes. Stereotyping people is a simplistic and lazy substitute for getting to know and understand them. By studying people carefully and focusing on the common ground between them and ourselves, we can reduce conflict and misunderstanding. Establishing a mutually respectful and trusting relationship between law enforcement and the communities they serve helps protect civil order.

KEY TERMS

culture
diversity equity
ethnicity
prejudice
race
stereotype
visible minority

REFERENCES

Baxter, P. (2003). A portrait of Canadian diversity: The 2001 census and its implications for multiculturalism. In *Issues in diversity and First Nations policing*. Unpublished manuscript. Georgian College, Barrie, ON.

Belanger, A., & Malenfant, B.C. (2005, Winter). Ethnocultural diversity in Canada: Prospects for 2017. *Canadian Social Trends*. Statistics Canada, Catalogue no. 11-008. http://www.statcan.gc.ca/pub/11-008-x/2005003/article/8968-eng.pdf.

Berry, J.W., & Laponce, J.A. (1994). Evaluating research on Canada's multiethnic and multicultural society. In J.W. Berry & J.A. Laponce (Eds.), *Ethnicity and culture in Canada* (pp. 3–16). Toronto: University of Toronto Press.

Brant, C.C. (1990). Native ethics and rules of behaviour. *Canadian Journal of Psychiatry, 35*, 534–539.

Canada, Minister of Indian Affairs and Development. (1997). Gathering strength: Canada's Aboriginal action plan. http://www.ahf.ca/downloads/gathering -strength.pdf.

Canadian Council on Social Development. (2003). Census shows increasing diversity of Canadian society. http://www.ccsd.ca/home.htm.

Canadian Heritage. (2004). Canadian diversity: Respecting our differences. http://www.pch.gc.ca/index_e.cfm.

Chui, T., Tran, K., & Flanders, J. (2005, Spring). Chinese Canadians: Enriching the cultural mosaic. *Canadian social trends*. Statistics Canada—Catalogue no. 11-008. http://www.statcan.gc.ca/pub/11-008-x/2004004/article/7778-eng.pdf.

Employment Equity Act. (1995). SC 1995, c. 44.

Henry, F., & Tator, C. (2005). *The colour of democracy: Racism in Canadian society* (3rd ed.) Toronto: Nelson Thomson.

Indian Act. (1985). RSC 1985, c. I-5.

Kallen, E. (2003). *Ethnicity and human rights in Canada: A human rights perspective on race, ethnicity, racism and systemic inequality*. New York: Oxford University Press.

Kazarian, S.S., & Evans, D.R. (1998). Cultural clinical psychology. In S.S. Kazarian & D.R. Evans (Eds.), *Cultural clinical psychology: Theory, research and practice*. New York: Oxford University Press.

Kazarian, S., Crichlow, W., & Bradford, S. (2007). *Diversity issues in law enforcement* (2nd ed.). Toronto: Emond Montgomery.

Linton, R. (1945). *The cultural background of psychology.* New York: Appleton-Century.

Milan, A., & Tran, K. (2004, Spring). Blacks in Canada: A long history. *Canadian Social Trends.* Statistics Canada—Catalogue No. 11-008. http://www.statcan .gc.ca/pub/11-008-x/2003004/article/6802-eng.pdf.

Moynes, J. (1999). *Social competence and deviant behaviour. Native Community Care, Counselling and Development.* Hamilton, ON: Mohawk College.

Moynihan, D.P. (1993). *Pandaemonium: Ethnicity in international politics.* Oxford: Oxford University Press.

Multicultural Canada. (n.d.). Arabs. In *Encyclopedia of Canada's peoples.* http://www.multiculturalcanada.ca/Encyclopedia/A-Z/a21.

Statistics Canada. (2001). Canada's ethnocultural portrait: The changing mosaic. http://www.statcan.ca/menu-en.htm.

Statistics Canada. (2006a). Aboriginal Peoples in Canada in 2006: Inuit, Metis, and First Nations, 2006 census: Highlights. http://www12.statcan.ca/ census-recensement/2006/as-sa/97-558/p1-eng.cfm.

Statistics Canada. (2006b). Canada's ethnocultural mosaic, 2006 census: National picture. http://www12.statcan.ca/census-recensement/2006/as-sa/97-562/ p5-eng.cfm.

Statistics Canada. (2006c). Canada's ethnocultural mosaic, 2006 census: Provinces and territories. http://www12.statcan.ca/census-recensement/2006/ as-sa/97-562/p11-eng.cfm.

Statistics Canada. (2006d). Ethnic origin reference guide, 2006 census. http://www12.statcan.ca/census-recensement/2006/ref/rp-guides/ ethnic-ethnique-eng.cfm.

Statistics Canada. (2006e). Table: Visible minority population by age group, 2006 census. http://www40.statcan.ca/l01/cst01/DEMO50A-eng.htm.

Statistics Canada. (2007a). The Arab community in Canada. http://www.statcan. gc.ca/pub/89-621-x/89-621-x2007009-eng.htm.

Statistics Canada. (2007b). Immigration and citizenship. http://www12.statcan.ca/ census-recensement/2006/rt-td/immcit-eng.cfm.

Sustainability Reporting Program. (2006). The urbanization of Canada. http://www.sustreport.org/signals/canpop_urb.html.

Tran, K., Kaddatz, J., & Allard, P. (2005, Autumn). South Asians in Canada: Unity through diversity. *Canadian Social Trends.* Statistics Canada—Catalogue no. 11-008. http://www.statcan.gc.ca/kits-trousses/pdf/social/edu04_0128a-eng.pdf.

Triandis, H.C. (1995). A theoretical framework for the study of diversity. In M.M. Chemers, S. Oskamp, & M.A. Costanza (Eds.), *Diversity in organizations: New perspectives for a changing workplace* (pp. 11–36). Thousand Oaks, CA: Sage.

REVIEW QUESTIONS

TRUE OR FALSE?

_____ 1. The terms *culture, ethnicity, race,* and *minority* are often used interchangeably.

_____ 2. In its anthropological sense, culture is synonymous with ethnoculture.

_____ 3. Ethnicity can be symbolic or behavioural.

_____ 4. Aboriginal people are considered one of Canada's visible minorities.

_____ 5. The Aboriginal population in Canada is growing almost twice as fast as the rest of the population.

_____ 6. The English and French in Canada are considered non-visible ethnic minority peoples.

_____ 7. The term *South Asian* identifies a single ethnic group from the Indian subcontinent.

_____ 8. A stereotype is an adverse judgment or opinion formed beforehand or without knowledge or an examination of facts.

_____ 9. Slavery had been practised in Canada since the early years of the 17th century and wasn't abolished in the British Empire until 1834.

_____ 10. Studying other people carefully and focusing on the common ground between them and ourselves can help reduce conflict and misunderstanding.

MULTIPLE CHOICE

1. Both English and French people belong to the same
   (a) paralanguage group
   (b) ethnocentral group
   (c) cultural majority
   (d) Caucasian race

2. *Culture* can be narrowly defined as
   (a) historical tradition
   (b) a socialization group
   (c) a generalization
   (d) folk tradition

3. *Ethnicity* refers to
   (a) the cultural origin with which a person or group identifies within a multicultural context
   (b) a factor of globalization
   (c) a person's colour
   (d) a pattern of behaviour

4. *Race* is a means of categorizing people according to
   (a) religion
   (b) gender
   (c) common beliefs and practices
   (d) common ancestry or origin

5. A nuclear family structure is
   (a) a characteristic of Asian racial minority cultures
   (b) a social pattern of behaviour
   (c) an attempt to ensure the survival of a culture
   (d) a characteristic of an individualist culture

6. Australians in Canada are an example of
   (a) a non-visible ethnic minority
   (b) a visible ethnic minority
   (c) a non-visible ethnic majority
   (d) a visible ethnic majority

7. African slaves were brought to Canada in the early 1600s by the
   (a) English
   (b) French
   (c) Norsemen
   (d) Portuguese

8. The first Chinese immigrants came to Canada in 1860
   (a) to build the railway
   (b) to farm
   (c) to prospect for gold
   (d) to work as pedlars

9. The first South Asians who came to Canada were
   (a) Vietnamese
   (b) Sikhs
   (c) Chinese
   (d) Laotians

10. Diversity equity refers to a core value according to which
    (a) all cultural groups should earn the same amount of money
    (b) there are no superior or inferior cultural groups
    (c) different laws for different cultural groups should prevail
    (d) some cultural groups should be considered as potential terrorists

FILL IN THE BLANKS

1. The _____ and the _____ have been called Canada's two founding races.

2. Individuals have unique world views that are shaped by their _____.

3. Race is not an absolute marker of identity but a _____ concept that can be rejected as a means of categorizing people.

4. A minority group within a society is subordinate to the majority in terms of _____ _____.

5. Fifty-four percent of Aboriginal people live in _____ across Canada.

6. Teaching in Aboriginal cultures is done by _____ rather than by commanding or dictating

7 The fastest-growing visible minority group in Canada are people of _____ heritage.

8. _____ falsify reality through overgeneralization and strip their subjects of individuality.

9. _____ _____ are now the largest visible minority group in Canada.

10. All of the provinces with significant Black populations had _____ laws on the books for most of the last century.

Religious Diversity

4

INTRODUCTION

This chapter discusses the concept of religion and describes the beliefs and religious practices of a number of communities in our society, with the aim of enlarging your understanding of them. It also examines the post-9/11 experiences of Muslims and discusses the significance of these experiences for policing in Canada, and how police services can respond effectively in the post-9/11 environment.

Canada is a multicultural, multi-ethnic, multilingual, and multi-faith country, one of the most religiously diverse countries in the world. New immigrants to Canada have brought not only new cultures and languages, but also new faiths. In 2001—the last year for which Statistics Canada has data concerning religion—43 percent of the population in Canada identified itself as Roman Catholic, 29 percent as Protestant, 2 percent as Muslim, and 1 percent each as Buddhist, Hindu, and Sikh. But immigration is continually changing Canada's religious makeup; the demographic trends of the last decade suggest that the number of Canadians reporting Protestant and Catholic religious affiliations is bound to decrease even as the numbers reporting Islam, Sikhism, and Buddhism increase.

Some recent religious trends in Canada, according to Ontario Consultants on Religious Tolerance (2009), include the following:

- The percentage of Christians is dropping about 0.9 percent annually, which amounts to a decrease of almost 10 percent over a decade.
- Small non-Christian faith groups are increasing in number and popularity.
- The percentage of atheists, agnostics, humanists, and people of no religious adherence is increasing rapidly.
- Many Canadians no longer attend religious services.

WHAT IS RELIGION?

religion
a spiritual belief system that addresses matters of ultimate reality, such as life and death, and instructs people in how to live

All human beings have basic spiritual needs that **religion** offers ways of satisfying. The spiritual needs identified and the solutions offered vary according to religion; each religious tradition evolves in a unique historical context. For example, Christianity identifies sin as a fundamental human problem and offers salvation from sin through Jesus Christ as a solution. Buddhism, on the other hand, regards ignorance, not sin, as the fundamental problem and prescribes enlightenment as the solution and the goal. In their rites, religions use sacred speech and narrative (myth, prayer, song), sacred acts and rituals, and they designate sacred places for religious expression (Forman, 1993).

Let us define *religion*, then, as a set of teachings and/or rituals that address issues of ultimate reality—the meaning of life, for example—and that try to tell us how to find fulfillment, spiritual health, and salvation within our mortal existence and beyond it (Religion Facts, 2010).

EXERCISE 1

How might religious diversity affect both individual police officers and police services?

RELIGIOUS BELIEFS AND PRACTICES

Religion plays a significant role in the lives of many people. Each religion has its own world view and its own concept of a higher power. Within a religious family, the members' common faith gives them a link to their past and to their future (White, 1997). However, **religious beliefs** and **religious practices** in pluralistic societies have the potential to create divisiveness, animosity, and intolerance. People tend to misunderstand one another's religious beliefs and to view their own as the only valid one. For example, many Americans interviewed by CNN after the 9/11 terrorist attacks believed that what America needed to do was go into Iraq and turn all Iraqi Muslims into Christians so as to "save" and "humanize" them.

religious beliefs
tenets of particular faiths

religious practices
concrete expressions of religious beliefs

Powerful nations have always sought to impose religious conversion on the peoples they oppress and colonize. Consider, for example, the colonists' attempts to Christianize Canada's Aboriginal peoples. Throughout history, conquered peoples have been forcibly converted to new religions, and these coercive conversions have left scars. Understanding an ethnocultural group's history of religious struggle can give us clues about its attitudes—its levels of trust and resistance—toward being integrated into mainstream society. Generally speaking, if we know something about the major religions and about the beliefs and practices associated with them, we will better understand the cultures within our society that these religions inform and influence.

atheist
a person who professes no particular religion and does not believe in a higher power

agnostic
a person who believes it impossible to know God or to determine how the universe began

Needless to say, not everyone has a religion or professes religious beliefs. For example, **atheists** profess no particular religion and do not believe in a higher power. Similarly, **agnostics** believe it impossible to know God or to determine how the universe began. Nonetheless, atheists and agnostics have their own values and individual codes of ethical conduct. They deserve as much recognition, respect, and protection as those with strong religious beliefs and practices. It has been estimated (Religion Facts, 2010) that there are nearly 1.1 billion atheists and agnostics worldwide.

The religions discussed in this chapter are listed in Table 4.1. Needless to say, all religions cannot be discussed in a single chapter, and those that have been included here have not been chosen because they are superior to or more significant than others.

EXERCISE 2

1. In the following section, you will learn about a variety of religious beliefs and practices. Do you currently have any impressions of the following people? Share your reactions.
   a. a Muslim woman wearing a *niqab*
   b. a Chinese Buddhist
   c. a Christian Scientist
   d. a Jehovah's Witness
   e. a traditional Aboriginal man
   f. a Sikh wearing a turban
   g. a Hindu woman wearing a sari
   h. a Muslim man with a beard
   i. a white Protestant woman
   j. a Roman Catholic priest
2. Identify factors that may have contributed to your impressions. Identify which factors are irrational, and which are rational.

Bahá'í Faith: Embracing All Nations, Creeds, and Colours

The Bahá'í Faith was founded by a Persian religious leader named Bahá'u'lláh. A Bahá'í is a follower of Bahá'u'lláh. It is a religion associated with a trinity of onenesses: the oneness of God; the oneness of all religions, which is revealed progressively by God; and the oneness of humanity, all of whose members are equal in the sight of God. The basic principles and the ideals of the Bahá'í Faith are as follows (New York City Bahá'í Community, 1999):

- the unity (oneness) of humankind;
- the unity in the foundation of all religions, which express a single divine plan;
- religion as the source of unity;
- religion as a progressive and evolutionary process;
- the compatibility of science and religion;
- the need for an independent investigation of truth;
- the equality of men and women;
- the elimination of all forms of prejudice;
- universal peace;
- universal education;

Table 4.1   Some Religions of the World

Religion	Number of believers in the world
Atheists and agnostics	1.1 billion
Bahá'í	5 to 7 million
Buddhism	360 million
Christian Scientists	150,000–400,000
Christianity	2.1 billion
Hinduism	900 million
Islam	1.5 billion (Sunni: 940 million)
Jehovah's Witnesses	6.5 million
Judaism	14 million
Shintoism	3.4 million
Sikhism	23 million
Taoism	20 million

Source: Religion Facts, Religion Statistics by Adherents.

- a universal auxiliary language—in other words, an international language that everyone learns in addition to his or her mother tongue;
- spiritual solutions to economic problems; and
- an international tribunal.

The Bahá'í do not have a clergy. They consider the family the foundation of human society, marriage a means for the spiritual development of both partners, and morality as a source of spiritual development and happiness. In addition to the Ten Commandments (see Table 4.2 on page 84), the moral code of the Bahá'í Faith prescribes the following practices:

- avoid backbiting and gossip, promiscuity, gambling, and alcohol and drug use;
- practise daily prayer and the reading of holy writings;
- practise fasting;
- observe Bahá'í holidays;
- maintain chastity before marriage;
- teach the cause of God;
- contribute to the Bahá'í Fund, which supports the work of the faith;
- consider work a form of worship; and
- respect and obey the government of the land.

Buddhism: Seeking Enlightenment

In 2001, over 300,000 Canadians identified themselves as Buddhists, who number 360 million worldwide. Buddhism was founded in northern India by the ascetic Siddhartha Gautama (566–480 BCE). Gautama, who was from an aristocratic family, discovered suffering as a young man and left home to search for redemption from it. As he sat under a tree in deep meditation, he saw the true path to salvation and on the basis of this wisdom became Buddha, "the enlightened one."

Buddhism is not a religion in the Western sense; Buddhists do not worship a creator God. Instead, they follow a path of spiritual development in search of the following:

- the full development and freedom of the individual's body, speech, and mind, so that his or her awareness, kindness, and wisdom are enhanced;
- insight into the true nature of life; and
- Enlightenment, or Buddhahood.

The three basic tenets of Buddhist teaching are that nothing is fixed or permanent (the principle of *impermanence*), that *actions have consequences*, and that *change is possible*. There are different types and levels of Buddhism, but all promote nonviolence, lack of dogma, tolerance of differences, and the practice of meditation.

In addition to these basic tenets, there are Four Noble Truths associated with Buddhism (Boeree, 2000):

1. Suffering is inherent in life.
2. Attachment to things and the craving of sensual pleasures are causes of suffering.
3. Release from suffering (Nirvana) is achieved by eliminating selfish, sensual, and material desires.
4. There is an Eightfold Path to achieving Nirvana:
    a. right view—understanding the Four Noble Truths;
    b. right aspiration—sincerely wanting to overcome attachment;
    c. right speech—avoiding slander and gossip;
    d. right action—conducting oneself morally;
    e. right livelihood—doing work that harms no one;
    f. right effort—focusing on good thoughts and nurturing good qualities;
    g. right mindfulness—integrating thoughts, body, and feelings to overcome desire; and
    h. right concentration—disciplining the mind through meditation.

The Four Noble Truths and the Eightfold Path translate into five rules of Buddhist living:

1. Avoid harm and be kind.
2. Avoid taking what is not given, and be generous.
3. Avoid sexual misconduct and excess, and be content.
4. Avoid false speech and be truthful.
5. Abstain from intoxicants and be aware.

The Buddhist moral code forbids killing, stealing, lying, and sexual promiscuity. In marital relationships, husbands are expected to be respectful, faithful, and supportive of their wives. Wives are expected to be diligent and hospitable to relatives, as well as faithful, respectful, and supportive to their husbands.

Christian Science: Healing Through Divine Laws

Christian Science aims to save the universe from evil and to heal disease by spiritual means alone. It is based on the words and works of Jesus Christ, draws its authority from the Bible, and follows the teachings of its founder, the American Mary Baker Eddy (1821–1910). Eddy's personal experience with spiritual healing through divine laws led to her discovering the Science of Christianity, by whose principles, she believed, Jesus lived and taught. In 1875, she wrote and published *Science and Health with Key to the Scriptures* (1875/1994), which is used as a textbook by Christian Science practitioners as they prepare to minister Christian healing.

Christian Scientists, whose numbers have declined in the last few years, subscribe to the belief that moral, spiritual, and physical healing can occur through *divine laws*—that is, through scientific prayer and spiritual communion with God. Scientific prayer is based on the idea that an ill person has direct access to God's love and that God, or divine Mind, is the only healer. This prayer brings the transforming action of Christ and the idea of divine Love to the ill person's consciousness, and the transformed consciousness that results from this process brings about a change in the person's physical condition (The First Church of Christ, Scientist, 2001).

Christian Science allows its members the freedom to choose their own form of health care and it acknowledges the interests of health-care professionals. It is a principle of Christian Science, originating with its founder, Mary Baker Eddy, that Christian Scientists should obey the law where health matters are concerned—for example, with respect to quarantines. At the same time, many Christian Scientists opt for prayer before any other kind of treatment, for themselves and for their children, and find it effective.

Christian Science teaches strict adherence to the moral code of the Ten Commandments (see Table 4.2) and to the tenets of Christ's Sermon on the Mount, which preaches the following:

- seek spirituality;
- be mild-tempered, peaceable, merciful, and a lover of righteousness;
- love those who are disliked;
- give to the needy;

Table 4.2   The Ten Commandments

1. I the Lord am your God. ... You shall have no other gods beside Me.
2. You shall not make for yourself a sculptured image. ... You shall not bow down to them or serve them.
3. You shall not take in vain the name of the Lord your God.
4. Remember the Sabbath day and keep it holy.
5. Honour your father and your mother.
6. You shall not murder.
7. You shall not commit adultery.
8. You shall not steal.
9. You shall not bear false witness against your neighbour.
10. You shall not covet.

- be non-judgmental; and

- treat others as you would like to be treated yourself.

The sermon also condemns murder, wrath, adultery, lustful thoughts, and careless divorce actions.

Christianity: Love Your Neighbour

Christianity is the most popular religion in the world. About 33 percent of the world's population is Christian, and there are over 34,000 separate Christian groups in the world (Ontario Consultants on Religious Tolerance, 2009). Jesus of Nazareth is the central figure in Christianity, which became a moral force in the first century CE.

The basic Christian beliefs are stated in the Nicene Creed. Christians believe in one God, who has three modes of being: God the Father; Jesus Christ, the son of God and the saviour whose birth, death, and resurrection provide hope for eternal life with God; and the Holy Spirit. The principle of love ("love your neighbour as yourself") represents the fundamental ethical instruction for Christians.

A number of branches of Christianity date back to Christ's disciples (for example, the Catholic and Orthodox churches). The Roman Catholic Church is the most popular and widespread of the Christian churches. In 2001, 43 percent of Canadians identified themselves as Roman Catholic. The head of the Catholic Church is the Pope (Latin for "father"). The Catholic Church opposes premarital sex, birth control, abortion, and the ordination of women as priests.

In 2001, Protestant denominations comprised 29 percent of the Canadian population (Statistics Canada, 2001). Protestantism began with Martin Luther (1483–1546), a German monk and reformer who sparked a major schism in the Catholic Church, a split known as the Protestant Reformation. Luther advanced the idea that the Bible, not the Pope or Church administrators, is the only true authority for Christian faith and practice, and that ordinary Christians are competent to profess their faith without subjecting themselves to church authorities. Luther's reforms resulted in the establishment of non-Catholic sects. Today, there are over 1,000 Protestant Christian denominations.

During the 20th century, prior to 1990, Christianity's popularity was stable in North America. About 87 percent of adults identified themselves as Christian. After 1990, however, substantial numbers of people began to disaffiliate themselves with Christianity and other organized religions. By 2008, the number of Christians in North America had fallen to about 76 percent (Ontario Consultants on Religious Tolerance, 2009).

Hinduism: Museum of Religions

In 2001, 297,200 Canadians identified themselves as Hindu. There are 900 million Hindus worldwide. *Hindu* is the Persian word for "India," and India and the Ganges River make up the sacred geography of Hinduism—Hindus believe that God lives on the Ganges. Hinduism is called a "museum of religions" because of the immense diversity of its beliefs and practices. There is no recognized founder of Hinduism, nor any single holy book that stands as the religion's basic scriptural guide. At the same time, there is a large body of sacred texts classified as "Hindu."

Hinduism has four primary denominations: Saivism, Vaishnavism, Shaktism, and Smartism. All four denominations rely on the Vedas—the most sacred books of Hinduism—as scriptural authority, but all four hold divergent beliefs and are considered independent religions. Nevertheless, all four denominations share beliefs in the following:

- dharma,
- all-pervasive divinity,
- one supreme being that is manifested in many deities (gods and goddesses),
- reincarnation,
- sacraments,
- the guru tradition, and
- yoga.

Dharma is a central concept in Hinduism. It refers to the eternal law of the cosmos, upheld by the gods but not created or controlled by them; it is a divine order or pattern that we can seek to follow ourselves through the ritualization of daily life and the self-actualization that follows from this.

No single deity is central to Hinduism. Hindus may worship a particular god (for example, Krishna) or goddess; a spirit, trees, and animals; or a Supreme Spirit. Of all the deities, the following three are the most significant:

- *Brahma*, the creator of the universe and life;
- *Vishnu*, the preserver of life, the guide of the cycle of birth and rebirth, and the saviour of the world from evil; and
- *Shiva*, the destroyer of all evil.

reincarnation
the belief that the soul, after the body's death, comes back to life in a new form

Reincarnation is a basic tenet of Hinduism—the belief that the soul, after the body's death, comes back to life in a new form. The soul, gaining wisdom through progressive reincarnations and realizing that the true self is not the body but the immortal soul, eventually tires of the cycle of birth and death, and seeks to escape into *moksha*, or liberation. By this process, *kharma* is resolved through successive lives. *Kharma* is the law of cause and effect, and Hindus believe that each person creates a personal destiny through his or her thoughts, words, and actions.

Gurus are teachers with superior spiritual knowledge, and they are considered essential guides for attaining that knowledge. The word *yoga* means union, and it is a philosophy and discipline whose purpose is to unite the person's consciousness with divine consciousness. There are several levels, or types, of yoga (Himalayan Academy, 2000).

The following are some other other basic principles of Hinduism (Himalayan Academy, 2000):

- Spiritual transformation comes from personal discipline, good conduct, and meditation.
- All life is sacred, so individuals must practise non-injury.
- No particular religion is above all others.

Islam: There Is No God but God

Like Judaism and Christianity, Islam is **monotheistic**—in other words, a religion that worships a single god—and it is the second most popular religion in the world. A global faith that spans diverse races, nationalities, and cultures, Islam may become the dominant religion of the world during the 21st century. One out of five people in the world is a Muslim. Islam is one of the fastest-growing faiths in Canada, North America, and the Caribbean. In Canada, the Muslim population more than doubled in the decade between 1991 and 2001, with 579,200 people identifying themselves as Muslims in 2001 (Statistics Canada, 2001). The number of Muslims in Quebec increased by almost 50 percent between 1991 and 2001, due largely to Muslim immigration from South Asia, North Africa, and the Middle East ("Islam fastest," 2001).

In Arabic, the word *islam* means "submission." In Muslim theology, the word means submission (surrender, obedience) to Allah (God) and commitment to His guidance, actions which lead to spiritual peace. A *Muslim* is a person who has surrendered to the will of God. A person becomes a Muslim by believing and proclaiming that "There is none worthy of worship except God," and that "Muhammad is the Messenger of God." Muslims do not worship the Prophet Muhammad, but they do follow his teachings.

The **Koran** ("recitation") is the holy text of Islam. Muslims believe that the Koran contains the words of God communicated to Muhammad through the archangel Gabriel. They also believe that the Koran does not contradict but completes the Jewish and Christian scriptures.

Belief in fate is seen in the Islamic doctrine of predestination ("Nothing will befall us but what God has written down for us"). At the same time, the Islamic doctrine of the hereafter, with its stress on reward and punishment, also requires that people assume responsibility for their deeds.

The two main Islamic sects are Sunni and Shiite, but there are other sects as well, including Sufi, Ismaili, and Druze. The five basic religious practices of Islam are listed in Table 4.3.

Islam is not just a religion; it is a way of life. There is no division between the secular and the sacred for Muslims; law is not separate from religion. Religious law, *fiqh*, relies on five sources: the Koran, Muhammad's way of life, oral traditions, reasoning, and community consensus. Proper food is known as *halal*. Muslims are prohibited from eating pork and from consuming blood, alcohol, and animals that have not been slaughtered properly or those that have died of natural causes. Parents are highly respected, and caring for them in old age is seen as an honour and a blessing for the caregiver. Consequently, institutional homes for the elderly are virtually unknown in the Muslim world.

The Muslim community has identified the following as the leading falsehoods or myths about Islam (Forman, 1993):

- Muslims worldwide threaten a "new world order." This conspiracy theory comes from the Western media's careless use of such terms and phrases as *jihad* (Holy War), *Islamic fundamentalism, Islamic terrorism,* and *Islamic militia,* which convey stereotypes.

monotheistic
a religion that worships a single god

Koran
the holy text of Islam

Table 4.3   The Five Pillars: Basic Religious Practices of Islam

Iman (faith)	Iman signifies the belief that the sole purpose of life is to serve and obey God through the teachings and practices of Muhammad. Muslims are required to declare their faith by bearing witness that there is no God but Allah and that Muhammad is his final messenger.
Salat (prayer)	Muslims are required to pray five times a day: at dawn, noon, afternoon, evening, and night.
Zakat (alms giving)	A certain percentage of earnings is expected to go to the poor or needy. This obligation is based on the belief that everything belongs to Allah.
Siyam (fasting)	Fasting is beneficial for health, self-purification, and self-restraint; it reminds Muslims of their purpose in life and promotes empathy for poor and hungry people. All adult Muslims are expected to fast (abstain from food, drink, and sexual relations) from sunrise to sunset during the holy month of Ramadan.
Hajj (pilgrimage)	Adult Muslims with the physical and financial means are required to make at least one pilgrimage to Mecca (in Saudi Arabia), the birthplace of Islam, during the 12th month of the Islamic calendar.

- The "sword of Islam" is forcing people to accept Islam.
- Muhammad is God's final messenger (in fact, Jesus is held in high esteem by Muslims).
- The God worshipped by Muslims is separate from the God of the Jews and Christians.
- All Muslims are Arabs.
- Islam oppresses women.

The West commonly associates Islam with the subordination of women. According to the Koran, however, men and women are equal before God and their roles are complementary. Muslim theologians have pointed out that it is governments, not Islam, that oppress women.

Jehovah's Witnesses: Spreading the Word

Most of us know Jehovah's Witnesses by their religious practice of going from house to house or standing on the streets with Bibles, Bible literature, and *Watchtower* and *Awake!* magazines. This religion originated in the United States; its founder was Charles Taze Russell (1852–1916), a minister whose goal was to reform the Christian church by returning it to its earliest form, which he considered pure and uncorrupt. Jehovah's Witnesses have published and use their own version of the Bible, known as the *New World Translation of the Holy Scriptures*. They have elders but no clergy. The following are the basic beliefs and practices of Jehovah's Witnesses (Watch Tower Bible and Tract Society of Pennsylvania, 2001):

- There is only one God, Jehovah. Jesus is Jehovah's son and is subordinate to Him.
- The Bible is Jehovah's word and is the truth.
- The end of the world is imminent. God's Kingdom will be ushered in when the wicked are destroyed in the battle of Armageddon, which is God's war to end wickedness. Armageddon will restore paradise, purify the world, establish God's Kingdom on earth for 1,000 years, and destroy Satan, his demon forces, and all rebels against God.
- Accepting blood orally or intravenously violates God's divine command to "abstain from blood." For this reason, Jehovah's Witnesses refuse to accept blood transfusions.
- The Memorial of Christ's Death is recognized at Passover, which, for Jehovah's Witnesses, is the only religious day that requires celebration. Other holidays are considered worldly or pagan.
- Jehovah's Witnesses dissociate themselves from politics because they regard the world as being under Satan's control; they refuse formal allegiance to political systems and view pledges of allegiance to national symbols as idolatry. Jehovah's Witnesses do not run for public office, join the military, salute the flag, or vote in elections. They believe they must keep separate from the world.
- Human beings were created by God; they did not evolve from primitive forms of life.
- Jehovah's Witnesses must maintain spiritual cleanliness, moral cleanliness, mental cleanliness, physical cleanliness, and cleanliness of speech. In keeping with their understanding of the Bible's teachings, Jehovah's Witnesses are expected to respect marriage, teach their children ethical principles, and value family.
- Jehovah's Witnesses believe that, as Christians, it is their duty to publicly testify to spiritual truth, and that the more individuals and families they influence to live by Christian principles, the less crime, delinquency, and immorality will exist in society.

Judaism: First Monotheistic Religion

Judaism is centred on God, the Torah, and Israel. It prescribes a way of life based on the relationship between God and the Jewish nation and their mutual obligations. The Hebrew Bible is called the *Tanach*. It consists of the Torah ("teaching"), the *Neviim* (prophets), and the *Ketuvim* (writings, or wisdom literature). The central symbol of Judaism is the Torah, which contains the 613 *mitzvot* (plural of *mitzvah*, commandments or divine rules of conduct) that God gave to the Jewish people. Ten of those *mitzvot*, the Ten Commandments, are listed in Table 4.2, above.

Relative to other religions, Judaism is based more on actions than on belief, but it does uphold several principles of faith:

- God exists.
- God is one and unique, incorporeal, eternal; all-knowing about the thoughts and deeds of every person; rewarder of the good and punisher of the wicked.

- Prayer is directed to God alone and to no other. (Even in prayer, Jews do not address God by name because naming God is an act of idolatry, which the Torah prohibits.)

- Moses's prophecies and the words of the prophets are true.

- The written Torah and the oral Torah (teachings contained in the *Talmud* and other writings) were given to Moses (the greatest of the prophets), and there will be no other Torah. The *Talmud* ("study") contains commentaries on and interpretations of Jewish law, in addition to proverbs and parables.

- The Messiah will come, and the dead will be resurrected.

Judaism is defined by a set of rules and practices known as *halakhah*, which means law, or "the path that one walks." Observing *halakhah* enables a person to lead a spiritual life. *Halakhah* consists of the 613 *mitzvot*, of laws instituted by the rabbis (teachers), and of long-standing customs. *Halakhah* addresses many aspects of a person's life, including his or her practice with respect to the following:

- God, the Torah, other people, and animals;
- clothing;
- prayers and blessings;
- food;
- marriage, divorce, family, and sexual relations; and
- criminal law.

Halakhah requires that food be *kosher*—in other words, fit to be eaten according to the dietary law of *kashrut*. Pork is prohibited, as are wild birds, insects, shellfish, and all animals that do not chew their cud. Strictly followed, *halakhah* regulates women closely (as it does men), but women are highly regarded in Judaism; their status is equal to men's. This equality is in keeping with the idea—another tenet of Judaism—that God has no body and has no distinct gender, possessing both masculine and feminine qualities.

With respect to women and in general, Jewish law is less oppressive than it seems. *Halakhah* is detailed and exacting, but it is not followed inflexibly. In the whole context of Judaism, observing Jewish law is less important than preserving and honouring life. For example, on the **Shabbath** (Saturday, which the *halakhah* prescribes as a day of rest), an Orthodox Jewish surgeon will go to the hospital and perform a surgery if doing so will save a life.

Shabbath
Saturday, prescribed in Jewish law as the day of rest

The four major movements or groups within Judaism are as follows:

- *Orthodox Judaism* is the most traditional and restrictive of the four groups. With the rationale that God gave the Torah to Moses, Orthodox Judaism views the Torah's 613 *mitzvot* as divine law and the *halakhah* as binding on all Jews. Men and women sit separately to worship, and women are not ordained as rabbis.

- *Conservative Judaism* views *halakhah* as binding on Jews, but believes in the evolutionary nature of the Torah. Unlike Orthodox Jews, Conservative Jews change religious rules and practices over time. For example, Conservative Judaism allows its members to ride in a car to attend service on the Shabbath (the day of rest, Saturday), permits the ordination of women as rabbis, and allows men and women to sit together during worship in Conservative synagogues. On the other hand, Conservative rabbis are unlikely to perform or attend a marriage between a born Jew and an unconverted non-Jew.

- *Reform Judaism* is a liberal religious movement that views Jewish law as non-binding. It allows individual autonomy and choice regarding the authority of religious laws.
- *Reconstructionist Judaism* views Judaism as a civilization that is progressively evolving. It is not dogmatic in its religious principles; it allows for considerable theological diversity. It does not view Jews as the chosen people and does not consider Jewish law to be binding.

Shintoism: The Way of the Gods

Shintoism is an ancient religion of Japan; historically, it was Japan's state religion. Today it has 13 denominations.

Shinto means "way of the *kami*." *Kami*, which translates as "God" or "divinity," are "the sacred spirits that exist both in the celestial realm and in nature and human beings" (White, 1997, p. 98). Shintoism is an animistic religion that sees the sacred in all things, including animals and plants, trees, and mountains. Human ancestors are also held in high regard. All forms of life are celebrated in Shinto, as is the connection among gods, people, and the world.

Shintoism has no written scriptures, formal teachings or dogma, or group worship. Instead, small shrines believed to be the homes of the *kami* are places for individual worship. Shinto festivals and rituals replace the sermons and the study of scripture that characterize other religions. There are three elements of Shinto worship:

- purification, usually with water;
- offerings to the *kami*, usually money or food; and
- prayer or petition (a request for something).

Shintoism promotes respect for life, appreciation of beauty, and love of purity and simplicity.

Sikhism: Religion of Disciples

In 2001, 278,400 Canadians identified themselves as Sikhs (Statistics Canada, 2001). There are 23 million Sikhs worldwide. Sikhism is the religion of the state of Punjab in northern India. In Punjabi, *Sikh* means "disciple" or "learner." Sikhism was founded by Guru Nanak in 1469. He was succeeded by nine more gurus (teachers or authorities), the last of whom, Guru Gobind Singh, appointed as his successor not a person but a text—the *Guru Granth Sahib*, which is the Sikh holy book and contains the writings of all ten gurus. These scriptures constitute the main authority of the Sikh religion; there are no clergy in Sikhism. Table 4.4 lists the five principles of faith, the five stages of spiritual development, the five virtues, and the five vices associated with Sikhism. Sikhs believe in human unity and equality of the sexes. They are anti-class and anti-hierarchy, and strive to eliminate all prejudices based on race, colour, and religion (Brar, 1998a).

Table 4.4   Doctrines of Sikhism

Principles of faith	Stages of spiritual development
Human equality	Duty
Worship of God	Knowledge
Charity for the poor	Effort
Dignity of work	Grace
Service to others	Truth

Virtues	Vices
Faith	Lust
Truth	Greed
Compassion	Materialism
Patience	Conceit
Self-control	Anger

Khalsa
the collective body of Sikhs who have undergone a baptism ceremony signifying dedication to the principles of Sikhism

The **Khalsa** is the collective body of Sikhs who have gone through a baptism ceremony signifying dedication to the principles of Sikhism. The word *Khalsa* means "pure." All Sikhs are expected either to be initiated into the order of Khalsa or to be working toward initiation. A male initiate is titled a *Singh*; a female initiate is titled a *Kaur*. The Sikhs of the Khalsa must wear five articles of faith (Brar, 1998b):

- *Kesh*: Uncut hair, a symbol of spirituality and dedication. Sikh men must wear a turban, a symbol of royalty and dignity; it is optional for Sikh women. The turban cannot be covered by anything else and cannot be replaced with a hat.
- *Kangha*: Comb, a symbol of cleanliness and discipline.
- *Kara*: Steel bracelet, to remind its wearer to show restraint.
- *Kachha*: Undergarments, a symbol of self-control and chastity.
- *Kirpan*: Ceremonial dagger or sword, a symbol of dignity and the Sikh struggle against injustice. The *kirpan* is a religious symbol only and is never used as a weapon.

Taoism: Universal Energy in Balance

Taoism is China's oldest religion, dating back to 206 BCE. It is believed that Lao Tzu, who wrote the *Tao Te Ching*, founded this religion. The word *Tao* comes from a Chinese word for "the way." Taoism is a philosophy of life that places great emphasis on non-aggression, non-competition, balance, the pursuit of health, and the quest for longevity. Its influence can be seen in such practices as acupuncture, Chinese herbal medicine, meditation, and the martial arts.

Until the 20th century, Taoism was the state religion of China. However, from 1911 on, because of political upheaval and the growth of Confucianism and Buddhism in China, Taoism began to wane. During the Chinese communist years, which began in 1949, religion was banned, many Taoist monks were imprisoned or killed, and Taoist temples were destroyed. Taoism almost died out entirely, but it has been resurgent since the 1980s (The Taoist Restoration Society, 1999).

According to Taoist belief, **Tao** is an energy force that flows through all life. The goal of life is harmony between the individual and this universal energy. The ancient *yin* and *yang* symbol represents *Tao*. *Yin* is the dark side and *yang* is the light side. The two sides symbolize pairs of opposites: good and evil, feminine and masculine, and so on. Taoists believe that *yin* and *yang* must be in balance in people. This balance is achieved through mental, physical, and spiritual health. Illness is believed to be caused by a lack of balance in the body's energy (*ch'i*). Practices such as meditation and Tai Chi help to restore the balance (Ontario Consultants on Religious Tolerance, 2000).

Tao
the energy source that flows through all life, according to Taoist belief

Aboriginal Spirituality

After landing at Gaspé in 1534, Jacques Cartier erected a wooden cross and preached a sermon, thereby introducing Christianity to the Aboriginal peoples. Like most Europeans, Cartier assumed that the Aboriginal peoples were "pagans"; he failed to acknowledge their complex spiritual tradition. While many Aboriginal peoples (First Nations, Métis, Inuit) are Christian, their ancestors having been converted by missionaries, many others follow the "old ways." These old ways involve teachings about spirituality and the environment.

Aboriginal spiritual practice consists of two main elements: mythic traditions (creation myths, ritual myths, institutional myths); and religious ceremonies and practices. Aboriginal creation myths account for the origins of things—of humans, for example, who were transformed from animals by the Great Spirit, according to some myths; and of the sun, moon, and stars. They also account for significant elements of the human experience, such as death. An example of a creation myth is the earth-diver narrative, common among eastern woodlands and northern plains Aboriginal people. According to this creation story, a deity called the Great Spirit or the Transformer dove—or, in some variations of the story, ordered animals to dive—into the primeval waters to bring mud to the surface, from which the deity then formed the earth.

Institutional myths explain the beginnings of significant religious ceremonies, such as the Sun Dance, while ritual myths preserve and explain the ceremonies and rituals surrounding rites of passage such as birth, death, and tribal initiation. Significant Aboriginal rituals and ceremonies include the following:

- The Sweat Lodge, a ceremony—common among the Great Plains and eastern Woodlands nations—that involves a ceremonial sauna within a hut or other dwelling and is thought to cleanse the individual both physically and spiritually.

- The Morning Dance, performed every spring by the Anishnabe (Ojibwa) people, which pays homage to "the tree of the universe."

- The Shaking Tent, a ritual in which a person—the shaking-tent seer— enters the tent and communicates with spirits beyond this world.

- The Sun Dance, a summer festival that takes place over 8 to 16 days and that, until 1978, was prohibited in the United States as a "pagan," "barbaric" ceremony.

- The Potlatch ceremony, which involves, among other activities, feasting, redistributing (and sometimes destroying) wealth, and sharing songs and stories. The Canadian government made this ceremony illegal in the late 1800s, viewing its anti-capitalist basis as subversive and uncivilized (Aboriginal Spirituality, 2011).

In the Aboriginal world view, there is no separation between the natural and the supernatural worlds. Natural elements, such as rocks and trees, can take on mystic significance and spiritual power and are sometimes invested with personality and the power to act. Sacred objects used in ceremonies also have mystical powers and meaning.

Aboriginal peoples believe that offending the spirits of animals or showing disrespect for sacred tribal objects and natural phenomena can bring trouble to individuals and communities. To prevent such occurrences, Aboriginal peoples rely on **guiding spirits**. Each individual possesses a guiding spirit, which he or she can discover only by undertaking a guiding spirit quest. This involves the person's isolating him- or herself and praying, fasting, and undergoing purification rites in the hope of receiving a vision or an encounter with the guiding spirit. The guiding spirit often takes the form of an animal or a person from the band's mythology, or spiritual tradition.

Belief in an afterlife and in a soul that survives death is part of Aboriginal spirituality. The place of the dead is thought to be a great distance from this life, reached by a long and perilous journey after death. Not just humans but non-human objects, too, are believed to have souls that survive death—a belief known as **animism**. Aboriginal groups also believe in reincarnation or rebirth (Aboriginal Spirituality, 2010).

guiding spirits
personal spirits that are believed, by Aboriginal peoples, to protect individuals from bringing trouble to themselves or to their communities

animism
the belief that non-human objects have souls that survive death

---

EXERCISE 3

Revisit your responses to Exercise 2, and consider what images you now have of the following individuals after reading about their respective religions. Have your perceptions changed? Discuss.

a. a Muslim woman wearing a *niqab*
b. a Chinese Buddhist
c. a Christian Scientist
d. a Jehovah's Witness
e. a traditional Aboriginal man
f. a Sikh wearing a turban
g. a Hindu woman wearing a sari
h. a Muslim man with a beard
i. a white Protestant woman
j. a Roman Catholic priest

RELIGIOUS DIVERSITY: POLICE ABILITIES, KNOWLEDGE, AND SKILLS

Police officers need to be aware of the important role that religious beliefs and practices often have in the lives of those they serve and protect. Police officers may sometimes have to intervene in conflicts that have religious overtones, and they can be subject to accusations of racism if these situations aren't handled with awareness and sensitivity. Knowledge of religion can assist police in resolving these kinds of conflicts successfully and can help them, more generally, in the practice of community policing and in their interactions with community members.

There are practical strategies available to law enforcement. Faced with a conflict involving someone from a particular religious group, for example, police will find that calling on religious leaders and those who understand the religious group in question can reduce conflict and enhance the community's trust in police. Another effective tool is alternative dispute resolution, which involves having the community deal with the dispute rather than sending it before the courts. One advantage of this approach is its familiarity; it is a practice traditionally used by many ethnocultural groups to solve certain kinds of internal conflicts.

In the post-9/11 environment, the religion most in need of understanding by police is the Muslim faith practised by Arab and other communities. Law enforcement agencies need to do what they can to cultivate good relations between Muslims and their host cultures. Police also need to separate, in their own minds, the Muslim people and their Islamic religion from the concepts of terrorism and suicide bombers. One constructive measure in this regard would be to eliminate the practice of racial profiling, by which Arabs and Muslims are automatically seen as threats to national security. In fostering good relations between themselves and the Arab/Muslim communities, police need to be aware that very few Muslims and Arabs are terrorists. There is currently a struggle within Islam between moderates and radicals, and the vast majority of Muslims identify with and support the moderates. Law enforcement agencies need to recognize that cultivating good relations with Muslims is good business for law enforcement, both in general and as a counterterrorism measure. It is also a good way to nourish a culture of peace. Reaching out to Muslims in the post-9/11 climate—trying to understand their culture and to create dialogue with their communities—should be seen as a duty for law enforcement.

Religious beliefs strongly influence an ethnocultural group's values, moral code, and social conduct. How their religious beliefs are viewed by others, especially by those in the host culture, also strongly affects such groups. Police may find the beliefs and practices of various religions puzzling or objectionable. But for a police officer to give way to such personal disapproval—to label these unfamilar practices primitive or savage—would be irresponsible. Religious intolerance in any form is wrong.

National and international strategies for intelligence gathering are important, as are cutting-edge technologies in border security and counterterrorism. Equally important, however, is some understanding of the "clash of civilizations" within our multicultural society. Such understanding can contribute to a trusting relationship between law enforcement and our society's diverse cultural and religious communities.

EXERCISE 4

Police may refer troubled families to their local clergy for help and guidance or they may use clergy to calm highly charged emotional situations. Do you believe there is any benefit to police collaborating with clergy or even forming police–clergy teams to respond to crisis situations? Why or why not?

EXERCISE 5

Some religious groups in our society have survived official persecution in their countries of origin, persecution in which police were involved. Consider some of these groups, and consider what core values and beliefs contributed to their persecution. How might this past mistreatment affect their attitudes and behaviour in their new country, and what might be the consequences for policing in Canada?

EXERCISE 6

An important issue for policing in a diverse society is how far people of diversity should adapt their ways to the host culture and how far police need to accommodate the diversity of those they serve and protect. For example, it could be argued that individuals from a religious group ought to abide by all the laws of the country (for example, enlisting in the army during a war) even though these laws may be contrary to their religious beliefs and practices.

Debate this topic by dividing the class into two groups. Have one group take the position that religious groups need to adapt their ways to those of the host culture. Have the second group argue that the police need to accommodate the religious beliefs and practices of every community. Follow the debate with a general class discussion.

CHAPTER SUMMARY

Pluralistic societies include many religions. The beliefs and practices of a particular religious group may be at odds with those of an individual police officer, with those of other minority religious groups, or with those of the host nation. Police need to understand and respect various religions; they need to be able to resolve religious conflict effectively; and they need to be willing to consider proactive approaches to preventing religious conflict. At the same time, police must combat the threat of terrorism. Balancing these mandates is no easy task. Police who are dedicated to their profession transcend cultural and religious differences; they serve and protect, indiscriminately, members of all religions and cultures.

KEY TERMS

agnostic
animism
atheist
guiding spirits
Khalsa
Koran
monotheistic

reincarnation
religion
religious beliefs
religious practices
Shabbath
Tao

REFERENCES

Aboriginal spirituality. (2011). [PowerPoint]. http://www.markville.ss.yrdsb.edu.on.

Boeree, C.G. (2000). The basics of Buddhist wisdom. An introduction to Buddhism. http://www.ship.edu/~cgboeree/buddhaintro.html.

Brar, S.S. (1998a). Introduction to Sikhism. http://www.sikhs.org/summary.htm.

Brar, S.S. (1998b). The Khalsa. http://www.sikhs.org/khalsa.htm.

Eddy, M.B. (1994). *Science and health with key to the scriptures.* Boston: The First Church of Christ, Scientist. (Original work published 1875.)

The First Church of Christ, Scientist. (2001). Questions and answers. http://www.tfccs.com.

Forman, R.K.C. (Ed.). (1993). *Religions of the world* (3rd ed.). New York: St. Martin's Press.

Himalayan Academy. (2000). Hinduism: The basics. http://www.himalayanacademy.com/basics.

Islam fastest growing religion in Canada. (2001). http://www.islamawareness.net/NorthAmerica/Canada/caislam2.html.

New York City Bahá'í Community. (1999). Beliefs and practices. http://www.bahainyc.org/.

Ontario Consultants on Religious Tolerance. (2000). Taoism. http://www.religioustolerance.org/taoism.htm.

Ontario Consultants on Religious Tolerance. (2009). Number of adherents of world religions. http://www.religioustolerance.org/worldrel.htm.

Religion Facts. (2010). The big religion comparison chart. http://www.religionfacts.com/big_religion_chart.htm.

Roberts, J. (2006). *First Nations, Inuit, and Métis peoples.* Toronto: Emond Montgomery.

Statistics Canada. (2001). Overview: Canada still predominantly Roman Catholic and Protestant. http://www12.statcan.ca/english/census01/Products/Analytic/companion/rel/canada.cfm.

The Taoist Restoration Society. (1999). Introduction. http://www.monclair.net/trs/frameset.html.

Watch Tower Bible and Tract Society of Pennsylvania. (2001). What Jehovah's Witnesses believe. http://www.watchtower.org/library/br78/index.htm.

White, G.C. (1997). *Beliefs and believers.* New York: Berkley Books.

REVIEW QUESTIONS

TRUE OR FALSE?

T   1. Each religion has its own world view.

T   2. Atheists do not believe in a higher power.

F   3. The Bahá'í faith teaches that people are unequal in the sight of God.

T   4. In Buddhist marital relations, husbands are expected to be respectful, faithful, and supportive of their wives.

___   5. Christian Science teaches strict adherence to the Ten Commandments.

F   6. *Hindu* is the Persian word for "China."

___   7. The word *yoga* means "union."

F   8. All Muslims are Arabs.

T   9. Muslims are prohibited from eating beef.

T   10. Judaism was the first monotheistic religion.

MULTIPLE CHOICE

1. The largest religious group in Canada is the
   (a) Roman Catholics
   (b) Protestants
   (c) Muslims
   (d) Buddhists

2. The fundamental religious issue for Buddhism is
   (a) sin
   (b) ignorance
   (c) sacred acts
   (d) religious expression

3. The foundation of human society for the Bahá'í is
   (a) the law
   (b) fasting
   (c) religious conversion
   (d) the family

4. Christian Science aims to heal disease by
   (a) the restorative power of the human body
   (b) spiritual means alone
   (c) a reliance on the latest medical technology
   (d) blood transfusions

5. The Protestant Reformation was sparked by

   (a) Martin Luther

   (b) Martin Luther King

   (c) King Charles II

   (d) Emmanuel Kant

6. All four Hindu denominations believe in

   (a) reincarnation

   (b) a basic scriptural guide

   (c) a single deity

   (d) the divinity of the guru

7. For the Jehovah's Witness, the only holiday that requires celebration is

   (a) Easter

   (b) The Memorial of Christ's Death

   (c) Christmas

   (d) Lent

8. The central symbol of Judaism is

   (a) the Bible

   (b) the Torah

   (c) the Ten Commandments

   (d) the *Talmud*

9. To avoid bringing troubles on themselves and their communities, Aboriginal individuals rely on

   (a) medicine men

   (b) the Potlatch ceremony

   (c) guiding spirits

   (d) creation myths

10. For police, creating a dialogue with the Muslim community is a

   (a) conflict

   (b) moral imperative

   (c) form of prejudice

   (d) duty

FILL IN THE BLANKS

1. Religion is a set of _____ and/or rituals that address issues of ultimate reality.

2. Christianity identifies _____ as the fundamental human problem.

3. Agnostics believe in the _____ of knowing God.

4. Buddhism is not a _____ in the Western sense.

5. The most common religion in the world is _____.

6. _____ are Hindu teachers with superior spiritual knowledge.

7. Islam is one of the _____-growing faiths in Canada.

8. According to the Koran, men and women are _____ before God.

9. Jehovah's Witnesses have _____ but no clergy.

10. The Canadian government made the _____ ceremony illegal in the late 1800s.

Family Violence, Mental Health Issues, and Developmental Disabilities

5

INTRODUCTION

Everyone has the right to a safe home environment, one that is free from neglect and from economic, physical, psychological, and spiritual abuse. But there are people who lack such an environment and are exposed to neglect, intimidation, domination, and physical or sexual assault. These people have the right to protection and assistance, as do people who suffer from mental illness. This chapter discusses family violence and mental illness from the perspective of diversity policing. The chapter's aim is to help you better understand the realities of family violence and mental health issues, and the ways in which police can respond most appropriately to them.

DEFINITION OF FAMILY VIOLENCE

The term **family violence** covers the many different forms of abuse, mistreatment, or neglect that adults or children may experience in their intimate, kinship, extended, or dependent relationships (Department of Justice Canada, 2006a). While family violence typically involves either the abuse of one partner in a relationship by the other or the abuse of a child by a parent, it can also entail the abuse of children by a caregiver or the abuse of a parent by a child.

Abuse in families may take a variety of forms, including physical assault, physical neglect, sexual assault, sexual exploitation, emotional and psychological abuse, financial abuse, and spiritual abuse. Physical assault may range in degrees of violence, from bruising to murder. Sexual assault may range from the victim's being forced to participate in an unwanted sexual activity, to rape, to the sexual abuse of children. Psychological abuse may range from emotional or mental violence (verbal abuse, putdowns, humiliation, threats, and intimidation through the damage or destruction of property) to excessive possessiveness, forced isolation from friends

> **CHAPTER OBJECTIVES**
>
> After completing this chapter, you should be able to:
> - Understand how various groups in Canada are affected by family violence.
> - Understand various mental illnesses and their characteristics.
> - Understand intellectual and developmental disabilities, and how they are defined.
> - Identify police strategies for addressing family violence and for responding to individuals with mental health issues.

family violence
the different forms of abuse, mistreatment, or neglect that adults or children may experience in their intimate, kinship, extended, or dependent relationships

and family, and harassment. Spiritual abuse may involve denigrating a person's religious beliefs and practices or not allowing that person's spiritual needs to be met. Finally, the following kinds of excessive control can qualify as economic abuse:

- withholding money to buy food or medical treatment,
- imposing a financially dependent relationship,
- controlling bank accounts and paycheques,
- making grocery lists and making sure that no money is spent on anything else,
- checking the gas gauge in the car to ensure that no extra trips are taken,
- denying access to finances, and
- preventing a person from working.

FAMILY VIOLENCE AND THE LAW

Although the *Criminal Code* does not refer specifically to family violence offences, there are many general offences defined under the Code that could be involved in family violence—for example, assault, sexual assault, stalking, threatening, and murder. The Code provides for measures to safeguard victims of family violence, such as protection orders and other procedures (Department of Justice Canada, 2011).

Ontario's *Child and Family Services Act* protects the well-being of children and contains provisions requiring that services to children and their families be administered in a manner that respects these families' "cultural, religious and regional differences" (s. 1(a)). The *Criminal Code* and the *Canada Evidence Act* include provisions concerning family violence and are amended periodically to address growing concerns in the area of family violence, such as child pornography, sexual exploitation of youth, the luring of children on the Internet, child sex tourism, and the admissibility of testimony from child victims and witnesses (Department of Justice Canada, 2006a).

HOW BIG A PROBLEM IS FAMILY VIOLENCE?

Family violence is a pervasive social and policing problem in Canada, but the real extent of it is unknown. That is because the victims often do not report the problem to police, and because most victims who do report it have suffered multiple incidents before coming forward. The Government of Canada is working to increase public awareness of family violence by doing research, studies, and surveys (Department of Justice Canada, 2011).

Abuse Among Adults

spousal abuse
violence or mistreatment suffered at the hands of a marital, common-law, or same-sex partner

Spousal abuse is violence or mistreatment suffered at the hands of a current or former marital, common-law, or same-sex partner. It may involve spiritual, emotional, psychological, sexual, or economic abuse, or varying degrees of physical violence. It is more likely to occur between ex-spouses or partners than between current spouses or partners (Statistics Canada, 2011, p. 9). In 2007, over 40,000 incidents of spousal violence were reported to police. This represents about 12 percent of all violent crime reported to police in Canada. The incidence of spousal violence remained stable in Canada between 2004 and 2009, at about 6 percent of the adult population (Statistics Canada, 2011, p. 5).

Spousal violence is suffered by both sexes, but women experience more serious forms of it than men do (Statistics Canada, 2011, p. 10). Common assault (in other words, the least violent kind of assault; it includes pushing, grabbing, slapping, and face-to-face threats) is the most frequent type of spousal violence, accounting for nearly two-thirds of offences, followed by major assault, uttering threats, or stalking. Socio-demographic factors—education and income levels, for example— have no influence on spousal violence rates; it is as common among the affluent as among the financially disadvantaged (Statistics Canada, 2011, p. 11).

Children and Youth

Child abuse is a generic term for different forms of physical and psychological abuse committed against children below the age of 14. *Psychological abuse* involves emotionally damaging acts of omission and commission—for example, rejection, isolation, exploitation, and poor socialization. It is important to differentiate between the harm done to children by acts that are prohibited, deliberate, and preventable, and harm that is due to economic disadvantage—for example, poverty.

Child sexual abuse refers to the sexual exploitation of children under the age of 18, deemed to occur when they are made to participate in "sexual activities they do not fully comprehend, are unable to give informed consent to, and that violate the social taboos of family roles" (Schecter & Roberge, 1976). The psychological and behavioural consequences of child sexual abuse include post-traumatic stress disorder and disturbed interpersonal relations.

Police-reported data for 2009 indicate that children and youth under the age of 18 are most likely to be physically or sexually assaulted by someone they know (85 percent of incidents). Nearly 55,000 children and youth were victims of police-reported assault in 2009, with about 3 in 10 incidents perpetrated by a family member. When children and youth were victims of family violence, a parent was identified as the abuser in nearly 6 of 10 incidents (Statistics Canada, 2011, p. 5).

Girls under the age of 18 reported higher rates of both physical and sexual assault by a family member than boys did; in 2009, the rate of family-perpetrated sexual assault was 4 times higher for girls than for boys (Statistics Canada, 2011, p. 21). Male family members were identified as the accused in 96 percent of sexual and 71 percent of physical assaults against children and youth (see Table 5.1).

Older Adults

Elder abuse is the physical, sexual, emotional, or psychological abuse or neglect, or the financial exploitation (fraud and theft), of an older person by

- a caregiver (spouse or partner, adult child, or relative);
- a staff member in an institution, such as a nursing home; or
- a criminal.

child abuse
physical and psychological abuse of children below the age of 14

child sexual abuse
the sexual exploitation of children under the age of 18

elder abuse
the physical, sexual, emotional, or psychological abuse or neglect, or the financial exploitation, of an older person by a caregiver, staff member in an institution, or a criminal

Table 5.1 Accused Perpetrators of Family Violence Against Children and Youth by Relationship to the Victim, Sex of the Accused, and Type of Assault, 2007

Accused by relationship to victim and sex	Total assault		Sexual assault[1]		Physical assault[2]	
	number	percent	number	percent	number	percent
Total family	11,621	100	3,217	100	8,404	100
Female	2,604	22	130	4	2,474	29
Male	9,017	78	3,087	96	5,930	71
Parent[3]	6,454	56	1,094	34	5,360	64
Female	1,748	15	50	2	1,698	20
Male	4,706	40	1,044	32	3,662	44
Sibling[4]	2,380	20	887	28	1,493	18
Female	420	4	32	1	388	5
Male	1,960	17	855	27	1,105	13
Extended family[5]	2,440	21	1,218	38	1,222	15
Female	416	4	46	1	370	4
Male	2,024	17	1,172	36	852	10
Spouse/ex-spouse[6]	347	3	18	1	329	4
Female	20	0	2	0	18	0
Male	327	3	16	0	311	4

Notes:
1. Includes sexual assault (level 1), sexual assault with a weapon or causing bodily harm (level 2), aggravated sexual assault (level 3) and the "other sexual crimes" category, which includes sexual interference, sexual touching, sexual exploitation, incest, etc.
2. Physical assault includes common assault (level 1), assault with a weapon or causing bodily harm (level 2), aggravated assault (level 3), unlawfully causing bodily harm, discharge firearm with intent, criminal negligence causing bodily harm, and other assaults.
3. Includes a small number of cases where age or the relationship between the accused and the victim may have been miscoded.
4. Includes natural, step, half, foster or adopted siblings.
5. Includes others related by blood, marriage, adoption or foster care.
6. Includes legally married and common-law partners and ex-spouses. Rates are calculated per 100,000 population for the geographic areas policed by the Incident-based Uniform Crime Reporting Survey respondents. Population counts by marital status are not available for this geographic level.

Children and youth include all those under the age of 18. Excludes incidents where the sex and/or age of the victim was unknown. Data are not nationally representative. The Incident-Based Uniform Crime Reporting Survey collected data from 153 police services representing approximately 94 percent of the population of Canada in 2007. The Hamilton Police Service is excluded from the analysis due to data quality of the relationship variable. Rate per 100,000 population for the geographic areas policed by the Incident-Based Uniform Crime Reporting Survey respondents, based on populations provided by Demography Division, Statistics Canada.

Source: Statistics Canada, Canadian Centre for Justice Statistics, Incident-Based Uniform Crime Reporting Survey. http://www.statcan.gc.ca/pub/85-224-x/2009000/t020-eng.htm.

For the victims of elder abuse, the psychological effects may include—apart from the trauma of the abuse itself—feelings of shame, embarrassment, self-blame, and inadequacy.

In 2009, police reported over 2,400 incidents of family violence against seniors (Statistics Canada, 2011, p. 5). To put this number in context, adults aged 55 to 64 experienced twice as much family violence as seniors did, while the rates for adults aged 25 to 34 were 8 times higher than those for seniors. Current or ex-spouses and adult children were the family members most likely to commit violence against senior women (see Figure 5.1), while adult children were most often accused of violence against senior men. Family violence accounted for more than one-third of all violent acts committed against older adults. Just over half of police-reported family violence incidents against seniors were common assaults (Statistics Canada, 2011, p. 6).

DIVERSITY AND FAMILY VIOLENCE

People of diversity, whatever the basis of their minority status—age, gender, ethnocultural identity, educational deficit, socio-economic status, occupation, race, religion, sexual orientation, physical or developmental disabilities—may be especially vulnerable to family violence (Green, 1996; Biesenthal et al., 2000; Law Commission of Canada, 2001). Members of the gay and lesbian communities are more than twice as likely as heterosexuals to report having experienced spousal violence, as are members of the Aboriginal community (Statistics Canada, 2011, p. 11). In many cultures, family violence tends to be kept secret; people are embarrassed by it and do not want to discuss it. As a result, no one really knows exactly how many

Figure 5.1   Relationship of Accused to Senior Victim, 2007

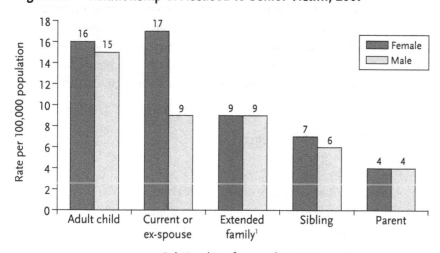

Relationship of accused to victim

Notes:

1. Extended family includes aunts, uncles, cousins, sisters or brothers-in-law, etc.

Data are not nationally representative. The Incident-Based Uniform Crime Reporting Survey collected data from 153 police services representing approximately 94 percent of the population of Canada in 2007. The Hamilton Police Service is excluded from the analysis due to data quality of the relationship variable. Excludes incidents where the victim's sex, age, and/or relationship of the accused to the victim was unknown.

Source: Statistics Canada, Canadian Centre for Justice Statistics, Incident-based Uniform Crime Reporting Survey. http://www.statcan.gc.ca/pub/85-224-x/2009000/ct011-eng.htm.

people are victims or survivors of this kind of violence. Table 5.2 lists some myths associated with family violence.

EXERCISE 1

Consider the myths about family violence listed in Table 5.2. Does it surprise you to see that certain of the statements refer to myths rather than facts? How might a belief in some of these myths affect the way in which police respond to perpetrators and victims of family violence?

Gender and Family Violence

While women and men experience similar levels of violence and emotional abuse in their relationships, the violence experienced by women tends to be more severe and more often repeated than the violence directed at men. Women are 6 times more likely than men to report being sexually assaulted, 5 times more likely to report being choked, 5 times more likely to require medical attention as a result of an assault, and 3 times more likely to be physically injured by an assault (Statistics Canada, 2011, p. 10).

Immigrants and Refugees and Family Violence

Western conceptions of acceptable behaviour, including what constitutes violence and abuse, differ from accepted norms in other cultures. For example, early marriage is a common practice in many parts of the world, especially Africa and South Asia, but in the West the practice is considered a form of sexual violence; forcing young girls into marriage and sexual relations poses risks to their health, including exposure to HIV/AIDS, and decreases their chance of attending school.

When considering what constitutes "abuse," we must apply the currently accepted legal definitions as applied in this country, and require that *all* Canadians act in accordance with them. At the same time, we must recognize that there are

Table 5.2   Myths About Family Violence

- Family violence is rare.
- Family violence is confined to lower socio-economic classes.
- Family violence happens only in heterosexual relationships.
- People with disabilities are unlikely to be victims of family violence.
- Substance abuse is the real cause of family violence.
- Victims of family violence have masochistic personalities.
- Victims of family violence exaggerate the abuse.
- Abusers have a licence to use violence.
- Abusers cannot control their abusive behaviours.
- Victims of family violence provoke the abuse.
- Victims of family violence consider abuse a sexual turn-on.
- Diversity (for example, culture, disability) is the root cause of family violence.

cultural practices—the piercing of infant girls' ears, for example, or the circumcision of infant boys—that, while considered objectionable by some, do not qualify as "abuse."

Immigrants and refugees from diverse cultures bring with them a variety of attitudes, beliefs, and practices that must be understood when examining family violence in a Canadian context. Not all cultures, for example, espouse the equality of men and women or have a conception of women's rights; some sanction or regard as minor crimes practices such as honour killing, virgin suicides, and female genital mutilation, which are considered reprehensible in the West and constitute serious crimes.

Most common in the Muslim world, so-called "honour" killing is the murder of a female family member by a male family member, usually a brother, for having, in the family's eyes, tarnished the family's honour. Acts that have given rise to "honour" killings include but are not limited to a girl or woman having been raped, engaging in consensual sex out of wedlock, going out alone, refusing an arranged marriage, eloping, committing adultery, wearing revealing clothing, flirting, and attempting to escape an abusive relationship. The belief is that killing the girl or woman will restore the family's name in the community. In such cases, girls and women are often killed based solely on the suspicions of a family member, without being given an opportunity to defend themselves. The simple fact of the allegation is considered enough to defile the family's honour, and therefore sufficient justification for the killing. Typically, those who commit such murders in their countries of origin go unpunished or receive reduced sentences.

Although "honour" killings are associated primarily with conservative Islam, it is important to note that many Muslims strongly condemn the practice, holding that it is contrary to Islam and in no way justified by Islamic law.

Related to the practice of "honour" killing is the practice of "virgin suicides." The two practices are related insofar as the latter omits the need for the former (thus ensuring that no male relative will risk punishment for the murder). The term "virgin suicides" refers to the compelled suicide of girls who, from the perspective of their family's culture, have dishonoured themselves and their families. The families lock their daughters in a room for days with lethal weapons—rat poison, a pistol, or a rope—and tell them that death is the only thing that can redeem their disgrace ("Virgin Suicides," 2006). Virgin suicides enable the parents to dispense with the daughter without sacrificing the son or other male family member.

Significant domestic tensions can arise when traditionalist families, accustomed to controlling their children according to strict familial and religious codes, suddenly find themselves in a liberal, secular environment where women have considerable freedom. Under these circumstances, conflict can arise between women and their families, and the conflict may result in violence. Police services and governments across Canada are attempting to increase awareness of human rights in the West, particularly women's rights, and urging community groups to help fight such crimes.

EXERCISE 2

List strategies that might enable police to help people from other cultures address family violence in their communities.

EXPLANATIONS FOR FAMILY VIOLENCE

In a society composed of diverse cultures, family violence is a complex social issue and can be a product of various factors:

- dislocation from one's culture, one's language, one's kin and community;
- historical oppression, as with the European subjugation of Aboriginal people;
- racism;
- sexism;
- homophobia;
- poverty; and
- isolation.

Explanations for family violence involving the abuse of women tend to fall into four categories. The *personal view* points the finger at women and suggests that they provoke men into abusing them. The *chemical view* blames abusive behaviour on the use of alcohol and illicit drugs. The *social view* points the finger at several factors: stress, economic hardship, men's hunger for control and power, women's fear of disclosure (which can prolong the abuse), and society's lax attitude toward abusers (Champagne, Lapp, & Lee, 1994). The social view identifies patriarchy as the main culprit, arguing that patriarchal societies institutionalize the social control of women and perpetuate their lack of power in relation to men. Religion, too, can be a factor in domestic violence. Some religions may practise **gendered apartheid**, based on the belief that women are morally inferior to men and constitute a subordinate class of human being (Okin, 1999). Gendered apartheid is opposed by feminism, which views women and men as moral and human equals and promotes a culture in which women have the same advantages and opportunities as men (Okin, 1999).

gendered apartheid
a policy of segregation, followed in certain religions, based on a belief that women are inferior to men and constitute a subordinate class of human being

---

EXERCISE 3

1. Identify factors that police should consider when trying to help a new immigrant who is in an abusive relationship.
2. List factors that need to be considered by someone creating a safety plan for victims of family violence. Assume that these victims have children.

BARRIERS TO LEAVING VIOLENT RELATIONSHIPS

Women, as well as some men, are silent about and tolerant of abuse for complex reasons that may include the following:

- a sense of privacy or shame,
- a fear of social stigma falling on the family and a desire to keep up appearances,
- a desperate need to be in a relationship,
- fear of reprisal and harm to the children,

- financial or emotional dependence,
- lack of social support, and
- inadequate support from the criminal justice system.

The Canadian government has funded projects through the Family Violence Initiative aimed at helping people leave abusive relationships. These projects have developed, among other things, information for victims regarding how to get safely out of a violent relationship, as well as resources for people encountering victims of family violence (Department of Justice Canada, 2006b).

SOCIAL RESPONSES TO FAMILY VIOLENCE

Canada supports a policy of zero tolerance for all types of violence. This policy dictates that

- all perpetrators of violence face appropriate consequences from the criminal justice system,
- victims receive necessary protection from the criminal justice system, and
- victims and survivors of violence be provided with diversity-sensitive supports and services in their communities.

In the past, community supports and services for victims of family violence didn't take the issue of diversity much into account. This *adiversity* (as in "asocial") tradition is changing; programs are gradually becoming more diversity-oriented. Specialized community-based programs are following a support-and-service philosophy that aims to do the following:

- respect diversity, individual autonomy, and safety;
- support a community-wide response to reduce violence against women; and
- promote systemic change at the legal and medical levels and in our society's overall response to victims.

An important government program is the Family Violence Initiative, which represents an ongoing federal commitment to address the deeply entrenched problem of family violence with numerous social, legal, and health measures. The long-term goal of the Family Violence Initiative is to reduce the occurrence of family violence in Canada (Department of Justice Canada, 2011).

Supports and Services

Organizations providing community support and services are essential for an effective response to family violence. Shelters for abused women, in particular, fulfill an important role; they provide refuge and services to women and children fleeing family violence. In 2008, the 569 shelters serving abused women across Canada recorded admissions of more than 101,000 women and children. As in previous years, almost half of the shelters were transitional facilities providing abused women with short- to moderate-term housing, while about one-quarter were facilities offering short-term, emergency refuge. These shelters provide a range of services to those they admit, including transportation, counselling, advocacy, housing referral, and life skills training, as well as services and programs for residents' children. They also provide continued support for former residents (see Figure 5.2).

Organizations providing community support and services to victims of family violence need to recognize diversity as a factor. For example, gay and lesbian victims of family violence can feel ill at ease in mainstream shelters where they may be fearful of encountering homophobia. There have been a number of diversity-oriented initiatives. One project developed by the government's Family Violence Initiative is a culturally sensitive resource guide. Entitled *Guidelines for Service Providers: Outreach Strategies for Family Violence Intervention with Immigrant and Minority Communities*, this resource guide identifies outreach strategies that mainstream service agencies can use to encourage minority communities and their leadership to address family violence issues (Changing Ways, 2010; Department of Justice Canada, 2006b).

It has been noted (Justice Institute of British Columbia, 2007; Kazarian & Kazarian, 1998) that abused immigrant and refugee women have unique vulnerabilities, including the following:

- worries about their immigration status (for example, their lack of permanent status or the threat of their abuser's sponsorship being withdrawn if they complain), about their work permits, and about deportation;

- lack of knowledge about host country laws (for example, women from some cultures may not realize that wife assault is a criminal act) and about the personal rights and freedoms they are entitled to in this country;

- lack of familiarity with the system and its available community supports and services; and

- language barriers.

Figure 5.2   Most Common Shelters for Women, 2008

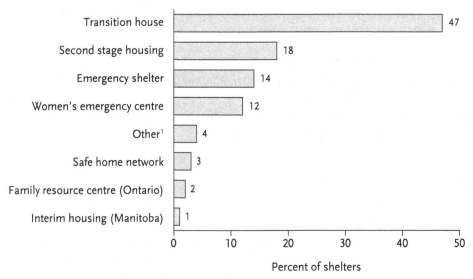

Note:

1. Includes other facilities not otherwise classified.

Source: Statistics Canada, Canadian Centre for Justice Statistics, Transition Home Survey, 2007/2008. http://www.statcan.gc.ca/pub/85-224-x/2009000/ct001-eng.htm.

The various needs of abused immigrant and refugee women are listed in Table 5.3. Canadians should view it as a social responsibility to inform immigrant women in abusive relationships that Citizenship and Immigration Canada does not expect them to remain silent about their partners' violent behaviour or to live in danger.

POLICE RESPONSE TO FAMILY VIOLENCE

Police have had three major response policies regarding family violence: the mediative policy, the pro-arrest policy, and the mandatory arrest policy. The **mediative policy**, which is now obsolete, favoured a non-arrest, hands-off approach by police. In other words, police officers responding to family violence calls mainly tried to get everyone in the household to calm down. Then they left it to the family to resolve their difficulties or they referred the offender or victim to social agencies.

mediative policy
a non-arrest police approach to family violence calls

The mediative approach to family violence was based partly on the fact that, in the past, police did not consider violence in intimate relationships a real crime. Two mindsets prevailed in this regard, the practical and the patriarchal. The following assumptions informed the practical mindset:

- the victim probably does not want the offender arrested;
- the victim depends financially on the offender and can't afford to have him or her arrested;
- the offence may be culturally acceptable;
- the offender may cause harm to the victim once he is released;
- arrest may have the unfortunate effect of breaking up the relationship; or
- the court is likely to dismiss charges when the victim chooses not to prosecute.

The patriarchal mindset resulted from a police officer's having been socialized in a patriarchal and hierarchical societal structure in which sexist attitudes prevailed, including the assumption that men should have power and control over

---

Table 5.3   Major Needs of Abused Immigrant and Refugee Women

1. Accessible information about Canadian laws and rights, social infrastructure, and available services

2. Help from interpreters or service providers who speak the languages of the immigrant women and who can help them leave abusive relationships, maintain their health and safety, and realize their rights

3. Help in addressing sponsorship and immigration barriers, with specific information about these matters and about the rights of women as immigrants or refugees

4. Material assistance in meeting a wide range of interrelated practical and material needs, including pre-employment or bridging programs, employment, income assistance, child care, transportation, affordable housing, and medical care

5. Assistance from the community to overcome their (the women's) isolation and self-blame for the abuse.

Source: Justice Institute of British Columbia (2007).

women. Police officers with this mindset had little interest in enforcing laws against men who abuse women, because they viewed such abuse as natural.

Since the mid-1970s, there have been major changes in the way police respond to family violence. Two policies now prevail. The **pro-arrest policy** encourages arrest in family violence cases, but it leaves the decision about arrest to the discretion of the officers. The **mandatory arrest policy**, on the other hand, dictates that arrest must take place whenever probable cause exists, even in the case of less serious offences. Police services in many countries, including Canada, have adopted a policy of laying criminal charges in family violence cases. Nonetheless, many police officers are still reluctant to take this approach.

Projects funded by the Department of Justice Canada, under the Family Violence Initiative, have aimed at having the police work with social agencies in matters of family violence. Family Service Regina Inc., for instance, as part of its Domestic Violence Program, received funding to continue working with the Regina Police Service, Regina Probation Services, and the Crown Prosecutor's Office to develop a strategy for immediate intervention—in the case of extremely high-risk relationships—between victims of domestic violence and their abusers. This initiative involves developing an individualized intervention plan for each victim as well as a collaborative community effort to facilitate and assist in the gathering of evidence from victims. The project concluded in February 2010 (Department of Justice Canada, 2006b).

pro-arrest policy
a policy that favours arrest in family violence cases but leaves the decision to the discretion of the officers

mandatory arrest policy
a policy dictating that arrest must take place in family violence cases

---

EXERCISE 4

As a police officer, what would you do in the case of the following disclosure? Role-play the scenario, demonstrating a diversity-competent approach to responding to family violence calls. Be aware of your verbal and non-verbal messages.

I am a physically disabled newcomer to this country. My husband has sponsored me and my three children. I have no one here other than my husband and my children. I have been beaten by my husband, as have my children, and I am scared. I finally had the courage to call the police to help me. They are my only hope.

MENTAL ILLNESS

mental illness
a group of disabilities marked by disturbances in thinking, feeling, and relating

Mental illness is more common than many people think, and traditionally has not been discussed openly. It is estimated that 20 percent of Canadians are likely to experience mental illness during their lifetime, and that the remaining 80 percent are likely to be affected by a family member, friend, or colleague who is mentally ill (Canadian Mental Health Association [CMHA], 2011b). Police have frequent contact with mentally ill people, and this contact is on the rise. A CMHA study found that over 30 percent of people with serious mental illness had contact with police (CMHA, British Columbia Branch, 2005). New psychiatric and psychological treatment approaches to mental illness have contributed to the deinstitutionalization of the mentally ill and their reintegration into the community. However, shortcomings in the community mental health services, including insufficient funding for health and social services, have led to increased police involvement in calls from the community concerning mental health episodes.

An issue related to mental illness is **homelessness**. Homelessness is significantly correlated with diagnoses of mental illness and substance abuse, although it is not clear whether mental illness and substance abuse is a factor contributing to homelessness or whether the opposite is true—that homelessness is a cause of mental illness and substance abuse. Two acknowledged facts are that a history of mental illness or substance abuse increases the *risk* of homelessness, and that the increased stress and anxiety associated with homelessness can lead to mental health issues, and can cause individuals to use substances as a coping strategy (Mental Illness Awareness Week, 2010).

This part of the chapter focuses on policing mental illness; its aim is to increase your understanding of mental illness and to consider how police can respond more effectively in situations involving mental illness.

The Concept of Mental Illness

Mental illness is a generic term for a variety of disorders. The Police Executive Research Forum (1997) has defined mental illness as a group of distinct disabilities marked by disturbances in thinking, feeling, and relating. The Public Health Agency of Canada (2011) has stated that mental illnesses are characterized by alterations in thinking, mood, or behaviour (or some combination thereof), alterations that are associated with significant distress and impaired functioning over an extended period of time.

Although mental illness causes disturbances in behaving, feeling, relating, and thinking, such disturbances can also be caused by other factors, including head injury, medical conditions such as diabetes and epilepsy, and substance abuse. For example, people who use cocaine may experience **formication**, a hallucinatory experience in which the users feel that insects or snakes are crawling over or under their skin. Similarly, people in the aftermath of a cocaine high may become irritable and depressed.

Mental illness ranges from mild to severe. Severe mental illness includes schizophrenia, mood disorders, organic brain syndrome (a general term referring to physical disorders that negatively affect brain function), as well as paranoia and other psychoses. According to the Public Health Agency of Canada (2011), mental illness can occur in the form of

- mood disorders,
- schizophrenia,
- anxiety disorders,
- personality disorders, and
- eating disorders.

Mental disturbances can be categorized as *non-psychotic* or **psychotic**; the latter involves losing touch with reality. Hallucinations and delusions are the two most common symptoms of a psychotic mental disturbance. Anxiety and depression are the two most common symptoms of non-psychotic mental disturbance.

homelessness
the condition of having no fixed, regular, and adequate address

formication
a hallucinatory experience, sometimes undergone by cocaine users, that involves feeling that insects or snakes are crawling over or under one's skin

psychosis
a form of mental disturbance that involves a person's losing touch with reality

Following are some other facts about mental health and mental illness (CMHA, 2011a):

- Mental illness indirectly affects all Canadians at some time through a family member, friend, or colleague.
- Mental illness affects people of all ages, education and income levels, and ethnocultural backgrounds.
- Anxiety disorders causing mild to severe impairment affect 5 percent of the people living in households.
- A complex interplay of genetic, biological, personality, and environmental factors causes mental illness.
- Almost 50 percent of people who have experienced depression or anxiety have never consulted a doctor about the problem.
- Stigma and discrimination and the community's non-acceptance of mental illness constitute a serious barrier to diagnosis and treatment.
- Mental illness can be treated effectively.
- The economic cost of mental illness to the Canadian health-care system was estimated to be at least $9.7 billion at the turn of the century.
- Also at the turn of the century, $6.3 billion was spent on uninsured mental health services and on time off work for mental health needs that were not treated by the health-care system.
- As well, 3.8 percent of all admissions in general hospitals (1.5 million hospital days) were due to mental illness.

MENTAL HEALTH LEGISLATION

When the *UN Principles for the Protection of Persons with Mental Illness and the Improvement of Mental Health Care* were adopted by resolution of the UN General Assembly on December 17, 1991, the international community officially recognized the fundamental right of mentally ill people to be protected from discrimination (Office of the United Nations High Commissioner for Human Rights, 1991). Despite this development, the mental health legislation in many countries still allows the removal of the civil liberties of people with mental illness (Persad & Kazarian, 1998). The essential criteria determining whether someone should be forcibly confined in a psychiatric hospital concern whether that person is a danger to self, a danger to others, or is incompetent to care for him- or herself.

Mental Health Act: Ontario

The Ontario *Mental Health Act* (1990, amended 2010) regulates the administration of mental health care, including the involuntary admission of people into a psychiatric hospital. This Act was amended (Bill 68) and passed as *Brian's Law* on June 23, 2000, and amended again in 2010. Brian Smith was a popular sportscaster and former National Hockey League player who was shot and killed by a man with a history of serious mental illness. *Brian's Law* enables seriously mentally ill people to be treated in a community setting that is less restrictive and less intrusive than a psychiatric hospital. Other provinces (for example, Saskatchewan) have similar laws.

The power of a police officer to admit people against their will to psychiatric hospitals or psychiatric units of hospitals is dealt with under s. 17 of the Act. New amendments to the Act state that a police officer must stay with a person who has been involuntarily admitted until the facility decides whether or not to admit the person (s. 33).

Brian's Law also stipulates that a justice of the peace may issue an order authorizing a police officer to take a person in custody to an appropriate place for examination by a physician, provided that—based on information that the officer must give under oath—there is evidence of *threat* and *mental disorder* (s. 16). As evidence of *threat*, the statute requires information to the effect that (1) the person has threatened or attempted or is threatening or attempting to cause bodily harm to herself or himself; (2) the person has behaved or is behaving violently toward another person or has caused or is causing another person to fear bodily harm from her or him; and (3) the person has shown or is showing a lack of competence to care for herself or himself. As to taking a person into custody on the grounds of mental disorder, the statute requires information, based on the officer's reasonable cause or belief, that the person's mental disorder is of a nature or quality that will result in (1) serious bodily harm to the person, (2) serious bodily harm to another person, and (3) serious physical impairment of the person.

Finally, *Brian's Law* stipulates that a police officer may take a person into custody provided the police officer has reasonable and probable grounds to believe that disorderly conduct has occurred and has reasonable cause to believe that the person fulfills the conditions of threat and mental disorder described above.

MENTAL DISTURBANCES AND POLICE RESPONSE

In their day-to-day duties, police are very likely to encounter people with one (or a combination) of the following conditions: a substance-related disorder, a mood disorder, schizophrenia, or an intellectual disability. Police are also very likely to deal with mental disturbances in connection with

- suicidal behaviour;
- threatening, destructive, assaultive, or violent behaviour;
- psychotic thinking and ideation (losing touch with reality);
- confusion in thought or action; and
- strange or unusual behaviours that exceed public tolerance.

Substance-Related Disorders

About 20 percent of people with a mental disorder also have a substance abuse problem. One in ten Canadians 15 years of age and older report symptoms consistent with alcohol or illicit drug dependence. Overall, men were 2.6 times more likely than women to meet the criteria for substance dependence (CMHA, 2011b). People with **substance-related disorders** may show mental disturbances of both the psychotic and the non-psychotic types. For example, consuming alcohol can have serious effects such as blackout and aggression. Angel dust (PCP, phencyclidine) is known to produce severe anxiety, depression, disorientation, unpredictable aggression, and paranoid thoughts (Levinthal, 1996). Alcohol and drug abuse are also associated

substance-related disorders
mental disorders caused by substance dependence and abuse, and by substance withdrawal

with crime and social violence such as robbery, burglary, shoplifting, pimping, prostitution, and the trafficking and distribution of illicit drugs for income.

In responding to a person with a substance-related disorder, police need to

- ensure their own safety and the safety of others,
- recognize the symptoms the person is displaying,
- expect irrational behaviour,
- decide whether the situation is a medical emergency, and
- ensure that an interim use of physical restraint is safe and unlikely to cause the person added harm.

Mood Disorders and Suicidal Behaviour

mood disorders
mental disorders, including depression and bipolar disorder, that affect a person's mood

depression
a mood disorder characterized by extended periods of despair and hopelessness and a lack of interest in life

bipolar disorder
a mood disorder, previously known as manic depression, that involves emotional swings between depression and mania

mania
a mood disorder characterized by an emotional high, agitation, and impulsivity

Mood disorders include depression and bipolar disorder. No one is immune to depression, which affects children as well as adults. Women are diagnosed with depression more often than men are. Approximately 8 percent of Canadians will experience major depression at some time in their lives, while about 1 percent of Canadians will experience bipolar disorder (CMHA, 2011b). **Depression** is characterized by extended periods of despair and hopelessness and a lack of interest in life. Contrary to popular belief, it is not simply sadness or feeling down. People who suffer from depression may have trouble facing each day. They often experience problems with sleeping (either sleeping too much or too little), eating (overeating or loss of appetite), and feeling alienated or separate from the rest of society.

Bipolar disorder, previously called manic depression, is a condition in which a person has emotional swings between depression and mania. **Mania** is a mood state of emotional high, agitation, and impulsivity. Men and women are equally prone to bipolar disorder. Table 5.4 lists the symptoms of depression and mania.

Table 5.4   Symptoms of Depression and Mania

Depression	Mania
• Feelings of sadness or emptiness	• Inflated self-esteem or grandiosity
• Loss of interest or pleasure	• Talkativeness
• Sleep disturbance (too much or too little sleep)	• Extreme irritability
• Change in eating habits (increase or decrease in appetite)	• Distractibility
• Change in weight (loss or gain)	• Decreased need for sleep
• Psychomotor disturbance (agitation or slowness in movement)	• Increased sexual, social, school, and work activities
• Fatigue or loss of energy	• Increased pleasurable activities (overspending, sexual indiscretion)
• Loss of self-esteem	
• Feelings of guilt or self-blame	
• Cognitive disturbance (poor concentration, indecisiveness)	
• Suicidal or homicidal thoughts	

People with mood disorders may exhibit psychotic or non-psychotic symptoms. The psychotic symptoms tend to be consistent with their mood state. For example, a man in a manic state may have the psychotic belief that his blood can cure all the sicknesses in the world, and he may insist, in his elated mood, that as much blood as possible be drawn from his arm and taken around the world to cure people of their diseases.

Knowledge of a mentally ill person's medication may be useful to police when they are responding to a mental health call. Ideally, police should know about drug therapy, psychotherapy (cognitive, interpersonal, supportive), psychoeducation for patient and family, and community supports and services.

Suicide is usually a consequence of mood disorder, and the symptoms of suicidal mood disorder include *ideation* (thinking about suicide), *threat* (expressing the intention to commit a self-destructive act), *gesture* (a self-destructive act with little or no death intent), *attempt* (a self-destructive act with clear death intent), or *completed suicide*.

suicide
a consequence of mood disorder, with suicidal mood disorder taking the possible forms of ideation, threat, gesture, attempt, and completed suicide

People with mood disorders are at a particularly high risk of suicide. Studies indicate that more than 90 percent of suicide victims have a diagnosable psychiatric illness, and suicide is the most common cause of death for people with schizophrenia. Major depression and bipolar disorder account for 15 to 25 percent of all deaths by suicide in patients with severe mood disorders (CMHA, Ontario, 2011).

In 2007, the latest year for which figures are available, 3,611 people in Canada (2,727 male and 884 female) committed suicide (Statistics Canada, 2010). Suicide accounts for 24 percent of all deaths among 15–24 year olds and 16 percent among 25–44 year olds. Men succeed in killing themselves four times more than women do (CMHA, Ontario, 2011), even though women attempt suicide more often than men do. Methods of suicide commonly used by men and women are as follows (Statistics Canada, 2010):

- hanging (46 percent for men, 37 percent for women),
- use of firearms (20 percent for men, 3 percent for women),
- poisoning (20 percent for men, 42 percent for women), and
- other (14 percent for men, 18 percent for women).

A person's religious beliefs may protect him or her from suicide to some extent, but no religion provides complete immunity. And suicide exists in all cultures.

Table 5.5 lists risk factors for suicidal behaviour. It is interesting to note that the media rarely report on public suicides—cases where people jump in front of trains or jump off bridges. Even cases with sensational circumstances may not make it into the media. The assumption is that publicizing suicide and making notorious those who commit it may encourage others to follow in their footsteps.

In responding to a depressed and suicidal person, police need to

- avoid telling the person to cheer up or snap out of it;
- assess the risk of suicide by asking direct questions and making explicit use of the words "kill" or "die" (for example, "Are you thinking of killing yourself?" "Have you made plans to kill yourself?" "Why do you want to die?");

Table 5.5   Risk Factors for Suicidal Behaviour

- Suicide plan
- History of past suicide attempts
- Absence of community support
- Recent loss (actual, threatened, or imagined)
- Physical illness, including AIDS or other terminal illness
- Change in lifestyle, behaviour, or personality
- Giving away possessions or valuables
- Putting personal affairs in order (for example, making a will)
- Depression, including feelings of hopelessness and helplessness
- Postpartum depression
- Substance use
- Recent discharge from psychiatric hospital care
- Psychosis
- Anniversaries (birthday, wedding, death of a loved one)

- take suicide threats seriously;
- be empathic (for example, "I would like to help because I know you are in pain");
- avoid promising secrecy;
- not leave the person alone;
- draw on the person's social support system (family, friends, counsellor); and
- present the person with two options to choose from (for example, "Would you like to go to the hospital with me, or would you rather I called an ambulance?").

In responding to a manic person, police need to

- reduce all extraneous stimulation (for example, noise from a TV);
- avoid arguments;
- allow the person to discharge energy in appropriate ways, such as by pacing;
- be firm, empathetic, and direct;
- draw on the person's social support system; and
- present the person with options to choose from.

EXERCISE 5

You receive a call from a family in the Aboriginal community informing you that a 17-year-old male has committed suicide by shooting himself. The surviving family members include a father, mother, and a seven-year-old sister. What would you do to assist the surviving family members in the short and the long term?

Schizophrenia

Schizophrenia, which afflicts 1 percent of the Canadian population (CMHA, 2011b), causes psychotic mental disturbances. Men are afflicted by it at a younger age than women are. Its symptom patterns differ from those of mood disorders insofar as the psychotic symptoms of schizophrenia tend to be inconsistent with the person's mood state. For example, a person suffering from schizophrenia may break into laughter and show signs of elation while discussing some delusional event—the imaginary death of a parent, for example—that would normally bring feelings of sadness or distress. Table 5.6 lists major symptoms of schizophrenia.

Thought disorders are ideas and speech that make sense to the schizophrenic person but not to others. **Hallucinations** are delusional sensory experiences that are often disturbing to the person having them. Things that appear in hallucinations can be felt, heard, seen, smelled, or tasted. Hearing voices and seeing things are the most common forms of hallucination. People who are hallucinating may talk to themselves, show concentration problems, or make head movements toward the source of the voices they hear. A person who is having visual hallucinations may jerk the eyes or the head. **Delusions** are ideas that have no basis in reality, and they are another common symptom of schizophrenia. A person with paranoid schizophrenia may believe, for example, that he is Jesus and the subject of persecution, or that valuable thoughts are being sucked out of his mind and stolen. A variety of psychotropic drugs are used in the treatment of schizophrenia (for example, clozapine). When schizophrenics discontinue taking their medication, they may do things that lead to a need for police intervention. Most police officers believe that incidents involving schizophrenics and police could be avoided if the schizophrenics stayed on their medication (McAndrew & Sutton, 2004).

In responding to a person showing psychotic symptoms, police need to

- be firm, empathic, reassuring, and helpful;
- avoid using deception or humour;
- validate and acknowledge the person's hallucinatory experience (do not argue against it), but also communicate that the experience is in fact a hallucination and doesn't correspond to reality (for example, "I don't see the man, but I understand that you do");
- avoid invading the personal space of a paranoid person and avoid implying special knowledge of the person's paranoid beliefs;
- employ the standard Use of Force Continuum if a schizophrenic person presents a threat;

schizophrenia
a serious mental illness marked by a breakdown in the connection between thoughts, feelings, and actions, and often accompanied by strong psychotic disturbances and delusions

thought disorders
ideas and speech make sense to a schizophrenic person but not to others

hallucinations
delusional sensory experiences that may be disturbing to the person having them; a common symptom of schizophrenia

delusions
ideas that have no basis in reality; a common symptom of schizophrenia

Table 5.6   Excess and Deficit Symptoms of Schizophrenia

Excess symptoms	Deficit symptoms
• Hallucinations	• Mood disturbances
• Thought disorders	• Impaired interpersonal functioning
• Delusions	• Lack of motivation

- draw on the person's social support system, if necessary; and
- offer the person options to choose from.

Intellectual and Developmental Disabilities

intellectual disability
a condition characterized by significantly subaverage intelligence, significant limitation in adaptive functioning, and onset before the age of 18 years

Intellectual disability, formerly known as "mental retardation," is not the same as mental illness. Three criteria are used to establish intellectual disability: significantly subaverage intelligence (an IQ below 70), significant limitation in adaptive functioning, and onset before the age of 18 years. *Intellectual disability* is the current term for the condition. Terms that were previously used, the main one being "mental retardation," are increasingly out of favour (Surrey Place Centre, 2009).

The terminology surrounding these kinds of disabilities can be confusing. Although *intellectual disability* and *developmental disability* are sometimes used as synonyms, the latter is, in the current usage, a much broader term; it is used in reference to a variety of disabling conditions, including intellectual disability, Autism Spectrum Disorders (Autistic Disorder and Asperger Disorder), cerebral palsy, fetal alcohol syndrome, and Down Syndrome, as well as to physical disabilities, such as congenital blindness. In other words, intellectual disability is a subcategory of developmental disability. A person may have more than one developmental disability, and they may be related; a person with the developmental disability of Down Syndrome, for example, is very likely to have an IQ below 70, which meets the criteria for intellectual disability. On the other hand, a person with cerebral palsy or Asperger Disorder, which qualify as developmental disabilities, may have very strong cognitive functioning (American Association on Intellectual and Developmental Disabilities, 2011).

The communication development and behavioural development of people with intellectual disability may be limited in a variety of ways. They may have a short attention span, impaired speech, or difficulty understanding or answering questions. They may act inappropriately with peers or with the opposite sex, become easily frustrated, be excessively eager to please, or be easily influenced by others. Finally, they may have difficulty carrying out the activities of daily living, such as using the telephone and telling time.

In responding to a person with an intellectual disability, police need to

- treat the person with respect and dignity,
- use simple language and short sentences,
- be patient but firm, and
- avoid asking confusing or leading questions.

EXERCISE 6

For each of the situations described below, indicate what course of action you would take. Options you should consider include the following: asking the person to go with you voluntarily to a hospital for assessment; laying a charge and taking the person to hospital; taking the person to hospital without laying a charge; laying a charge and bringing the person before a justice of the peace;

diverting the person to a home (family, relatives), a community program, or a community agency for care and safety; and referring the person to a diversion program that involves the criminal justice system and mental health agencies.

1. A mentally ill man has committed a serious crime and is clearly showing signs of mental illness.
2. A homeless man has committed a violent crime and is clearly showing signs of a mental disorder.
3. A mentally ill woman has committed a serious crime but has been functioning adequately.
4. A mentally ill person has committed a minor offence and is clearly showing signs of a serious mental disorder.
5. A homeless man has committed a non-violent offence and has been functioning adequately.
6. A mentally ill woman has committed a minor offence but poses no threat to public safety.

FAMILY VIOLENCE AND MENTAL HEALTH ISSUES: POLICE ABILITIES, KNOWLEDGE, AND SKILLS

Police, Crown attorneys, judges, probation officers, victim-witness assistance personnel, and correctional personnel provide supports and services in the area of family violence, and they develop resources on the topic for distribution. It has been noted (Department of Justice Canada, 2006b) that policing in Canada is becoming more responsive to family violence issues; police executives attend national forums on family violence with the following goals in mind:

- to educate themselves about facts, initiatives, and approaches related to family violence;
- to learn about effective police and community responses to family violence; and
- to develop—with other police chiefs, professionals, and government agencies—networks for dealing with family violence.

Police are also becoming more effective in responding to family violence calls. Most have shifted from a victim-blaming approach to an approach that holds the abuser accountable. Traditional victim-blaming attitudes not only failed to intercede against the abuser; they also revictimized the victim by giving tacit approval to the abuse.

Police are recognizing that they can't fight family violence alone and that they need community support systems. Among the positive changes police have made in this regard are

- organizing family-response teams,
- identifying at-risk households on the beat, and
- providing the community with family violence training programs.

In addition to developing these outward initiatives to address family violence in the community, police services are acknowledging the need for internal initiatives.

They are recognizing that police are not immune to the problems of family violence in their own lives.

Policing mental illness is challenging for several reasons. Many of the incidents to which police are called involve mental illness, and such incidents are on the rise. If the police response is not successful, the outcomes of these incidents can be tragic. Also, such incidents call for a specialized response from police. When police respond to a person in a mental health crisis in the same way they respond to a typical emergency criminal situation (that is, with a show of force and authority), they may in fact escalate the situation to the point of putting people at risk of injury or death (CMHA, British Columbia Branch 2005).

Cases where police have injured or killed mentally ill people indicate the need for specialized police training in mental health (Commission for Public Complaints Against the RCMP, 2003). The Ontario Ministry of the Solicitor General *Policing Standards Manual* (2000) has advised chiefs of police to ensure that their police services' training programs teach officers about conflict resolution in connection with the mentally ill or the emotionally disturbed.

The Commission for Public Complaints Against the RCMP (2003) identified several Canadian police services that have implemented special training policy guidelines and/or specialized intervention teams for managing incidents involving the mentally ill. These police services include the following: Ottawa-Carleton, Toronto, Niagara, Guelph, Ontario Provincial Police, Hamilton-Wentworth Regional Police Centre, and Chatham-Kent. The specialized approach entails teaching police officers about mental health legislation and mental disturbances, and about specific interventions, such as

- tactical communication;
- crisis resolution;
- containment of potentially volatile situations (for example, a mentally ill person threatening other people with a gun); and
- partnership with available community supports and services.

The supports and services available in the community may include advocacy representatives, consumer and family education, family support, medical and dental services, medication, peer support, police support, and rehabilitation centres (Fernando & Kazarian, 1995; Kazarian & Joseph, 1994). Many of these support systems, including crisis response services (crisis lines, mental health teams, hospital emergency wards), are insufficiently funded; the deinstitutionalization movement has caused a sharp increase in the demand for such resources and has led to shortages in certain areas, such as hospital beds. To function effectively and efficiently, community support systems also require skilled coordinators.

The British Columbia Branch of the Canadian Mental Health Association (2005) has identified several programs, developed through a collaboration between police and mental health service providers, for helping people with mental health crises. These programs include

- mobile teams of police and mental health professionals;
- police "reception centres" where police can take a person who shows signs of mental illness for further assessment and referral;

- "crisis intervention teams" within each police catchment area to respond to mental health crises;
- joint protocols between police and the local mental health centre;
- ongoing mental-health awareness training for all officers and specialized crisis-intervention skills training for specialized officers;
- an information system that tracks crisis interventions and outcomes and trains dispatchers to recognize and address mental health issues.

EXERCISE 7

Identify strategies that enable police to work in partnership with the mental health system and diverse groups in the community to deal with mental health calls.

EXERCISE 8

Analyze each of the following scenarios and role-play them. Consider reversing the roles and re-enacting the scenes.

1. A 24-year-old man is threatening to punch his mother. As the police officer on the scene, you assess the situation and decide that the man is unlikely to act out his anger, and that there is no real possibility that anyone will get hurt. You say, "If you don't stop threatening your mother, you'll have a real battle on your hands. Now what's it going to be?"

What is the problem, what are the issues, what are the solutions? Is your response appropriate? If not, what would an appropriate response be?

2. A 28-year-old homeless woman has been drinking and is now threatening passersby with a knife. As the police officer on the scene, you decide that the woman is unlikely to attack anyone or hurt anyone accidentally. You say, "All you homeless people are drunk. What are we going to do with you?"

What is the problem, what are the issues, what are the solutions? Is your response appropriate? If not, what would an appropriate response be?

3. You are called to an incident involving a teenager who tells you that the dentist put a microchip in his mouth when he went for a filling, so now everyone can hear his private thoughts all the time. You say, "You believe people are spying on you. That must be very scary."

What is the problem, what are the issues, what are the solutions? Is your response appropriate? If not, what would an appropriate response be?

4. A 65-year-old mentally ill woman tells you that her husband and children are trying to get rid of her by poisoning her food. You tell the family that the woman is "psycho" and that you have to take her to the "nuthouse."

What is the problem, what are the issues, what are the solutions? Is your response appropriate? If not, what would an appropriate response be?

Finally, police are not immune to mental health issues of their own. It may be difficult for police to accept this reality, since it shatters the image of their invulnerability and indomitable emotional strength (Violanti, 1996). But police are no less susceptible to problems of this sort than other people are. Furthermore, police work involves confronting trauma and adversity on a regular basis, and these experiences can affect even the most resilient minds. Initiatives for promoting the mental well-being of police are absolutely necessary.

CHAPTER SUMMARY

Family violence is a serious problem for society and for policing. It affects both men and women. Effective policing requires seeing this kind of violence for the criminal action that it is, understanding family violence in the context of Canada's ethnocultural diversity, and forming partnerships with community supports and services.

In preparing to police mental illness, police must gain as great an understanding as they can of the various types of illnesses, common symptoms, and most appropriate responses, and recognize the established connections between mental illness, substance abuse, and homelessness. Police must also understand how mental illness differs from intellectual and developmental disabilities, and how to best respond in situations involving the latter. To serve and protect *all* people effectively, police need to work in partnership with families, professionals, and community services.

KEY TERMS

bipolar disorder	gendered apartheid	mood disorders
child abuse	hallucinations	pro-arrest policy
child sexual abuse	homelessness	psychosis
delusions	intellectual disability	schizophrenia
depression	mandatory arrest policy	spousal abuse
elder abuse	mania	substance-related disorders
family violence	mediative policy	suicide
formication	mental illness	thought disorders

REFERENCES

American Association on Intellectual and Developmental Disabilities. (2011). Developmental disabilities. http://www.aamr.org/.

Biesenthal, L., Sproule, L.D., Nelder, M., Golton, S., Mann, D., Podovinnikoff, D., Roosendaal, I., Warman, S., & Lunn, D. (2000). *The Ontario rural woman abuse study: Final report.* Ottawa: Department of Justice Canada.

Canadian Mental Health Association. (2011a). Fast facts about mental illness in youth. http://www.cmha.ca/bins/content_page.asp?cid=6-20-23-44.

Canadian Mental Health Association. (2011b). Mental health/mental illness. http://www.cmha.ca/bins/content_page.asp?cid=6-20-23-43.

Canadian Mental Health Association, British Columbia Branch. (2005). Police and mental illness: Increased interactions. http://www.cmha.bc.ca/files/1-increased_interactions.pdf.

Canadian Mental Health Association, Ontario. (2011). Suicide statistics. http://www.ontario.cmha.ca/fact_sheets.asp?cID=3965.

Champagne, C., Lapp, R., & Lee, J. (1994). *Assisting abused lesbians: A guide for health professionals and service providers*. London, ON: London Battered Women's Advocacy Centre.

Changing Ways. (2010). *Guidelines for service providers: Outreach strategies for family violence intervention with immigrant and minority communities*. London, ON: Author.

Child and Family Services Act. (1990). RSO 1990, c. C-11, as amended.

Commission for Public Complaints Against the RCMP. (2003, October 20). *Report into a complaint concerning RCMP treatment of a person experiencing a mental health crisis*. http://www.cpc-cpp.gc.ca/prr/anr/2003-2004-eng.aspx#toc3.1.

Commission for Public Complaints against the RCMP. (2011). http://www.CPC-cpp.gc.ca.

Criminal Code. (1985). RSC 1985, c. C-46, as amended.

Department of Justice Canada. (2006a). About family violence in Canada. http://www.justice.gc.ca/eng/pi/fv-vf/about-aprop/index.html.

Department of Justice Canada. (2006b). Projects funded by the Department of Justice Canada under the Family Violence Initiative (April 2008–March 2009). http://www.justice.gc.ca/eng/pi/fv-vf/rep-rap/appro/a2008_09.html.

Department of Justice Canada. (2011). Family Violence Initiative. http://www.justice.gc.ca/eng/pi/fv-vf/index.html.

Fernando, M.L.D., & Kazarian, S.S. (1995, April). Patient education in the drug treatment of psychiatric disorders: Effect on compliance and outcome. *CNS Drugs, 3*, 291–304.

Green, K. (1996). *Family violence in Aboriginal communities: An Aboriginal perspective—Information from the national clearinghouse on family violence*. Ottawa: Health Canada.

Justice Institute of British Columbia. (2007). *Empowerment of immigrant and refugee women who are victims of violence in their intimate relationships: Final report*. New Westminster, BC: Author.

Kazarian, S.S., & Joseph, L.W. (1994). A brief scale to help identify outpatients' level of need for community support services. *Hospital and Community Psychiatry, 45*, 935–937.

Kazarian, S.S., & Kazarian, L.Z. (1998). Cultural aspects of family violence. In S.S. Kazarian & D.R. Evans (Eds.), *Cultural clinical psychology: Theory, research and practice* (pp. 316–347). New York: Oxford University Press.

Law Commission of Canada. (2001). *Restoring dignity: Responding to child abuse in Canadian institutions*. Ottawa: Minister of Public Works and Government Services.

Levinthal, C.F. (1996). *Drugs, behavior, and modern society.* Needham Heights, MA: Allyn and Bacon.

McAndrew, A., & Sutton, E. (2004). *Searching for solutions: The front line police perspective on mental health interventions in Simcoe County.* Paper for the Research Analyst Program, Georgian College, Barrie, ON.

Mental Health Act. (1990). RSO 1990, c. M.7, as amended. Amended and passed as *Brian's Law* on June 23, 2000. Amended 2010.

Mental Illness Awareness Week. (2010). Homelessness and mental illness. http://miaw.ca/en/mental-illness/what-is-mental-illness/homelessness.aspx.

Office of the United Nations High Commissioner for Human Rights. (1991, December 17). Principles for the protection of persons with mental illness and the improvement of mental health care. http://www2.ohchr.org/english/law/principles.htm.

Okin, S.M. (Ed.). (1999). *Is multiculturalism bad for women?* Princeton, NJ: Princeton University Press.

Ontario Ministry of the Solicitor General. (2000, February). Police response to persons who are emotionally disturbed or have a mental illness or a development disability, section 29. *Policing Standards Manual.* Toronto: Queen's Printer for Ontario.

Persad, E., & Kazarian, S.S. (1998, November). Physician satisfaction with review boards: The provincial psychiatric hospital perspective. *Canadian Journal of Psychiatry, 43*(9), 905–909.

Police Executive Research Forum. (1997). *The police response to people with mental illnesses.* Washington, DC: Author.

Public Health Agency of Canada. (2011). *A report on mental illness in Canada.* http://www.phac-aspc.gc.ca/publicat/miic-mmac/index-eng.php.

Schecter, M.D., & Roberge, L. (1976). Sexual exploitation. In R.E. Helfer & C.H. Kempe (Eds.), *Child abuse and neglect: The family and the community* (pp. 127–142). Cambridge, MA: Ballinger.

Statistics Canada. (2010). Suicides and suicide rate, by sex and by age group. http://www40.statcan.ca/l01/cst01/hlth66a-eng.htm.

Statistics Canada. (2011). *Family violence in Canada: A statistical profile.* Catalogue no. 85-224-X. http://www.statcan.gc.ca/pub/85-224-x/85-224-x2010000-eng.pdf.

Surrey Place Centre. (2009). Developmental disabilities. http://www.surreyplace.on.ca/Developmental-Disabilities/Pages/Home.aspx.

Violanti, J.M. (1996). *Police suicide: Epidemic in blue.* Springfield, IL: Charles C. Thomas.

"Virgin suicides" take place of "honor killing." (2006, July 13). *International Herald Tribune*, pp. 1, 5.

REVIEW QUESTIONS

TRUE OR FALSE?

_____ 1. Abuse of a parent by a child is not included in the definition of family violence.

_____ 2. Psychological abuse may involve forced isolation from friends or family.

_____ 3. In Canada, family violence is against the law only in Ontario.

_____ 4. Child sex tourism is not addressed in the _Criminal Code_ of Canada.

_____ 5. Child sexual abuse refers to the exploitation of children or adolescents under the age of 16.

_____ 6. Family violence tends to be kept secret in many cultures.

_____ 7. It is a myth that substance abuse is the real cause of family violence.

_____ 8. Fear of social stigma is one of the reasons why women endure family violence.

_____ 9. Gay and lesbian victims of family violence sometimes feel ill at ease in mainstream shelters.

_____ 10. Policing is becoming less responsive to family violence issues.

MULTIPLE CHOICE

1. Psychological abuse may involve
   - (a) humiliation
   - (b) sexual abuse of children
   - (c) withholding money to buy food
   - (d) discrediting a person's religious beliefs

2. Legal provisions to deter family violence are found in the
   - (a) Constitution
   - (b) _Highway Traffic Act_
   - (c) _Criminal Code_
   - (d) _Canadian Bill of Rights_

3. _Child abuse_ is a generic term for abuse of children under the age of
   - (a) 10
   - (b) 12
   - (c) 14
   - (d) 16

4. According to the chemical view, family violence is caused by
   - (a) substance abuse
   - (b) stress
   - (c) provocation by women
   - (d) lack of spirituality

5. In the past, community supports for victims of family violence gave little thought to

   (a) consequences under the *Canadian Bill of Rights*

   (b) the financial implications of family violence

   (c) the issue of diversity

   (d) effective responses to family violence

6. A major concern of abused immigrant or refugee women is their

   (a) children

   (b) spiritual beliefs

   (c) immigration status

   (d) parents

7. One police response to family violence is the mediative policy, which involves

   (a) leaving an arrest to the discretion of officers

   (b) mandatory arrest

   (c) encouraging arrest

   (d) a hands-off, non-arrest approach

8. *Mental illness* is a generic term for

   (a) a variety of disorders

   (b) a specific disorder

   (c) issues relating to family violence

   (d) the disorders of homeless people

9. *Formication* is a hallucination involving

   (a) snakes and insects

   (b) dead relatives

   (c) heights

   (d) suicide

10. In responding to a depressed and suicidal person, police need to

    (a) tell the person to cheer up

    (b) be empathic

    (c) leave the person alone

    (d) use their firearms as required

FILL IN THE BLANKS

1. Family violence is a pervasive _____ and policing problem in Canada.

2. Mistreatment at the hands of a common-law partner in a relationship is considered _____ abuse.

3. Elder abuse can be carried out by a _____ , _____ or institutional staff member.

4. Men and women experience _____ levels of both violence and emotional abuse in their relationships.

5. Western concepts of _____ may be different from those of other cultures.

6. Canada supports a policy of zero tolerance for all types of _____.

7. As one of the three major police response policies for cases of family violence, the pro-arrest policy encourages arrest, but leaves this to the _____ of officers.

8. Shortcomings in community mental health services have led to increased _____ involvement in mental health calls.

9. Bipolar disorder was previously called _____ _____.

10. In responding to a manic person, police need to present the person with _____ to choose from.

Policing with Diversity Competency

6

INTRODUCTION

Police and the communities they serve have common goals. Both want safe, crime-free neighbourhoods and a good quality of life. A police officer whom the community views as an ally is more likely to be effective in policing communities; when people respect the police, they are more likely to assist them. In Canada's pluralistic, multicultural society, the communities served by law enforcement are very diverse. In the 2006 census, there were 223 different ethnic origins reported in Canada, from English (6,570,015 persons) to Dinka (495 persons) (Statistics Canada, 2006a). Amid this diversity, police and police services have been rethinking how they can

- better represent the diverse ethnic backgrounds and diverse groups they serve;
- perform their jobs in a way that respects diversity;
- cultivate and maintain the resources—the confidence, openness, education, support, and cultural awareness—to serve their diverse communities effectively; and
- address issues of diversity in policing proactively (Durham Regional Police Service, 2010).

This chapter focuses on several related topics: perceptions of police in the community, the evolution of policing culture, the benefits and challenges of diversity for policing today, and the strategies, structures, and skills needed for policing with **diversity competency**—in other words, policing with an inclusive, responsive attitude to diversity.

PERCEPTIONS OF POLICE

How well a free society administers justice is one measure of its health. Within the criminal justice system, the police are the only element that has a direct relationship with the community. What is the role of police in relation to the community?

CHAPTER OBJECTIVES

After completing this chapter, you should be able to:

- Describe self-perceptions of police and community perceptions of police.
- Explain the difference between the police force approach and the police services approach.
- Understand the principles of community policing.
- See how diversity can be both a challenge and a strategic advantage for police.
- Describe some of the initiatives police services have taken to diversify the face of policing and to reach out to minority communities.
- Understand how police training in race relations, cultural sensitivity, and diversity awareness are increasing their diversity competency.

diversity competency
possessing the cultural knowledge and understanding to serve diverse communities effectively

We can consider this question from two perspectives: police perception of themselves and the community's perception of police.

Self-Perception of Police

The acronym ZAC represents the three images, past and present, that police have tended to have of their role. The acronym stands for

- zookeeper,
- avenger of the Lord, and
- champion of the people.

According to the zookeeper self-image, the community is not a natural habitat for police but "a large zoo where the ferocious animals must not only be fed and watered but also must be watched every moment and allowed only that limited freedom which the zoo keeper's security can stand" (Steinberg & McEvoy, 1974, p. 149). The image of police as avengers of the Lord comes from the evangelical minister Billy Graham, who proclaimed that police are "the sword of the Lord, avenging the wickedness of this world" (Steinberg & McEvoy, 1974, p. 148).

In Canada, these antagonized old self-images of police are mostly obsolete; they have little relation to the realities of 21st-century policing. Police officers in this country spend most of their time in a helpful role, and they see themselves, justifiably, as champions of the people. Contemporary data regarding what police officers actually do on the job reflects this more recent self-image, as do some of the professional watchwords adopted by police services—"To Serve and Protect" (Toronto); "People Helping People" (Waterloo).

Community Perception of Police

A positive public image is good for police in several ways:

- it enhances self-respect and job satisfaction;
- it makes policing a safer profession; and
- it makes police more effective in combatting crime.

Most people in our society are satisfied with police most of the time. Some years ago, an international survey involving 11 Western industrial nations showed that satisfaction with police performance was highest in Canada. In fact, the study found that "Canadians love their cops far more than the English love their famed British Bobby" (Durkan, 1998, p. A9). More recently, in 2011, the preliminary results of an Ontario Provincial Police Community Satisfaction Survey found that 98.2 percent of respondents (5,361 people were surveyed) felt safe in their community; 90.5 percent were satisfied or very satisfied with the OPP's ability to work with local communities to solve local problems; and 92.7 percent were satisfied or very satisfied with the level of service offered by the OPP (Ontario Provincial Police, 2011).

A community's personal interactions with police officers will determine its perception of them. It is a circular process that can work for or against police. The police set the tone. If they show positive, helpful attitudes toward the people they serve, the community will view them favourably—-and this public approval will, in turn, reinforce the positive attitude taken by police. On the other hand, antagonistic encounters between police and community will generate negative perceptions on both sides. This reciprocal relationship is at the core of police–community relations (Coffey, 1990).

Negative Perceptions of Police

The majority of Canadians view police as their allies in maintaining order and upholding their rights, not as overbearing zealots of law enforcement; the public perception of police in this country is generally very positive. Certain kinds of police conduct, however, are extremely damaging to the image of police in the community. People particularly object to rudeness and authoritarianism. Rudeness is one of the most common complaints. Such complaints come not from people arrested for serious crimes but from ordinary citizens—from people involved in traffic stops, from those reporting crimes, or from those simply seeking directions. People object to **authoritarianism** from police—that is, "badge-heavy" conduct that insists on obedience. Such conduct is appropriate and necessary in certain situations, such as when police are confronted by violence or when they are interrogating a suspect, handling a crime scene, conducting an investigation, or resolving a domestic dispute. But if it appears too often or in situations where it is not called for, authoritarian conduct will prevent a strong police–community alliance. Most situations that police find themselves in are better served by cooperation and compromise. Visibility, accessibility, problem-solving ability, fairness, and openness to partnership—these are what communities want from police.

authoritarianism
policy of demanding
obedience to authority

EXERCISE 1

Suppose that police–community relations in your neighbourhood are very poor. The neighbourhood is tense because of recent accusations that police have used excessive force against members of visible minorities and have harassed mentally ill and homeless people. What actions would you take to ease tensions in the short term? Consider establishing a police–community diversity coalition. What goals would this coalition pursue?

TWO APPROACHES TO POLICING: POLICE FORCE VERSUS POLICE SERVICES

Many police services in North America have adopted the motto "to serve and protect." In Canada, these serving and protecting functions must be extended to all community residents, regardless of their culture, race, ethnic origin, religion, sex, age, sexual orientation, or physical or mental ability. Police in Canada are fulfilling this mandate successfully. At the same time, in Canada as in other multicultural contexts, there have been questions about how police should interact with our diverse communities. Among the leading concerns of police departments in this regard are how best to organize themselves internally and how to relate to the communities they serve and protect.

EXERCISE 2

What does the motto "to serve and protect" mean to you? Discuss this motto in a diversity context.

police force approach
the approach to policing that emphasizes the crime-control, enforcement aspect of the job, on the assumption that police need to be hard on crime

Two approaches have come to dominate the culture and management structure of policing worldwide: the authoritarian police force approach and the police services approach (Fleras, 1992; Williams & Henderson, 1997). A summary of both approaches is provided in Table 6.1. The **police force approach** is based on a reactive, crime control mandate that calls on police to be warriors, their effectiveness measured by

- the number of patrols they carry out to deter criminal activity,
- their response rate to police calls,
- their tally of arrests and convictions, and
- citizen satisfaction surveys (Fleras, 1992).

An underlying assumption of the police force, or crime control, approach is that only a strong, centralized police department, with an organizational culture that is hard on crime, can keep order in streets and neighbourhoods. The trouble with this approach is that it can lead to an us-versus-them mentality that isolates police from the communities they serve.

A skeptic might argue that police work is by its nature adversarial, necessarily coercive, and that this limits the potential for positive police–community relations. From this perspective, enforcing the law precludes cordiality and makes isolation from the community inevitable. And it is true that with certain kinds of criminals and in tough, urban neighbourhoods, confrontation and coercion do play a role in police work. Nonetheless, the adversarial model of police–community relations is not, in the end, the most valid model. As Banton (1963) has suggested, the police officer actually spends very little time pursuing people or locking them up. Practically speaking, it is misleading even to describe a police officer's job as "law enforcement." The police officer spends most of his or her time helping citizens in distress. In day-to-day police work, an officer's decisions are determined much more by common-sense ethics than they are by legal dictates (Banton, 1963).

police services approach
the approach to policing that emphasizes the helpful, supportive aspect of the role, with a focus on problem solving, crime prevention, and partnership between police and communities

The **police services approach** has evolved partly in reaction to the police force approach and the shortcomings of authoritarian crime control. It is an approach that emphasizes the helpful, supportive aspect of policing rather than the law-enforcement aspect, and it calls for an organizational structure and culture geared toward finding new ways—new core knowledge, skills, and abilities—for police to perform their duties. The police services approach promotes the following:

- proactively identifying and solving problems,
- trying to understand and resolve the underlying causes of disputes,
- trying to prevent recurrences of problems and disputes, and
- not making arrests except when necessary (Clyderman, O'Toole, & Fleras, 1992).

Table 6.1 Police Force Approach Versus Police Services Approach

Police force	Police services
Crime fighting	Crime preventing
Incident-driven	Problem-driven
Reactive	Proactive
Us versus them	Partner with community
Centralized	Decentralized
Hierarchical	Egalitarian
Diversity-blind	Diversity-sensitive
Inwardly focused	Outwardly focused

Community Policing

Community policing principles, also known as problem-solving policing principles, are a key element in the police services approach. Community policing involves policing for and with communities by actively involving them in police matters. Examples of community policing programs are Crime Stoppers and Neighbourhood Watch. One of the assumptions of community policing is that a police service can most effectively keep order in streets and neighbourhoods if it welcomes input from its own rank and file and from the communities it serves. Table 6.2 provides a list of principles associated with community policing.

On a practical level, community policing involves the following:

- making an effort to establish friendly contact with community members from diverse backgrounds;

- trying to show the positive side of law enforcement by allowing the public to see the police as much as possible in a services (in other words, assistance) role rather than a law-enforcement (that is, authoritarian) role;

- making a consistent effort to treat all members of the community justly and fairly;

- remembering that criminal activity is not linked to any particular ethnocultural group;

- not discussing a suspect's racial or cultural background with the public;

- taking time to explain the role of the police officer and police procedures to members of immigrant communities; and

- taking the initiative to improve relationships with all ethnocultural groups within the community (Shusta, 2005, p. 31).

Today, community policing continues to be the standard model of service delivery for most police organizations in this country. The 1997 Speech from the Throne, which confirmed community policing as the model of choice for police in Canada, still applies today: "Safe communities—a hallmark of Canada—depend on strong crime prevention efforts. There is a growing commitment and belief that effective policing can only be achieved when there is ongoing co-operation and partnership between police and the community" (McKim, 1999).

community policing principles
principles that are associated with the police services approach and with the mandate of policing for and with communities

Table 6.2   Principles of Community Policing

- Empowering police officers and supervisors to solve community issues without having to seek a stamp of approval from the police hierarchy.

- Actively listening, at all police levels, to community issues, concerns, and solutions.

- Providing needs-based police services determined by public input.

- Adopting a style of internal police management that is responsive to the recruitment of police with attributes and skills conducive to effective community-oriented policing.

- Applying a people-oriented philosophy to the organization of police services, to law interpretation, and to law enforcement.

- Communicating with citizens in languages they understand, including mandatory police acquisition of second languages for the purposes of communication and the minimization of conflict, doubt, and distrust.

- Selecting and training police officers to ensure that the best people are entrusted with the job of policing.

- Using police officers as effectively as possible with respect to the jobs and neighbourhoods to which they are assigned.

- Ensuring that the employees of a police service reflect the cultural diversity of the community served.

- Assigning officers to work with residents, schools, and community groups for the purpose of resolving community issues.

- Treating employees of police services fairly by fostering an environment within the ranks that is free of sexual harassment, discrimination, and bias.

Source: Williams & Henderson (1997, pp. 219–220).

POLICE SERVICES IN A DIVERSITY CONTEXT

Police in Canada serve and protect a diverse public. In their day-to-day working lives, police officers will encounter individuals who vary widely from one another—and from the officers themselves—in terms of cultural background, language, gender, age, socio-economic class, religion, sexual orientation, physical and mental ability, and psychological well-being. In response to the increased diversity of Canada's population and to other national initiatives, police services across the country are increasingly adopting a diversity-oriented policing structure and function.

There are both ideological and practical reasons for doing so. Adopting such an approach will, first of all, keep police services in line with Canada's official diversity initiatives. The Government of Canada's current multiculturalism program lists the following as priority areas (Leman, 1999):

- developing strategies to facilitate the full and active participation of ethnic, racial, religious, and cultural communities in Canada;

- supporting collective community initiatives and responses to ethnic, racial, religious, and cultural conflict and hate-motivated activities;

- improving the ability of public institutions to respond to ethnic, racial, religious, and cultural diversity;

- encouraging and assisting in the development of inclusive policies, programs, and practices; and

- increasing public awareness, understanding, and public dialogue with respect to multiculturalism, racism, and cultural diversity in Canada.

Police also have strong practical reasons for adopting a diversity policing framework and for developing their diversity competency. Among these reasons are the following:

- fewer injuries to both law enforcement officers and citizens,

- fewer citizen complaints and lawsuits against police,

- improved police–community relations, and

- improved ability to respond to major demographic changes in communities served.

Diversity-Related Challenges for Police

For the most part in this country, there is goodwill between police and the communities they serve, with community members respecting the work of police and police increasingly working to acknowledge and accommodate diversity in the communities. Nonetheless, relations between police and people of diversity have been strained at various times and for various reasons.

Racial Bias

One source of strain is racial profiling, which, in the past decade, has been a topic of dispute in more than one police service. Six years ago, police statistics in Kingston, Ontario, revealed that police in that predominantly white city were 3.7 times more likely to stop a Black person than a Caucasian person for a traffic offence, and 1.4 times more likely to stop an Aboriginal person than a white person (CBC News in Depth, 2005). Many Kingston residents, including but not limited to the Black and Aboriginal communities, were extremely concerned about what these statistics suggested about police tactics.

In 2002, the *Toronto Star* ran a series that reported a racial bias in the Toronto Police Service (Rankin et al., 2002). The *Star*'s statistical analysis of Toronto crime data focused on arrests for simple drug possession over a six-year period. The report claimed that Black individuals arrested by Toronto police were treated more harshly than were white individuals, based on the following facts:

- According to the latest census figures available at the time of the report, Blacks made up 8.1 percent of Toronto's population. But of the more than 10,000 individuals arrested for simple drug possession, 63.8 percent were classified by police as white, 23.6 percent as Black.

- When white persons were charged at the scene with simple drug possession, 76.5 percent of the time they were permitted to go home; when Black individuals were charged under the same circumstances, only 61.8 percent of the time were they immediately released.

- Of those arrested and taken to the station, only 7.3 percent of white persons were kept in jail to await a bail hearing, while 15.5 percent of Black individuals were held.

The *Star* also looked at Toronto police traffic-offence data and found that a disproportionate number of Black persons were ticketed for "out-of-sight" violations; these offences typically surface during stops that are supposedly random.

Toronto's police chief at that time, Julian Fantino, responded to the *Star*'s findings with an adamant denial that racial profiling was occurring at the Toronto Police Service, and he firmly stated that he was opposed to such profiling. Of course, the *Star*'s findings should be viewed with caution, as should any claim based on the interpretation of statistics. What the news story and Fantino's strong reaction revealed was the sensitivity surrounding questions about race and diversity within policing. Indeed, the dispute suggested that the following may be the case: a police service's official policy may prohibit racial profiling, but racial profiling is not easy to eradicate.

Police Culture

white machismo culture
a culture that values white skin colour, masculinity, and hierarchy while devaluing non-whites, women, and non-traditional sexual orientation

In Canada, police services now strive to represent in their own rank and file the diverse communities they serve and protect. This has not always been the case. In pluralistic Western countries, including Canada, Australia, the United Kingdom, and the United States, white males have historically been overrepresented in police services. As a result, these services have been seen as having a **white machismo culture**—in other words, a culture that values white skin colour, masculinity, and hierarchy while devaluing non-whites, women, and non-traditional sexual orientation. Police officers who subscribe to this "culture of masculinity" have typically had a "gladiator mentality" and "a crime-fighting mission that provides ideological justification for authority that is exercised against fellow citizens" (Waddington, 1999).

Canada has made progress in moving away from a male-dominated police culture, but a gender imbalance persists. In 2006, for instance, only 11,211 police officers out of nearly 70,000 were women, which is about 1 in 7 (Statistics Canada, 2006b). Police services in Canada continue to recruit women in order to overcome this gender imbalance.

Other people of diversity—for instance, Aboriginal peoples and members of minority immigrant groups—are also underrepresented in law enforcement. Law enforcement services themselves are not entirely to blame for this situation; it is at least partly due to the perception in some cultures that law enforcement is not an appropriate career choice. In some cases, immigrant families have had negative experiences with law enforcement in their countries of origin. And members of visible minority immigrant families may have the mistaken impression that *all* law enforcement agencies are pervaded by the "white machismo culture." Another factor is that immigrant communities sometimes know little about career opportunities in policing, or else they assign higher status to traditional professions—the legal or medical professions, for example—than they do to policing.

EXERCISE 3

Some soul searching is required in this exercise. Do you consider law enforcement to be a male-dominated profession? In other words, is it still a white machismo culture? Are law enforcement agencies recruiting women and visible minorities from a genuine wish to truly overcome gender and diversity inequality? Or are these recruiting efforts merely window dressing—in other words, cynical attempts to deflect criticism of law enforcement hiring practices? If you believe that the white machismo culture still prevails, do you think that this culture will disappear as older law enforcement officers retire, or is the culture ingrained in law enforcement?

Positive Diversity Management in Policing

Police services organizations in 21st-century Canada have come to see our society's diversity as a strategic advantage for them. A number of factors, including the following, have contributed to this perception:

- changes in immigration and the growing pluralism of Canadian society,
- globalization,
- advances in technology,
- an aging workplace,
- the *Canadian Charter of Rights and Freedoms* and case law decisions related to it, and
- terrorist events, such as 9/11.

Police services' pursuit of the advantage offered by diversity is increasingly reflected in their recruitment, promotion, and career-development strategies (Durham Regional Police Service, 2010), as well as in their emphasis on diversity competency in policing. Four core values are identified with such diversity competency: affirming and valuing diversity; assuming a police-community climate that validates diverse perspectives; empowering diverse voices within and outside the police service in goal setting, problem solving, and decision making; and promoting a police culture that respects the rights of people of diversity, police safety, and the individual.

On the national level and within individual police services, there have been efforts to implement a diversity policing framework. In 2003, the Canadian Association of Chiefs of Police, supported by the Multiculturalism Program of Canadian Heritage, assumed responsibility for the Law Enforcement Aboriginal Diversity (LEAD) unit, with the following goals in mind (Canadian Heritage, 2006; Taylor, 2004):

- to help law enforcement officers across the country develop better working relationships with the ethnocultural and Aboriginal communities they serve;
- to offer training and information on delivering bias-free policing services; and
- to help law enforcement institutions become more diverse through recruitment and retention.

An important aspect of the LEAD initiative has been the development of a website (www.lead-alda.ca) that is a forum for discussing the most effective approaches to diversity and that provides resources regarding such areas as hate crimes, national crime statistics, and community and police partnerships (Taylor, 2004).

In their philosophies, codes of conduct, and administrative selections, police services across Canada are promoting diversity competency and the need for community policing. The Ottawa Police Service (2010), for example, has affirmed the following:

> building partnerships with our community is an important part of community policing. It is a successful way to establish clearer communication and trust between police and Ottawa's increasingly diverse community. By mobilizing community resources and working together, community-police partnerships can play an active role in problem solving and crime prevention.

Some services have a diversity component as part of their officers' yearly evaluations. The section of the Hamilton Police Service evaluation form relating to diversity is shown in Figure 6.1. Diversity is the subject of two of the six principles of the Ontario *Police Services Act*: the fifth principle mandates the need for "sensitivity to the pluralistic, multiracial and multicultural character of Ontario society," while the sixth principle recognizes the need "to ensure that police services are representative of the communities they serve" (s. 1). Table 6.3 lists a number of the particular initiatives that have been taken to increase diversity among police services employees and to address diversity issues in policing.

In Toronto, the hiring of Bill Blair as chief of police in 2005 represented a renewed effort to address diversity-related shortcomings in the Toronto Police Service. When the police board began searching for a new chief, its priority was to find someone with a commitment to diversity issues. Chief Blair, successor to Julian Fantino,

Table 6.3   Diversity Initiatives in Policing

- Relaxing weight and height requirements for recruits
- Increasing recruitment of people of diversity (for example, women and those from diverse cultures and sexual orientations) and those with higher education
- Introduction of race relations training programs
- Introduction of cultural awareness training programs
- Introduction of diversity awareness training programs
- Implementation of anti-racism and anti–sexual harassment programs
- Improvement in communication between police and people of diversity
- Increased citizen participation in crime prevention initiatives
- Increased community involvement in review of police activity (for example, civilian review boards)
- Introduction of police, ethnic, and cultural exchange (PEACE) programs
- Creation of Aboriginal policing programs to improve Aboriginal–police relations and quality of policing services to Aboriginal peoples
- Inclusion of courses on diversity issues in policing as part of police foundations programs

Figure 6.1   Diversity Component of Hamilton Police Service Officers' Evaluation

10 Valuing Diversity:

Valuing Diversity is the ability to understand and respect the practices, customs, values and norms of individuals, groups and cultures other than one's own. It is not restricted to employment equity, but includes the ability to respect and value diverse points-of-view, and to be open to others of differing backgrounds or perspectives. It includes seeing diversity as beneficial to the Hamilton Police Service. It also implies the ability to work effectively with a wide cross-section of the community representing diverse backgrounds, cultures, and/or socio-economic circumstances.

Expectations:	☐ Requires Improvement ☐ Meets Exceeds: ☐ (d) ☐ (e)
(a) Accepts Diversity	Is willing to accept and respect the practices, customs, values and norms of other individuals or groups. Is open to others of different backgrounds or perspective. Responds openly when approached by others.
(b) Values Differences or Diversity	Values diversity and actively seeks out opportunities to gain new knowledge and understanding of individuals/groups through learning and active community participation and involvement. Recognizes prejudices and systemic barriers which may exist within the current environment.
(c) Monitors and Modifies Own Behaviours	Monitors and evaluates own beliefs and behaviours with regard to prejudices and personal bias. Practices new behaviours that reflect an understanding and appreciation of diversity.
(d) Challenges Others	Openly and directly addresses issues or situations that may not support diversity and tolerance of others. Holds people accountable for their actions to ensure that their behaviour reflects an appreciation and acceptance of diversity. Educates others of the value of diversity, and teaches tolerance and openness to diverse ideas and backgrounds.
(e) Actively Promotes Diversity	Actively promotes the value of diversity through planned and visible activities aimed at building sensitivity to, and support for, others. Actively promotes and supports programs that are designed to increase diversity within the Hamilton Police Service.

Supporting Evidence:

Comments:

acknowledged that there might be racial bias in the police force: "Racism is a hu-man failing. Racial profiling can occur. We've acknowledged that right upfront and that has really enabled us to work with our community partners to do something about it" (Doolittle, 2009, p. A01). Blair's acknowledgment was a positive step to-ward raising awareness of diversity matters in the Toronto Police Service.

Inward Initiatives: Recruitment

A number of police services in Canada have taken steps to increase the diversity of their workforce. In the past decade, the Toronto police board, in addition to bringing in diversity-minded leadership, has made changes in its human resources practices. One of the new recruitment and promotion strategies is to have officers go door-to-door in different ethnic residential areas to promote careers in policing and offer information to potential recruits. The Toronto Police Service has also begun holding women-only recruitment sessions. These initiatives, implemented after the arrival of Chief Blair in 2005, have produced remarkable changes in re-cruitment patterns. Previously, white males accounted for 85 to 90 percent of the average class of recruits; by 2009, women and visible minorities accounted for 40 to 60 percent of new officers (Doolittle, 2009, p. A01).

Inward initiatives to increase diversity are occurring in other police services as well. In 2007, the Halton Regional Police Service began offering an Enhanced Language Training (ELT) program that provides employment-specific language training and mentorship opportunities to new Canadians who have law enforcement or security backgrounds in their countries of origin and are interested in policing careers. ELT participants are able to develop the required knowledge and skills by meeting with Halton Multicultural Council facilitators and Halton Regional Police officers and recruiters (Halton Regional Police Service, n.d.). In the Vancouver Police Department, one of the initiatives for recruiting a diverse workforce is the Aboriginal Cadet Program, which mentors Aboriginal youth who are interested in becoming police officers (Vancouver Police Department, n.d.b).

Another example of a police service that has gone the extra mile with respect to recruitment is the Ottawa Police Service. This service has developed a unique program called "Outreach Champions," which involves using "recruitment champions"—volunteers from the diverse communities—to assist in recruiting members from diverse backgrounds (Ottawa Police Service, 2009). These volunteers are responsible for identifying candidates for recruitment to the Ottawa Police Service and for help-ing these candidates apply. Recruitment champions include immigrants from Haiti and from the Caribbean, members of the Gay-Lesbian-Bisexual-Transgendered community, and members of the Sikh and Chinese communities. Collectively, recruitment champions contribute a wide variety of languages, along with culturally specific social skills, to the cause of "changing the make-up of the police service."

Outward Initiatives: Police–Community Partnership

Many police services in Canada have some form of diversity and race relations unit. These units are responsible for implementing initiatives like the ELT and Aboriginal Cadet programs, ensuring that police services reflect at all levels the diverse communities they serve, and trying to make policing bias-free. Following are some examples of diversity and race relations units in different Canadian police services:

- Diversity Relations Unit (Peel Regional Police)
- Diversity Management Unit (Toronto Police Service)
- Diversity and Aboriginal Policing Section (Vancouver Police Department)
- Diversity and Cultural Resources Bureau (York Regional Police)
- Diversity Resources Team (Calgary Police Service)
- Diversity and Race Relations Section (Ottawa Police Service).

As well as addressing diversity-related recruitment concerns, these units provide outward initiatives—that is, initiatives enabling police to reach out to communities and forge partnerships with them. Many of these units operate committees dedicated to community consultation. These committees enable police services to fulfill effectively their community-based policing mandate, which is focused on prevention rather than on enforcement.

Many diversity and race relations units also address hate crimes. According to Statistics Canada (2009), the number of hate crimes reported to the police increased 42 percent in 2009, after a 35 percent increase in 2008. More than half (54 percent) of hate crimes reported to police in 2009 were centred on race or ethnicity; 29 percent were centred on religion; and 13 percent on sexual orientation. Many diversity and racial relations units include a hate crimes section and a newcomer outreach section. Their aim is to educate vulnerable populations as well as the general public about what constitutes a hate crime, how a hate crime should be reported, and what police services are available to address these problems.

A community-based policing model calls for proper community awareness and engagement. Police services in Toronto and Vancouver, for example, have community consultation committees made up of both volunteer citizens and police representatives. These committees function as advisory bodies to their respective forces. In 1996, the Vancouver Police Department created the Diversity Advisory Committee (DAC), which explores diversity issues in police activities. The DAC develops initiatives to improve police relations and communications with the diverse populations of the city (Vancouver Police Department, n.d.a). The Toronto Police Service, too, reinforces its community policing efforts with a community consultation process. Community Police Liaison Committees (CPLCs), whose members reflect the demographics of each local community, exist for each of the 17 divisions throughout Toronto. Promoting community and police cooperation, CPLCs help to identify and address local policing issues by being proactive in community relations, crime prevention, education, mobilization, and community initiatives (Toronto Police Service, 2011).

Some diversity and race relations units in Canadian police services provide for outreach to specific minority populations. The task of Vancouver Police Department's Diversity and Aboriginal Policing Section (DAPS) is to address the needs of specific populations within Vancouver that have significant safety concerns. These are populations that are vulnerable owing to culture, economic situation, ethnicity, sexual or gender orientation, race, religion, or to other characteristics that might cause them to be marginalized. Reaching out to them occurs via community forums, workshops, and rallies, as well as through the various community groups with which DAPS maintains relations. These groups enable DAPS to hold regular meetings with representatives from the different populations. In these meetings, DAPS and the various representatives address together the populations' public safety concerns. By reaching out in this way, DAPS builds the communities' trust in police and thereby improves police–community relations.

One such community is the significant Aboriginal population in Vancouver. DAPS includes an Aboriginal liaison officer who works directly with the urban Aboriginal community and is involved with the Aboriginal Community Policing Centre as well as with Aboriginal youth. Another population in Vancouver with significant safety concerns is sex industry workers, chronic victims of violence. DAPS participates in the Sex Industry Workers Safety Action Group, which addresses this violence. In 2008, Vancouver police reached out to another minority community, collaborating with members of Qmunity—a resource centre representing British Columbia's lesbian, gay, bisexual, transgendered, and queer (LGBTQ) populations—to conduct a series of public forums that addressed discrimination, domestic violence, and the underreporting of violence against and within the LGBTQ communities (Vancouver Police Department, n.d.b).

In Toronto, the police service has created Community Consultative Committees (CCCs) to supplement the Community Police Liaison Committees (CPLCs) already in place. The CCCs are different from the CPLCs in that they are meant to serve specific communities on a city-wide basis; they have credibility because they include representatives from different organizations within each community. The Toronto Police Service has CCCs for the Aboriginal, Black, Chinese, French, LGBTQ, Muslim, and South and West Asian communities. The chief of police assigns a senior officer to each CCC to ensure an effective flow of information between the executive branch of the police service and the committees. Consultation through these CCCs informs wider policing initiatives such as training, recruiting, professional standards, and community mobilization (Toronto Police Service, 2011).

Outward initiatives in Canadian policing, such as the formation of DAPS and CCCs, ensure that police attend to the unique needs and problems of specific populations or communities. While certain problems persist, such as hate crimes and violence against sex industry workers, reaching out to people of diversity is a valuable step for policing.

Cross-Cultural Criminal Investigations

Efforts to bring diversity training to community policing are also based on the importance of diversity factors in cross-cultural criminal investigations. For such investigations to be successful, police must have

- an understanding of diversity as a factor in crime;
- personnel from diverse communities who can interact with and gain the confidence of these communities and their leaders and thereby secure critical information for the investigation; and
- policies that require investigators or cultural experts to work with leaders of communities that are likely to be affected by an investigation (Perry, 2004).

An underlying assumption of cross-cultural criminal investigations is that if police engage in open and honest dialogue with community leaders, identify problems specific to the leaders' particular culture, and involve these leaders in the investigative process, they will not only have a successful investigation but will establish strong, long-lasting relationships with the community.

Police Training

Training police properly is the key to instilling in them an effective awareness of diversity and an understanding of how to act on this awareness. In the past decade, police training in diversity issues has moved from piecemeal training to diversity-based programs that are fully integrated into police training programs and police organizations.

The goal of **diversity awareness training** in policing is to prepare police and police organizations to become culturally competent, so they can deal more effectively with the diverse communities they protect and serve. The current training programs are integral to policing culture, founded on the principle that diversity is something valuable—a strategic advantage for police. Today's diversity training programs are practical and relevant to police work rather than esoteric.

It has been suggested (Pruegger, 2003) that an effective police diversity training program should be integrated within a larger diversity training plan and should

- be grounded in supportive policy,
- cover all aspects of policing,
- provide targeted training for all levels of service,
- allow on-the-job training and mentoring of cross-cultural competence, and
- have an anti-racism focus.

As well, the diversity training curricula should rely on a variety of instructional approaches, including guest speakers and role-playing.

Diversity awareness training in policing used to be a supplement to police officers' core training. Recruits would have brief training sessions on race relations, cultural awareness, and cross-cultural interaction. (Some of these earlier training programs are discussed below.) Today, diversity training is seen not as supplementary but as integral to the strategic planning of police services.

Race Relations Training

Race relations training programs used to be focused on understanding particular attitudes to do with race, on increasing awareness of race-related beliefs, and on the requirements of the law in general, especially **employment equity** legislation. These early efforts did not inspire confidence among police trainees, who viewed them as touchy-feely and irrelevant to real police work, as well as confrontational and ineffective (Harris & Currie, 1994; Pruegger, 2003, Rees, 1992; Ungerleider, 1992).

The limitations of these early programs (see Table 6.4) led to a rethinking of their goals and, in time, to a new strategic focus on changing police organizations themselves—in other words, systemic change—rather than on changing the feelings

---

diversity awareness training
training in how to be culturally competent so that the trainee can deal more effectively with diversity issues in all their forms

race relations training
training in how to deal more effectively with race-related issues, on the assumption that racism is a social disease that can be cured through education

employment equity
the principle, defined in Canadian law by the *Employment Equity Act*, according to which employers are required to increase the representation of women, people with disabilities, Aboriginal peoples, and visible minorities

and behaviours of individual police officers. Some race-relations training programs now focus on both kinds of change, individual and systemic (see Table 6.5).

Race relations training is currently a formal, short-term program designed to prepare police officers to deal more effectively with race-related issues. It does not pretend to offer immediate solutions to racism or racism in policing. This training approach considers racism a social disease that requires the antidote of awareness and education about race relations.

Cultural Awareness Training

cultural awareness training
a formal, short-term program
that prepares police to deal
more effectively with cultural
issues, either in general or in
terms of a particular culture

Cultural awareness training is a formal, short-term program that prepares police to deal more effectively with cultural issues. Some cultural awareness training programs focus on both culture and race (Hennessy, Warring, & Arnott, 1994). Table 6.6 summarizes the important differences between cultural awareness training and race relations training. There is no standardized, universal cultural awareness training program. A particular training program may be general in focus or it may focus on a particular culture.

Police need cultural awareness or sensitivity training for several reasons. First, they spend a significant amount of time on the job—both within the communities

Table 6.4   Limitations of Early Police Race Relations Training Programs

- Use of non-needs-based content (that is, without surveying the needs of police)
- Time-limited training, which precludes meaningful integration and practice
- Passive instructional approach (one-way lectures)
- Confrontational learning environment and teaching style (for example, white bashing and assumption that all white participants are racist)
- Lack of differentiation of training programs from orientation, briefing, and education programs
- Inadequate knowledge and skill of instructors
- Programs not specific to rank in the police organization (for example, new recruits or veterans)
- General programs rather than programs specific to policing structure and functions
- Lack of serious administrative support
- Absence of short- and long-term impact evaluations

Table 6.5   Goals of Recent Police Race Relations Training Programs

- Change in the organizational structure of police services to promote employment equity and to eliminate systemic barriers to recruitment, selection, retention, and—promotion of visible minorities
- Change in the police organizational climate to reduce racism and race-based conduct
- Change in the behaviour of those who work in police organizations
- Social change—for example, in socio-economic conditions—to eradicate racism

Table 6.6 **Cultural Awareness Training Versus Race Relations Training**

	Cultural awareness training	Race relations training
Personal growth	Increased understanding of one's own culture	Increased understanding of the dynamics of racism
Interpersonal growth	Increased cognitive and emotional understanding of other cultures	Increased competence in combatting racially based discrimination and harassment
Interpersonal effectiveness	Increased competence in cross-cultural communication	Ability to effect structural changes in institutions to remove systemic barriers
		Ability to effect social change to eradicate racism

they serve and, increasingly, within the police service itself—interacting with people of diversity. Carelessly conducted, these interactions can produce misunderstanding and conflict (Triandis, 2000). Training can give police the necessary tools to manage intercultural encounters effectively. Second, most complaints levelled against police concern their interpersonal conduct rather than their professional performance. Third, police themselves want to be more competent in human relations. Fourth, police can increase their effectiveness and the quality of their work life by improving their relations with multicultural groups.

Anti-Racism Training

Anti-racism training is an action-oriented, educational, and political strategy for institutional and systemic change; it addresses the problem of racism and related systems of social oppression such as sexism, classism, heterosexism, and ableism (Dei, 1996). Anti-racism training provides police with information—academic but also practical—to help them practise good, culturally sensitive policing. Furthermore, an anti-racism framework is critical for police officers' understanding of race, class, gender identity, and equal representation in connection with organizations other than law enforcement—for example, educational institutions and immigration agencies.

anti-racism training
training that addresses issues of racism and related systems of social oppression and that involves an action-oriented, educational, and political strategy for institutional and systemic change

Cross-Cultural Training

Cross-cultural training programs prepare an individual for living in another country and for relating to people of diverse cultures in his or her own country (Bhawuk & Brislin, 2000). They help people to manage emotional experiences that arise from negative intercultural encounters, including clashes in cultural values, and help them to address the stereotypes and prejudices they may be exposed to—or may harbour—themselves. Brislin and Horvath (1997) introduced a "CAB" approach to cross-cultural training—that is, cognitive (thinking), affective (emotions), and behavioural (what is actually done).

The *cognitive component* focuses on increasing people's knowledge of culture, cultural differences, and the problems they may face in intercultural encounters.

cross-cultural training
training that prepares an individual for living in another country and for relating to people of diverse cultures in his or her own country

The goal is to increase participants' understanding of people from other cultures so that they can understand other points of view and thereby increase the sensitivity of their thinking.

The *affective component* focuses on the feelings and emotions generated in intercultural encounters. Unfamiliar habits, customs, and values—and even differences in physical features—may stimulate negative emotions in police when they are dealing with individuals from other cultures. A negative reaction to an individual from a certain culture may lead to a police officer's having a generally negative attitude toward everyone from that culture. Such attitudes can interfere with police performance and contribute to police–community hostilities. The goal of affective cultural training is to help police develop effective strategies for rethinking and reframing their negative emotions.

The *behavioural component* of cross-cultural training focuses on actual behaviours in intercultural encounters. The goal of behavioural cultural training is to teach police the appropriate behaviours for successful intercultural exchanges.

CROSS-CULTURAL COMMUNICATION

A valuable new element in cross-cultural training is teaching police about cross-cultural communication, so they can understand the verbal and non-verbal communicative patterns of people from diverse cultures. Communication is always a critical issue for police, but especially so in a culturally diverse community. Conflict may result from misunderstandings over language and over unfamiliar cultural behaviours. Every culture has its own behavioural norms. For example, where Middle Eastern people may take time to warm up to and trust people, North Americans often try to rush right into social intimacy. In some cultures, you are expected to wait for an invitation to join others in an activity; in others, you are considered aloof for not joining in.

misattribution
the misinterpretation of a message or behaviour; a common occurrence in cross-cultural communication

A common type of cross-cultural miscommunication is **misattribution**—the misinterpretation of a message or behaviour. Police often encounter situations in which a person's accent (or the officer's own accent) or inability to speak or understand a language is a barrier to communication and to police performance of duties. Non-verbal communication is important, too, and it has traditionally been neglected in many cultural awareness training programs even though it is estimated that up to 93 percent of a message's social meaning is delivered non-verbally (Singelis, 1994).

paralanguage
the non-verbal features of speech, such as tone, loudness, speed, and the use of silence

kinesics
physical communication, including look and appearance, eye contact, facial expressions, posture, body movements, and touching

Paralanguage, which refers to the non-verbal features of speech (for example, tone, loudness, speed, and the use of silence), is an element of communication that varies from culture to culture. So do the conventions of **kinesics**, which is physical communication: look and appearance, eye contact, facial expressions, posture, body movements, and touching. Six facial expressions of emotion are universal, signifying the same thing in all cultures: anger, fear, happiness, sadness, surprise, and disgust. However, the rules associated with displaying emotions are culture-specific. Some cultures discourage the public display of emotions, whereas others consider it acceptable and normal. In some cultures—for example, French, Middle Eastern, and Latino—touching is more common and socially acceptable than it is in other cultures. In North America, direct eye contact is a sign of respect and attentiveness, whereas in other cultures (for example, Laotian) downcast eyes are the norm for showing respect and attentiveness.

Proxemics refers to the conventions surrounding the physical distance between people. These conventions, too, vary from culture to culture. Hall (1966) identifies four kinds of physical distance:

- *intimate distance*, as in comforting, lovemaking, and wrestling
- *personal distance*, which refers to the comfort zone of about 0.5 to 1 m separating one person from another
- *social distance*, at which one person is far enough from another that touching cannot occur
- *public distance*, which is a distance of 4 m or more between two people.

Understanding proxemics in relation to culture makes police less liable to misjudgment in their intercultural encounters. For example, it helps a police officer to know that a man who is standing very close as he speaks to her is doing so for cultural reasons, not because he means to be threatening. Conversely, a culturally sensitive police officer can avoid intruding on an individual's personal distance and thereby making that person feel uncomfortable or even threatened.

Singelis (1994) has described four dangers involved in non-verbal communication: missing signals, confusing context, misattribution, and sending wrong signals. Misattribution, as explained earlier, is the misinterpretation of a message or behaviour. Here are some examples of misattribution in the context of non-verbal behaviour, all of them relevant to police work:

- interpreting a person's impassive expression as a sign of deceit or obstruction
- interpreting a person's silence as a sign of disrespect or an admission of guilt
- interpreting touching as a sexual advance
- interpreting loud speech and physical closeness as threatening
- interpreting a woman's downcast eyes as a sign of deceit and guilt.

Sensitivity to non-verbal communication can help police in all areas of diversity awareness. In communications with the physically disabled or mentally ill, for instance, it is sometimes the case that the meanings we typically associate with a particular posture, expression, or other non-verbal cue may not apply.

proxemics
the conventions surrounding the physical distance between people

EXERCISE 4

Role-play each of the following situations. Have observers watch the verbal and non-verbal communication of the participants. First, role-play the situations according to the scripts set out below, in which police are behaving incompetently. After the class has given feedback, re-enact the situations, with the "police officers" now using culturally competent verbal and non-verbal communication.

Observe the responses of the role players in relation to

- tone of voice
- hand gestures, including touching
- facial expression

- turn-taking rules
- eye contact
- expression of emotions
- body posture and movement
- empathy
- physical distance
- persuasive disclosure

Situation 1: Police officer stops a teenager on the street.

Black teenager to police officer: "I was doing nothing wrong."

Police officer: "Listen, boy, with an attitude like yours you're going to be a loser for the rest of your life."

Situation 2: Police officer to white woman who is involved in an argument with another white woman: "You better shape up, bitch, or else I'm going to lock you in the slammer for good."

Situation 3: Police officer called to school to deal with an incident in which a straight student called a gay student a "fag." Police officer to gay student: "What's the big fuss, boy? You have to stop carrying a chip on your shoulder and learn to get along with all the straight students in school."

Situation 4: A 14-year-old has called police because his father slapped him in the face for getting home after his 2 a.m. curfew. Police officer to father: "You may be allowed to slap your son in your country, but here in my country we do things differently."

Situation 5: A 13-year-old Arab teenager calls police and complains that her father is not allowing her to go out on a date with a 16-year-old from the neighbourhood. Police officer to father: "This is not the Middle East. When are you going to do things our way?"

Situation 6: A Bosnian family calls police. On arrival, the police officer is told that the family is concerned because the daughter should have been home from school five hours ago. Police officer to distressed mother: "Stop being overprotective. She's probably just having fun with her friends."

POLICING WITH DIVERSITY COMPETENCY: POLICE ABILITIES, KNOWLEDGE, AND SKILLS

As we suggested earlier, a police officer's day-to-day activities have more to do with exercising common-sense discretion and morality than with enforcing the letter of the law and putting people in jail. In a diverse society, cultural knowledge at the police level is a real advantage. Police have significant control over their interactions with the community members they encounter on the job. Individual officers have the opportunity to create positive public relations if they demonstrate cultural sensitivity and understanding toward members of a minority community. Policing with diversity competency involves, among other things, acquiring knowledge of ethnic communities and establishing in these communities a positive, trustworthy image of police.

Understanding diversity, being competent in dealing with its issues, and knowing how to work with minority communities—these abilities can help police do their jobs well and can contribute to their own safety and reputation in the communities they serve. On the other hand, a failure by police in these regards will contribute to misunderstanding, miscommunication, tension, and conflict between police and community. Negative encounters with people of diversity also reduce police officers' job satisfaction while increasing their exposure to complaints and lawsuits—not to mention irate taxpayers and bad press.

The past three decades of policing in Canada have seen an increasing focus on diversity-awareness programs for police services employees. Where the police training programs of three decades ago merely encouraged sensitivity to diversity, police services nowadays view diversity as a positive strategic advantage. As some have noted (Perry, 2004; Pruegger, 2003; Taylor, 2004), this perception has led to

- the establishment of human rights offices and diversity units in police services,
- numerous diversity training initiatives,
- participation in the Law Enforcement Aboriginal Diversity (LEAD) network and Data Collection Strategy on Hate-Motivated Crime Initiatives (Canadian Heritage, 2006),
- the RCMP's drafting of the Bias-Free Policing Policy, and
- the application of diversity principles to cross-cultural criminal investigations.

CHAPTER SUMMARY

While diversity was once considered purely a challenge for police, it is now seen as offering benefits and strategic advantages for policing culture, for police–community relations, for criminal investigations, and, ultimately, for public safety. In short, the diversification of policing makes police more effective. Traditional police training programs in race relations and cultural awareness were limited in scope and utility. Today, the most effective police training programs in diversity competency are part of a police-sponsored diversity awareness training plan and are integral to police culture.

Policing has come a long way in recognizing the value of diversity. Police services have changed their traditional "white machismo face," benefiting both police and society through the cultural competence they have acquired. There is always room for improvement, but Canadian police organizations have made great strides in diversifying the face of policing.

KEY TERMS

anti-racism training	kinesics
authoritarianism	misattribution
community policing principles	paralanguage
cross-cultural training	police force approach
cultural awareness training	police services approach
diversity awareness training	proxemics
diversity competency	race relations training
employment equity	white machismo culture

REFERENCES

Banton, M. (1963, April). Social integration and police. *Police Chief,* 10–12.

Bhawuk, D.P.S., & Brislin, R.W. (2000, January). Cross-cultural training: A review. *Applied Psychology: An International Review, 49*(1), 162–191.

Brislin, R.W., & Horvath, A.M. (1997). Cross-cultural training and multicultural education. In J.W. Berry, M.H. Segal, & C. Kagitcibasi (Eds.), *Handbook of cross-cultural psychology: Social behaviour and applications.* (Vol. 3, pp. 327–369). Needham Heights, MA: Allyn and Bacon.

Canadian Heritage. (2006). Annual report on the operation of the *Canadian Multiculturalism Act* 2004–2005. http://dsp-psd.pwgsc.gc.ca/Collection/CH31-1-2005E.pdf.

Canadian Press. (2011, June 7). Race the No. 1 motivator as police-reported hate crimes rise 42% in 2009: StatsCan. http://ca.news.yahoo.com/race-no-1-police-reported-hate-crimes-123740738.html.

CBC News in Depth. (2005, May 26). Racial profiling. *CBC.ca.* http://www.cbc.ca/news/background/racial_profiling/.

Clyderman, B.K., O'Toole, C.N. & Fleras, A. (1992). *Police, race and ethnicity.* Toronto: Butterworths.

Coffey, A. (1990). *Law enforcement: A human relations approach.* Englewood Cliffs, NJ: Prentice Hall.

Dei, G.S. (1996). *Anti-racism: Theory and practice.* Halifax: Fernwood.

Doolittle, Robyn. (2009, September 30). Racial bias exists on police force, chief says. *The Toronto Star,* A01.

Durham Regional Police Service (DRPS). (2010, May 20). 2005-2010 diversity strategic plan. http://www.drps.ca/internet_explorer/whatsnew/whatsnew_view.asp?ID=16989.

Durkan, S. (1998, March 24). Canadian cops top the list in most-popular survey. *The London Free Press,* p. A9.

Fleras, A. (1992). From enforcement to service: Community policing in a multicultural society. In B.K. Clyderman, C.N. O'Toole, & A. Fleras (Eds.), *Police, race and ethnicity* (pp. 69–126). Toronto: Butterworths.

Hall, E.T. (1966). *The hidden dimension.* New York: Doubleday.

Halton Regional Police Service. (n.d.). Enhanced language training. http://www.hrps.on.ca/Diversity/ELT/Pages/default.aspx.

Harris, E.V.C., & Currie, G.A. (1994). An integrated anti-racism training model: A framework for positive action. *Crime & Justice: The Americas, 7,* 11–14.

Hennessy, S.M., Warring, D.F. & Arnott, J.S. (1994). *A cultural awareness trainer's manual for law enforcement officers.* Scottsdale, AZ: Leadership.

Laws, J. (2005, February 4). Durham Regional Police Service (DRPS): 2005–2010 diversity strategic plan. Ottawa: Graybridge Malkam.

Leman, M. (1999, February 15). Government of Canada. Depository Services Program, 93-6E. Canadian multiculturalism. http://dsp-psd.pwgsc.gc.ca/Collection-R/LoPBdP/CIR/936-e.htm.

McKim, E. (1999). Policing in Canada today. http://ssrsbstaff.ednet.ns.ca/aripley/Law12/.../Policing_in_Canada_Today_1.doc.

Ontario Provincial Police. (2011, June 7). OPP western region community satisfaction survey results. http://www.cnw.ca/en/releases/archive/June2011/07/c3544.html.

Ottawa Police Service. (2009). Outreach champions. http://www.ottawapolice.ca/en/community/diversitymatters/recruitment/champions.aspx.

Ottawa Police Service. (2010). Diversity matters. http://www.ottawapolice.ca/en/Community/DiversityMatters/index.aspx.

Perry, D. (2004, Fall). Complexities of cross-cultural investigations. *Canadian Police Chief Magazine*: 22–24.

Police Services Act. (1990). RSO 1990, c. P.15.

Pruegger, V. (2003, February). *Community and policing in partnership*. Paper for the Policing in a Multicultural Society Conference, Ottawa.

Rankin, J., Quinn, J., Shephard, M., Simmie, S., & Duncanson, J. (2002, October 19). Singled out: Star analysis of police crime data shows justice is different for blacks and whites. *The Toronto Star*, p. AO1.

Rees, T. (1992). Police race relations training. *Currents: Readings in Race Relations, 7*, 15–18.

Shusta, R.M. (2005). *Multicultural law enforcement* (3rd ed.). Upper Saddle River, NJ: Pearson/Prentice Hall.

Singelis, T. (1994). Nonverbal communication in intercultural interactions. In R.W. Brislin & T. Yoshida (Eds.), *Improving international interactions: Modules for cross-cultural training programs* (pp. 268–294). Thousand Oaks, CA: Sage.

Statistics Canada. (2006a). Ethnic origins, 2006 counts, for Canada, provinces and territories – 20% sample data. http://www12.statcan.ca/census-recensement/2006/dp-pd/hlt/97562/pages/page.cfm?Lang=E&Geo=PR&Code=01&Data=Count&Table=2&StartRec=1&Sort=3&Display=All&CSDFilter=5000.

Statistics Canada. (2006b). Police resources in Canada. Table 5: Male and female police officers by rank, 1986 to 2010. http://www.statcan.gc.ca/pub/85-225-x/2010000/t006-eng.htm.

Statistics Canada. (2009). Police-reported hate crimes. http://www.statcan.gc.ca/dailyquotidien/110607/dq110607a-eng.htm.

Steinberg, J.L., & McEvoy, D.W. (1974). *The police and the behavioural sciences*. Springfield, IL: Charles C. Thomas.

Taylor, N. (2004, Fall). Policing with cultural competency. *Canadian Police Chief Magazine*, 14–19.

Toronto Police Service. (2011). Community consultative process. http://www.torontopolice.on.ca/communitymobilization/ccc.php.

Triandis, H.C. (2000). Culture and conflict. *International Journal of Psychology, 35*(2), 145–152.

Ungerleider, C. (1992). *Issues in police intercultural and race relations training in Canada.* Ottawa: Canadian Centre for Police–Race Relations.

Vancouver Police Department. (n.d.a). Diversity advisory committee (DAC). http://vancouver.ca/police/organization/public-affairs/diversity-aboriginal-policing/index.html.

Vancouver Police Department. (n.d.b). Diversity and Aboriginal policing section. http://vancouver.ca/police/organization/public-affairs/diversity-aboriginal-policing/index.htmlhttp://vancouver.ca/police.

Waddington, P.A.J. (1999). Police (canteen) sub-culture. *British Journal of Criminology, 39*, 287–309.

Waterloo Regional Police Service. (2010). Member showcase. http://www.wrps.on.ca/careers/member-showcase.

Williams, W.L., & Henderson, B.B. (1997). *Taking back our streets: Fighting crime in America.* New York: Lisa Drew/Scribner.

REVIEW QUESTIONS

TRUE OR FALSE?

_____ 1. Regarding their role in the community, police used to see themselves as zookeepers.

_____ 2. It is misleading to describe a police officer's job as law enforcement.

_____ 3. Authoritarian conduct is what the community wants and expects from police.

_____ 4. Race relations training programs take the approach that racism is a social disease that requires the antidote of awareness and education about race relations.

_____ 5. Cross-cultural training is not necessary for police when dealing with intercultural encounters.

_____ 6. Efforts to bring diversity training to community policing demonstrate the importance of diversity factors in the conduct of cross-cultural criminal investigations.

_____ 7. Diversity training curriculums should rely on a single instructional approach.

_____ 8. Police are unlikely ever to encounter a situation where a person's accent is a barrier to communication.

_____ 9. Paralanguage refers to non-verbal features of speech such as tone and loudness.

_____ 10. A person's passive facial expression may be seen by a police officer as a willingness to cooperate.

MULTIPLE CHOICE

1. Police officers in Canada today tend to see themselves as
   - (a) security guards
   - (b) avengers of the Lord
   - (c) champions of the people
   - (d) babysitters

2. Most people are satisfied with police
   - (a) most of the time
   - (b) some of the time
   - (c) all of the time
   - (d) very little of the time

3. It can be argued that the functions police perform are by necessity
   - (a) coercive
   - (b) antagonistic
   - (c) secretive
   - (d) passive

4. A significant source of strain between police and people of diversity is
   - (a) overuse of firearms by police
   - (b) noisy community festivals
   - (c) racial profiling
   - (d) language barriers

5. People can better deal with emotional experiences that arise from intercultural encounters by
   - (a) using employment equity on the job
   - (b) taking race relations training
   - (c) taking cultural awareness training
   - (d) taking cross-cultural training

6. Cross-cultural training prepares people for
   - (a) running a marathon
   - (b) marrying someone from a different culture
   - (c) relating to people from diverse cultures
   - (d) seeking refugee status in Canada

7. The affective component of cross-cultural training for police focuses on the
   - (a) career choices open to them
   - (b) negative emotions felt by people of diversity
   - (c) negative attitudes police have toward extra training
   - (d) feelings and emotions generated in intercultural encounters

8. *Misattribution* is
   (a) failing to give a source for quoted material
   (b) identifying someone incorrectly
   (c) failing to give credit where credit is due
   (d) misinterpreting a message or behaviour

9. *Proxemics* refers to
   (a) the nearness of a neighbour whose culture is different from yours
   (b) an approximation of the cultural differences between groups
   (c) physical contact between people, such as touching
   (d) the conventions surrounding physical distance between people

10. A person's loud speech and physical closeness may be interpreted by a police officer as
   (a) friendliness
   (b) threatening behaviour
   (c) disrespectful behaviour
   (d) deceptiveness

FILL IN THE BLANKS

1. The police are the only element in the criminal justice system that has a _____ relationship with the community.

2. Police officers in this country spend most of their time in a _____ role.

3. A positive public image is good for police because it makes policing a _____ profession.

4. Two approaches have come to dominate policing worldwide: the authoritarian police force approach and the _____ _____ approach.

5. Examples of _____ policing programs are Crime Stoppers and Neighbourhood Watch.

6. In pluralistic Western countries, _____ _____ have historically been overrepresented in police services.

7. Policing in Canada in the 21st century sees diversity as a strategic _____.

8. In the past decade, police training in diversity issues has moved from _____ training to programs that are fully integrated into police training curricula.

9. The goal of diversity awareness training in policing is to prepare police and police organizations to become _____ competent.

10. The physical distance between two people who are wrestling is an example of _____ distance.

PART II

First Nations Issues in Canada

Creation and Contact

7

INTRODUCTION

This chapter contrasts pre-contact Europe and pre-contact America to the end of understanding what the two cultures were like before they collided. Identifying the differences between their respective world views is crucial to any such understanding.

We gain insight into a culture's world view by examining its creation story. This first chapter will look at Aboriginal creation stories and at Western European creation stories. We will reflect briefly on Western creation stories, despite the fact that Canada is widely considered to be a cultural mosaic. Not all Canadians today are familiar with Christian religion. But at the time of colonization and well into the 20th century, the majority of Canadians were people of Western European origin— that is to say, overwhelmingly Christian. Their European culture was the dominant culture in Canada during colonization and arguably remains so today. The fundamental principles of Aboriginal culture have always been quite different from the European principles that underlie the mainstream world view in Canada.

After examining the creation stories and differences in world view between Aboriginal culture and mainstream culture, we will examine the relationship between Aboriginal people and Europeans as it developed from the time of first contact through to the period in which Aboriginal people declined from partners in trade and allies in war to displaced and subjugated peoples.

CHAPTER OBJECTIVES

After completing this chapter, you should be able to:

- Identify the differences between the Western European world view and the world view of First Nations people.

- Understand how a people's world view affects all aspects of its culture, from religion to technology.

- Consider how differences in world view will affect the continuing relationship between the mainstream culture and the First Nations culture.

- Identify the core issues in the longstanding debate over Aboriginal claims to land and authority in the Americas.

- Discuss the relationship between the new European arrivals and the First Nations people in Canada up to the time of the *Royal Proclamation of 1763*.

WORLD VIEW

A world view is the set of assumptions and beliefs on which a people's comprehension of the world is based. The stories, symbols, analogies, and metaphors that compose a people's mythology express a world view in coded form. Such expression occurs in informal, formal, unconscious, and conscious ways through family and community, through arts and media, and through economic, spiritual, governmental, and education institutions. (Cajete, 2000, p. 62)

What distinguishes the world view of the dominant culture in Canada? Amid the many cultures that compose Canada there is a dominant, mainstream culture. Members of a mainstream culture are sometimes hardly aware of its existence, but people from outside that culture tend to be acutely aware of it. According to Cajete, our culture gives us a particular world view that affects the way we live and our social and political actions. What are the stories, metaphors, symbols, and myths that express the mainstream Canadian world view?

FOUNDATIONS OF THE MAINSTREAM CANADIAN WORLD VIEW

The foundations of the mainstream Canadian world view include stories of creation, 17th-century philosophy, structures of governance, and capitalist assumptions about land and property.

Religious Creation Story

Our society is still deeply influenced by the Christian religion. The Christian belief is that humans are created in the image of God and that they, alone among the world's creatures, are endowed with a spirit. God has given humans "dominion over the fish of the sea, and over the fowl of the air, and over the cattle, and over all the Earth" (Genesis 1:25). This belief has profoundly shaped the mainstream culture's view of humanity's relationship with the natural world. The Bible's assertion that humans were made to cultivate the earth is in part responsible for the emphasis on agriculture in Western European society, while the biblical view that the human purpose is to populate the earth was, historically, one of the factors in the high populations of Western European societies.

Our conceptions of justice are rooted in religion. Until very recently, our principles of sentencing for criminal offences were based on notions of retribution and punishment that are biblical in origin. Although the purpose of sentencing, as expressed in section 718 of the *Criminal Code*, is now more in line with modern thinking, various signs and symbols within mainstream culture (for example, in film, books, and stories) still promote a biblical, "eye for an eye" view of justice.

Finally, the Christian faith is a proselytizing religion, based on the belief that there is only one God and one true religion and that others must convert to it or be damned. At the same time, it contains many factions. This state of affairs produced much religious intolerance and dissension and conflict in Europe, one of the many reasons Europeans came to settle in new lands. Christianity's proselytizing tendency has affinities with ethnocentrism—the idea that others must live as we do because ours is the best way to live and all other ways are inferior. Not just First Nations people but all people from cultural traditions outside the mainstream one will have come across this ethnocentric propensity in members of the cultural majority.

Scientific Creation Story

Mainstream culture has a second creation story, the scientific one based on Charles Darwin's theory of evolution. This story locates the creation of humanity in the Fertile Crescent of Africa. (According to Christian scientists seeking to validate the biblical story, this is the true site of the Garden of Eden.) It is a story that has humans evolving through several stages of development to their final form, then migrating outward to occupy the earth in a gradual process.

Darwin's theory of evolution has had a huge impact on mainstream culture's world view. That impact is reflected in colloquialisms such as "dog eat dog" and "only the strong survive." The creation story based on Darwin's theory has profoundly affected the way we see both ourselves and life on this planet. It supports our view that life is about competition for resources and survival. For mainstream culture, the scientific view of creation has displaced to some extent the religious view of creation.

PHILOSOPHY AND GOVERNANCE

Philosopher Thomas Hobbes wrote *Leviathan* in 1660, after the discovery of the Americas but prior to their full-scale colonization. Hobbes theorized that life in a state of nature, where there is no strong centralized government with absolute power, is "nasty, brutish, and short." His view of human nature was not a positive one. He presumed that men would kill one another in order to survive. He advocated investing absolute power in a sovereign in order to maintain both structure and peace in society. Hobbes's historical circumstances influenced his opinion. Europe in that period experienced political instability, war, and plagues that wiped out huge portions of the population. There were huge class divisions between the wealthy and the poor, with wealth concentrated in the Church and monarchy. Europe was a long way from democracy. The Church and the sovereign were seen as one concentrated source of power, while ordinary people had very little political control. It was a top-down structure of governance. This is the conception of government that Europeans subscribed to when they embarked on the process of colonization.

Our political structure today is very different. Many academics maintain that our current form of democratic government was to some extent modelled on the forms of government practised by First Nations peoples at the time of their first contact with European explorers.

Locke's Theory of Landownership

When we discuss land rights, we tend to think in terms of rights to private ownership of property; that is our cultural understanding of people's relationship to land. This understanding is rooted in biblical texts and in political structures that date back to medieval times. Early in European history the division of the "haves" and "have-nots" was determined by private landownership. By the time the Americas were "discovered," most of the land in Europe was already in the hands of private landowners. Those who worked the land for landowners would almost certainly never own land; they would be labourers their entire lives. When the Americas were discovered, philosopher John Locke wrote a theory of landownership that reinforced the established Western European notion of man's relationship to land. Locke's theory would rationalize the European seizure of land in the Americas. In brief, his theory went like this:

1. All land is owned by all of mankind.
2. Land can be transferred from general to private ownership by mixing one's labour with it.
3. Once converted to private ownership, land requires delineated boundaries (physically represented by fencing).
4. In order to have delineated boundaries, a society must have an established government and laws for enforcing private ownership.
5. Proviso: A man could take as much land as he required, provided he left "enough, and as good" for others. (Bishop, 2003)

Locke's theory is an important one: it will come up again later in this book in connection with the clearing of Aboriginal people from the land and our society's justifications for doing so. It is also relevant to our discussion later in this chapter; it provides a contrast to Aboriginal concepts of land and methods of government.

The concepts we have discussed thus far should be very familiar to all members of mainstream Canadian culture. They are the building blocks of our society's world view. Many other concepts could be discussed, particularly the rise of capitalism, but space limitations preclude a fuller treatment. Now we must look at another world view, one that is very different from the mainstream one.

ABORIGINAL WORLD VIEW

Before Europeans arrived on the shores of what would become Canada, there were self-governing nations of people living in organized groups throughout the land. The land sustained 500,000 to 2,000,000 people in all (archeologists cannot provide more exact numbers) (Dickason, 1997, p. 43). These nations have rich histories that are tens of thousands of years old; conservative archeological estimates put First Nations occupancy at 15,000 years. (According to Aboriginal people, they have been here since time began.) In other words, European history on the continent represents less than one-tenth of the histories of these nations (see Figure 7.1), who occupied every territory of the continent, using natural resources for sustenance.

In the 16th century, an estimated 2,200 languages were spoken across the continents of Central and South America (Dickason, 1997, p. 5). In what would become Canada, 50 languages were spoken, which have been classified into 11 language families. Not all people who speak the same language can understand one another. Many languages have a number of different dialects—variations of a common language. Since language is the conduit of culture, we know that the cultures are as diverse as their languages. Often we approach Aboriginal people across Canada as if they are all part of one homogeneous group. This misconception often damages relationships between Aboriginal people and mainstream Canadians.

ORAL TRADITION

Language conveys culture from one generation to the next. Aboriginal culture accomplishes this through an oral tradition in which storytelling is the means of conveying values, social expectations, history, and knowledge. Storytellers hold a special place in Aboriginal communities; storytelling is a tremendous responsibility that is taken very seriously. Stories are not passed down in a spontaneous manner;

Figure 7.1   Cultural and Language Groups Prior to Contact

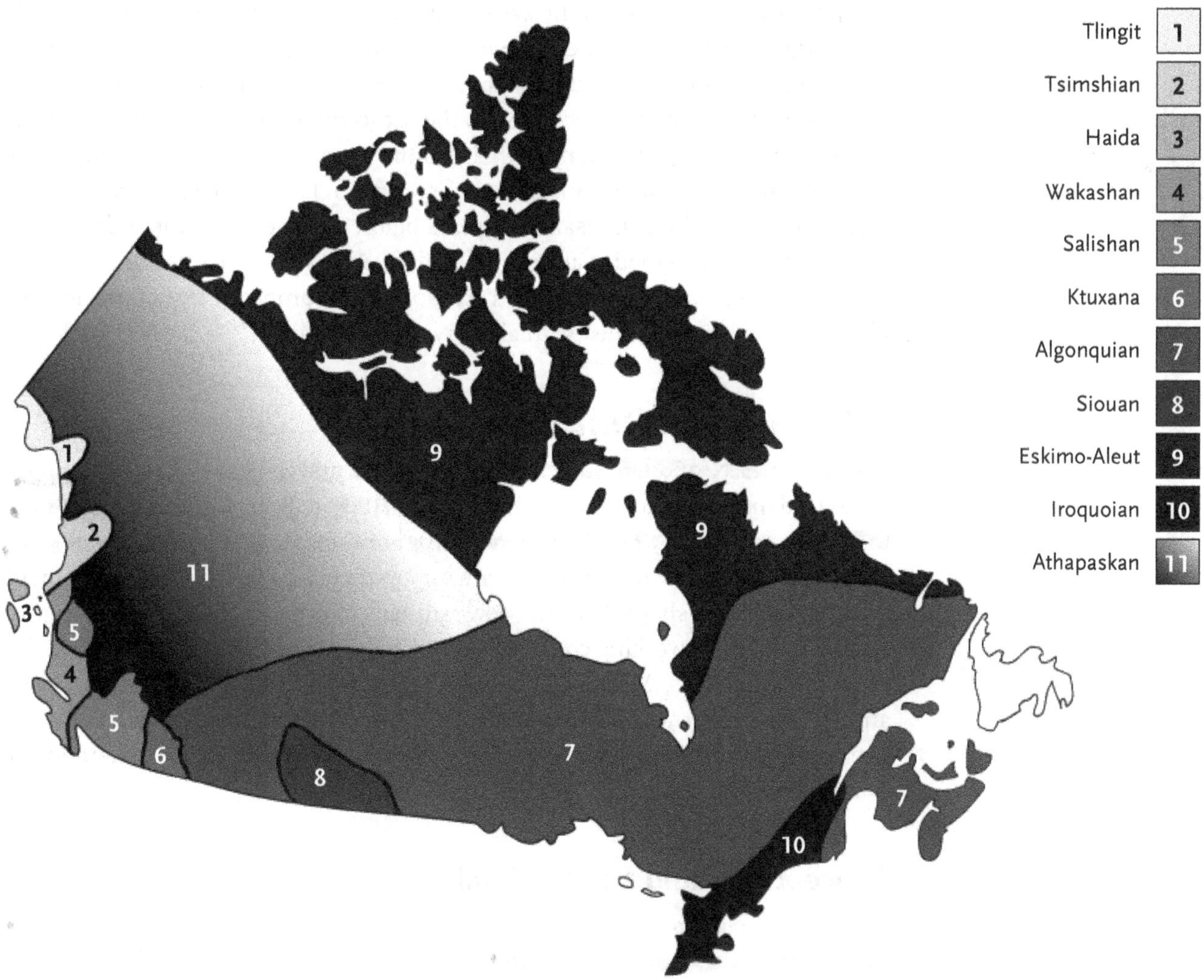

Tlingit	1
Tsimshian	2
Haida	3
Wakashan	4
Salishan	5
Ktuxana	6
Algonquian	7
Siouan	8
Eskimo-Aleut	9
Iroquoian	10
Athapaskan	11

they are told and retold by the storyteller in teaching circles and formal ceremonies. Traditionally, few Aboriginal cultures found a need to write; their storytellers have always been like living books. The stories they tell have certain features in common:

- They include various aspects of the storyteller's physical environment—the people, the local animals and plants. Mythical creatures in the stories combine human characteristics with characteristics of local animals.

- They provide spiritual guidance and ethical instruction, exemplifying cultural values and expectations. (See Appendix 7.1 for two conservation stories from Alaskan oral tradition.)

- They often include places that would be familiar to the listeners, and places that would have spiritual significance for them.

- They are rich in symbolism that sheds light on the origin of the people as well as on their world view.

European historians have tended to question the reliability of oral histories, believing that they are susceptible to being embellished, misinterpreted, or misunderstood.

But they have found that the earliest recordings of Aboriginal stories, which were compiled by Jesuit priests in the early 1600s, are identical to the stories being told by Aboriginal elders and other storytellers today. This attests to the accuracy and completeness of oral transmission from one generation to the next, and to the fact that these stories are timeless. Heirs to the text-centred European tradition would do well to remember that many of their culture's central narratives—the Bible, for example, and the seminal works of Homer—were in fact derived from oral renderings that subsisted for thousands of years before anyone wrote them down. The oral and the written modes are not as distinct as is sometimes assumed. Stories about the Garden of Eden and Noah's ark, and other European creation stories, are, like Aboriginal stories, filled with allegory and symbolism.

CREATION STORIES

One of the most important subjects in First Nations and Inuit stories is their origins. Where did the people come from? In all stories, the people were either created from the land in which they have traditionally lived or they came to the land from some other spiritual place. Creation stories are important to a culture because they situate it in the world and shape its world view. Animals figure prominently in Aboriginal stories of creation, working collaboratively with humans. (See Appendixes 7.2, 7.3, and 7.4 for Iroquois, Mi'kmaq, and Cree creation stories.) Not only humans but animals and other natural elements are endowed with spirit by the Creator. The Creator gives humans stewardship of the natural world and compels them to live in harmony with it.

Concepts of Land and Spirituality

From these creation stories come foundations for a distinct world view. Intrinsic to this view is the connection to land. In these stories, land is more than merely a geographic territory or a potential source of wealth. It is Land—a sacred living entity, with its own rhythms and cycles. The life and spirituality of First Nations peoples have always been connected to the land in a close, symbiotic relationship. They believe that because the people were born with the land as part of the common creation, they cannot be separated or differentiated from it.

All Aboriginal peoples' spirituality is connected to the land. Their spiritual practices developed to reflect this connection, and these practices are as diverse as the nations themselves.

Community Organization

Aboriginal people organized themselves in different ways depending on their unique environments and spiritual beliefs. Generally, they organized themselves into communal groups that were egalitarian, self-sufficient, and connected to the land and its resources. Often they were connected to other specific nations in cooperative relationships for trade and the sharing of resources. These relationships were often set out in treaties that outlined each nation's responsibility to the others and, at times, delineated territorial boundaries for the purpose of resource management and harvest. Several nations would often be unified in a confederacy.

The Haudenosaunee, for example, were a collection of five nations: the Mohawk, Seneca, Oneida, Onondaga, and Cayuga. Each nation had its own distinctive clan system. The Mohawk were bear, turtle, or wolf clan. The other nations had their respective clans. The Five Nations were united in a "League of Peace," otherwise known as the Iroquois Confederacy. The Confederacy was governed by a council of 50 chiefs representing the participant nations. Decisions were made by consensus among the chiefs and by the chief's consultation with the people whose interests he represented. Women had tremendous influence in the governmental system since they selected the chiefs and had the right also to remove a chief who proved to be unsatisfactory. Clarkson, Morrissette, and Régallet (1992, p. 16) have described the Aboriginal decision-making process as follows:

> [W]hen decisions had to be made that affected the whole community, each clan would sit around a central fire with all other clans. Decisions the clan made to-gether may include when to move, conservation of the resources of the territories, the striking of alliances and relationships with other nations and how to imple-ment these decisions. Usually after much discussion and further consultation with their clan members, decisions would be made that would respect the inter-ests of all clans and their members. Decisions were not arrived at in the same manner as western society today through majority vote. When decisions had to be made it would be through a consensus process. All people had to agree with the action or no action would be taken.

These forms of government indicate that cooperation and consensus are among the foundations of the Aboriginal world view. Their spiritual teachings, by advis-ing that decisions be made in the best interests not only of all living people but also of all people of the next seven generations, encourage a farsighted concern for the community. Aboriginal forms of governments are based on equality and on balancing individual interests against group interests, with group interests always taking precedence.

Because everything is connected in the Aboriginal world view, spirituality influ-ences land use, and both influence governance structures. There is no separation between these elements as there is in mainstream tradition. The conception of indi-vidual rights is not alien to the Aboriginal system of social organization; it just holds a place of less importance than group or collective rights. Negotiated rights to harvest territories are not individual rights; they are collective rights of the group. The har-vest does not belong to the individual harvester but to the collective group, and is distributed according to subsistence needs. The focus of Aboriginal teachings is the individual's responsibilities to the group rather than the individual's rights within the group.

International Organization

Individual Aboriginal Nations did not exist in a vacuum. They were very aware of one another and entered into relationships to exchange knowledge and to trade material goods. In this way, they influenced one another's cultures. Sometimes nations traded for natural resources not available within their own territory. Agri-cultural societies such as the Iroquois traded their excess agricultural products. Trade took place over vast areas of the Americas.

CONTACT

First contact with Aboriginal peoples in what would become Canada was not by the British or the French, but by Vikings travelling from Greenland. They arrived in Newfoundland sometime between the 11th and 13th centuries. They settled at L'Anse aux Meadows at the northern tip of Newfoundland, which is today a Canadian World Heritage Site. The Vikings were drawn by the great supply of fish, which later drew many more Europeans, but they arrived just prior to a global shift in weather. As temperatures dropped, they abandoned their settlement and returned to Greenland.

Little is known about the presence of the Vikings in North America; however, they did make records of their encounter with the indigenous people of Newfoundland, whom they referred to as the "Skraelings." Although this indigenous group is known by several names, the most common is the Beothuk. Little is known about the Beothuk. Historians estimate there were 2,000 to 5,000 members of this community. They were hunter-gatherers, making seasonal movements to the coastline in summer for fishing and sealing, to the interior in winter to hunt game. They were very dependent upon the coastline for the fish and seals that they stored for consumption throughout the winter.

Explorer John Cabot arrived on the coast of Newfoundland in 1497, then carried news of the rich fishing waters back to Europe. It was said at that time that the fish were so numerous you could walk across the ocean on cod. Many Europeans were drawn by the opportunity to make their fortune exporting fish to Europe. In 1501, Portuguese explorer Gaspar Cortes Real captured 50 Beothuk and took them back to Europe as slaves. Likely due to this incident, the Beothuk subsequently avoided contact with whites.

By 1578, over 400 European fishing ships came to the region every summer. They began to occupy the coastline to dry fish, limiting the Beothuk's access to the ocean and pushing them further inland. According to European accounts, the Beothuk would help themselves to fishing equipment left behind over the winter when the ships returned to Europe. This caused great hostility among the whites toward the Beothuk. In 1613, a French fisherman shot a Beothuk he believed to be stealing from him. The Beothuk people retaliated, killing 37 Frenchmen. As a result, the French and English began to shoot the Beothuk on sight, believing them to be a threat. The Beothuk were forced inland and, without access to the resources of the sea, they faced great hardship.

The French, British, and Dutch fought over the ownership of Newfoundland for the next 100 years. In 1713, the French were expelled and moved to Cape Breton, giving the British title to the island. The British increased their coastal settlements, further limiting the Beothuk's access to the ocean and to the resources that had sustained them for thousands of years. After taking control of the land and the resources, the decision was made to attempt to protect the remaining Beothuk, whose population the British recorded in 1768 as a mere 400. In 1810 the British sent a search party to make contact, but two members of the search party were killed by the Beothuk. The British captured the last few Beothuk a short time later. The last known Beothuk Indian, Nancy Shanawdithit, died of tuberculosis in 1829. Thus ends the story of the Beothuk people as it is recorded in European history (Dickason, 1997, pp. 73–74).

The first true voyage of discovery into what would become Canada occurred when Jacques Cartier explored the Gulf of St. Lawrence in 1534. He, like Christopher Columbus, was intent on finding a passageway through to the Orient. Failing that, he hoped to find gold for France as the Spanish were busy doing in Central America. Cartier met with the St. Lawrence Iroquois on his journey and engaged in trade with them. He gathered information from them regarding the route to the interior of the continent, where he hoped to find gold. The friendship became strained when Cartier took—perhaps kidnapped (the historical record is unclear)—Chief Donnaconna's two sons back to Europe with him at the end of the season. The two survived their trip to Europe and returned the following summer to act as interpreters and guides to assist Cartier in his quest for the route into the heart of the continent.

With the help of his Iroquois guides, Cartier made it all the way to Hochelaga, present-day Montreal. He wrote extensively of his voyage. He counted 14 villages on the north shore, of which Hochelaga was the largest, numbering 50 longhouses, with an estimated population of 1,500. Cartier engaged in trade but was forced to return to France as winter set in. He annoyed the Iroquois by setting up a cross to claim the land in the name of France, and then forcibly taking several of the Iroquois headmen back to France.

Cartier returned on a third voyage, this time bringing settlers; however, the relationship between the two groups was by this point sufficiently strained that the Iroquois killed the settlers, forcing Cartier to return to France with a ship full of iron pyrite (fool's gold).

The Europeans continued to arrive on Canada's eastern shores, drawn by a variety of hopes—of growing wealthy through the region's natural resources, of acquiring land, or of escaping poverty or religious persecution in the Old World. These Europeans continued to make contact with various Aboriginal nations, each with its own form of governance and economic system.

Initially, contact involved a spirit of cooperation between the Aboriginal groups and the colonists, and respect for one another's sovereignty. The reasons were three-fold, and quite practical: (1) the Aboriginal nations vastly outnumbered the colonists, who were poorly equipped for the harsh conditions of the land; (2) the economic interests of the newcomers depended on maintaining a good relationship with the Aboriginal communities, who in turn benefited in terms of trade; and (3) Aboriginal people were desperately needed as military allies by the French and the English in their wars against each other, and, later, against the newly independent United States. In the relationship between the Europeans and the Aboriginal nations, the latter clearly had the upper hand at this point.

This was made most clear in the Two Row Wampum, or the *Guswentha*, the first agreement entered into between the Five Nations of the Iroquois and the British. To the Iroquois, the *Guswentha* was international law, recorded in wampum beads as was their custom. The two coloured rows of wampum represented an English trading ship and an Iroquois canoe. They travel parallel paths along the river of life. These paths never meet; the two nations are bound together in peace and friendship, with an agreement for reciprocal aid and defence. At the same time, neither nation is to interfere with the other or attempt to impose laws on it.

This agreement is well documented by the British, referred to as the "**covenant chain**." The covenant chain was a clear recognition by both sides that their political

covenant chain
first agreement entered into between the Five Nations of the Iroquois and the British; a clear recognition by both sides that their political systems would remain separate even as their systems of trade and alliance bound them

systems would remain separate even as their systems of trade and alliance bound them. The British historical record, until it reaches the early 1800s, contains many references to this agreement. One such reference is made in a speech by an Onondaga speaker named Sadakanahtie in 1694 addressing Benjamin Fletcher, governor of New York and Pennsylvania (quoted in Venables, 1992):

> When Christians first arrived in this country, we received them kindly. When they were but small people, we entered into a league with them, to guard them from all enemies whatsoever. We were so fond of their society that we tied the great canoe that brought them, not with a rope made of bark to a tree but with strong iron chain fastened to a great mountain. Now before the Christians arrived, the general council of the five nations was held at Onondaga, where there has, from the beginning, a continual fire been burning: it is made of two great logs whose fire never extinguishes. As soon as the hatchet makers (Christians) arrived, this General Council at Onondaga planted this pine tree at Albany (New York), whose roots and branches have spread as far as New England, Connecticut and Pennsylvania; under the shade of this tree all these English colonies have been frequently sheltered.
>
> Then he renewed the Chain and promised as they likewise expected, mutual assistance in case of any attack by an enemy.

This military alliance with the Iroquois served the British well and led to their defeat of the French in 1760. The French and British continually accused one another of bribing their allies with gifts and also of using Aboriginals, who during battles sustained great losses on the front lines, as "cannon fodder."

Aboriginal nations on both sides considered the battle to be between the French and the English and allied themselves with their traditional trade partners, viewing the outcome as a matter of trade dominance alone; they had no concept that their lands were at stake. They viewed the land as their sacred territory, which they had allowed Europeans to settle on under certain terms and conditions, such as trade alliances and gift distributions.

Upon the defeat of the French, many Aboriginal leaders remarked to the English that it was not the Aboriginals that were conquered but the French. Ojibwa Chief Minweweh, whose warriors had fought on the side of the French, reminded the English: "Although you have conquered the French you have not conquered us. We are not your slaves. These lakes, woods and mountains were left us by our ancestors. They are our inheritance, and we will part with them to none" (Dickason, 1997, p. 155).

To address the Aboriginals' fears concerning the loss of their ancestral lands, the British included article 40 in the Capitulation of Montréal between the French and English. This section guaranteed Aboriginal nations protection of their lands from the encroachment of new settlers. It immediately proved difficult to enforce, however, as settlers began to pour in once peace had been established. Colonial governments displayed little will to enforce the legislation (Dickason, 1997, p. 153).

After the defeat of the French, Aboriginal nations found their position worsening. They had been holding the balance of power between two rivals, but now found themselves becoming irrelevant to both the British and the French. Gift distributions ended quickly, as did the supply of guns and ammunition. The Europeans no longer respected boundaries that Aboriginal nations set out as hunting grounds or sacred territories. Discontent among various nations led to a formidable uprising led by a remarkable man named Pontiac, an Odawa war chief, who was able to unite a number of nations in his quest to defeat the Europeans and drive them from the land. Within the span of two months in 1763, nine British forts fell to Pontiac with almost no casualties sustained by his men. The British feared being overrun and resorted to the first ever recorded case of biological warfare. They distributed smallpox-infected blankets to Aboriginal settlements, wiping out entire communities, including women, children, and elders.

In this intense political climate, the British made efforts to justify their acquisition of land in the Americas. It was apparent to them that the land was in fact occupied by organized nations of people, albeit non-Christians. How could the British reconcile their principles of justice with the acquisition of this land for resource extraction and for settlement?

Acquiring the land for these purposes would be impossible without the help of the Aboriginal nations. Britain was facing a growing rebellion in the 13 colonies and would require the allegiance of Aboriginal nations again in war or would face the loss of the New World altogether. Britain would never be able to secure the necessary allegiance if Europeans continued to trespass on the Aboriginals' territories, which was causing great animosity toward the British.

THE ROYAL PROCLAMATION

In 1763, the British drew up an important piece of legislation to address the dilemma. The ***Royal Proclamation of 1763*** would become the cornerstone of Aboriginal land claims today. This document has been called the "Magna Carta of Indian Rights" and has been deemed by the courts to have the "force of a statute which has never been repealed."

The first purpose of the *Royal Proclamation* was to reserve a large piece of land for Aboriginal occupation and use. The second purpose was to appease Aboriginal leaders in order to secure military allegiance and to stop the mounting Aboriginal resistance movement. The third purpose was to create a treaty process by which the Crown alone could purchase Aboriginal land for settlement.

Consider the wording of the *Royal Proclamation* itself:

> And We do hereby strictly forbid, on Pain of our Displeasure, all our loving Subjects from making any Purchases or Settlements whatever, or taking Possession of any of the Lands above reserved [for Indians], without our especial leave and Licence for that Purpose first obtained.
>
> And We do further strictly enjoin and require all Persons whatever who have either wilfully or inadvertently seated themselves upon any Lands within the Countries above described, or upon any other Lands which, not having been ceded to or Purchased by Us, are still reserved to the said Indians as aforesaid, forthwith to remove themselves from such Settlements.
>
> And whereas great Frauds and Abuses have been committed in purchasing Lands of the Indians, to the great Prejudice of our Interests, and to the great Dissatisfaction of the said Indians: In order, therefore, to prevent such Irregularities

Royal Proclamation of 1763
the cornerstone of Aboriginal land claims today; has been called the "Magna Carta of Indian Rights" and has been deemed by the courts to have the "force of a statute which has never been repealed"

for the future, and to the end that the Indians may be convinced of our Justice and determined Resolution to remove all reasonable Cause of Discontent, We do, with the Advice of our Privy Council strictly enjoin and require, that no private Person do presume to make any purchase from the said Indians of any Lands reserved to the said Indians, within those parts of our Colonies where We have thought proper to allow Settlement: but that, if at any Time any of the Said Indians should be inclined to dispose of the said Lands, the same shall be Purchased only for Us, in our Name, at some public Meeting or Assembly of the said Indians.

This powerful piece of legislation has never been repealed and therefore is still in effect and legally binding. The 13 colonies were very displeased with the limitations the Proclamation imposed on them; it became one of the many reasons for their rebellion against the British. The *Royal Proclamation* is legislation, drawn up by an imperial power, designed to protect the rights of First Nations to their land. As you continue to read, consider whether the British enforced the terms of the Proclamation. Are we honouring these terms today?

The *Royal Proclamation* did accomplish what it set out to do: it drew a line between British territory and Aboriginal land, and it convinced Aboriginal people of Britain's "Justice and determined Resolution to remove all reasonable Cause of Discontent" where the Aboriginal people were concerned. Its reassurances secured Aboriginal support for the British in the upcoming American War of Independence and in Britain's later battles to repel the American invasion of what would become Canada.

The British government's third objective in setting up a treaty process to acquire land was to give the Crown a monopoly over land sales in Canada; it established itself as the only legal purchaser of Aboriginal land. This was a source of enormous wealth for the British. In some of the first treaties in Ontario, the Crown was able to purchase land for settlement for a mere 3 pence an acre from Aboriginals, who could not drive up the prices of their land by selling to any other party. The British then sold the land to private investors for settlement for 6 to 15 pence per acre, making a healthy profit.

The *Royal Proclamation* does not refer to Aboriginal nations as sovereign nations, but it doesn't refer to them as subjects of the Crown, either. We may ask ourselves when the Crown began to assert control or jurisdiction over Aboriginal people.

THE FUR TRADE

During the early period of European–Aboriginal contact, when settlement was still sparse, the fur trade was well under way. The French allied with the Huron and other East Coast nations, and the English allied with the Iroquois and their Aboriginal allies. Both in trade and in war, the British and the French managed to exploit the divisions that had existed among Aboriginal nations prior to contact.

The British set up the Hudson's Bay Company and the French the Compagnie du Nord. The companies were in direct competition for the harvest and export of furs. Both attempted to extend their trade northward so as to gain control over trade routes. As early as 1632, the French were exporting up to 15,000 kilograms of furs a year. The French had 500 to 700 men on the canoe routes travelling to Huronia. Furs were the next best thing to gold (Dickason, 1997, p. 103).

The balance of power at this time was still very much in favour of the Aboriginal nations. Consider, for example, that in 1633 the French had 3,000 people in their colonies, while the Huron nation alone numbered over 30,000. However, the Huron would shortly experience a rapid population decline as a result of European diseases brought by the missionaries and traders.

The French established a system of **seigniorial farms**, in which one man, usually a soldier, was granted land in the name of France. The soldier would bring over his family from France to labour on the farm to produce food for the fledgling colonies. The French did not enact any treaties to acquire this land for farming; they simply considered themselves as sole proprietors of the land by their mere presence. They declared the land to be *terra nullius*—empty land. The French did not recognize indigenous nations as rightful possessors of land, on the grounds that the Aboriginal people were not Christian. The French were, however, very careful to maintain good relationships with Aboriginal nations and never made any open assertions to them about the ownership of the land on which they settled. They did not enter any treaties or legal arrangements to clear the land of Aboriginal title. This became problematic later; upon the defeat of the French, the British also did not enact any legislation to clear the land of Aboriginal title, assuming that the French had already done so.

> **seigniorial farms**
> a system in which a man, usually a soldier, was granted land in the name of France

As the fur trade expanded, forts were erected to house staff and government officials. The fur trade extended into northern Ontario in search of fresh supplies, and to the end of advancing British interests. The fur trade was not conducted at a sustainable rate; beavers were all but extinct south of today's Canada–US border and soon neared extinction in southern Ontario once the traders moved in.

The trading posts created new, non-Aboriginal communities in Aboriginal territory in the North, and had an impact on Aboriginal people who came to sell furs. Posts were often established in strategic proximity to Aboriginal campsites, and Aboriginal groups who had traditionally been hunter-gatherers, travelling continuously with the seasons, began to create permanent dwellings around the trading posts.

Aboriginal people began to trade for objects such as sewing needles, copper pots, knives, and hatchets, through a barter system. This improved their immediate quality of life; they traded for items they could not produce themselves, lacking the technology. This trading system, however, did not have the potential to create long-term economic prosperity in Aboriginal communities. The real profits were being exported back to Europe in the form of furs, and the resources that had sustained Aboriginal people for thousands of years were quickly being depleted beyond recovery.

CHANGES TO ABORIGINAL COMMUNITIES

Contact with Europeans brought fundamental changes to Aboriginal communities. For example, they began to develop notions of cumulative wealth. Before contact, Aboriginal people had never viewed furs in terms of wealth. Animals were killed for food, shelter, clothing, and tools. Anything that the hunter did not need would be given to another family. The proceeds generated by the hunt were shared among community members. Hunting for more than the community needed simply did not make any sense; collecting and storing hides was ill-adapted to the Aboriginals' traditional wandering lifestyle.

Economic imperatives, previously non-existent, began to influence the process by which Aboriginal leaders were selected. The clan system, which had previously maintained the groups' cohesiveness by maintaining strict rules, values, and social mores, slowly lost its influence.

Aboriginal groups became increasingly dependent on European traders, and less reliant on their own natural environment and on the traditional web of trade established between Aboriginal nations prior to contact. The introduction of alcohol through trade created new societal problems that have persisted to this day in some Aboriginal communities. For many Aboriginal nations, this dependence on European trade became entrenched; for others it remained nominal. Europeans were eager to foster this dependence as it provided an advantage in trade. For Aboriginal people, the fur trade did not provide economic stability; prices of furs were dependent upon the whims of fashion, and the fur harvest fluctuated according to environmental conditions and animal populations. The rate of harvest was unsustainable, and the fur trade was destined to collapse.

Many indigenous animals hunted for their fur neared extinction by the early 1800s. As a result, many trading posts closed, bringing extreme hardship to those Aboriginal people who had become reliant on their commerce. Many faced starvation, and diseases unknown to them pre-contact. The government provided food and other necessities, but could never restore the economy of Aboriginal people. Animal resources had been depleted beyond recovery in the first phase of harvest. Aboriginal people later underwent a second harvesting of natural resources in the form of logging and mining, which proved no less devastating to their society.

Along with trade goods, Europeans brought Christian religion—English Protestant and French Catholic—and missionaries to spread the faith. Aboriginal people were not eager to accept missionaries or their faith. Traders brought practical benefits such as guns and copper pots, but new spiritual beliefs were something Aboriginal people simply did not value. Eventually, however, most Aboriginal groups began to accept missionaries into their communities, sometimes for self-serving reasons. In some instances, traders and missionaries assisted one another's causes; Aboriginal trappers who had converted to Christianity were often given better prices for their furs and were permitted to purchase guns and ammunition where their non-Christian peers were not. The missionaries often became frustrated with these incentives, believing that Aboriginal people were converting for convenience rather than from genuine desire for the Christian religion.

The Aboriginal conversions may often have been half-hearted or purely mercenary, but the impact of European religion on Aboriginal communities was unquestionably profound. Missionaries restricted or forbade Aboriginal ceremonies, traditions, and cultural practices, pronouncing them "from the devil." With these elements of their culture gone—elements that had been the foundations of their values, unity, and governance for thousands of years—Aboriginal communities began to unravel. Differences arose between those who accepted European religion and those who did not, and this disrupted communities and families. In extreme cases, the churches or religious orders were given authority to govern reserve land and resources. Resources were extracted, and the churches reaped the financial profits while the Aboriginal people were driven into poverty.

CONCLUSION

Although the mainstream political structure in Canada today has borrowed heavily from Aboriginal government structure, the two systems are based on different conceptions of the world. The Aboriginal peoples, as their creation myths demonstrate, have traditionally seen themselves as having a profound connection to the land. More than a geographic territory, more than a thing merely owned, the land is a sacred, living entity to which they are connected symbiotically. And yet, at the time of first European contact, Aboriginal people were certainly occupying the land in the Lockean sense. They lived in politically organized groups, in territories with boundaries which, though fluid, they had negotiated with other nations on this continent. And they managed the resources within their respective territories, "mixing their labour with the land" and thus meeting another Lockean criterion for ownership. The main difference between Aboriginal and European conceptions of landowning consists in Locke's emphasis on the individual nature of landownership. Aboriginal people had a government structure in which individuals were part of a collective whose well-being was primary rather than secondary. From the Aboriginal perspective, no individual owned the land; the collective did. These differing emphases—on collective rights in Aboriginal culture and on individual rights in European culture—have complicated the relationship between settler nations and Aboriginal people since first contact.

The Aboriginal peoples initially held significant political power in their relations with the Europeans, but they quickly moved from a position of power to a position of subservience, both politically and in their trade relationships. The fur trade, prone to fluctuations beyond their control, could not ensure long-term economic stability for their communities. At the same time, Aboriginal peoples were decimated by new diseases and by wars in which European powers involved them. The *Royal Proclamation of 1763* was seen as guaranteeing Aboriginal rights to land and, therefore, to basic subsistence. However, the ruling powers' reluctance to enforce its provisions tended to nullify any advantage the Proclamation conferred on Aboriginal people. The European presence severely disrupted traditional Aboriginal ways of living in harmony with their environments and of governing by consensus. The influence of European values, such as materialism, upset the balance in Aboriginal society between individual and communal needs.

KEY TERMS

covenant chain
Royal Proclamation of 1763
seigniorial farms

REFERENCES

Axtell, J. (Ed.). (1981). *The Indian peoples of Eastern America: A documentary history of the sexes.* New York: Oxford University Press. http://www.ucalgary.ca/applied_history/tutor/firstnations/earth.html.

Berger, T. (1999). *The long and terrible shadow: White values, Native rights.* Vancouver/ Toronto: Douglas & McIntyre.

Bishop, J.D. (2003). The Lockean basis of Iroquoian land ownership. In R.B. Anderson & R.M. Bone (Eds.), *Natural resources and Aboriginal people in Canada: Readings, cases, and commentary*. Toronto: Captus Press.

Cajete, G. (2000). Philosophy of native science. In G. Cajete, *Native science: Natural laws of interdependence*. Santa Fe, NM: Clear Light.

Clarkson, L., Morrissette, V., & Régallet, G. (1992). *Our responsibility to the seventh generation: Indigenous peoples and sustainable development*. Winnipeg: International Institute for Sustainable Development. http://www.iisd.org/pdf/seventh_gen.pdf.

Dickason, O.P. (1997). *Canada's First Nations: A history of founding peoples from earliest times* (2nd ed.). Toronto: Oxford University Press.

Ellis, C.D. (Ed.). (1995). *Cree legends and narratives from the west coast of James Bay*. Winnipeg: University of Manitoba Press.

Frideres, J.S. (1997). *Aboriginal peoples in Canada: Contemporary conflicts* (5th ed.). Scarborough, ON: Prentice Hall.

Parfit, M. (2000, December). Hunt for the first Americans. *National Geographic, 198*(6).

Royal Proclamation of 1763. (1970). RSC 1970, app. II, no. 1.

Smelcer, J.E. (1996, Summer). Two conservation myths from Alaska Native oral tradition. *Literary Review, 39*(4), 478–481.

Venables, R. (1992). *The founding fathers choosing to be the Romans*. Ithaca, NY: Akwekon Press, Cornell University.

Whitehead, R.H. (Ed.). (1991). *The old man told us: Excerpts from Micmac history, 1500-1950*. Halifax: Nimbus Publishing. http://www.ucalgary.ca/applied _history/tutor/firstnations/mikmaq.html.

REVIEW QUESTIONS

TRUE OR FALSE?

F 1. Canadian mainstream culture is no longer influenced by its religious roots.

F 2. Prior to European arrival in what today is Canada, there were 20,000 people living on this land mass.

T 3. In the oral tradition, spoken language is used to convey culture from one generation to the next.

T 4. Before European contact, in First Nations communities the interests of the group took precedence over the interests of the individual.

F 5. The idea of collective rights was more prominent in European culture than in First Nations culture.

F 6. The Beothuk of Newfoundland are currently negotiating land claims in that region.

T   7. According to Iroquois history, the Two Row Wampum is an agreement between the British and the Iroquois to respect each other's sovereignty and to form a military alliance.

T   8. The *Royal Proclamation of 1763* is deemed to carry the force of law and has never been repealed.

F   9. The *Royal Proclamation of 1763* explicitly refers to Aboriginal nations as subjects of the Crown, defining the moment clearly when the British began to assert authority over Aboriginal nations.

T   10. The French in Canada did not enter into treaties or legal arrangements to clear the land of Aboriginal title.

MULTIPLE CHOICE

1. First Nations creation stories most often assert that
   - (a) they travelled across the Bering Sea
   - (b) they travelled across the Atlantic Ocean
   - (c) the people were born from the land or came to the land from a spiritual place
   - (d) they travelled from the South Pacific on ocean currents

2. Many academics assert that our current form of democracy was influenced by
   - (a) Locke's theory of landownership
   - (b) First Nations forms of government at the time of European contact
   - (c) Thomas Hobbes's philosophy
   - (d) Charles Darwin

3. Across Central and South America there were approximately _____ languages spoken in the 16th century.
   - (a) 10
   - (b) 200
   - (c) 500
   - (d) 2,200

4. According to John Locke, all land is owned by all of mankind, but land can be converted to private ownership through
   - (a) standing on it
   - (b) buying it
   - (c) mixing one's labour with it
   - (d) placing No Trespassing signs on it

5. Women possessed a high degree of political power pre-contact in
   - (a) many First Nations cultures
   - (b) the European tradition
   - (c) nowhere
   - (d) all societies

6. In Europe, the Christian religion was a "proselytizing religion." This means that

   (a) Christians believed in one God manifested in many forms

   (b) Christians believed that others must convert to Christianity or be eternally damned

   (c) Christians were very tolerant of others' spiritual beliefs

   (d) the Christian religion was not central to European culture at any time in history

7. The first foreign people to arrive in the Americas were

   (a) the Dutch

   (b) the British

   (c) the French

   (d) the Vikings

8. After Cartier's voyages to the Gulf of St. Lawrence and Hochelaga, Europeans continued to arrive on Canada's eastern shores to

   (a) escape adverse social and economic conditions

   (b) escape religious persecution

   (c) find wealth in natural resources such as the fur trade

   (d) all of the above

9. Which of the following is not true of the outcomes of the fur trade as it affected Aboriginal people?

   (a) Aboriginal people became increasingly dependent on European traders for goods.

   (b) Many animal species neared extinction due to overhunting.

   (c) Aboriginal people incorporated the accumulation of wealth into their culture, which upset traditional balances.

   (d) The fur trade created long-term and permanent economic stability for Aboriginal nations.

10. The term *terra nullius* means

   (a) empty land

   (b) unfertile land

   (c) land whose ownership is contested

   (d) lawfully purchased land

APPENDIX 7.1

TWO CONSERVATION MYTHS FROM ALASKA

The Indigenous Peoples of Alaska have long known that natural balance, indeed their very subsistence lifestyles, depends much upon how the land is treated. Whereas the Western philosophy of environmental usage was, and still is to an extent, "Take everything and give nothing," the natives of Alaska, like most Native American Indian Peoples, have traditionally regarded the land as both provider and protector. To them, the land and its resources are sacred and the connection between human actions and the Earth's welfare is clear.

From this understanding, numerous taboo myths and legends, didactic in function, exist to illustrate and warn that the land must be treated with respect and stewardship. In these narratives from long-lived oral traditions, the consequences of violating the land and its many resources are portrayed in such horrific accounts that young listeners will remember the lessons throughout their lives and pass on the moralistic message to the next generation.

The following two narratives, "The Ptarmigan Story" from Inupiaq Eskimo and "The Squirrel Shaman" from southeast Alaska Tsimshian, show what happens when nature is destroyed indiscriminately.

THE PTARMIGAN STORY

When young boys are trained to hunt and fish, one of the first lessons they are taught is to respect and care for the game they hunt. If animals are mistreated, then they may no longer allow themselves to be killed for food and clothing, and the Eskimos would certainly die of hunger or freeze to death. Therefore, fathers always tell their children to show respect when they kill an animal.

One day, though, two young brothers left their village to check ptarmigan snares. As they approached the traps, they saw one white bird caught by the leg in one of the snares. The bird was frightened and tried to escape. It jumped up and down and tried to fly away, but the string was very tight around its leg.

The brothers watched the bird and then one spoke to the other.

"I wonder if ptarmigan can fly straight without eyes?" he asked.

The other brother laughed and poked the bird's eyes out with a small branch. Then he threw the blind ptarmigan into the air. It tried to fly but because it could not see, it kept crashing into the hillside and into small bushes. The brothers chased it and they laughed aloud.

Then the other brother asked, "I wonder if ptarmigan can fly without feathers?"

They began to pluck the blind bird while it was still alive! Then they threw it up into the air as before, but each time it just fell to the frozen ground. They did this many times until the bird was nearly dead. When it was time to check the other snares they dropped the poor bird and left it to die without even taking its meat for food.

The next morning both boys awoke feeling very sick. They had the fever and they kept throwing up. The shaman was sent for, but he could do nothing for them. He gave them special medicine, but nothing stopped their suffering. Soon, blood began to pour from their eyes!

The shaman told the parents that the sickness was too great. He said that they must have broken a powerful taboo.

That night the two boys, who had shown such great disrespect to the ptarmigan, died in terrible agony.

THE SQUIRREL SHAMAN

In a small village upon the Skenna River, three young brothers would hunt and kill squirrels. They hung the tiny furs to dry and collected the tails. Together they had killed so many squirrels that they had to go farther and farther away from home to find more.

One day, one of the boys was hunting alone far from the village when he saw a perfectly white squirrel running along the trunk of a very tall tree. The boy raised his bow to shoot, but he saw that it was so pretty that he could not kill this one.

The white squirrel ran into a hole in the tree and turned around and motioned for the boy to follow. The handsome young man approached and looked inside. He saw that it was a house with a great many empty beds. It was a community house for many people, but there was no one inside. It was entirely empty except for the white squirrel who stood in the middle waving at him to come inside.

"I cannot come in," said the Tsimshian boy. "I am much too big." "Lean your bow against the Great House, and then you will be able to come inside," replied the white squirrel.

The boy did so and to his surprise he became small enough to walk into the empty hall. He saw that the white squirrel was a beautiful young woman who was wearing a white fur coat. She told the boy to follow her up to the top of the Great Tree. When they arrived, an old man who looked like a chief spoke to him.

"I have been waiting for you to come. Why have you killed all of my people? All of my children and grandchildren are gone except for my favorite granddaughter who led you to the Great House. Why have you done this?"

The young man looked around and saw that this room too was empty, and then he answered the old chief, "I have not killed your people. I have never killed a person before. I do not know what you are saying, old father."

"Look around you," said the chief. "See how we are alone here now where once these halls were full of my people."

The boy looked again and replied, "But I did not kill anyone."

The old man came close to the boy and spoke to him again, "I am the chieftain of the Squirrel People. You and your brothers have killed all of my children and now their skins hang outside your house."

Suddenly the boy understood what had happened. He looked at the girl and saw that she was indeed very beautiful. He felt ashamed and saddened.

"We did not know that you live like people. We did not know that you love your children and grandchildren. I am sorry. Forgive me. I will tell my brothers not to hunt your people any longer."

But the chief was still sad. "It is too late to stop killing us. We are all dead now. My granddaughter and I are all that is left."

"But I did not mean to kill you all!" exclaimed the young hunter as a tear filled his eye. "Is there not something I can do?" he asked the old father Squirrel.

"There is a way," said the chief. "I can make you a great shaman and you can return my people."

The young Tsimshian agreed, and so the old man began to work his powerful magic. He took the boy outside and tied his limbs to the tree. Then he pushed sharp needles with string through his skin and pulled them tight in every direction. There was a piercing needle for every dead squirrel. The boy screamed in pain, but the old man said that the pain was part of the power. When he was finished, the chief left the boy hanging for three days. On the third day he returned and sang his magic song for three more days. He did not rest, and he did not eat or drink either. After that, the chief left the boy alone.

One day, the boy's two younger brothers were out hunting squirrels when they came across the carcass of their brother who had been lost for six days. It was hanging in a tall tree just as they had hung the squirrel furs at their house. They cut him down and took his body home.

That night, after they arrived with their dead brother, a magic filled the entire village and all of the dead squirrels came back to life.

They ran back to the Great House and told the chief what had happened. After all of the squirrels were returned, the spirit of the young man flew back into his dead body and returned him to life. From that time on, he was a great and powerful shaman and the Tsimshian did not kill squirrels.

Source: Smelcer, J.E. (1996, Summer). Two conservation myths from Alaska Native oral tradition. *Literary Review, 39*(4), 478–481.

APPENDIX 7.2

IROQUOIS CREATION STORY—EARTH DIVER

The first people were the Sky People, they lived beyond the sky because there was no earth beneath. One day the chief's daughter became very ill and no one was able to provide a cure for her sickness. A wise elder was consulted and he told them to dig up a tree and lay the girl beside the hole that remained. The Sky People respected the elder and began to dig up the tree. Suddenly the tree fell down through the hole and dragged the chief's daughter with it. As the girl fell she saw that below was only an ocean of water. Two swans were alarmed by the girl falling and decided she was too beautiful to drown so they swam to catch her. They landed her on the back of the Great Turtle, and all of the animals of the earth gathered. The Great Turtle counsels that the Sky Woman is a symbol of good fortune. He orders the animals to find where the Sky World tree had landed in the ocean and to bring it back with its earth-covered roots. The swans lead the animals to the place where the tree had fallen into the ocean. First otter, then muskrat, and then beaver dove in search of the tree. Each animal came back to the surface without the tree and died from exhaustion. Many other animals tried but they also died. An elder woman toad volunteered. She dove and remained below a long time. All of the animals thought she had been lost, when at last she surfaced and before dying managed to spit a mouthful of earth onto the back of the Great Turtle. This earth was magical and contained the power of growth. The island grew and grew until it was large enough for the Sky Woman to live on. The two swans set the woman upon the island and circled it encouraging it to grow into the world island it is today. Yet the world was dark. Again the Great Turtle called for the animals to gather. They decided to put a great light in the sky. A little turtle volunteered and climbed up to the sky with the help of the other animals' magic. Little turtle climbed into a black cloud and crawled around the sky collecting the lightning as she went. She made a big bright ball from the lightning and threw it into the sky. Then she collected more for a smaller ball which she also threw into the sky. The first ball became the sun, the second ball became the moon. Then the Great Turtle commanded the burrowing animals to make holes in the corners of the sky so that the sun and moon could go down through one and climb up again through the other as they circled. So there was day and night. The Sky woman lived on the island on top of the Great Turtle's back. She gave birth to twins, one good called Tharonhiawagon, one evil called Tawiskaron. From the breast of Sky Woman grows three sisters corn, beans, and squash.

Source: Axtell, J. (Ed.). (1981). *The Indian peoples of Eastern America: A documentary history of the sexes.* New York: Oxford University Press. http://www.ucalgary.ca/ applied_history/tutor/firstnations/earth.html.

APPENDIX 7.3

Mi'kmaq Creation Story—Two Creators and Their Conflicts

Before the earth was new, the sun was all that existed in the great universe. The sun divided the earth into several parts separated by many great lakes. In each part he caused one man and one woman to be born. They bore children and lived for many years. Wickedness pervaded this family, and slowly they killed one another. The sun wept and wept with grief. The tears became rain that fell from the skies until water covered the entire earth. The family had to set sail in bark canoes to save themselves from the flood. A violent wind overturned their boats. All perished in the sea but the old man and the old woman, who were best of all people, and it was they who populated the earth.

Source: Whitehead, R.H. (Ed.). (1991). *The old man told us: excerpts from Micmac history, 1500-1950.* Halifax: Nimbus. http://www.ucalgary.ca/applied_history/tutor/ firstnations/mikmaq.html.

APPENDIX 7.4

The Cree Creation Story

So then, I shall tell another legend. I'll tell a story, the legend about ourselves, the people, as we are called. Also I shall tell the legend about where we came from and why we came, why we who are living now came to inhabit this land.

Now then, first I shall begin.

The other land was above, it is said. It was like this land which we dwell in, except that the life seems different; also it is different on account of its being cold and mild [here]. So then, this land where we are invariably tends to be cold.

So that is the land above which is talked about from which there came two people, one woman and one man, ... they dwelt in that land which was above. But it was certainly known that this world where we live was there.

Now then at one time someone spoke to them, while they were in that land of theirs where they were brought up. He said to them, "Do you want to go see yonder land which is below?"

The very one about which they were spoken to is this one where we dwell.

"Yes," they said, "we will go there."

"That land," they were told, "is different, appears different from this one which we dwell in, which you dwell in now during your lifetime. But you will find it different there, should you go to see that land. It is cold yonder. And sometimes it is hot."

"It fluctuates considerably. If you wish to go there, however, you must go see the spider at the end of this land where you are. That is where he lives."

The spider, as he is called, that is the one who is the net-maker, who never exhausts his twine,—so they went to see him, who is called the spider. So they reached him.

Then he asked them, "Where do you want to go? Do you want to go and see yonder land, the other one which is below?"

"Yes," they said.

"Very well," said the spider. "I shall make a line so that I may lower you."

So then, he made a line up to,—working it around up to, up to the top.

"Not yet, not yet even half done," he said.

Then he spoke to them telling them, better for him to let them down even before he finished it the length it should be.

Then he told them, "That land which you want to go and see is cold and sometimes mild. But there will certainly be someone there who will teach you, where you will find a living once you have reached it. He, he will tell you everything so you will get along well."

So he made a place for them to sit as he lowered them, the man and the woman.

They got in together, into that thing which looked like a bag.

Then he instructed them what to do during their trip. "Only one must look," he said to them. "But one must not look until you have made contact with the earth. You may both look then."

So, meanwhile as they went along, one looked. At last he caught sight of the land.

The one told the other, "Now the land is in sight."

Again the first told the other, "Now the rivers are in sight."

They had been told however, that "if one, ... if they both look together, before they come to the land, they will go into the great eagle-nest and they will never be able to get out and climb down from there."

That's where they will be. That's what they were told.

Then the one told the other, "Now the lakes are in sight. Now the grass."

Then they both looked before they arrived, as they were right at the top of the trees. Then they went sideways for a short while; then they went into the great eagle-nest. That's where they went in, having violated their instructions.

Now then, "Look down!"

They saw all the creatures which live there on earth: the bear, the caribou, the beaver, the otter, the fisher, the mink, the wolverine, the lynx.

Then at one point the caribou walked there right across [from them].

They said to him, "Come and help us. We cannot get down."

The caribou said to them, "No. I never climb up."

He showed them what his hooves looked like.

Then the lynx came by.

So once more they said to him, "Come and help us."

"Never, ... not ever am I climbing," said the lynx.

He was not telling the truth. He was deceiving them. Then away he went again past them.

Then the bear arrived.

So he said to them, ... they said to him, "Come and help us."

The bear didn't listen for long; but then he started to get up on his hind legs to go and see them. Also another one, the wolverine as he is called. They made one trip each as they brought them down.

But the bear was followed by those people.

That was the very thing which had been said to them, "You will have someone there who will teach you to survive."

This bear, he taught them everything about how to keep alive there.

It was there that these people began to multiply from one couple, the persons who had come from another land. They lived giving birth to their children generation after generation. That is us right up until today. That is why we are in this country.

And by-and-by the White People began to arrive as they began to reach us people, who live in this country.

That is as much as I shall tell.

Source: Ellis, C.D. (Ed.). (1995). *Cree legends and narratives from the west coast of James Bay*. Winnipeg: University of Manitoba Press. Used by permission of University of Manitoba Press.

Western Expansion and Treaties

INTRODUCTION

Following the American Revolution, a massive influx of settlers into Upper Canada began. Land was needed for settlement, and in keeping with the *Royal Proclamation of 1763* the British began the tedious process of acquiring Indian land through treaty. Although Aboriginal people did not have a full understanding of the treaty-making process, they had no choice but to engage in it; with Canada competing with its US neighbours for occupancy and therefore title over lands and access to resources, the British felt pressure to expand westward.

Once occupancy was established, the "Indian question" remained. What would the colonies do with regard to the Indians with whom they had entered into treaties? The newly formed government of Canada chose to embark upon a journey of forced assimilation by carefully enacting legislation designed to eliminate the Indians as a special group within Canadian society.

TREATIES BACKGROUND

Most **treaties** in Canada were signed between 1800 and the early 1900s. They are documents drawn up by the government of Canada during this period as purchase agreements for land recognized as having Aboriginal title. In 1982 the treaties were protected in s. 35 of the *Canadian Charter of Rights and Freedoms*, which reads as follows: "The existing aboriginal and treaty rights of the aboriginal peoples of Canada are hereby recognized and affirmed." This is a recent affirmation of the legitimacy of these documents. Aboriginal people continue to petition the government of Canada to fulfill its treaty promises and to have the original spirit of the treaties interpreted by the courts to uphold Aboriginal rights to resources and land.

Treaties were not unknown to Aboriginal people prior to the arrival of Europeans. Since time immemorial, treaties had been made among Aboriginal nations to settle wars, delineate harvest territories, and facilitate trade alliances. The records of these treaties were passed down orally and were honoured by the groups who entered into them. The most frequent subject matter of treaties related to peace and friendship, military alliance, boundaries, or trade.

CHAPTER OBJECTIVES

After completing this chapter, you should be able to:

- Discuss Western expansion and relate it to the Western European cultural world view.
- Understand the treaty-making process, and the benefits and disadvantages for the British and the First Nations involved.
- Identify the assimilation policies and legislation set out by the Dominion of Canada with regard to First Nations people.
- Discuss the legal, moral, and ethical implications of those policies.

treaty
an agreement between two states that has been formally concluded and ratified

When Europeans arrived, Aboriginal people entered into treaties with them as well, including the Two Row Wampum treaty between the Iroquois and the British, which we read about in the previous chapter. Another example of a peace and friendship treaty was the one made between the British and the Mi'kmaq of Nova Scotia in 1725. The British secured military neutrality and assistance from the Mi'kmaq in their war against the French in exchange for facilitating trade and guaranteeing protection of the Mi'kmaq people's traditional economy of hunting and fishing.

Aboriginal people expected that the principles that had governed their earlier agreements—treaties of peace and friendship; military and trade alliances—to carry over into their negotiations with the Europeans over land. To them, mutual respect and understanding were essential components of negotiations. And they assumed, in keeping with the principles of their oral culture, that terms negotiated by way of discussion would be included in the final agreement.

This was not the case for Europeans; they had a different conception of written documents as opposed to spoken assurances, and different goals for the negotiations. Aboriginal people believed that no one could own the land in the European sense of ownership. The land was a gift from the Creator, and they were stewards of the land, not owners of it. Aboriginal people viewed the treaties as laying out the terms of a mutual sharing of resources, including their own compensation for consenting to share with Europeans.

Europeans understood the treaties, according to their own cultural context, as requiring Aboriginal people to yield the land to the Europeans, thus giving the Europeans absolute ownership of the land. The intention was to erase Aboriginal title to the land so that it could be parcelled out for ownership. Although both parties had interpreters present, it was difficult to translate the European understanding of ownership into terms the Aboriginal negotiators would grasp. In retrospect, too, one must wonder how diligent the Crown was to convey its intended meaning; a full understanding on the part of the Aboriginal people would most certainly have brought negotiations to an unsuccessful conclusion. Many times it was not until the Europeans began the process of removing Aboriginal people from their land that the latter fully understood what they had signed.

There are three categories of treaties in Canada: (1) pre-Confederation treaties, which were entered into before 1867; (2) numbered treaties, signed between 1871 and 1921, and intended to unite the interior of Canada and formally recognize these territories as part of Canada, as well as to clear title to build a railway to facilitate the extraction of resources; and (3) land claims agreements, which were made after 1973 when the government established a formal land claims policy.

All treaties before 1973 were initiated by Europeans. Aboriginal people never began any negotiations to sell their land. Following the defeat of the British in the American Revolution of 1776, the British sought land to compensate both their Aboriginal allies—primarily, the Six Nations (Mohawk, Onondaga, Cayuga, Seneca, Oneida, and Tuscarora), who performed military services for and sustained considerable losses for the British—and their other military allies. In 1874, Frederick Haldimand purchased 3 million acres (1.2 million hectares) from the Mississauga for £1,180 worth of goods to facilitate the settlement of the Loyalists. The Iroquois loyalists were granted a tract 6 miles (10 kilometres) wide on either side of the Grand River, a total of almost 1.2 million hectares in what is today southwestern

Ontario. This is known today as the Haldimand Grant, which provided a land base for the Six Nations reserve. In Chapter 11, we will look at this grant and discuss its implications for today.

Until 1798, the government had no problem obtaining Indian land, through treaty, for about 3 pence per acre in either cash or goods, then selling that land for a healthy profit to private investors and settlers for 6 to 15 pence per acre. By 1912, there were 483 treaties listed for Canada, comprising a considerable body of law (Dickason, 1997, p. 163).

Aboriginal allies became the deciding factor in yet another war—the War of 1812—as the newly independent United States attempted to make its way north into British-held territory. The British were victorious and in the end established a border between the United States and Canada. In the following years of peace, the European population in Canada once again exploded. Between 1821 and 1851, the European population rose from 750,000 to 2.3 million (Dickason, 1997, p. 198). Once again the Crown was desperate for land to accommodate the population growth. With peace in sight, the British had less need of their Aboriginal allies, who thus lost one of their key means of maintaining a balance of power. The government began to offer Aboriginal people annuities for their land rather than the considerably larger one-sum payments. This was a more economical way for the Crown to obtain land through treaty, as the annuities could be paid from the profitable sale of the land to settlers.

The treaty-making process was quite irregular. The Crown representative was included as a negotiator, but otherwise there seems to have been no standard policy, especially concerning the price of land. In 1790, for example, 2 million acres were purchased by the Crown for £1,200 from the Ojibwa and Odawa in southern Ontario. Two years later, 3 million acres (1.2 million hectares) were purchased from the same group for the same amount (Dickason, 1997, p. 164). Many of these land transactions were not properly recorded or were imprecise in their terms regarding boundaries, giving rise to later disputes. For example, one treaty, aptly named the "gunshot treaty," describes a boundary as being "from the lakeshore to as far back as you can hear a gunshot." Many of the original treaties were lost. By the mid-1830s, a sequence of over 30 treaties had been concluded, effectively covering southern Ontario.

NUMBERED TREATIES

Following Confederation in 1867, treaty negotiations with a large number of Aboriginal groups across Canada began. These treaties are referred to as the "numbered treaties"; they were made in the interest of nation building and to acquire land for a national railway. The terms of the 1850 Huron Robinson treaty became a precedent for the other numbered treaties. These terms included the following:

- Sale of reserved lands and mineral rights was to be conducted by the government for the sole use and benefit of the Indians.
- Negotiations were to be open and accessible to the public.
- Land was to be surrendered only to the Crown.
- Annexed to each treaty, a schedule of reserves was to be held in common by each group affected by the treaty.

- Annuities were to be paid in cash to signing members.
- Aboriginal peoples "retain the full privilege to hunt over territory ceded by them, except such lands as are sold by private individuals."

The numbered treaties based the quantity of land reserved for Aboriginal people on their population in the treatied area at the time. These populations were smaller than pre-contact populations, as Aboriginal peoples had sustained at least an 80 percent death toll due to European diseases. Agreements regarding schooling, annuities, and agricultural equipment for Aboriginal peoples were included, among other things, in most numbered treaties.

This brings us to a common misconception among Canadians. Some believe that federally funded education, housing, or taxation exemption are special and generous provisions from the federal government for Aboriginal people. This is not the case; the federal government has frequently tried to escape these obligations but has been instructed by the courts that the treaties hold the force of law and must be honoured. These benefits were granted Aboriginal people in negotiated treaties by which the Crown acquired the land that is now Canada. In the words of the treaties, these terms are to be upheld "as long as the grass is green, as long as the sun shines and the rivers flow."

There were many problems with the treaty process. First, as discussed previously, there was the problem of making the Aboriginal people understand such concepts as exclusive possession of property. Second, there was the government's tendency to be unscrupulous in weighting the written terms of the agreement more heavily than the oral ones that the Aboriginal negotiators considered binding. Today, efforts have been made to research the recorded minutes of council meetings before and after the signing of the treaty. This research has brought to light promises that were clearly made by the government but never written into treaty documents, which were then signed by individuals who could not read. Third, there was the problem of obtaining signatures from the leaders of Aboriginal groups affected by the treaty. Many Aboriginal nations were left out of the treaty-signing process simply because government officials did not know they were there. With a stroke of a pen, the government seized the land of these people without their permission or signatures. Adhesions had to be made later to the treaties to include some groups who had been overlooked.

WESTERN EXPANSION

The pressure to populate the West with white settlers intensified following the conclusion of the American Revolution in 1783. It was apparent that the western lands and all the wealth and resources therein would belong to whoever could get there first and be prepared to defend it. The newly independent United States had severed its ties with Britain and therefore was no longer bound by the *Royal Proclamation*. The United States embarked on a series of wars against the original inhabitants of the West in order to clear them from the land. Twice the Americans were defeated, but they managed to break through in the battle of Fallen Timbers in 1794. The British chose not to come to the aid of their former Aboriginal allies; in fact, they closed the gates of the forts closest to the battle.

The British colonies created incentives for immigrants and other white settlers to move west, enticing agricultural settlers with 64 hectares of free "Crown land." Rapid work was required to obtain that land from the current occupants by way of treaty. The protection of this western land would be provided in part by the Indians themselves. Recall that the United States concluded terms of independence in 1783. After this, the British were concerned about the Americans moving west and northward, as well as about the possibility of an American attack on the remaining British colonies, which would ultimately happen in 1812. The British had learned a valuable lesson in their wars against the French: the side with the most Aboriginal allies would win. Between 1784 and 1788, the British spent £20,000 on gift distributions to Aboriginal people, hoping to secure military allegiance as they moved westward. This was more than the British had paid to secure land through most of the treaties to that date. They were successful in securing the allegiance of Tecumseh, who was a powerful Aboriginal leader. He sided with the British and united more than 30 nations to lead in the defence of British-held territories. Together they helped the British repel the Americans in the War of 1812. Tecumseh sided with the British not only for the gift distributions but also because he believed them to be the lesser of two evils, as the British continued to make assurances of protecting Indian lands, an assurance that the United States would not make. Consider what Tecumseh said in 1795:

> My heart is a stone. Heavy with sadness for my people; cold with the knowledge that no treaty will keep the whites out of our land; hard with determination to resist as long as I live and breathe. Now we are weak and many of our people are afraid. But hear me; a single twig breaks but the bundle of twigs is strong. Someday I will embrace our brother tribes and draw them into a bundle and together we will win our country back from the whites.

Following the War of 1812, western expansion accelerated again. Northwestern Indians such as the Sioux, Blackfoot, and Plains Cree, as well as the Métis, had built an economy based on the buffalo. Upon the arrival of traders, a market was quickly created for buffalo products. The hides became fashionable to wear, and the bones were exported to create bone china, popular in Europe. In less than a century, by 1835, the number of buffalo had been reduced from 70 million to 635. Needless to say, this caused extreme hardship among the Aboriginal peoples of the plains at a time when treaty negotiations were fully under way.

Ultimately, Europeans made it all the way to the West Coast of Canada. In 1785 the first trading ships arrived, drawn by the lucrative trade in sea otter pelts. Contact and trade were done by ship because an overland route was not found until 1804. Within the first 100 years of contact, West Coast peoples suffered an 80 percent population decrease due to European diseases, one of the most dramatic declines in an Aboriginal population since first contact (Dickason, 1997, p. 180).

Sea otter pelt trading was in full swing by 1792, and by 1825 the sea otter population was decimated. One trader, John Kendrick, reported that he traded £100 worth of chisels and iron tools for 200 sea otter pelts. He then received £8,000 for the pelts in Europe (Dickason, 1997, p. 181).

In 1852, Vancouver Island had only 500 settlers; however, the discovery of gold led to the convergence of 25,000 miners on Queen Charlotte Island in 1858. Salish First Nations and miners clashed regularly, sometimes violently. The destruction of Aboriginal territories was rapid, and their land base eroded with the building of roads and mines.

Salmon resources were being exploited for export to European markets. Salmon was a main source of subsistence for many First Nations such as the Nisga'a, and the depletion of this resource caused them significant hardship.

James Douglas, governor of Vancouver and the British Columbia mainland at this critical time, attempted to acquire land by way of treaty. He had signed 14 treaties with Salish bands on the Island of Vancouver by 1854, but this amounted to only 3 percent of the island's territory. Aboriginal people were not eager to enter into treaties, and James Douglas quickly ran out of money. Although the colony offered no further finances, Douglas was undeterred and continued to establish reservations for the First Nations people based on their favourite locations and on their numbers. He allotted 200 acres (91 hectares) per head of family, then simply assumed the rest of Vancouver and British Columbia to be territory of the Crown. He retired in 1864 and was succeeded by Frederick Seymore, who appointed a commissioner of Crown lands, Joseph Trutch. Trutch refused to recognize the legitimacy of the reserves established by Douglas, and was hostile to Aboriginal land claims. He wrote:

> The Amerindians have no rights to the land as they were of no actual value to them, and I cannot see why they should either retain these lands to the prejudice of the general interests of the colony. Or be allowed to make a market of them to either the government or individuals. (Dickason, 1997, p. 234)

Trutch proceeded to reduce the size of the reserves surveyed by Douglas from 81 hectares per head of family to 4, again without compensation.

British Columbia entered Confederation with Canada in 1871 and was allowed to retain control over "Crown land." But the federal government assumed responsibility for Indians and lands reserved for Indians as per the *British North America Act* of 1867. Arguments between provincial and federal governments began over how much land was to be granted for reserved land for Indians. British Columbia tried to reduce the lands even further, to 4 acres (1.6 hectares) per head of family, but the federal government insisted on 80 acres (32 hectares). British Columbia persisted in assigning reserves for Aboriginal nations without compensation, and by 1900 there were over 90 reservations established at an average of 75 hectares per reserve (Dickason, 1997, p. 234–235).

Note the emerging pattern here with regard to the seizure of land and resources. Most of the resources were exported to Europe; however, much of the wealth thereby produced went toward building what is now our very affluent country. In fact, Canada is still reliant for its wealth on natural resources such as timber, oil, and gas; owners of land often grow wealthy from its natural resources. Unfortunately, Aboriginal peoples generally do not share in this wealth. As we will see in Chapter 10, Aboriginal people still suffer from higher than average levels of poverty and today live on only one-half of 1 percent of Canada's land mass.

EXERCISE 1

Read Appendix 8.1 as a class. Discuss the word "progress" from different cultural world views.

VANISHING RACE

The sizing of almost all reserves through the treaty process was based on the population of the Aboriginal group at the time of the treaty. But Aboriginal populations were low during this period, and the treaties made no provision for an increase in numbers. This seems evidence of a strong belief that Aboriginal people were vanishing. And in fact they were dying at a rapid rate from disease, and many were lost in the numerous wars among the colonists. It was generally believed that within three generations of treaty making there would be no Indians left; they would either die of disease or be assimilated into mainstream Canada.

The Canadian government's intent regarding Aboriginal people was never made so clear as it was by Deputy Superintendent of Indian Affairs Duncan Campbell Scott in 1920 (quoted in Leslie & Maguire, 1978):

> I want to get rid of the Indian problem. I do not think as a matter of fact that this country ought to continually protect a class of people who are able to stand alone. That is my whole point. ... That has been the whole purpose of Indian Education and advancement since earliest times. One of the very earliest enactments was to provide for the enfranchisement of the Indian. So it is written in our law that the Indian was eventually to become enfranchised. ... Our object is to continue until there is not a single Indian in Canada that has not been absorbed into the body politic and there is no Indian question, and no Indian department, that is the whole object of this Bill.

Scott's view was reflected in the actions of certain Canadians during this period. Aboriginal graves, often fresh, were dug up so that the remains could be put on display at Wild West shows. Spiritual and cultural artifacts still in use by Aboriginals were taken and sold to collectors, who anticipated their value increasing as the Aboriginal people themselves vanished. Today, Aboriginal nations have undertaken serious efforts to repatriate these items and bring them back to their communities from museums around the world.

The idea of the Aboriginal peoples' vanishing was appealing to the British for one very important reason: the treaties they had entered into with these nations were binding in perpetuity. The British could see that the cost of maintaining these promises forever could be high, particularly because the depletion of resources was impoverishing Aboriginal nations and creating a need among them for the relief assistance guaranteed by the treaties. Assimilation of those who survived disease and poverty became a paramount concern for the British in the years to come. The complete assimilation of Indians meant no obligation to honour treaties, and it meant free access to reserve lands.

EXERCISE 2

As a class, read and discuss Appendix 8.2. Consider the author's political position. Consider the meaning of the poem.

THIRST FOR LAND

During the treaty process and later, it proved difficult to keep settlers and resource speculators off reserve land. Several British parliamentary inquiries were undertaken to address this problem. One, in 1830, found that people were circumventing the *Royal Proclamation* and fraudulently purchasing reserve land. Furthermore, squatters were settling on the land and, as time passed, laying claim to it. The *Royal Proclamation* contributed to the problem of squatting; it stated that all purchases of Indian land had to go through the Superintendent of Indian Affairs. Since there was only one superintendent for the colonies, purchasing was a lengthy process in a system that was desperately underfunded.

To address this problem, the Crown drafted the *Crown Lands Protection Act, 1839*, declaring Aboriginal reserve lands to be Crown lands. This entrenched the emerging idea of wardship and removed Aboriginal peoples' authority to make decisions about their own land use. Nonetheless, the Crown was unable to stop the encroachment onto Aboriginal lands. In 1842, the Bagot Commission reaffirmed the *Royal Proclamation*, asserting that Aboriginal people must be compensated for any land lost to settlement or resource harvesting. This commission's work was cited later when new legislation was passed in 1850 in an attempt to control the intrusion of loggers into reserve areas in Temiskaming and the Ottawa Valley.

Its attempts to protect Indian reserve land led to the Crown's having to define an "Indian." Prior to 1830, Aboriginal people were self-defining, as any self-governing body of people are. They determined membership in their group and the transfer of members in and out of the group. When the Crown took on the paternalistic role of controlling the land, it needed to define *Indian*, since it set out clearly that only Indians of the band could reside on the reserve. The following were considered Indians under the definition fashioned by the Crown:

- All individuals of Indian blood belonging to a tribe, band, or body of Indians and their descendants.

- Any person residing among such Indians whose parents were or are descended on either side from Indians, and the descendants of this person.

- All women lawfully married to an Indian and their children. Aboriginal women who married non-Aboriginal men would not be entitled to be Indian; nor would their children.

In 1830, the British began attempts to assimilate Aboriginal people into mainstream culture, pushing them to become agriculturalists, to set up communities similar to white settlements, and to adopt Christian religions and ways of life. Some Aboriginal nations accepted this transition and requested assistance with it; they recognized that the industrialization of their lands would make the hunting way of life impossible. Furthermore, they believed that conversion to the "ideal" might help protect their lands. Model villages were set up and overseen by missionaries; many were quite successful. However, regardless of their success, as white communities expanded, the model villages experienced loss of land, and many were relocated. The genius of this plan was that the finances required to set up these communities and begin the "civilizing" process would come from the funds generated through the sale of reserve land or through the extraction of resources such as lumber from reserve lands. In effect, Aboriginal people would pay their own way to "civilization" (Dickason, 1997, p. 199).

In 1836, Upper Canada, under the leadership of Sir Francis Bond Head, intended to move all these settled communities to the isolation of Manitoulin Island. Head managed to secure Manitoulin Island from the Ojibwa with the simple promise that it would be protected by the Crown against settler encroachment. No payment accompanied that promise. He then secured an agreement from the Saugeen Ojibwa from the Bruce Peninsula to trade 1.5 million acres (0.6 million hectares) of the Saugeen tract's fertile land for the northern tip of the Bruce Peninsula. Head advised them that he could not control the squatters settling on their land and therefore they must relocate to Manitoulin Island or the northern tip of the Bruce Peninsula. In effect, they received granite rocks and bog land in exchange for their fertile territory in the Saugeen tract (Dickason, 1997, p. 211).

ASSIMILATION LEGISLATION

The Crown passed legislation in 1857 called the *Gradual Civilization Act* to create a process of enfranchisement for Aboriginal people, so that they could cease being Aboriginal. Enfranchisement began as a voluntary process. The legislation set out that if an Aboriginal male was self-supporting, debt-free, and deemed by the superintendent to be a suitable candidate for enfranchisement, he could forfeit his status as an Indian and receive 20 hectares of land cut from his people's reserve. Furthermore, he would thereafter have all the rights of a regular citizen, including the right to vote in provincial and federal elections. This legislation, if it had been successful, would have eroded the reserve land base as well as Aboriginal sovereignty (Dickason, 1997, p. 225).

This enfranchisement plan was less than successful, however; only one person applied to be enfranchised, Elias Hill from the Six Nations Reserve in southwestern Ontario. He lost his status but never received the promised 20 hectares of land because the Six Nations Council, seeing the legislation for what it was, refused to surrender the land.

In 1869, the *Enfranchisement Act* was introduced to limit blood quantum to one-quarter Indian in order to qualify to remain a status Indian. All others would be removed automatically from treaty entitlements. The purpose of this legislation, in the words of a bureaucrat in 1871, was "to lead the Indian people by degrees to mingle with the white race in the ordinary avocations of life" (Miller, 2004). The result would be fewer treaty Indians. Amazingly, this focus continued to be central to all legislation designed to administer Indian people until 1985.

During Confederation in 1867, at a time when efforts were focused on nation building, the Canadian government passed the **British North America Act**. Aboriginal people were not consulted in the creation of the Act, and the Act did not recognize the right of Aboriginal self-government. Section 91(24) of this Act gave Canada authority over Indians and lands reserved for Indians. Many historians believe this was a turning point in history that marked the beginning of an era of serious oppression of Aboriginal people in Canada. Through the BNA Act, the power of Aboriginal governments was reduced to less than that of a municipality. Power would be held by the federal government with no regard to the diversity of Aboriginal people,

British North America Act
a statute enacted on March 29, 1867, by the British Parliament providing for the confederation of Canada

their culture, or their historical relationship with the Crown. They would all be treated as one homogeneous group and governed by a one-size-fits-all policy. They would no longer have the right to negotiate with the British Crown in regard to legislation affecting them or their lands; rather, they would have to negotiate with the federal government, which had a keen interest in acquiring the lands occupied by Aboriginal people.

THE INDIAN ACT

Indian Act
a statute created in 1876 to consolidate all policies aimed at the administration of Indian populations in Canada and giving the federal government exclusive jurisdiction over Indians and reserves

Within nine years of Confederation, the legislation regarding Indians was consolidated into one act called the **Indian Act**. The *Indian Act* retained the earlier definition of an Indian but, continuing to broaden its scope of authority, now defined a band as well (Dickason, 1997, p. 259). According to the *Indian Act*, a "band" is

a body of Indians

(a) for whose use and benefit in common, lands, the legal title to which is vested in Her Majesty, have been set apart before, on or after September 4, 1951,

(b) for whose use and benefit in common, moneys are held by Her Majesty, or

(c) declared by the Governor in Council to be a band for the purposes of this Act.

The lands referred to in paragraph (a), above, refer to a reserve. Many Aboriginal groups are still awaiting designation as bands in accordance with this legislation; without such designation, the government does not afford them any benefits or protection. There are currently 633 recognized bands in Canada and 116 in Ontario.

The *Indian Act* did not include the Inuit because there was little contact between Canada and the Inuit at the time. The government was intent on reducing rather than increasing the number of Indians. So when the Inuit question arose in the 1930s, Ottawa's position was that since the Inuit are not culturally Indians, they were not included in the *British North America Act*, s. 91(24), which designated the federal government's responsibility for Indians. In the 1930s, the Inuit were hard hit by a scarcity in the game that were their traditional source of sustenance, and they needed relief assistance. Neither level of government wanted any responsibility to provide this assistance, even though fur traders, miners, and whalers had spent decades extracting resources from Inuit land without compensating the land's inhabitants. The Quebec government took the federal government to court, arguing that the Inuit were Indians for all intents and purposes and should fall under the authority of the federal government. In 1939, the Supreme Court of Canada ruled that the Inuit, although culturally distinct, would be considered Indians, but would not be included in the *Indian Act*.

Despite the Inuit's being legally classified as Indians, the government neglected them until after the Second World War, when the need arose for military expansion into the North. Between 1941 and 1970 the federal government used a disk system to identify those Inuit for which it accepted responsibility. The disk bore the Canadian coat of arms and a number by which the wearer could be identified; it had a hole punched in it so it could be fastened by a string around the neck. This simplified record keeping, since the naming system used by the Inuit was unfamiliar to the government. The disk evolved into proof of status; those who had disks were eligible for government services, those without were not.

Other groups were also left out of the legislation aimed at Indians, including the Innu of Newfoundland and Labrador. When these territories entered Confederation in 1949, the rights of Indians to be defined and dealt with in accordance with Canadian legislation such as the *Indian Act* were originally included in the documents but were pencilled out prior to ratification, leaving the Innu with no protection for their territories and no guarantees of any assistance in times of need.

Imposed System of Government

The *Indian Act* quickly provided for the removal of Aboriginal peoples' traditional systems of governance and replaced them with a system called the band council. It is similar in nature to municipal governments in that it comprises one chief and several councillors through an election process that is strictly regulated by the Act. This system was implemented for all Aboriginal groups in a "one size fits all" fashion with no consideration given to the diverse forms of government and culture across First Nations groups. Furthermore, a person called the Indian agent (a white government official set in place to oversee the functions of the reserve) had authority, set out in the Act, to remove the chief or council members for any number of reasons.

Some nations resisted this intrusion on their established systems of government, the Six Nations being one of them. This band tried to resist the transition to an elected band council by agitating for change to the system and petitioning the Queen, insisting they were allies, not subjects, of the British Crown, and had never given up their sovereignty. In 1924, Deputy Superintendent General of Indian Affairs Duncan Campbell Scott ordered the overthrow of the Six Nations' traditional council by force.

Lt. Col. Morgan was charged with the responsibility of overseeing troops provided by the RCMP to overthrow the traditional council and oversee the institution of the first elected band council for the Six Nations.

Gender Discrimination Within the Act

Aboriginal women who had lost their status and that of their children by marrying non-Aboriginal men began to appeal their situation in the mid-20th century; they asserted that this loss was discrimination under the *Canadian Bill of Rights*, which guaranteed the equality of women under the law. These women argued their case on the grounds that Aboriginal men who married non-Aboriginal women did not lose their status and that, furthermore, their non-Aboriginal wives were given status as Indians. Their appeals were unsuccessful; an astonishing 5:4 ruling by the Supreme Court of Canada in the 1974 case *Attorney General of Canada v. Lavell* ruled that the *Indian Act* took precedence over the *Bill of Rights*.

An appeal was made to the United Nations Human Rights Committee, which found Canada was in violation of the *International Covenant on Civil and Political Rights* in denying women their rights to status because of marriage. This was very embarrassing to Canada, a country renowned for its work and advancement in the area of human rights. The result was the passing of Bill C-31 in 1985, which allowed those Aboriginal women who had lost their treaty rights through marriage to re-apply.

The federal government estimated that there would be about 50,000 women who would qualify for reinstatement and that about 20 percent of them would apply. However, over 100,000 people applied, and by 1991 almost 70,000 had been reinstated on application, increasing the number of status Indians dramatically. Nevertheless, a funding increase did not accompany the increase in population. Many people who had regained status through Bill C-31 returned to overcrowded reserves looking for shares in treaty benefits such as housing and education. Their return effectively overwhelmed already insufficient resources, and caused division between long-standing status Indians and those newly created through Bill C-31. The Bill left the decision regarding band membership up to individual bands. Some bands that control their membership have refused to allow Bill C-31 Indians to rejoin the band and thereby refused them residency on the reserve. Under Bill C-31, it is now possible to be a status Indian but not a member of a band. Furthermore, the Bill did not rectify the inequities completely; the passing of status from an Indian recognized by Bill C-31 is limited to the third generation, depending on the status of their chosen life partner. This is often referred to as the double-grandmother clause. Changes have been passed again in 2010 to address the continuing inequities in the Act. The changes will be discussed in Chapter 10.

Another inequity within the Act with regard to women was their exclusion from taking part in decisions regarding the surrender of band land. This was included in the original Act and not changed until 1951 when the Act was overhauled. This goes against many Aboriginal societies' understanding that women play a significant role in decisions over land management and are in fact known to be capable guardians of the land.

Tax Exemption

The *Indian Act* included laws surrounding taxation. Aboriginal people living on reserves were not to be taxed either on any purchases they made while living on a reserve or on income generated from on-reserve activities. This provision was included in recognition of the special status accorded to "Reserved Territories" and was rooted in principles concerning Nationhood and self-government. This tax exemption still exists today and is misunderstood by some non-Aboriginals, who perceive it as an unfair advantage. Many Aboriginal people assert that this tax exemption signifies that Aboriginal land is sovereign land and not a part of Canada, based on the fact that Aboriginal people have never surrendered their sovereignty and right to self-government. Many non-Aboriginal people overestimate the benefits of tax exemption. It is only for people living on the reserve and does not provide exemption for income earned off-reserve. Since on-reserve employment is hard to find and on average generates income levels that are less than half the average Canadian income, most Aboriginal people work off-reserve and are subject to income tax and all other taxes that other Canadians pay.

As we will discuss later, 60 percent of Aboriginal people live off-reserve and therefore work off-reserve. Since tax-exemption status is attached to the territory of a reserve, not to the person, fully 60 percent of Aboriginal people pay all of the taxes that other Canadians pay, apart from the 6 percent provincial sales tax (PST) on purchases. Status Indians living off-reserve do not access provincial dollars to obtain services as other non-Aboriginal members of the community do. They are the sole responsibility of the federal government and therefore must access federal funds allocated through Indian Affairs for services. For example, the province funds non-Aboriginal education, while the federal government funds Aboriginal education. It makes sense, then, that Aboriginal people are not forced to contribute to a provincial tax base that they are unable to access for services.

Changes Through Time

The first change to the *Indian Act* in 1880 was to withdraw "half-breeds" (mixed-blood Indians) from treaty agreements. This measure was calculated to quickly reduce the number of Indians that held status and therefore had treaty rights. At the same time, treaty making was ongoing in the Western plains area. The government could see that the buffalo population was in sharp decline and that the Métis, a distinguishable group who had already asserted their right to land, would require assistance in rebuilding their economy. In order to avoid any obligation of assistance, the government encouraged the Métis to accept **scrip**—a one-time payment and small land allocation—in lieu of the assistance they would have been entitled to as treaty Indians.

scrip
a one-time payment issued to Métis to discharge treaty rights

In the same year, the Indian Branch became its own department, with inside staff based in Ottawa, including a superintendent general, a chief clerk, an accountant, and clerical staff, as well as an outside staff comprising 460 field workers responsible for the implementation of policies directed at Indians. These outside workers were called **Indian agents**, and were invested with tremendous authority over the reservation and the people with whom they worked.

Indian agent
a federal employee of Indian Affairs in charge of administration on reserves

A 1958 job study lists the authorities of the Indian agent as follows: dealing with the recording of property; registering births, deaths, and marriages; administering band funds; and holding elections. The Indian agent interviewed people who needed farming equipment, those who complained about land encroachments, and those applying for loans. He encouraged people to marry legally and to enlist in the armed forces. He adjusted property when members left or joined the band. He dealt with the estates of the deceased and supervised the building of infrastructure, including schools. He negotiated the surrender of band lands for highways or other purposes, and applied for relief funds to house those in need. He informed the court of matters concerning Indians who were on trial for criminal matters. He was the justice of the peace and the health inspector for the community and, later, for the schools. He presided over band council meetings and could vote to break a tie. Finally, he enforced the *Indian Act* and policies directed at Indians.

In some cases, Indian agents were capable people with integrity; in others, they were not. In all cases, they were non-Indians. This continued for decades. Slowly, bands have wrested authority for these matters back from the federal government.

In 1880 the "unmaking" of Indians continued, with mandatory enfranchisement of an Aboriginal person if that person held a university degree, joined the clergy or the armed forces, or voted in a federal election. The 1880 changes to the *Indian Act* dispensed with recognition of hereditary chiefs and recognized only elected band council chiefs. Aboriginal peoples in the West were prohibited from selling their agricultural products because the government did not want them to purchase liquor or other "worthless" things.

In 1884, Aboriginal people complained that the government was not fulfilling the treaty agreements that would enable them to use the land; agricultural equipment promised in the treaties was not delivered. The government conceded that this was a legitimate complaint but excused the breach, explaining that the bands were not sufficiently advanced to benefit from the promised tools, livestock, and schools.

The potlatch and other Aboriginal ceremonies were banned in 1884, with a two- to six-month jail term for those who contravened this prohibition. This prohibition was included in the Act but was not enforced until the 1920s under the leadership of Deputy Superintendent General of Indian Affairs Duncan Campbell Scott. Cultural practices and ceremonies went underground to avoid the watchful eye of the Indian agent. These practices had always played a critical part in the Aboriginal oral culture, conveying to the next generation the people's history, their principles of governance, and their spirituality. Repressing these practices resulted in the beginning of loss of culture.

In 1889, the *Indian Act* was amended to allow the federal government to override a band that did not wish to lease land. By 1894, any Indian lands that were not worked (agriculturally) due to illness or injury could be leased to non-Aboriginal Canadians under the authority of the superintendent. Idle or surplus Indian land was also seen as fair game.

In 1911, s. 46 of the *Indian Act* allowed portions of land to be taken by municipalities or companies for roads or railways without consent of the band but with permission of the superintendent. Section 46(a) permitted the removal of Indians, against their wishes, from any reserve next to or partly within a town of 8,000 inhabitants. For example, a Mi'kmaq reserve in Sydney, Nova Scotia and the Songees reserve in Victoria, British Columbia were moved outside these cities to free up urban land for development. In the West, between July 1, 1896, and March 31, 1909, Aboriginal peoples received $74,343 for surrendered land. The Department of Indian Affairs subsequently received $2,156,020 for that land.

The promise of reserved lands through treaty was in some cases not fulfilled; in other cases, the power given to the Indian agent through the *Indian Act* resulted in large sections of reserved lands, coveted by settlers and resource speculators, being carved out of the Aboriginal group's territory, sometimes without compensation. Railways expropriated reserved lands freely, often splitting communities down the centre. The railway towns that were springing up often grew to displace Aboriginal people, and more land was seized, often without compensation, as the towns expanded.

In 1918, the enfranchisement of Aboriginal people was made easier for those who wished to apply; however, the plan still did not meet with success. Subsequently, in 1921, legislation changed to provide the Indian agent with the authority to enfranchise any Indian who was deemed suitable regardless of his or her wishes. In other words, without giving consent, an Indian could lose his or her status with the stroke of a bureaucrat's pen.

You may be wondering why Aboriginal people did not rebel against this oppressive legislation and continued seizure of their lands. In fact they did respond and organize resistance, but it seemed futile. In 1880, in response to political movement in the West to oppose land seizure, a pass system was implemented requiring any Indian leaving the reserve to have a pass issued by the Indian agent. The goal of the system was to inhibit Aboriginal people's mobility and discourage an Aboriginal alliance that might threaten Canadian authority. Many reserves were impoverished due to the depletion of resources, and any sign of political activism was quickly met with governmental threats of withdrawing its relief funds.

In 1927, in a heavy-handed response to Six Nations resistance to coming under the authority of the Act and the West Coast Nisga'a's continued appeals to England, the *Indian Act* was again amended to proclaim that no person could raise money to fund any form of claims to land against the federal government without the express permission of the Indian agent.

EXERCISE 3

The legislated disempowerment of Aboriginal people through legislation such as the *Indian Act* has led to the federal government assuming fiduciary responsibility for First Nations in Canada. **Fiduciary responsibility** is the legal or ethical responsibility to manage something, usually money or property, in trust for another person (or people) and act in their best interests. Discuss as a class whether the federal government has fulfilled this duty. Why or why not?

fiduciary responsibility
the legal or ethical responsibility to manage something, usually money or property, in trust for another person (or people) and act in their best interests

1951: CHANGES TO THE ACT

The *Indian Act* was overhauled in 1951 in an attempt to create a more equitable piece of legislation. The ban on potlatches and other traditional dances and ceremonies was lifted. Over the previous 30 years, however, the passing of Aboriginal culture and oral history to new generations, which was a central function of these practices, had been seriously disrupted.

The Act established the Indian Register as a centralized record of all individuals entitled to be registered. The registrar was given authority to add or delete names from the general band lists. In response to complaints from Indians who were unilaterally removed from the band list or who could not be included on the band list because their births had never been registered, new rules were put in place to require the posting of the band list. An appeal process was instituted for those who were removed from the list, with a limit of six months for appeal.

Despite the overhaul of the Act, there was still no agreement to set up a land claims commission as requested by Aboriginal people. Furthermore, the 1951 revisions to section 88 of the Act allowed "all laws of general application in force in any Province to apply as well to Indians on and off reserves." This was undoubtedly a precursor to the federal government's intention to slowly devolve the responsibilities for Indians on to the provinces. The problem with this amendment was that certain provincial laws, such as hunting and fishing regulations, if applied to Indians, were in violation of rights accorded under treaty. Today, Canadian courts are attempting to navigate their way through layers of treaty and provincial law to provide an equitable interpretation of that law, and to define Aboriginal rights in Canada.

It was not until the early 1960s that Aboriginal people were given the right to vote in federal elections. Soon after, they would use this right to become politically active in opposing the White Paper, proposed by then Liberal Indian Affairs Minister Jean Chrétien. This paper proposed the elimination of the *Indian Act*, the elimination of reserved land for Indians, and the elimination of the special legal category of Status Indian. It further proposed to transfer all responsibilities for Aboriginal people to the provinces and promised to look into land claims. Although assertions were made that the paper was introduced as a path to equality for Aboriginal people in Canada, they viewed it as the final stroke of assimilation. The National Indian Brotherhood stated the following: "We view this as a policy designed to divest us of our aboriginal, residual, and statutory rights. If we accept this policy, and in the process lose our rights and our lands, we become willing partners in culture genocide. This we cannot do" (Dickason, 1997, p. 364).

Once again, a policy had been created with little consultation with Aboriginal people. In the words of Dave Courchene, president of the Manitoba Indian Brotherhood from 1967 to 1974: "Once again the future of the Indian people has been dealt with in a high-handed and arbitrary manner. We have not been consulted; we have been advised of decisions already taken. I feel like a man who has been told he must die and am now to be consulted on the methods of implementing that decision" (Dickason, 1997, p. 364). Cree leader Harold Cardinal stated, "We do not want the Indian Act retained because it is a good piece of legislation. It is not. It's discriminatory from start to finish. But it is a lever in our hands and an embarrassment to the government, as it should be. No just society with even pretensions to being just can long tolerate such a piece of legislation, but we would rather continue to live in bondage under the inequitable Indian Act than surrender our sacred rights. Any time the government wants to honor its obligation to us we are more than ready to help devise new legislation" (Cardinal, 1969, p. 140).

Many treaties had originally been made with the British, and legislation passed the responsibility to honour those treaties to the federal government upon the transfer of power during Confederation. The federal government could not simply exonerate itself of those obligations by passing them on to provincial governments. In 1971, the White Paper was abandoned by the federal government, but the idea of devolving responsibilities for Indians on to the provinces had not disappeared. It resurfaced in 1986, when the *Nielson Report* recommended that the cost of delivering services to Indians be shared by the provinces. This was motivated by the rising costs of program delivery as Aboriginal populations increased dramatically around this time, and their communities were suffering from the effects of the residential school system, which increased the need for social services. This recommendation was abandoned after much protest from Aboriginal people.

A positive change to the *Indian Act* resulted from the fight against the White Paper; for the first time, the federal government agreed to fund research into land claims and to set up processes by which those claims could be negotiated. We will discuss land claims in Chapter 11.

CONCLUSION

The dispossession and disempowerment of Aboriginal people in Canada has been a long process that has spanned generations. This dispossession was purposefully conducted by many levels of government to facilitate expansion and economic growth for Canada; however, First Nations people in Canada rarely benefited from the economic growth. Aggressive policies of assimilation were created to ensure that Status Indians with treaty entitlements would slowly disappear. Canada was unsuccessful in accomplishing that goal and so today we struggle to define Aboriginal rights in Canada in accordance with treaties. Aboriginal people in Canada struggle to reclaim authority over their own affairs, to reclaim lost culture, to rebuild healthy communities, and to create economic growth and prosperity for themselves within Canada.

KEY TERMS

British North America Act
fiduciary responsibility
Indian Act
Indian agent
scrip
treaty

REFERENCES

Armstrong, J.C. (1997). The history lesson. In D.D. Moses and T. Goldie (Eds.), *An anthology of Canadian Native literature in English* (2nd ed.). Toronto: Oxford University Press.

Attorney General of Canada v. Lavell. (1973). [1974] SCR 1349.

Bill C-31. *An Act to Amend the Indian Act.* (1985, April 17).

British North America Act. (1867). 30 & 31 Vict., c. 3.

Canadian Bill of Rights. (1960). SC 1960, c. 44.

Cardinal, H. (1969). *The unjust society: The tragedy of Canada's Indians.* Edmonton: M.G. Hurtig.

Dickason, O.P. (1997). *Canada's First Nations: A history of founding peoples from earliest times* (2nd ed.). Toronto: Oxford University Press.

Indian Act, RSC 1985, c. I-5.

Leslie, J., & Maguire, R. (Eds.). (1978). *The historical development of the Indian Act* (2nd ed.). Ottawa: Indian and Northern Affairs Canada.

Miller, J.R. (2004). *Lethal legacy: Current Native controversies in Canada.* Toronto: Macfarlane Walter & Ross.

Scott, D.C. (1926). The Onondaga Madonna. In *The poems of Duncan Campbell Scott* (p. 230). Toronto: McClelland & Stewart.

REVIEW QUESTIONS

TRUE OR FALSE?

F   1. Most treaties with Aboriginal peoples in Canada were entered into between 1800 and the early 20th century.

F   2. Through the *Indian Act*, the government recognizes traditional forms of Aboriginal government.

T   3. In 1974, a woman appealed to the Supreme Court of Canada in order to regain her Indian status after she lost that status through marriage to a non-Aboriginal man. She was denied re-instatement when the Supreme Court of Canada ruled that the *Indian Act* took precedence over the *Canadian Bill of Rights*.

T   4. The *Constitution Act, 1982* recognizes existing treaty rights.

_____ 5. Treaties are a strictly European creation; Aboriginal peoples never entered into treaties prior to European arrival.

_____ 6. From the first, there was a uniform practice in treaty making, with a set price per acre due in payment by the Crown.

_____ 7. As the British moved west throughout what would become Canada, Aboriginal leader Tecumseh united Aboriginal nations to defend British interests militarily, partly because the British had made assurances to protect Indian lands.

_____ 8. The extraction of natural resources by the British had little effect on Aboriginal economies.

_____ 9. It was not until the 1940s that Aboriginal people were given the right to vote in federal elections.

_____ 10. The White Paper of 1969 proposed the elimination of reserved lands for Indians.

MULTIPLE CHOICE

1. A treaty is

   (a) a promise that is not legally binding

   (b) an agreement between states in written form and governed by international law

   (c) an agreement that is informal in nature

   (d) an agreement between two states that has been formally concluded and ratified

2. Settlers came to Canada to

   (a) seek wealth

   (b) look for land to settle on

   (c) seek freedom from oppression

   (d) all of the above

3. The Huron Robinson treaty of 1850 set a precedent for all future treaties made to acquire lands for settlement. Which of the following is not true of those precedent-setting inclusions to treaties?

    (a) Sales of reserve lands and mineral rights were to be conducted by the government for the sole use and benefit of the Indians.

    (b) Land was to be surrendered only to the Crown.

    (c) Annuities were to be paid.

    (d) Aboriginal people were to forfeit hunting and fishing rights over the land that was ceded in the treaty.

4. Which of the following is not one of the three main problems with the numbered treaties?

    (a) It was difficult to obtain the signatures of all leaders of the groups affected by the treaty.

    (b) The government was unscrupulous in its interpretations of the terms of the treaty.

    (c) Violent reactions from Aboriginal people toward the treaty commissioners undermined the treaty process.

    (d) There were grave problems translating concepts such as exclusive landownership.

5. The government accepted fiduciary responsibility for First Nations people when it passed the *Indian Act*. Fiduciary responsibility means

    (a) the responsibility to cultivate the natural resources on land granted by the government

    (b) the responsibility to educate

    (c) the legal or ethical responsibility to manage something, usually money or property, in trust for another person (or people) and act in their best interests

    (d) the responsibility to civilize

6. The Indian agent assigned to a reservation in the 1950s had powers over which of the following?

    (a) registering births, deaths, and marriages

    (b) band funds

    (c) negotiations for the surrender of reserve lands

    (d) all of the above and more

7. Aboriginal people opposed Chrétien's White Paper, which proposed legislation that would in effect eliminate the *Indian Act*. Why?

    (a) Because they believed that the *Indian Act* was fair and equitable.

    (b) Because they were resistant to change of any kind.

    (c) Because the White Paper did not address the issue of land claims.

    (d) Because the White Paper proposed to eliminate reserve land and treaty status for Indians.

8. Special rights accorded to Aboriginal people in Canada today in the areas of education and taxation are

    (a) an attempt at reconciling the inequalities of the past

    (b) acts of generosity by the Canadian government

    (c) attempts to resolve social problems prevalent on reserves

    (d) obligations of the federal Crown that are rooted in treaty law

9. The concept of the vanishing Indian was important to the British after peace was established. By what means did they attempt to encourage the elimination of Status Indians?

    (a) enfranchisement

    (b) blood quantum definitions of Indians

    (c) both

    (d) neither

10. After the *Indian Act* was established, who had control over the sale of Indian reserve lands?

    (a) Indians

    (b) the federal government through the Indian agent

    (c) band-elected Aboriginal representatives

    (d) traditional councils established by the band

APPENDIX 8.1

THE HISTORY LESSON

By Jeannette C. Armstrong

Out of the belly of Christopher's ship
A mob bursts
Running in all directions
Pulling furs off animals
Shooting buffalo
Shooting each other
Left and right

Father mean well
Waves his makeshift wand
Forgives saucer eyed Indians

Red coated knights
Gallop across the prairie
to get their men
and to build a new world

Pioneers and traders
Bring gifts
Smallpox, Seagrams
And Rice Krispies

Civilization has reached
the promised land.

Between the snap crackle pop
Of smoke stacks and multi-coloured rivers
Swelling with flower powered zee
Are farmers sowing skulls and bones
And miners
Pulling from gaping holes
Green paper faces
Of smiling English lady

The colossi
In which they trust
While burying breathing forests and fields beneath concrete and steel
Stand shaking fists
Waiting to mutilate
Whole civilizations
Ten generations at a blow.

Somewhere among the remains
Of skinless animals
Is the termination to a long journey
And unholy search
For power
Glimpsed in a garden forever closed
Forever lost.

Source: Armstrong, J.C. (1997). The history lesson. In D.D. Moses and T. Goldie (Eds.), *An anthology of Canadian Native literature in English* (2nd ed.). Toronto: Oxford University Press.

APPENDIX 8.2

THE ONONDAGA MADONNA

By Duncan Campbell Scott, 1894
Deputy Superintendent of Indian Affairs, Canada

She stands full-throated and with careless pose,
This woman of a weird and waning race,
The tragic savage lurking in her face,
Where all her pagan passion burns and glows;
Her blood is mingled with her ancient foes,
And thrills with war and wildness in her veins;
Her rebel lips are dabbled with stains
Of feuds and forays and her father's woes.

And closer in the shawl about her breast,
The latest promise of her nation's doom,
Paler than she her baby clings and lies,
The primal warrior gleaming from his eyes;
He sulks, and burdened with his infant gloom,
He draws his heavy brows and will not rest.

Source: Scott, D.C. (1926). The Onondaga Madonna. In *The poems of Duncan Campbell Scott* (p. 230). Toronto: McClelland & Stewart.

Residential Schools

INTRODUCTION

From 1867 to 1945, Aboriginal children were not allowed to attend any schools other than those designated specifically for their education. These schools were provided by the Canadian government in conjunction with the Roman Catholic, Anglican, United, and Presbyterian churches. The purpose of the schools was assimilation through the teaching of farming for boys, domestic duties for girls, and religion. The schools were chronically underfunded, and the health conditions of the children suffered. Due to poor nutrition and substandard living conditions, many children died of diseases such as typhoid fever and tuberculosis. In these schools, many children suffered physical and sexual abuse, and many aspects of Aboriginal culture and language were lost. Today, some **residential school** survivors have sought to use civil and criminal law to hold the government of Canada and the churches involved accountable for their actions.

In the last five years, the government of Canada has made some major efforts to support the Aboriginal people in their journey of healing. The government has been involved, for example, in the creation of both the Aboriginal Healing Foundation and the Truth and Reconciliation Commission (TRC).

The government's past focus on Aboriginal children did not end with the residential school system but persisted into the mid-1980s. Well-intentioned social workers removed thousands of Aboriginal children from their communities in the belief that they were rescuing these children from a life of poverty and despair—from conditions that were, in fact, a legacy of the residential school system.

Some may question the decision to dedicate an entire chapter of this text to children's issues. The justification is as follows: the final report of the **Royal Commission on Aboriginal Peoples (RCAP)**, released in November 1996, gave society at large a clearer picture of the enormous damage done to Aboriginal communities by the long-standing maltreatment and abuse of their young. Aboriginal

CHAPTER OBJECTIVES

After completing this chapter, you should be able to:

- Explain the Dominion of Canada's rationale for implementing residential schools.

- Understand the magnitude of the damage done to Aboriginal societies by the schools.

- Understand why the Truth and Reconciliation Commission was created, what its goals are, and the degree to which it has been successful.

- Understand how the residential school experience led to the later seizure of children from Aboriginal communities during the 1960s to the 1980s.

- Discuss the moral, legal, and ethical issues related to accountability and healing, as well as the current efforts being made by the government of Canada, in partnership with the Aboriginal people, to promote healing.

residential schools
church-run, government-funded residential schools for Aboriginal children designed to prepare them for life in white society

Royal Commission on Aboriginal Peoples (RCAP)
commission established in 1991 to investigate the issues facing Aboriginal people in Canada

people who are working to heal their communities believe that the education system's part in this damage cannot be overestimated. This chapter will discuss the political environment that made this whole episode possible in a country today renowned for its attention to civil rights. To help us understand the survivors' pain, we will recount some of their stories. This chapter will also examine some of the efforts currently being made to help the Aboriginal people recover and to bring about reconciliation between them and the rest of Canada.

EDUCATION AS A TOOL FOR ASSIMILATION

An appreciation of and desire for education was common to both Aboriginal and non-Aboriginal people from an early point in their relations. As a result, guarantees for state-funded education were set out in certain treaties. The Stone Fort Treaty (1871), for example, stated the following: "And further, Her Majesty agrees to maintain a school on each reserve hereby made, whenever the Indians of the reserve should desire it" (Morris, 1971, p. 315). Aboriginal leaders recognized that their children would need new knowledge to cope with the rapidly changing environment. With the depletion of natural resources and with increasing white settlement, these leaders saw that their traditional hunting and trapping lifestyles were going to be severely disrupted. They envisioned state schools that would be run in partnership with Aboriginal nations so as to preserve traditional Aboriginal culture while preparing children for new, non-traditional labour markets.

John Tootoosis (1899–1989), a prominent Cree First Nations leader, wrote the following in his biography:

> The Indians who at treaty time had asked that their children be educated were asking that they be taught to read and write, to learn to work with figures, to be trained into useful skills to enable them to compete on an equal basis for a way of making a living with the children of the white men. ... Poundmaker (chief at treaty time) had replied very clearly, "We want to be sure that life will be as good for them (our children) as it will be for your children." (Quoted in Goodwill & Sluman, 1982, p. 113)

The federal government had an altogether different vision for the schools; it viewed education as an efficient means of assimilating the Aboriginal people, a governmental ambition that we discussed in the previous chapter. While education in Canada has long been a provincial responsibility, the *British North America Act* gave the federal government jurisdiction over Aboriginal people in this regard, a responsibility it bears to this day.

As early as 1830, four mission schools for Aboriginal populations were established in Ontario. A leader in this initiative was an Ojibwa man, Peter Jones, who was also a Methodist missionary. He had founded an agricultural settlement for the Mississaugas on the Credit River (in present-day Toronto) and was providing education to young Aboriginal people through the Credit River School, which was reasonably successful. Jones wished to extend his education provisions to other Aboriginal nations by building residential schools that would also provide manual training. The Mohawk Institute, established in 1833 by the New England Company and dedicated to the Christianization, "civilization," and instruction of Aboriginal people, was a model for Jones. He asked four different bands in his area to help finance the schools by donating one-quarter of their treaty money. The Methodist church and the federal government also shared in the cost of establishing the schools. Jones had a vision that the schools would eventually be run by Christian Aboriginal people. Neither the federal government nor the church shared this vision.

Although Aboriginal people supported the schools initially, they soon discovered that the goals of the church and the government were inconsistent with their own. Aboriginal leaders recognized that schooling meant assimilation and a total rejection of all their own values and traditions. They stopped financial support to the schools and withheld their children from them. The experiment was deemed a failure, but the precedent had been set—of using partnerships with the church and missionaries in the education of Aboriginal children (Grant, 1996).

When the question of education for Aboriginal children arose again in 1870, the churches were recruited for the task, for two main reasons. The first was that the churches could be expected to inculcate Aboriginal children with the religious ideals of the day and have them reject all things associated with their own culture. The second reason for involving the churches was purely practical. The running of the schools and the instruction of the Aboriginal children promised to be an expensive endeavour for the Indian department; the free labour of missionaries and priests would significantly reduce the cost. The federal government, in turn, would provide funding in the form of land grants, per capita grants, and other material rewards to the four churches involved in Indian education. This partnership between church and state would last until 1969.

The decision to make education for Aboriginal children "residential" rather than provide day schools on reserves was driven by similar motives. First, the cost of building a day school on each and every reserve, according to the Department of Indian Affairs, was certainly too high (regardless of the wording within the treaty). Second, separating the children from the influence of their families and community was considered necessary if the children were to internalize the religious teachings of the church.

PROBLEMS WITHIN THE SYSTEM

One of the first problems to surface in this education system was poor attendance. Health conditions in the schools were not good, and many children died of diseases such as smallpox, tuberculosis, and polio. Rumours of abuse within the schools circulated quickly among parents, who also opposed the curricula, the purpose of which, they saw, was assimilation. For these reasons, many Aboriginal nations and Aboriginal parents chose to withhold their children from residential schools. Poor attendance resulted in a change to the *Indian Act* in 1894: school attendance became compulsory. Section 119 of the Act gave truant officers authority to enforce attendance in day schools by removing children forcibly, if necessary, from their homes and families. In 1920, the Act was amended to give truant officers the same authority with respect to residential schools, and to provide for parents' being convicted of summary offences if they withheld their children from the schools.

EXERCISE 1

Consider the quotations below, which are taken from records of the time, and then discuss them as a class. The first is from Sir Hector Langevin, secretary of state for the provinces, who argued before Parliament in 1883:

> Industrial schools have succeeded very well in the United States and it is quite likely they will succeed here as well. The fact is, that if you wish to educate the children you must separate them from their parents during the time they are being taught. If you leave them in the family, they may know how to read and write, but they will remain savages, whereas by separating them in the way proposed, they acquire the habits and tastes of civilized people. (Indian Tribes of Manitoba, 1971, p. 113)

The second is from the *Indian Affairs Annual Report 1889*:

> The boarding school dissociates the Indian child from the deleterious home influences to which he would otherwise be subjected. It reclaims him from the uncivilized state in which he has been brought up. ... By precept and example he is taught to endeavor to excel in what will be most useful to him. (Provincial Archives of Manitoba, RG 10, vol. 6040, file #160-4, part 1, C8153)

Hayter Reed, deputy superintendent general for Indian Affairs, said the following in 1894:

> The extension of the educational work is chiefly being carried out in the direction of Industrial and semi-Industrial Schools, in which children not only get the positive advantage of instruction superior to what they could be given on reserves, but are removed from the retarding influences of contact with them. ... How can improvement be looked for in a race of children, when out of school they are subject to such a degrading environment? (Provincial Archives of Manitoba, RG 10, vol. 6040, file #160-4, part I, C8153)

Another problem that immediately surfaced concerned questions about what type of education should in fact be delivered, by whom, and to whom. The various agencies involved disagreed with one another about these matters. Age of enrollment, for example, was a frequent source of dispute. Some Protestant ministers advocated enrolling students as young as three in residential schools, to "catch them early." Others argued that this would be a waste of money. Some argued the students should be kept until they were 14; some argued for 16, some 18, and some for 21. Enrollment ages did in fact change through the years. Bickering among the Catholic, Presbyterian, Anglican, and Methodist churches over who would get the students was common; each denomination viewed the contest for students as a battle for souls—or, in some instances, as a battle for per capita funding.

As far as curricula were concerned, some schools classed as "industrial schools" offered training in skilled trades such as carpentry, cabinet making, and tailoring. Some of these schools produced a well-educated and literate group of graduates. However, these successes created two problems. The first was that success in acquiring a skilled trade did not guarantee employment. In fact, there were no opportunities for employment. One agent wrote to the Department in December 1907,

"Race prejudice is against them and I am afraid that it will take time, under the circumstances, before they can compete with their white brothers in the trades" (quoted in Milloy, 1999, p. 158). Critics of the system insisted that the more costly industrial school training was a waste of resources, since people in mainstream Canada were not prepared to accept working alongside Indians. In response, the industrial schools were phased out.

The second problem with the early success of the schools was baldly expressed by the Minister of the Interior, Frank Oliver, in 1897: "We are educating these Indians to compete industrially with our own people, which seems to me a very undesirable use of public money" (quoted in Hall, 1983, p. 126). The attitudes expressed in these historical records may seem shocking to the average Canadian today, but they reflect the sentiments that were prevalent among many Canadians at the time. The status quo was being threatened by Aboriginals, who were showing that they could not only learn to read and write but could also become great craftsmen on par with non-Aboriginals and thus compete with the latter in the labour market for skilled jobs. It had to stop.

As industrial schools were phased out and the number of residential schools increased, the quality of the education declined. By 1932, at the end of Duncan Campbell Scott's career as deputy superintendent general of Indian Affairs, there were 17,163 students enrolled in residential schools. Scott viewed this increase in attendance as proof of his success in the assimilation process. It was more likely due to the compulsory attendance legislation enforced by his government. The flipside of this statistic is that three-quarters of students enrolled were in grades 1 through 3. In 1932, only 100 students reached grade 6 (Milloy, 1999, p. 171).

In his autobiography, Aboriginal scholar Basil Johnston (1989, p. 47) remembers having to repeat grades over and over in residential school and finally realizing, much to his dismay, that, as a matter of policy, Aboriginal students' discharge from the school at the age of 16 had to coincide with their graduation from grade 8. In other words, no matter how they performed academically, Aboriginal students were destined to repeat grades until they reached 16 and could be released from the school.

Cree writer and lawyer Harold Cardinal (1969, p. 54) has described his residential school experience as follows:

> In plain words, the system was lousy. The curriculum stank, and the teachers were misfits and second raters. Even my own elementary school days, in grade eight I found myself taking over the class because my teacher, a misfit, has-been or never-was sent out by his superiors from Quebec to teach savages in the wilderness school because he had failed utterly in civilization, couldn't speak English well enough to make himself understood. Naturally he knew no Cree. When we protested such inequities we were silenced as "ungrateful little savages who don't appreciate what is being done for you."

Bill Thomas (1991, p. 6), of the Peguis First Nation, has described staff in the schools as follows:

> The kooky clergy and even kookier staff make a shambles of any potential for effective development. ... For the most part the "dedicated" staff I knew in the

United Church school were old ladies trying to atone for earlier sins and mucking that up. Others were religious zealots or simply strange people who—under ordinary circumstances—could not get a job or fit in anywhere else.

These complaints about the staff from residential school survivors are corroborated by studies conducted in the early 1960s. These studies indicate that, with few exceptions, staff fell into three categories: first, relatively recent immigrants; second, Canadians from lower socio-economic backgrounds; and, finally, a few Aboriginal people. In 1967, researcher Richard King conducted a study of a Yukon Indian School at Mopass. King (1967) categorized staff as "generally deviant in the white-man society." He found that many of the teachers lacked qualifications and many could not even speak English well. It seems that the reasonably generous pay in the residential schools—generous by comparison with other jobs such people would have been qualified for—attracted poorly educated and deficient personalities to work in them. As early as 1910, letters sent to school administrators by the Department of Indian Affairs address concerns over the quality of its teachers (Grant, 1996, p. 143).

Also damaging the academic standards of the residential schools was the requirement—based on the department's desire that the schools be self-sufficient—that students do long hours of manual labour. The students were supposed to spend half the day in class and half the day in manual labour, but the latter often took precedence. The records show that field workers and school inspectors were concerned from the first about this over-emphasis on manual work. One letter, written in 1916, alerts the Department of Indian Affairs to the fact that the boys in one school had spent only 9 days out of 42 in class; the rest of their time was spent working on the farm to support the school (Milloy, 1999, p. 170). Poorly served by this regimen, many students left the school unable to read or even to converse well in English.

HEALTH CONDITIONS

The health of children in the schools was always a source of concern. Unsafe construction, overcrowding, and poor nutrition resulted in physical problems and a high death rate. The churches and the administrators at Indian Affairs were well aware of this, but funds were not readily available to provide more sanitary conditions in the schools through renovation. Dr. Peter Bryce was commissioned in 1903 to inspect residential schools and report on the health conditions. His report was scathing, indicating that some schools had a death rate of *50 percent*. He wrote as follows: "The sight of the ragged, ill-kempt and sickly looking children was enough to make me sick at heart." In 1910, an Indian agent named MacArthur reported a 50 percent death rate at the Duck Lake residential school. S.H. Blake (quoted in Milloy, 1999, p. 77), a lawyer, conducted a review of the Anglican missions and reported as follows to Minister of Indian Affairs Frank Oliver: "The appalling number of deaths among the younger children appeals loudly to the guardians of our Indians. In doing nothing to obviate the preventable causes of death, brings the department within unpleasant nearness to the charge of manslaughter."

Nutrition was lacking in many of the schools, and this left the children vulnerable to disease. In 1943, Dr. A.B. Simes conducted an inquiry into Elkhorn School in response to complaints from the Indians at The Pas, Manitoba. He reported

(Milloy, 1999, p. 114) that the children were dirty, their clothes disgraceful, and that 28 percent of the girls and 69 percent of the boys were underweight. The menu he forwarded to the Ministry had many omissions and few substitutions. Today, many residential school survivors remark about never having had enough to eat.

At File Hills Boarding school, Dr. Bryce found that 75 percent of the students on the discharge roll were dead. Of the 31 students on the roll, 15 had died in the school, and 7 had died at home within three years of discharge. At the time of first enrollment, all of these students had enjoyed good health. File Hills was certainly the worst case, but if its statistics are factored in with those of the other schools, the death rate in the 35 schools included in Dr. Bryce's study would be 42 percent. Those figures, projected throughout the 1907 school system, suggest that of the 3,755 children in the schools, 1,614 would die prematurely (Milloy, 1999, p. 90).

This information was not restricted to government officials. Dr. Bryce's report made headlines in the newspapers; in other words, the Canadian public knew about the horrific conditions in the schools and about the unacceptable death rate. One reporter wrote that the death rate would be unacceptable even in war. Other efforts were made to attract public attention to the appalling conditions of the schools, but to no avail. It seems that the Canadian public was content to be complicit in the brutality of this process of forced assimilation. Up to 1922, Dr. Bryce would continue to criticize the Ministry for doing nothing to improve sanitation. Bryce was successful only in ensuring that he did not secure a position in Duncan Campbell Scott's administration as the department's minister of health.

Ultimately, there were modest measures taken to improve the conditions in the schools. But the communications between school administrators and Indian Affairs indicate that high death rates and poor sanitary conditions were constant problems throughout the decades the schools were in operation. Four decades later, in 1948, Neil Walker (quoted in Milloy, 1999, p. 262), Indian Affairs superintendent, wrote as follows: "If I were appointed by the Dominion Government for the express purpose of spreading tuberculosis, there is nothing finer in existence than the average Indian residential school."

EXERCISE 2

Read Appendix 9.1 together as a class and discuss the government's guardianship position with respect to Indian children as well as its treaty obligation to provide education.

What value did mainstream society seem to place on Aboriginal children? Discuss.

Consider the mandatory attendance legislation instituted by government. How would you have felt about this legislation if you had been the parent of an Indian child in this era?

ABUSE WITHIN RESIDENTIAL SCHOOLS

Most people who write about abuse in residential schools divide the subject into four categories: sexual, physical, mental, and spiritual/cultural. Here, we will examine each category in turn, then look at the aftermath of the abuse and the efforts by the government and Aboriginal communities to reach some agreement on liability and possible compensation.

In 1964, 10-year-old Willie Blackwater was removed from his family home on Kisiox Reserve in British Columbia and taken to Port Alberni Indian residential school on Vancouver Island, 1,600 kilometres away. Immediately, Blackwater was singled out by dorm supervisor Henry Plint, who sexually abused the boy during his years at the school. Blackwater revealed the abuse to several authorities, including a government official, none of whom believed him. Furthermore, when news reached Plint that the boy had accused him of abuse, he beat the child so severely that Blackwater ended up in the infirmary. Blackwater, after suffering greatly as an adult trying to cope with his childhood, came forward again in the 1990s to initiate an investigation into his abuse at the school. Thirty other adult men also came forward in an attempt to make Plint accountable for his actions, and, after judgments against him in 1995 and 1997, Plint, at the age of 72, was convicted and sentenced to 12 years in prison; he showed no remorse. In his judgment, Supreme Court Justice Douglas Hogarth referred to Plint as a sexual predator and a sexual terrorist whose activities had been allowed to go on unchecked: "As far as the victims are concerned, the Indian residential school system was nothing more than institutionalized pedophilia" (quoted in Fournier & Crey, 1997, p. 72).

This is only one of the thousands of incidents of sexual abuse in residential schools across Canada that came to light in the 1990s. In 1990, the Manitoba Grand Chief of the National Assembly of First Nations talked publicly of his experience of sexual abuse while in residential schools in Manitoba. The Aboriginal community was divided in its response to sudden public scrutiny. Some felt these experiences were so painful and shameful that they should not be brought forward, since they caused victims to relive their pain. Others felt that the only way to begin the healing process was to openly face the harsh reality of what had been suffered.

The RCMP and other policing agencies became involved in uncovering information regarding past sexual assaults in the schools. They quickly uncovered thousands of victims. In 1994, the RCMP created a task force to deal with the many investigations required to address the complaints. Investigations were difficult because many of the perpetrators had died or could not be located. In some circumstances, victims who made disclosures to police were unable to cope with dredging up the past; some have committed suicide, and some have turned to alcohol and drugs in order to deal with their pain.

No one can know for certain how widespread the sexual abuse was; we can count only those who have come forward voluntarily. In 1990, when residential school abuse became part of the political landscape, *The Globe and Mail* reported that Rix Rogers, the special adviser to the minister of national health and welfare on child sexual abuse, had indicated, during a meeting of the Canadian Psychological Association, that the abuse revealed to that date was believed to be just the tip of the iceberg. He believed that "a closer scrutiny of the past treatment of native children at Indian residential schools would show 100 percent of children at some schools were sexually abused" ("Reports of sexual abuse," 1990, p. A3).

Physical abuse was also rampant within the schools; the application of corporal punishment was difficult to monitor or contain. There are many stories of children being forced to eat their own vomit, having their faces rubbed in human feces, and being beaten for minor infractions of school rules. Many incidents of abuse are recorded in the Department of Indian Affairs files. Teachers who were sympathetic to the children and described or reported abuse by other teachers were dismissed for disloyalty. One such letter (quoted in Milloy, 1999, p. 282) from a sympathetic teacher states the following:

> Children's faces are slapped, [they are] hit on the head, struck across the nose causing nose bleeds. ... One teacher said a boy in her classroom had a swollen face for two days from being slapped. Another teacher reported that one of her pupils was slapped because he couldn't read the small print in the hymn books. One of my grade 8 boys was slapped on the head until he was pale, he staggered, complained of feeling dizzy and his nose bled profusely. This was witnessed by most of the school boys. He fainted five days later in prayers and again in my classroom.

Eventually, in response to the various allegations and to the reports of the children's injuries, which were observed when the schools were inspected, the Department of Indian Affairs issued a number of regulations to address the use of corporal punishment. These regulations seem to have had little effect; school administrators continued on the old course of physical punishments, set as policy when the schools were first established.

In 1965, in response to the widespread allegations of physical abuse, the department solicited an evaluation of the residential school system, to be presented at the first Residential Principals' Conference. The department handpicked as witnesses six residential school graduates who were of "impeccable authority and character," each successful in public service, education, or church service. One respondent was a graduate of the Mohawk Institute in Brantford, Ontario and he described (quoted in Milloy, 1999, p. 284) the conditions there as follows: 90 percent of the children suffered from dietary deficiency, evidenced by boils, warts, and general ill health. He reported seeing children eating from the garbage and from the bin intended to feed the pigs. Lice infestations were common and so children's heads were frequently shaved. Captured runaways were brought back to run a gauntlet where they were hit with anything found on hand. He reported (quoted in Milloy, 1999, p. 284) that he had "seen boys crying in the most abject misery and pain with not a soul to care—the dignity of man!" The appraisal of the schools resulted in some positive comments; overall, though, the comments were unfavourable and difficult to ignore.

Emotional abuse is perhaps the most damaging kind of abuse, and it was constantly meted out in the residential schools. Students were made to endure humiliation and ridicule by staff. At one school, as a punishment for bedwetting, children were made to wear the wet sheet draped over their heads. In another school, female students were stripped of their underwear and struck on the bare buttocks in front of the class. This disclosure came from the principal of a northern school who believed the punishment to be reasonable. Children reported being locked in a room in only their underwear and restricted to a bread-and-milk diet as a punishment for running away. Two female runaways were forced to attend meals in the dining room in only their underwear. Children were ridiculed and taunted by staff and called derogatory names that specifically targeted their race.

The department was aware of the persistent problem of children running away. Many died while trying to escape, mainly due to exposure. The department also had to deal with the problem of children attempting suicide within the schools. These two problems were further symptoms of real problems within the school itself and the system at large. In 1920, nine boys attempted suicide by eating water hemlock; one died. In 1981, at Muscowequan school, five girls between the ages of eight and ten tied socks and towels together with a view to hanging themselves (Milloy, 1999).

Finally, spiritual and cultural abuse were implicit in the very purpose of the schools: assimilation. The schools were meant to eliminate the Aboriginal way of life for the next generation. Duncan Campbell Scott believed and hoped that within three generations the Indian race would no longer exist as a result of the government's assimilation policies; residential schools were seen as an effective means to this end. Ultimately, Scott was mistaken. Though several generations—as many as five, in some cases—of Aboriginal children did attend residential schools, Aboriginal nations are alive and persevering in Canada today.

Residential schools vigorously tackled the ambitious goal of eliminating Aboriginal culture. Many survivors report that the most severe punishments meted out by school staff were reserved for children who spoke their original language or attempted to carry on any Aboriginal tradition. As children arrived at the schools, their birth name was replaced with an identification number and a new Christian name. Many of them spoke little or no English and so could not communicate with staff. A few schools would assign an interpreter from the older student population, but most schools expected the child simply to stop speaking in his or her original tongue until he or she could acquire sufficient English to communicate. Isabelle Knockwood (1992, p. 81) has written of her experiences at Shubenacadie residential school in Nova Scotia: "When little children first arrived at the school we would see bruises on their throats and cheeks that told us that they had been caught speaking Mi'kmaw. Once we saw the bruises begin to fade, we knew they'd stopped talking."

The idea for such a forcible attack on the Aboriginal language came from the United States and that country's approach to Indian education. In 1867, President Grant called strongly for linguistic genocide:

> Through sameness of language is produced sameness of sentiment, and thought. ... In difference of language today lies two-thirds of our trouble. ... Schools should be established, which children should be required to attend; their barbarous dialect should be blotted out and the English language substituted. (Reyhner & Eder, 2004)

For the children, the psychological effects of this linguistic suppression were severe. As we will see in the next chapter, a study (Hallett, Chandler, & Lalonde, 2007) has shown that the continuation or retention of language is a factor in the well-being of individuals and communities, whereas loss of language has been linked to higher rates of youth suicide. Erasing the child's language meant erasing his or her identity, concept of self, and world view, as well as the child's sense of his or her place in the world. A saying from this era expresses the non-Aboriginal view of this erasure: "Kill the Indian and save the child/man." Once everything Indian in the child's life was destroyed, however, it was not replaced with any new values or world view. The original intention had been for Christianity to take the place of Aboriginal culture and values, but the coercive way in which Christianity was taught belied its own values and detracted from its validity in the children's eyes, so that few of them internalized its ideals.

For many children, acquiring a new language under such stressful circumstances was difficult. Many children simply stopped speaking and ceased to express emotions such as frustration, fear, and anger; they learned to internalize emotion rather than express it. These self-protective barriers to communication remained in place after the child was discharged from the school. As the children returned to their home communities, the first generation of survivors could not communicate with any members of their community, even their own families. They had lost their language and now spoke only English, not widely spoken by members of their community. The emotional isolation thus continued.

We know that language is both the basis of culture and its conduit, and that if a language is forever lost, as is a risk for many Aboriginal languages, the culture it conveys will be significantly diminished. Since the closure of the residential schools, various conditions have contributed to the decline of Aboriginal languages. For example, there has been a significant influx of Aboriginal people into large urban centres, where their mother tongues are inevitably eroded. In 1941, however, less than 10 percent of Aboriginal people claimed English as their first language. In 1971, by which point the schools had mostly been phased out after three generations of children had passed through them, 54 percent of Canadian Aboriginals reported English as their first language. By 1996, 75 percent of Canada's Aboriginal population listed English as their mother tongue. In the 2006 Aboriginal Peoples Survey of off-reserve Aboriginal children, 90 percent reported that English or French is the primary language used in the home. Only 1 percent of these children speak an Aboriginal language exclusively in the home (Statistics Canada, 2010).

EXERCISE 3

Read Appendix 9.2 and discuss the reading as a class.

AFTERMATH OF RESIDENTIAL SCHOOLS

The federal government undertook a review of Indian residential schools in 1948. The government found that the schools were a dismal failure and proposed phasing them out and integrating Aboriginal students into mainstream schools. The review of the schools found that an Aboriginal graduate from the residential school system was less prepared for life than an Aboriginal person who had never attended any formal education institution. The federal government began funding provincial schools on a per capita basis to include Aboriginal children. Nevertheless, many of the residential schools were kept open until the 1960s. The last one did not close until 1996.

The effect of the schools on Aboriginal communities has been devastating. As many psychological and sociological studies have shown, those who are abused often become abusers, particularly in cases of sexual abuse. Aboriginal leaders report that sexual abuse is like a disease ripping through their communities. A 1989 study commissioned by the Native Women's Association of the Northwest Territories found that 80 percent of girls under the age of eight and 50 percent of boys under the age of eight had been victims of sexual abuse.

Families have also been torn apart by violence—another legacy of the residential school experience. This system taught students that adults exert power and control over children by physical punishment, and the survivors of the system have carried this conditioning into Aboriginal communities where, traditionally, few would ever have thought to raise a hand against a child for punishment or for discipline. The cycle is difficult to break. Residential school survivors never experienced nurturing, respectful parenting, and many, as a result, have faced difficulties raising their own children. Until recently these struggles were being passed from one generation to the next without intervention.

In 1990, a First Nations leader wrote as follows to Minister of Indian Affairs Tom Siddon:

> Social maladjustment, abuse of self and others and family breakdown are some of the symptoms prevalent among First Nations baby boomers. The graduates of Ste. Anne's Residential school are now trying and often failing to come to grips with life as adults after being raised as children in an atmosphere of fear, loneliness and self loathing. Fear of caretakers. Loneliness in knowing that elders and family were far away. Loathing from learning to hate oneself, because of repeated physical, verbal or sexual abuse suffered at the hands of various adult caretakers. This is only a small part of the story. (Indian and Northern Affairs Canada, 1990)

Aboriginal leaders called for a public inquiry into the residential school system to determine the breadth and depth of the damage it caused and to suggest resolutions for their communities regarding how to deal with healing. Initially, the federal government did not agree to such an inquiry. In 1992, however, the Royal Commission on Aboriginal Peoples (RCAP) was established by the federal government in response to a land claims issue that erupted into violence. RCAP devoted considerable effort to the residential school issue. The final report, submitted by RCAP in 1996, contains the following recommendation (RCAP, 1996, p. 338):

> Our research and hearings indicate that a full investigation into Canada's residential schools system, in the form of a public inquiry ... is necessary to bring light and begin to heal the grievous harms suffered by countless children, families, and communities as a result of the residential school system. The inquiry should conduct public hearings across the country, with sufficient funding to enable those affected to testify. The inquiry should be empowered to commission research and analysis to assist in gaining an understanding of the nature and effect of residential school policies. It should be authorized to recommend whatever remedial action it believes necessary for governments and churches to ameliorate the conditions created by the residential school experience. Where appropriate, such remedies should include apologies from those responsible, compensation on a collective basis to enable Aboriginal communities to design and administer programs that assist the healing process and rebuild community life, and funding for the treatment of affected people and their families.

RCAP's findings put several processes in motion. One of these led, in 1998, to a carefully worded apology from the government to the Aboriginal community, and to the creation of a "healing fund" to finance the search for pathways to wellness in Aboriginal communities. Another process put in motion by RCAP's findings was the negotiation of a settlement for survivors. Both will be discussed later in this chapter.

ATTEMPTS AT RESOLUTION

Before discussing the attempts at resolution, it is important to note that Aboriginal communities and leaders agree that no amount of money can ever compensate Aboriginal people for the suffering they have endured. The question, then, is how Canadians ought to go about reconciling themselves with the past and partnering with Aboriginal people to promote the latter's recovery. It is a question of justice. What is the fair and just thing to do, considering all that has taken place? Financial compensation should not be construed as a punishment to Canada and viewed in terms of a fine; it must be perceived in the appropriate terms—that is, as a dedication of resources to help the sufferers overcome their pain and move toward health and wellness.

As discussed earlier in the chapter, Henry Plint was convicted of sexually assaulting Willie Blackwater and many other boys at Port Alberni Residential School during the 1960s. In 1995 and 1997, he was sentenced to 12 years in prison. In 1998, Blackwater and 30 other residential school survivors embarked on a civil suit against Plint, and the suit also named the federal government, which organized the residential school system, and the United Church of Canada, which ran the Port Alberni school. The trial was difficult for survivors to endure, as they faced hard questioning by government and church lawyers. In 2001, the complainants chose to take an out-of-court settlement for a reported $180,000 to $290,000 each in order to end the trial. But the questions remain: who is responsible for these atrocities? Is it Henry Plint alone or is it the entire Indian Affairs Department that appears to have turned a blind eye to the abuse of children? Is the government to be held fully responsible for setting up an education system with very few formal accountability processes, thereby creating a situation that was destined to foster abuse? The historical records of the Indian Affairs Department have now been extensively examined, and it is clear that the department attempted to document complaints of abuse. But its attempts to stop the abuse were modest, and they failed. Should churches share in the responsibility because they supplied the unqualified staff who were the abusers?

Survivors have tried a variety of methods of redressing the wrongs done them. The first method is the criminal prosecution of offenders. One problem with this method, as the Blackwater case showed, is that victims are forced to relive their traumatic experiences during the investigative and trial processes. Another problem is that police are frequently unable to locate the offenders, many of whom are now deceased.

The victims' second method of seeking redress—and the one that has proved most popular—has been civil litigation. There are several reasons for choosing this process, aside from the prospect of financial reparation. The first reason is that victory in the public forum of the court system signifies acknowledgment, on the part of Canada's mainstream judicial system, that a legitimate wrong has occurred and that a victim deserves compensation. This type of public recognition satisfies those who seek vindication on a matter of principle. Another reason for choosing civil litigation is that the court system is perceived as levelling the playing field between the plaintiff and the accused. Of course, the playing field cannot be perfectly level, since one side—in this case, the defendants (government and churches)—always has more financial resources for the litigation process than the other side. Still, in the case of civil litigation, the plaintiff can be assured that there will be no back-door, high-pressure negotiation, with the powerful strong-arming the powerless, as sometimes occurs—or is perceived to occur—in the alternative dispute resolution (ADR) process. The justice system, although imperfect, aspires to be unaffected by unequal distributions of power. Another reason for victims to choose civil litigation is that a court decision establishes precedents that other courts are bound to follow, thereby helping to ensure that victims will be treated equally.

The final reason for victims of the residential school system to seek redress through the civil litigation process is that they want their stories heard. This desire was clear in the findings of RCAP, which recommended a cross-country inquiry into the damage done by the residential schools—a recommendation that the federal government adamantly refused to follow. The victims desired to be heard and understood, and they wanted their experience to be registered in the consciousness of mainstream Canadian society. This could happen only if a resolution was sought in a public forum such as the court system, where the transcripts and outcome are part of the public record.

It is startling how many young adults today are only vaguely aware that Aboriginal children, until comparatively recently, were forced to attend residential schools. Non-Aboriginal Canadians have not been taught, or simply have not chosen to inquire, about the residential school legacy. This state of affairs is very unfortunate. Just resolutions and reconciliation in the issues involving Aboriginal people in Canada depend on all Canadians, Aboriginal and non-Aboriginal alike, having the same awareness of past and present.

For the Aboriginal plaintiffs, there were drawbacks to the civil litigation process. The most obvious was the cost. Some victims resolved this through the use of contingency fees, although they were sometimes charged up to half of their financial settlement in legal fees (Tibbetts, 2000). Another drawback to the civil-litigation route was that the acknowledgment of harm was offered only to the individual victim; there was no recognition of the harm done to the victim's family, to subsequent generations, and to the community. This second kind of recognition is particularly important to Aboriginal people and to their communities.

Despite the difficulties they faced in seeking restitution for past wrongs, a growing number of survivors came forward through the 1990s. As of July 2003, there had been 12,000 claims filed, very few of which had been resolved. Many prospective claimants were waiting to see what resolutions would be reached before filing their own claims. It was predicted at the time that the number of claims could reach 30,000. At its height, the residential school system included 88 schools across Canada, and the 1991 census reported that there were 105,000 residential school survivors alive at that time. It was estimated in 2003 that, if the number of cases continued to grow at the current pace, the pursuit of civil litigation could stretch the time frame for settlement to over 50 years, by the end of which almost all the plaintiffs would be dead.

In order to address these timing problems, the government embarked upon an ADR process. This process was slow because many matters had to be settled, not the least of which was the division of responsibility between church and state. The federal government announced, after negotiations stalled, that it would accept responsibility for 70 percent of the claim amount, leaving the churches responsible for the remaining 30 percent. The churches insisted that being made responsible for this amount could in fact leave them bankrupt. Another issue that arose in this process was the government's refusal to address the loss of culture and language suffered by Aboriginal people as a consequence of the residential school experience. The government insisted it would address those losses through government-funded initiatives for Aboriginal language and cultural renewal, and would provide compensation to victims only for sexual and physical abuse suffered in the schools.

A major shortcoming of the ADR process, at least where the residential schools survivors' case was concerned, is that it moved the negotiation of these matters from the public to the private forum, so that only those directly involved were included in the negotiations. In this way, the process became less accountable to the public, which could not be sure whether justice had in fact been served. The ADR process began in June 2001. In 2003, a lawyer representing some residential school survivors pointed out that of the $1.2 billion dedicated to the ADR process, $540 million were earmarked for legal costs rather than compensation (Frank, 2003). The survivors of residential schools grew older each year, and many passed away without closure to this most life-altering experience. On May 10, 2006, through the ADR process, the **Indian Residential Schools Settlement Agreement (IRSSA)** was reached. Under the agreement, Aboriginal people who could prove their attendance in the schools became eligible to receive a "common experience payment" (CEP) of $10,000 for the first year of attendance and $3,000 for each subsequent year. An estimated 79,000 living former students qualified (United Church of Canada, 2011).

Indian Residential Schools Settlement Agreement (IRSSA)
agreement by which Aboriginal people who could prove their attendance in the residential schools became eligible to receive a "common experience payment" (CEP)

The IRSSA, which is the largest lawsuit settled out of court in the history of Canada, began accepting applications in September of 2007. The application process had a number of components. First, survivors applied to Indian Residential Schools Resolution Canada, whose role was to verify the applicant's years of attendance in one or more of the recognized schools. Following the verification, letters were mailed out and payment was made.

For those who were denied payment or were not happy with the results of their application, there was an appeal process. This process was put in place because the registration records of many students had been lost by the government, and the onus was on the survivor to prove his or her attendance. It is necessary to verify attendance and years of attendance in order to calculate entitlement. Attendance claims that could not be easily verified through archived records required additional research on the part of Indian Residential Schools Resolution Canada.

Another point of contention was that certain schools were not included on the list of residential schools. This meant that the survivors of these excluded schools did not qualify for the settlement process. Among the schools excluded were the Stirland Lake and Cristal Lake residential high schools in Northern Ontario, which operated between 1971 and 1991. A 2011 decision by the Ontario Superior Court confirmed that Stirling Lake must be added to the list and that all of the attendees must be considered for the CEP since the school met the definition of an Indian Residential School (Nishnawbe Aske Nation, 2011).

Another component of the IRSSA was an independent assessment process for certain kinds of survivors—those who identified themselves as victims of sexual and physical abuse that had led to serious psychological trauma. In these cases, there was a hearing and an adjudicated judgment.

Throughout this process, there were support services put in place for the applicants, many of whom found that the application process triggered traumatic memories that led to feelings of depression, loneliness, fear, panic, and, in some cases, addictive behaviour and suicidal thoughts.

Another component of the IRSSA was the Aboriginal Healing Fund, administered by the Aboriginal Healing Foundation (AHF), which was assigned $125 million over five years to operate healing initiatives and supports for survivors. To date, the AHF has produced two volumes of reports on the healing process, and its third volume was released in July 2011. This third volume was dedicated to reconciliation and titled *Cultivating Canada: Reconciliation through the Lens of Cultural Diversity* (AHF, 2011).

One of the AHF's initiatives was an evaluation of the Common Experience Lump Sum Payment process. Its report was published in 2010, following interviews of 280 CEP recipients. The aim of these interviews was to determine whether the CEP had helped the survivors to heal and whether there were sufficient services in place to support them, practically and emotionally, in the application process.

The interviews conducted for this study produced many stories and reflections from survivors, some excerpts from which are included below. With regard to the application process, many found it straightforward enough, but some had difficulties on account of the poor education they had received in the residential schools. One survivor (AHF, 2010, p. 22) spoke as follows of his educational shortcomings:

> I didn't even get an education. I didn't go to a class or anything. ... They made you work down there all the time. I didn't do any learning. I was on the farm, that's all I was doing. ... There used to be rocks all over the fields, big boulders and they used horses and picked them all up. That's how they got that meadow there to make hay. We'd go out in the morning and first we'd clean the barn, pigs, chicken, we'd do that in the morning and then in the afternoon we'd go to the field. No time for the classroom. I can't even read or write, some of these heavy words [in the CEP application] I couldn't even understand.

A survivor in Nunavut (AHF, 2010, p. 29) spoke of the difficulty of finding school records to prove attendance at the schools, and of the skepticism with which their claims were often met:

> It was a waiting game, and you know, they don't believe you sometimes. They don't believe you went to the school. ... Like us from before in the early 70's, we never keep all our records and our parents just threw them away. And that's what they want and that was hard. And then our school burnt down and all our records

were in there and so for us around here it was kind of hard. I know there's still some people that are still waiting and trying.

Other survivors spoke about the long waiting times for the CEPs. Many of them—both for emotional reasons and for reasons of principle—were slow to apply, and then they had to wait a long time for the payment, sometimes for over a year. One survivor (AHF, 2010, p. 27) described this process as follows:

I heard about [CEP] and it took me a long time. A lot of people applied for it right away but I didn't for a long time because I was angry, and I still am at the government because of what they have done to our Aboriginal people. I said, "they aren't going to buy me for what they have done to me." You know, it never replaces what we have lost ... It took me quite a while and I thought about it for a long time. I wasn't going to apply for it in the beginning. No, I wasn't going to because I just felt that, "is that trying to replace what we lost?"

Another survivor described (AHF, 2010, p. 29) the emotional challenge of the application process, and the trauma of having to recall the details of his life in the school:

I waited a year and a half. It was a time consuming thing. They said to call back, asking the same questions over and over, and it was hard recalling names of people who died in school, who hung themselves, who died, who I grew up protecting. To bring it up again is kind of a hard thing to do.

The study asked participants whether the lump sum CEP had had, overall, a positive or a negative impact on their lives. Of the 281 participants, 77 reported an overall positive experience, 38 a negative one, and 130 a mixed experience (AHF, 2010, p. 43). The remaining participants either did not respond or reported that their experience had been neither positive nor negative. Figure 9.1 lists the positive and negative effects of the CEP as described by the applicants.

A British Columbia survivor (AHF, 2010, p. 45) offered the following negative account of his CEP experience:

I want to mention about the negative experiences. I have lost about half a dozen cousins since we have gotten [CEP]. In my home community we are having funerals all the time. I have one cousin now who has wet brain and is in the hospital and he doesn't remember us. He drank and drank and drank and drank when the money came in. His younger brother died shortly after that money came in. He was young—he was 34 or 35 and he just drank and drank and drank. You know there is a lot more than just the half a dozen in my family and a lot of the people dying are younger than me. I'm 52 and many of them are my cohorts and were my cohorts in residential school and some of them are younger. There are Elders as well who passed away as a result. It is a common refrain in our territory. In our area there are three bands that speak the same language but culturally we are different. In the three bands, we were just having funerals and funerals and funerals. It is like the support people at the funerals just can't keep up. It has really done a lot of damage and destruction to our villages ... Everyone keeps dying.

Figure 9.1   Positive and Negative Impact of CEP Experience on the Aboriginal Participants

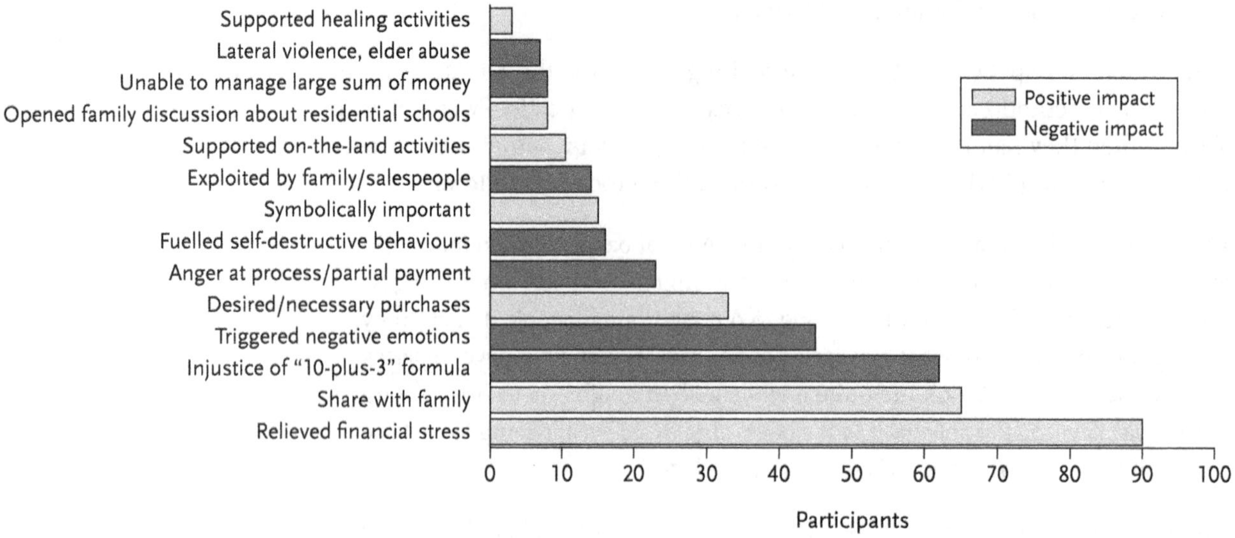

Source: Aboriginal Healing Foundation (2010, p. 44) http://www.ahf.ca/downloads/cep-2010-healing.pdf.

Those who saw the CEPs in symbolic terms—that is, as an official acknowledgment by the government of the wrong done the Aboriginal people—had a more positive experience of the process. The following quotation (AHF, 2010, p. 50) reflects a perspective of this sort:

My kids understand a little of what we went through. ... The impact of being in that place [residential school], they didn't realize it. They put you in a strange place, they didn't see that. ... My kids were helped in a lot of ways. In a lot of ways they understood where the money was coming from. Everyone thinks it's just money, all the pain you went through, that the CEP is just about money. It's not.

Those who reported positive experiences tended to emphasize the benefits of sharing pain openly and of family healing, and they said the process gave them hope for future reconciliation with non-Aboriginal Canada.

Survivors' efforts to heal themselves have taken various forms. Some have used Aboriginal healing methods such as sweat lodges, traditional medicines, and other techniques for cultural reconnection. Some have adopted Western traditions of healing, such as therapy and counselling. Figure 9.2 shows the extent to which the recipients of the CEPs have been engaged in the healing process and—in cases where they have been engaged—how successful the process has been. Figure 9.3 shows the effects the CEPs have had on this process, according to the survivors themselves.

In addition to the CEP, part of the IRSSA's mandate was to create the Truth and Reconciliation Commission (TRC). The TRC has a five-year mandate (TRC of Canada, 2011) to accomplish the following, and to do so without holding any formal hearings, or acting as a public inquiry, or conducting any formal legal process:

1. Acknowledge residential school experiences, impacts, and consequences;
2. Provide a holistic, culturally appropriate, and safe setting for former students, their families and communities as they come forward to the commission;

3. Witness, support, promote, and facilitate truth and reconciliation events at both the national and community level;

4. Promote awareness and public education of Canadians about the Indian residential school system and its impacts;

5. Identify sources and create as complete an historical record as possible of the Indian residential school [IRS] system and its legacy. The record shall be preserved and made accessible to the public for future study and use;

6. Produce and submit to the parties of the agreement a report including recommendations to the Government of Canada concerning the IRS system and experience including: the history, purpose, operation and supervision of the IRS system, the effect and consequences of IRS (including systemic harms, intergenerational consequences and the impact on human dignity) and the ongoing legacy of the residential schools;

7. Support commemoration of former Indian residential school students and their families in accordance with the Commemoration Policy Directive.

One of the TRC's main tasks has been to address concerns about the relative seclusion of the ADR negotiations—the fact that the records of abuse were not fully disclosed during this process. Canadians were not privy to the information that led to the various settlements. As previously mentioned, survivors want the rest of Canada to be aware of what they experienced in the residential schools. Only through a shared perspective—a common recognition of past and present—can Aboriginal and non-Aboriginal Canada be reconciled.

At the time of writing, The TRC is moving across Canada collecting statements from survivors of the residential schools. It will also support the missing children research project. This project is aimed at locating the remains of children who died at the schools but were not interred in the school graveyard. Once they are found, their bodies can be repatriated. At the conclusion of the TRC's five-year mandate

Figure 9.2   Residential School Survivors—Engagement in Healing

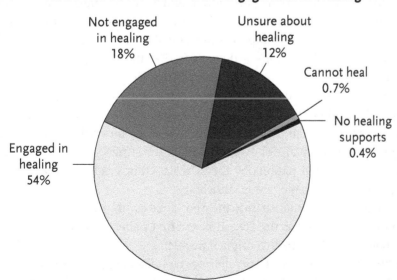

Source: Aboriginal Healing Foundation (2010, p. 78) http://www.ahf.ca/downloads/cep-2010-healing.pdf.

Figure 9.3   Effects of CEPs on Healing and Well-Being

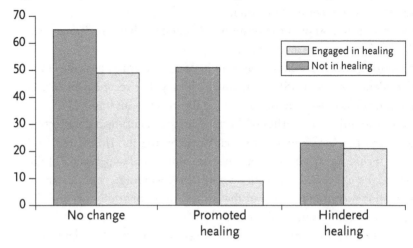

Source: Aboriginal Healing Foundation (2010, p. 86) http://www.ahf.ca/downloads/cep-2010-healing.pdf.

(2008–2013), a record of its findings will be established and a research centre created to mark the residential school system as part of Canada's history. It is hoped that much healing will have taken place by then in Aboriginal communities.

Whether the TRC is fulfilling all aspects of its mandate is open to question. One of its stated goals—to "promote awareness and public education of Canadians about the IRS [Indian residential school] system and its impacts"—seems far from being accomplished. Many young people are not even aware that this process is under way. In my own college teaching experience, only a handful of students know about the TRC, much less about its mandate, or the survivors' stories it has unearthed.

RECOGNITION OF WRONG

In 1998, the Canadian government issued a carefully worded apology, delivered by then Minister of Indian Affairs Jane Stewart and directed at those who had suffered physical and sexual abuse at the schools. At the time, an announcement was made that a new initiative would support community-based healing for people affected by residential schools, including those suffering the intergenerational impacts. This Aboriginal Healing Fund provided $350 million for use over ten years for counselling programs and culture recovery initiatives. Aboriginal people were divided in their sentiment regarding both the apology and the Aboriginal Healing Fund initiative. Many felt that the apology was a step forward; others felt that the healing fund was incapable of even scratching the surface of the social problems inflicted on Aboriginal nations by the schools. Others believed that neither the healing fund nor the apology was sufficient.

Despite the mixed response from the Aboriginal community, this was an historic occasion in Canada; it was the government's first public acknowledgment that its former policies had harmed Aboriginal people.

In 2008, Prime Minister Harper delivered a full apology in Parliament for Canada's role in the residential school system. He called on the government to partner with Aboriginal people in the healing of the latter's communities. Many survivors made their way to Parliament Hill to hear the apology in person, and they reflected that this was the most significant movement toward healing to date.

THE SIXTIES SCOOP

A discussion of the government's mistreatment of Aboriginal people and the terrible legacy of the residential schools would not be complete without addressing a more recent phenomenon—something that occurred as the schools were being phased out between the 1960s and 1980s. It has been dubbed the "**Sixties Scoop**" by sociologists, in reference to the practice of removing Aboriginal children from their communities and placing them in foster care or putting them out for adoption in non-Aboriginal homes.

Sixties Scoop
the practice of removing Aboriginal children from their communities and placing them in foster care or putting them up for adoption in non-Aboriginal homes

This phenomenon came about as the schools closed, and the question arose concerning what to do with the children of school age and younger. This emerged as a significant problem. After three or four generations of Aboriginal people had been raised in schools rather than in family homes, the ability of residential school survivors to raise their own children was severely handicapped. The prevalence of poverty, alcoholism, and other social problems on reserves left many children in need of protection or, at the very least, of intervention. After generations of the schools' efforts to break and destroy family ties, the communities had difficulty in rebuilding harmonious family lives.

In 1947, the Canadian Welfare Council and the Canadian Association of Social Workers presented a brief to a federal Special Committee asserting that, under provincial social legislation, Aboriginal children suffering from neglect were not afforded the same protections as white children. This was true: Aboriginal children fell under the authority of the federal government, which was in the process of dismantling the school system. Child welfare services were provided to the mainstream population through provincial funds and under provincial legislation. New changes to the *Indian Act* in 1951 addressed the concerns expressed by social workers. These changes provided that all provincial laws respecting child welfare were now to apply to Aboriginal children as well, effectively bringing child welfare services under the authority of provincial child welfare workers. The following question then arose: who would fund the provision of these services to the Aboriginal reserves and Aboriginal children? There was considerable debate over this issue, which resulted in the postponement of intervention for Aboriginal children. When the federal and provincial governments finally agreed to a cost-sharing process to finance these services, well-intentioned social workers quickly sprang into action. Although only 1 percent of all children in care in 1959 were Aboriginal, this number had risen, by the end of the 1960s, to 30 to 40 percent, even though Aboriginal people made up only 4 percent of the population.

Reasons cited for removing Aboriginal children from their communities included inadequate housing, unsafe drinking water, no running water, no available school, and poor health conditions. Instead of addressing these conditions, the federal government chose to remove the children from their communities. Services such as counselling and child care were not made available to intact Aboriginal families; these services could be funded only if the child became a ward of the state. Fournier and Crey (1997, p. 85) have described this situation as follows:

The caseloads in social service agencies were so high that workers did not have time to properly screen homes, nor was monitoring of either foster or adoptive homes usually feasible. But most social workers, none of whom were aboriginal, felt little harm could befall an aboriginal child rescued from poverty and placed with a nice, middle-class, white family. Yet behind the closed doors of their foster and adoptive homes, aboriginal children were even more isolated and vulnerable than they had been in residential school. ... In many cases, children were taken from parents whose only crime was poverty and being aboriginal.

In a holdover from the residential school days, siblings were separated. This was due not only to the large sizes of Aboriginal families but also to the belief that the individual children would adjust more quickly to their new homes and new environments without the influence of siblings.

Bridget Moran, a social worker in British Columbia at the height of the Sixties Scoop, writes in *A Little Rebellion* (2002) that social service workers had no resources available that might have helped keep Aboriginal families together. They had no family support workers, treatment centres, or transitional housing. Moran reports that when they found a child at risk, they had no alternative but to place the child in foster care. Ernie Klassen, former district superintendent for Indian Affairs, recalls that on one weekend a social worker chartered a bus to apprehend 38 children on the Spallumcheen reserve in British Columbia and was asking for 38 different foster homes to accommodate the apprehension (Fournier & Crey, 1997).

One result of the apprehension of the children was the intensification of social problems on reserves that were experiencing the loss of their young. Aboriginal leaders spoke out against the practice with vehemence, but their voices were rarely heard.

By the end of the 1970s, one in every four Status Indian children could expect to be separated from his or her parents for all or part of childhood. In British Columbia in 1997, one in three legal wards was of Aboriginal heritage. Many Aboriginal children were shipped out of province and many went to families in the United States. Some private adoption agencies, mostly of a religious nature, sprang up to secure Canadian Aboriginal children for adoption to US families. In all, Manitoba lost the greatest number of Aboriginal children, an estimated 20,000, of which 55 percent were sent out of province, in comparison with 7 percent of non-Aboriginal adoptions going out of province. In 1982, Manitoba judge Edwin Kimmelman was called in at the insistence of Aboriginal leaders to investigate the apprehension of Manitoba's Aboriginal children. He conducted his investigation and concluded that the child welfare services were well intentioned but misguided, and guilty of cultural genocide. In response to his findings, a moratorium was placed on out-of-province adoptions, and the wholesale removal of children was stopped in the mid-1980s.

Tragically, many of these adoptions failed, as many of the children suffered from an identity crisis in their teens. Many had to endure racism in schools and from society at large without the support of the Aboriginal community. Many had been subjected to abuse while they were in the foster system prior to adoption, and were unable to overcome that legacy. Others were suffering from health complications such as fetal alcohol syndrome and fetal alcohol effects that were not diagnosed prior to adoption, and newly adoptive parents were unable to cope with the challenges of raising such a child. Today our court system and our jails are filled with Aboriginal people who are casualties from this era.

CULTURAL GENOCIDE

The term **cultural genocide** has been used widely by academics studying the history of the relationship between Canada and First Nations peoples. *Cultural genocide* can be defined as the deliberate and systematic destruction of the culture, traditions, language, and ways of being of a specific cultural group. More recently, academics have applied this term to the experiences of First Nations people in Canada and around the world. In response to the discovery of the atrocities committed against Jews during the Second World War, the international community rallied together through the United Nations to create the Convention on the Prevention and Punishment of the Crime of Genocide. Canada participated in this Convention in 1948, more than 50 years after the establishment of residential schools and prior to the proposed closure of the schools. The Convention reads as follows:

cultural genocide
the deliberate and systematic destruction of the culture, tradition, language, and ways of being of a specific cultural group

> **Article 1:** The Contracting Parties confirm that genocide, whether committed in time of peace or in time of war, is a crime under international law which they undertake to prevent and to punish.
>
> **Article 2:** In the present Convention, genocide means any of the following acts committed with intent to destroy, in whole or in part, a national, ethnical, racial or religious group, as such:
>> (a) Killing members of the group;
>> (b) Causing serious bodily or mental harm to members of the group;
>> (c) Deliberately inflicting on the group conditions of life calculated to bring about its physical destruction in whole or in part;
>> (d) Imposing measures intended to prevent births within the group;
>> (e) Forcibly transferring children of the group to another group.
>
> **Article 3:** The following acts shall be punishable:
>> (a) Genocide;
>> (b) Conspiracy to commit genocide;
>> (c) Direct and public incitement to commit genocide;
>> (d) Attempt to commit genocide;
>> (e) Complicity in genocide.
>
> **Article 4:** Persons committing genocide or any of the other acts enumerated in Article 3 shall be punished, whether they are constitutionally responsible rulers, public officials or private individuals.

EXERCISE 4

Using information from chapters 7, 8, and 9, discuss as a class whether the UN Convention's definition of genocide fits the experiences of previous generations of Aboriginal people in Canada.

If you conclude that the definition does fit, discuss who should be held accountable and how. If you believe that the definition doesn't fit, give reasons.

CONCLUSION

All aspects of the assimilation process have been devastating to Aboriginal communities: the seizure of resources and territory, which forced economic dependence; the influence of missionaries in undermining traditional Aboriginal values and forcing an agricultural way of life; the suppression of culture through provisions of the *Indian Act*. But nothing has been so devastating to Aboriginal people as the residential school system, which targeted their youngest, most vulnerable members. Among its destructive consequences are broken families, violence, substance dependency, and ill health.

On a reserve in British Columbia, research was recently conducted to determine the health status and quality of life of Aboriginal residential school survivors compared with members of the community who did not attend residential schools. The results were not surprising; there was little difference between the two populations. Both groups, however, suffered from worse health and a lower quality of life than non-Aboriginal people. Researchers concluded that the effects of residential schools are disseminated through the community. In other words, the trauma of the residential school experience was a contagion, spreading to collateral victims and from generation to generation (Benton et al., 2005).

The AHF and the TRC continue working to help survivors of the residential schools and to educate Canadians about this dark episode in our past. And there is finally a real hope that Aboriginal and non-Aboriginal Canadians may reconcile their shared history and move forward into a brighter future. This can only happen if this history, rather than being suppressed or ignored, becomes part of the national consciousness.

KEY TERMS

cultural genocide
Indian Residential Schools Settlement Agreement (IRSSA)
residential schools
Royal Commission on Aboriginal Peoples (RCAP)
Sixties Scoop

REFERENCES

Aboriginal Healing Foundation. (2010). *The Indian Residential Schools Settlement Agreement's Common Experience Payment and healing: A qualitative study exploring impacts on recipients.* Aboriginal Healing Foundation research series. Ottawa: Author. http://www.ahf.ca/downloads/cep-2010-healing.pdf.

Aboriginal Healing Foundation. (2011). *Cultivating Canada: Reconciliation through the lens of cultural diversity.* Ottawa: Dollco Printing. http://www.ahf.ca/downloads/cultivating-canada-pdf.pdf.

Benton, S., et al. (2005, August). *Social Indicators Research, 73*(2), 295–312.

Cardinal, H. (1969). *The unjust society: The tragedy of Canada's Indians.* Edmonton: Hurtig.

Fournier, S., & Crey, E. (1997). *Stolen from our embrace: The abduction of First Nations children and the restoration of Aboriginal communities.* Vancouver: Douglas and McIntyre.

Frank, S. (2003, July). *Time Canada, 162*(4), 30.

Goodwill, J., & Sluman, N. (1982). *John Tootoosis: A biography of a Cree leader.* Winnipeg: Pemmican.

Grant, A. (1996). *No end of grief: Indian residential schools in Canada.* Winnipeg: Pemmican.

Hall, D.J. (1983). Clifford Sifton and the Canadian Indian Administration 1896–1905. In I.A.L. Getty & A.S. Lussier (Eds.), *As long as the sun shines and the water flows: A reader in Canadian native studies.* Vancouver: UBC Press.

Hallett, D., Chandler, M.J., & Lalonde, C.E. (2007). Aboriginal language knowledge and youth suicide. *Cognitive Development, 22,* 392–399.

INAC File 501/25-1-019, vol. 1. (1999). G.H. Marcoux Memorandum to Mr. R.S. Davis, October 21, 1953. Reprinted in John Milloy, *A national crime: The Canadian government and the residential school system 1879 to 1986* (pp. 259–260). Winnipeg: University of Manitoba Press.

Indian and Northern Affairs Canada. (1990, November 15). Letter to Tom Siddon, file E6575-18-2, vol. 4.

Indian Tribes of Manitoba. (1971). *Wahbung: Our tomorrows.* Manitoba: Manitoba Indian Brotherhood.

Johnston, B.H. (1989). *Indian school days.* Norman, OK: University of Oklahoma Press.

King, A.R. (1967). Case study of a Yukon Indian School: How education fails. *The school at Mopass: A problem of identity.* New York: Holt, Rinehart, & Winston.

Knockwood, I., with Thomas, G. (1992). *Out of the depths: The experiences of Mi'kmaw children at the Indian residential school at Shubenacadie, Nova Scotia.* Lockport, NS: Roseway.

Milloy, J.S. (1999). *A national crime: The Canadian government and the residential school system 1879–1969.* Winnipeg: University of Manitoba Press.

Moran, B. (2002). *A little rebellion.* Vancouver: Arsenal Pulp Press.

Morris, A. (1971). *The treaties of Canada with the Indians of Manitoba and the North West Territories.* Toronto: Coles.

Native Women's Association of the Northwest Territories. (1989). Child sexual abuse: A special newsletter of the Native Women's Association of the NWT.

Nishnawbe Aske Nation. (2011). Windigo and Nan applaud landmark decision for Stirland and Cristal Lake Schools. http://www.nan.on.ca/article/windigo-and-nan-applaud-landmark-decision-for-stirland-and-cristal-lake-schools-721.asp.

Provincial Archives of Manitoba. RG 10, vol. 6040, file #160-4, part 1, C8153.

Reports of sexual abuse may be low, expert says. (1990, June 1). *The Globe and Mail*, p. A3.

Reyhner, J., & Eder, J. (2004). *American Indian education: A history*. Norman, OK: University of Oklahoma Press.

Rita Joe. (1998). I lost my talk. In D.D. Moses & T. Goldie (Eds.), *An anthology of Canadian Native Literature in English*. Toronto: Oxford University Press.

Royal Commission on Aboriginal Peoples. (1996). *The Report of the Royal Commission on Aboriginal Peoples* (Parliamentary Research Branch of the Library of Parliament No. 99-24E). http://www.parl.gc.ca/Content/LOP/ResearchPublications/prb9924-e.htm.

Statistics Canada. (2010). Family, community, and Aboriginal language among young First Nations children living off-reserve in Canada. http://www.statcan.gc.ca/pub/11-008-x/2010002/article/11336-eng.htm#a14.

Thomas, W.C. (1991, January 7). Letter, *Western Report*, p. 6.

Tibbetts, J. (2000, August). Lawyers agree to stop swooping in on victims. *The Ottawa Citizen*, p. A4.

Truth and Reconciliation Commission of Canada. (2011). Our mandate. http://www.trc.ca/websites/trcinstitution/index.php?p=7.

United Church of Canada. (2011). Aboriginal peoples: Indian residential schools. http://www.united-church.ca/aboriginal/schools/.

United Nations. (1948, December 9). *Convention on the Prevention and Punishment of the Crime of Genocide*, adopted by Resolution 260(III) A of the United Nations General Assembly.

REVIEW QUESTIONS

TRUE OR FALSE?

_____ 1. Schools for Aboriginal children in Canada were originally wanted both by Aboriginal people and by the government of Canada.

_____ 2. Aboriginal education in Canada today is funded by the provincial and territorial governments.

_____ 3. Access to education for Aboriginal people is a treaty responsibility of the federal government.

_____ 4. From 1867 to 1945, Indian children were not permitted to attend any school other than those designated for Indian education.

_____ 5. In 1920 the *Indian Act* was amended to make attendance at residential school mandatory for all Indian children and provided for Indian parents to be charged criminally for withholding their children from the schools.

_____ 6. Training schools called industrial schools were set up to teach Indian children more advanced skills such as carpentry and cabinet making. These schools were phased out because the children were unable to learn those skills.

_____ 7. Under the leadership of Duncan Campbell Scott, attendance at residential schools increased and many students were registered in grades 6 to 8.

_____ 8. The decision to use clergy as instructors in residential schools stemmed from the genuine belief that they were the most skilled teachers and could provide the highest-quality education available.

_____ 9. Dr. Peter Bryce was commissioned in 1903 to inspect residential schools and report on health conditions. He found that the death rate of the student population exceeded 50 percent in some schools.

_____ 10. Under article 4 of the United Nations _Convention on the Prevention and Punishment of the Crime of Genocide_, constitutionally responsible rulers or public officials cannot be charged under any of the acts of genocide mentioned in article 3 of the convention.

MULTIPLE CHOICE

1. Those who write about abuse within Indian residential schools generally divide the abuse into four categories. Which of the following is not one of those categories?

   (a) physical

   (b) sexual

   (c) mental

   (d) financial

2. In the struggle to redress the abuses suffered at the residential schools, the federal government has agreed to discuss compensation for which of the following forms of abuse?

   (a) spiritual/cultural

   (b) sexual

   (c) physical

   (d) b and c only

3. The most popular method of seeking redress for individual victims of abuse is civil litigation. Which of the following are reasons for this choice?

   (a) They want recognition by the public court of the legitimacy of the claim.

   (b) They want their stories told.

   (c) They believe that the courts can level the playing field between themselves and a very well-funded church and government.

   (d) All of the above.

4. Which of the following are drawbacks of the civil litigation process?

   (a) The contingency fees that go to the lawyers can constitute up to half of the financial settlement.

   (b) It takes an inordinate length of time for a case to get to court.

   (c) There is no recognition of harm to the community and the victims' families.

   (d) All of the above.

5. Which of the following was not involved in the setup and administration of Indian schools?

   (a) the provincial government

   (b) the federal government

   (c) the Catholic Church

   (d) the United Church

6. Which of the following problems can be traced in some way to the residential schools experience?

   (a) rampant sexual abuse in Aboriginal communities

   (b) family dysfunction

   (c) culture and language loss

   (d) all of the above

7. There was a significant delay between the time that the need for child welfare services on reserves was established and the time that services became available. This delay was due to

   (a) Aboriginal people's refusal to allow service staff to help their children

   (b) the remote location of the reserves

   (c) the inability of the federal and provincial governments to agree to cost sharing to provide services

   (d) problems identifying children at risk on reserves

8. By 1996, what percentage of Aboriginal people claimed that English was their mother tongue?

   (a) 10

   (b) 50

   (c) 75

   (d) 100

9. The alternative dispute resolution process set up to deal with compensation finally produced a resolution in 2006 called the Indian Residential Schools Settlement Agreement. Under this resolution, how many residential survivors will qualify?

   (a) 79,000

   (b) all Aboriginal people who can prove their heritage

   (c) 10,000

   (d) 500

10. Article 2 of the 1948 United Nations convention on genocide identifies acts that, if committed with intent to destroy a national, ethnic, racial, or religious group, constitute genocide. Which of the following acts is not contained within the definition of genocide?

    (a) causing serious bodily or mental harm to members of a group

    (b) deliberately inflicting on a group conditions of life calculated to bring about its destruction in whole or in part

    (c) failing to provide education in the language of choice

    (d) forcibly transferring children of a group to another group

APPENDIX 9.1

INHUMANE CONDITIONS AT RESIDENTIAL SCHOOL

MEMO

TO: Mr. R.S. Davis
         The Department of Citizenship and Immigration
         Indian Affairs Branch
         Norlyn Bldg.
         Winnipeg Manitoba

FROM: G.H. Marcoux
         Regional Inspector of Indian Schools

DATE: October 21, 1953

RE: Situation at Residential School

I visited the school on October 19th and 20th and found the following situation:

From the front entrance to the corridor of the basement one was subjected to an unbearable odor. The floor of the boiler room was covered with liquid from the sewage system to a depth of 6 to 8 inches, some of the liquid was seeping into the boys' recreation room. At the other end of the building, in the girls' recreation room there are a number of trap openings on the floor. Upon opening these traps one could see the same kind of liquid containing raw sewage, direct from toilets, almost to the level of the floor.

It looks as if the entire sewage piping under the floor had collapsed and that the sewage piping leading to the outside has been blocked by some obstruction.

On Monday, October 19, the smell in the building was unbearable and no human being should be asked to live under such conditions. There is no doubt in my mind that such drastic action must be taken to remedy the situation and make sure it does not re-occur in the future. I, therefore, strongly recommend that the school be closed until such time as the necessary repairs are made. Should this condition continue or happen again at a later date, the health of the pupils and the members of the staff can be seriously affected. Furthermore, should there be an outbreak of disease in a school like this one, the Indian parents would blame the school and refuse to send their children there. This would be a ten year set back in the education plan.

This is respectfully submitted in the hope that the department be advised of the situation and that immediate appropriate action be taken.

Source: INAC File 501/25-1-019, vol. 1. (1999). G.H. Marcoux Memorandum to Mr. R.S. Davis, October 21, 1953. Reprinted in John Milloy, *A national crime: The Canadian government and the residential school system 1879 to 1986* (pp. 259–260). Winnipeg: University of Manitoba Press.

APPENDIX 9.2

I Lost My Talk

By Rita Joe, Mi'kmaq

I lost my talk
The talk you took away.
When I was a little girl
At Shubenacadie school.

You snatched it away;
I speak like you
I think like you
I create like you
The scrambled ballad, about my word.

Two ways I talk
Both ways I say,
Your way is more powerful.

So gently I offer my hand and ask,
Let me find my talk
So I can teach you about me.

Source: Joe, R. (1998). I lost my talk. In D.D. Moses & T. Goldie (Eds.), *An anthology of Canadian Native literature in English*. Toronto: Oxford University Press.

Current Socio-economic Issues

10

INTRODUCTION

The socio-economic issues facing First Nations people today are a legacy of colonization and forced assimilation. We have journeyed here together as mainstream Canada and First Nations people, but it is clear who is responsible for the journey's direction. As one Aboriginal speaker put it, "We were not standing on the shores of Eastern Canada waiting for the white man to arrive in his sailing ship carrying a welfare check" (Geddes, Doxtater, & Krepakevich, 1997). Aboriginal populations are growing rapidly, but economic growth in their communities is slow. In this chapter, we look at obstacles to that growth and to the ultimate goal of self-sufficiency for Aboriginal people. We examine their overall social and economic capacity, as well as the health and resilience of their communities. Our aim is to understand how they can achieve greater mental and physical health, positive economic growth, and increased community cohesion and strength.

CASE STUDY: GRASSY NARROWS

Prior to discussing demographics, let us look closely at a northern Ontario reserve—the Ojibwa community of Grassy Narrows—and at how this community came to its current socio-economic condition. There are many Aboriginal communities in Canada, each with a distinct individual history shaped by particular events and crises, and all deserve our attention. But space constraints prevent us from discussing more than one of them.

Grassy Narrows is located 80 kilometres north of Kenora, Ontario, near the Manitoba border. The Ojibwa community living on the reserve today consists of 630 people. Fifty-two percent of them are children or youth under 19 years of age.

The reserved area was set aside for the Grassy Narrows people in 1873, with the signing of Treaty No. 3. By this treaty, the people of this area relinquished 14 million hectares to the government while retaining their right to pursue their traditional occupations, such

CHAPTER OBJECTIVES

After completing this chapter, you should be able to:

- Identify the social and legal categories of Aboriginal people in Canada, and appreciate the challenges of researching Canada's diverse Aboriginal groups and communities.

- Discuss trends in Aboriginal educational achievement levels, population, income and labour market participation, health, language, living conditions, and social assistance, and the implications of these trends for Canada's future.

- Outline the contributing factors to the socio-economic trends analyzed in this chapter.

- Understand the connection between colonization and current challenges facing Aboriginal people.

- Identify the relationship between Aboriginal people, the federal government, and the provincial governments with regards to funding, provision of services, and plans for economic renewal for Aboriginal people in Canada.

- Understand the critical situation of many Aboriginal languages, and the link between language and Aboriginal well-being.

as hunting and fishing, on the surrendered tract of land, except on such areas as may "from time to time" be required for settlement, mining, or forestry. The government was to maintain schools for instruction, and pay annuities to the band in the amount of $5 per person per year.

Missionaries began work in the Grassy Narrows area in the 1840s, accessing the area by canoe. On their arrival, most of the Aboriginal people were out of their reach, following a traditional hunting and trapping way of life. The people would return from the traplines in May to their summer grounds where they would plant gardens and live in their spaciously distributed summer cabins. Those who were taken to the residential schools at McIntosh or Kenora were the ones most influenced by the missions.

Land development came with the building of a railway to access forestry products, but few Aboriginal people left the community. There was no welfare or social services; the Indian agent came to the reserve once a year to distribute treaty money. Until 1963, the relative isolation allowed the Aboriginal people of this area to preserve their culture, way of life, self-sufficiency, and freedom. The summer of 1963, Indian Affairs began the process of relocating the people of Grassy Narrows to a new community on the Jones logging road, which was linked to both the railway and the city of Kenora. Indian Affairs intended to provide the Aboriginal people with the benefits of modern life, and to end the isolation that had helped them resist assimilation.

The new community was built 8 kilometres from the old one, on the English Wabigoon River. The river was to supply their water needs (the government's promise of running water was not initially fulfilled). The housing provided on the new reserve was crowded and of poor quality. The hunting and trapping way of life became difficult to maintain; the government insisted that the children remain on the reserve and attend school, and this made the parents reluctant to leave for the traplines through the fall and winter.

Prior to the move, the government had been systematically dismantling the traditional economic system of the Ojibwa people. Harvesting wild rice for sustenance had been an activity of Ojibwa people from time immemorial. In the 1950s, however, the government began to issue licences for that harvest; the price of wild rice had increased, making it a possible source of income for the Ojibwa. Initially, the Ojibwa people were issued licences to harvest wild rice, but in the 1970s non-Aboriginal wild rice farmers took over many of those licences. Their mechanical methods of harvesting were more efficient than the traditional Ojibwa methods.

Access to the new reserve from Kenora made it easier for government officials to impose fishing regulations on the Grassy Narrows people. Amendments to the *Indian Act* made all laws of the province applicable not just to non-Aboriginal people but to Aboriginal people, too; this made the Ojibwa subject to fishing regulations even though this restriction was in direct violation of their treaty rights. Commercial fishing licences were issued to some Grassy Narrows people, but sport fishing licences were given priority because they brought more revenue to the area, predominately in white communities.

With limited access to paid employment and new constraints on their traditional means of sustenance, the community began to sink into despair. During this time of social upheaval and vulnerability, the Jones logging road, intended to bring the benefits of modern life to the people of Grassy Narrows, brought an unregulated flow of alcohol. Alcoholism, violence, and suicide spiralled out of control in the community, as is shown in Figure 10.1.

Studies conducted at Grassy Narrows in 1977–1978 concluded that 70 percent of adults in their child-bearing years and 80 percent in their child-rearing years were heavy drinkers. Alcohol has been, and continues to be, a disruptive influence on Aboriginal communities such as the one at Grassy Narrows, where the parents' drinking is largely responsible for the children's substance abuse and consequent failure to achieve academically (see Table 10.1). Gas sniffing, in particular, is a major problem among young people who live in these communities.

The Department of Indian Affairs and Northern Development (DIAND) brought extensive development to the North, in the form of forestry and mining, and by doing so brought more hardship to the people of Grassy Narrows. In the early 1920s, a pulp and paper mill was opened in Dryden, Ontario, 130 kilometres upstream from the traditional Grassy Narrows area. Between 1962 and 1970, Dryden Chemicals Limited pulp and paper mill, with the sanction of the Ontario government, dumped over 20,000 pounds of mercury into the river system, poisoning it. The commercial fisheries on the reserve had to be shut down, and the people were advised not to eat the fish. Those who held fishing licences were issued $300 in compensation for the loss of their livelihood. In the 1970s and subsequently, health officials conducted tests on the population and found that their mercury levels were 40 to 150 times higher than the average Canadian's, likely due to their consumption not only of fish but also of animals that had ingested the mercury in some form.

The government's expenditures on Grassy Narrows skyrocketed. Within 15 years of relocating the Grassy Narrows Ojibwa, DIAND was spending almost $1 million annually on health, food, and housing for a community formerly visited once a year by an Indian agent and requiring little in the way of health care (see Table 10.2).

Figure 10.1   Incidence of Violent Death at Grassy Narrows, 1959–1978

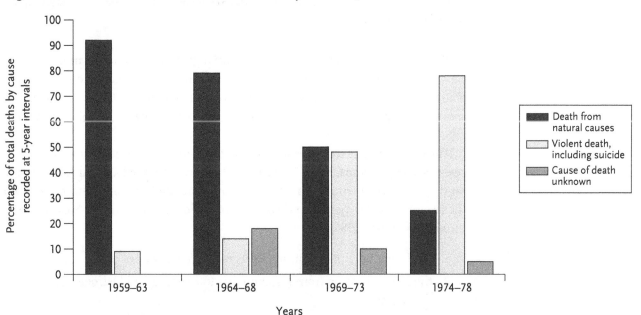

Source: Shkilnyk (1985).

Table 10.1   School Dropout Rate at Grassy Narrows, 1977–1978

Grade	Number of dropouts	Class size	Percentage of class
Kindergarten	10	20	50
1	3	16	18
2	7	24	29
3	9	17	53
4	7	17	41
5–8	10	24	42
4–6 (special class)	10	25	40

Note: Based on the records of attendance at the Grassy Narrows Federal Elementary School.
Source: Shkilnyk (1985).

Table 10.2   DIAND Expenditures at Grassy Narrows, 1969–1978

Fiscal year	Amount ($)
1969–70	37,600
1970–71	106,400
1971–72	143,100
1972–73	356,800
1973–74	413,300
1974–75	377,600
1975–76	442,135
1976–77	708,970
1977–78	950,900

Note: The data from 1969–70 to 1972–73 were provided by the Kenora district office of DIAND and correspond to band financial records. Data for 1973–74 on came from the band's audited financial statements.
Source: Shkilnyk (1985).

There were disputes between the provincial government and the mill as to who was responsible for the environmental disaster; neither wished to accept accountability. Because the mill had followed environmental practices that were acceptable according to provincial law, the band was ultimately unable to hold any agency accountable.

The band continued to appeal to the government for assistance in alleviating its severe social problems. In 1977, the federal government held a Royal Commission on the Northern Environment. The Commission cited the following reasons for the severe physical, mental, and spiritual breakdown in the Grassy Narrows community (Shkilnyk, 1985):

1. the intentional undermining of its religion and way of life;
2. the loss of income from trapping due to flooding and hydroelectric development;
3. the Jones logging road disrupting the community's isolation upon relocation;

4. new access to alcohol;

5. introduction of a foreign value system;

6. loss of commercial fishing due to mercury poisoning;

7. availability of welfare but no work; and

8. inability to hold any agency accountable for mercury disaster.

It was not until 1985 that the Grassy Narrows community received a negotiated settlement for the poisoning of their environment. By then, the community had already hit rock bottom and was beginning to recover. The situation at Grassy Narrows improved through the 1990s, and today the people are moving forward and taking control over many aspects of their community life. Currently, they are addressing logging issues in their traditional territories with some success. In April 2011, Grassy Narrows signed a memorandum of agreement with the province of Ontario over the management of the Whiskey Jack Forest resources. This forest, traditionally used by the Grassy Narrows First Nation, was licensed by the Crown to Abitibi Lumber until 2009, by which point 50 percent of the area had been clear-cut. For the ten years prior to 2009, the band had been blockading roadways in an effort to force a negotiation to preserve the forest and gain some control over the timber access on their traditional territory.

Conclusion

This has been a very brief look at the recent history of the Grassy Narrows people. You are encouraged to look into this history more deeply, on your own time. This community is an extreme case, but its dealings with non-Aboriginal Canada are typical in some respects of the Aboriginal experience in Canada. Almost every First Nations community in Ontario has been relocated at some point from its traditional territory, usually because the government or some private interest, such as a logging company, wants readier access to the region's resources. Some Aboriginal groups have been moved hundreds of kilometres from their traditional land. In almost all cases, relocation has brought severe social problems and economic hardship to those concerned. The Canadian government has known about the negative consequences of relocation since it first began to impose it on Aboriginal people in the 19th century. Until recently, however, the government has continued this destructive practice.

EXERCISE 1

As mentioned in Chapter 8, the federal government of Canada, through the treaty process, undertook the fiduciary responsibility for Aboriginal people. Discuss as a class whether you think the government met that responsibility in the case of Grassy Narrows.

Discuss as a class the name of the branch of the government charged with responsibility for Aboriginal people during the 1970s: *Department of Indian Affairs and Northern Development*. Separate that title into two distinct interests: "Indian Affairs" and "Northern Development." Discuss what these two had in common and the conflicts between the two.

ABORIGINAL ANCESTRY: SOCIAL AND LEGAL CATEGORIES

Trying to describe Canada's Aboriginal people in statistical terms can be very confusing; there are various categories of people with Aboriginal ancestry. Another complicating factor is that statistical data in this area comes from three sources—Statistics Canada, Indian and Northern Affairs Canada, and the Aboriginal Peoples Survey. Each of these organizations goes by a different classification system. Statistics Canada information is derived from the census survey, for which identification is voluntary. The census uses the umbrella term "Aboriginal Identity," which includes Métis, Inuit, and First Nations (status and non-status) peoples. Indian and Northern Affairs Canada, in its statistical surveys of the Aboriginal population, includes only those Indians who are registered under the *Indian Act*. The Aboriginal Peoples Survey is different again, including in its statistical count only Inuit, Métis, and *off-reserve* First Nations populations. Because of these divergent accounting systems, statistics regarding Aboriginal populations vary from source to source. This can become confusing to researchers and readers alike.

It is not surprising, then, that the number of registered Indians recorded by the Indian and Northern Affairs Indian Register differs from Statistics Canada's census counts of registered Indians; the two sources of data do not count registered Indians the same way or for the same reason. The Register is an administrative database, while the census is a statistical survey. To complicate matters further, although many registered Indians are members of one of the more than 600 bands in Canada, many others are not. Some band members are registered as Indians, but others are not. Some bands are connected to treaties and therefore sometimes referred to as Treaty Indians, but some bands have never signed onto any treaty (as discussed in Chapter 8). See Figure 10.2 for an overview of these categories.

There have always been significant statistical differences between Aboriginal people who live on-reserve and those who live off-reserve; therefore, Statistics Canada and Aboriginal Affairs and Northern Development Canada collect information for both of these categories. However, because the Aboriginal population tends to be more mobile than the non-Aboriginal population, these numbers change regularly, as the people move back and forth between reserved territories and cities.

There is such diversity among Aboriginal people that it is unwise to envision a homogeneous "Aboriginal" population in Canada. A snapshot of census data covering all 600 bands, the Métis, and the Inuit cannot possibly capture the profound differences in all data areas between the various Aboriginal groups. For example, there are profound differences between the Kanewake Mohawks of Quebec and the Lubicon Cree of Alberta, who differ from the Innu of Natuashish, or the Cree Nation of Saskatchewan.

SIZE OF THE ABORIGINAL POPULATION

In the 2006 census, 1,172,790 people identified themselves as having an Aboriginal identity, with 698,025 reporting as North American Indian, 389,780 reporting Métis, and 50,480 reporting Inuit ancestry. The number of Canadians reporting Aboriginal ancestry is growing rapidly (see Table 10.3). The population of Canada increased by 9.5 percent between 1996 and 2006; in the same period, the number of persons

Figure 10.2   Social–Legal Categories of Aboriginals Residing in Canada

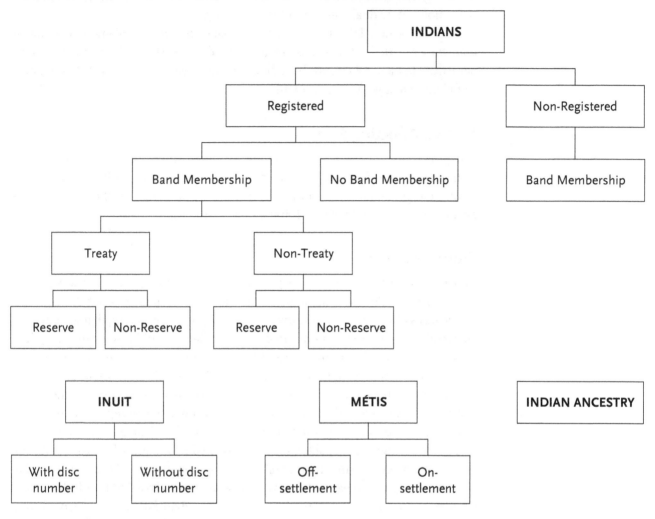

Source: Frideres & Gadacz (2008, p. 30).

Table 10.3   Size and Growth Rate of Aboriginal Populations in Canada

Aboriginal identity population	2006 counts	Distribution (%) (2006)	Growth (%) (2001 to 2006)	Growth (%) (1996 to 2006)
Total population of Canada	**31,241,030**	**100.0%**	**5.4%**	**9.5%**
Aboriginal identity population	1,172,790	3.8%	20.1%	44.9%
Non-Aboriginal identity population	30,068,240	96.2%	4.9%	8.4%
Total Aboriginal identity population	**1,172,790**	**100.0%**	**20.1%**	**44.9%**
North American Indian	698,025	59.5%	14.6%	29.1%
Métis	389,780	33.2%	33.3%	90.9%
Inuit	50,480	4.3%	12.0%	25.5%

Source: Statistics Canada (2008a, p. 10). http://www12.statcan.ca/census-recensement/2006/dp-pd/hlt/97-558/pages/page.cfm?Lang=E&Geo=PR
&Code=01&Table=3&Data=Count&Sex=1&StartRec=1&Sort=2&Display=Page.

reporting Aboriginal ancestry rose by 44.9 percent, with a staggering 90.9 percent rise among individuals reporting Métis identity.

It should be noted that the actual Aboriginal population numbers may be higher than those reported in the census, because 22 Indian reserves and settlements did not participate in the 2006 census. In addition, some individuals may have chosen not to self-identify to government workers.

Factors Affecting Size

The growth rate of Canada's population is affected primarily by two factors: the birth rate and the death rate. (A third factor is immigration.) The growth rate of Aboriginal populations is significantly affected by three factors: the birth rate, the death rate, and the rate at which individuals gain or lose status.

Status Loss and Gain

Canadian laws defining whom the government would recognize as Indians predate the *Indian Act*. The earliest statutory definition of "Indian" did not discriminate on the basis of sex, but in 1869 provisions were introduced stating that women who "married out"—that is, who married a non-Indian—would lose status, and their children would not be granted status. On the other hand, Indian men who married non-Indian women would not lose status. The 1876 *Indian Act* maintained these provisions; moreover, the 1876 Act also provided that an "Indian" included any woman who was married to "any male person of Indian blood reputed to belong to a particular band," whether or not the woman was Indian (Hurley & Simeone, 2010).

The new *Indian Act*, enacted in 1951, established a national registry, with entitlement linked to band membership; it also maintained the provisions that discriminated, on the basis of sex, against women who married non-Indian men. Children born to an Indian mother and a non-Indian father were deemed non-Indian. However, the status of children born to an Indian father was determined by the "double mother rule," which stated that if the child's mother and paternal grandmother had a right to Indian status only through having married an Indian man, the child had Indian status only up to the age of 21.

Prior to 1985, these provisions were strongly criticized by First Nations women's groups, human rights groups, and others, but these criticisms were ignored. However, when s. 15 of the Charter came into force in 1985, the provisions were in clear violation of the new equality rights—which made it illegal to discriminate based on various categories, including sex. At this point, the government could not wait any longer to take action. In 1985, Bill C-31, An Act to Amend the *Indian Act*, was passed. Three principles guided the changes: (1) removing discriminatory clauses; (2) restoring status and membership rights; and (3) increasing control of Indian bands over their own membership (Aboriginal Affairs and Northern Development Canada, 2010b).

With regard to entitlement to registration, ss. 6(1) and 6(2) provided the following:

- Individuals entitled to registration prior to 1985 (including non-Indian women married to Indian men, and their children) retained full status (s. 6(1)(a)).

- Women who had lost status through marrying out or through an order of enfranchisement, and persons who had lost status at 21 through the double mother rule, regained status (s. 6(1)(c)).

- Individuals with one parent entitled to registration under s. 6(1) acquired status under s. 6(2); persons with one parent registered under s. 6(2) and one non-status parent were/are not entitled to registration.

Figure 10.3 shows the percentage change in Canada's registered Indian population from 1981 to 2003, and the effects of the 1985 amendments to the *Indian Act*.

The requirement that children registered under s. 6(2) must partner with a registered Indian in order for the children to be entitled to registration is often referred to as the "second generation cut-off rule." This requirement was a primary target for charges that there was residual sex discrimination in the Act, and there were calls for the removal of this requirement (Hurley & Simeone, 2010). In a 2005 statement, the Assembly of First Nations commented that "[t]he bill has not resolved any of the problems it was intended to fix ... Significant gender discrimination still remains, control over Indian status is still held by the Crown, and the population of Indians is declining as a direct result of Bill C-31" (Assembly of First Nations, 2005).

According to Indian and Northern Affairs Canada (INAC) (2009, p. 3), since Bill C-31 came into force, over 117,000 persons who had lost status under discriminatory status provisions, as well as their descendants, have regained or acquired status. However, projections made several years ago warned of a "rapid decline" in the number of individuals entitled to registration. This decline would result from the s. 6 rules and from marrying out, with one source predicting that sometime around the end of the fifth generation, the number of children born who would be entitled to Indian registration would fall to zero (Hurley & Simeone, 2010).

Until recently, it was believed that applications for reinstatement had slowed to a trickle and that population growth in the future would no longer be affected by

Figure 10.3   Percentage Change in Registered Indian Population, Canada, 1981 to 2003

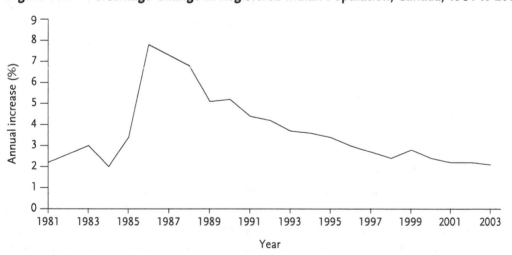

Source: Indian and Northern Affairs Canada (2005, p. 2). http://dsp-psd.pwgsc.gc.ca/collection_2008/inac-ainc/R12-7-2004E.pdf.

status reinstatement applications under Bill C-31. If this ultimately turns out to be the case, it will be largely owing to the 2009 BC Court of Appeal ruling in *McIvor vs. Canada*, which has had a significant effect on the number of individuals who are eligible for registration.

To summarize the *McIvor* case, Sharon McIvor was not registered as an Indian prior to 1985. Had she been registered, she would have lost her registration because she married a non-Indian. Ms. McIvor became registered after 1985 under s. 6(2), on the basis of having one parent registered under s. 6(1) and one non-Indian parent. Her son, Jacob Grismer, has a child with a non-Indian woman. Because Ms. McIvor was registered under 6(2) of the Act, her grandchild (Mr. Grismer's child) could not be registered as Indian.

The core of McIvor's argument on behalf of her grandson's registration was that if she had not been removed from status prior to 1985, she would have been registered as a s. 6(1) Indian and thereby able to pass status on to her grandchild. If Ms. McIvor had been male (the court made use of a "hypothetical brother" of Ms. McIvor in considering this), she—or rather, "he"—would have maintained status and been registered as a s. 6(1) Indian once the changes to the Act took place in 1985. Any grandchildren of this hypothetical brother would be entitled to be registered. The BC Court of Appeal held that the "preferential treatment" enjoyed by Indian men who married prior to 1985—and whose grandchildren were afforded "enhanced status" as compared to those of a female who had married prior to 1985—was a violation of s. 15 of the Charter. The court gave the Government of Canada until April 2010 to amend the unconstitutional provisions in the Act.

In 2010, the government introduced amendments ensuring that eligible grandchildren of women who had lost status as a result of marrying non-Indian men would be entitled to registration under the Act. The current version of the Act, which came into force in January 2011, incorporates these amendments, in s. 6(c.1). At the time of writing, the amendments do not extend to other situations (such as the second-generation cut-off), but other constitutional challenges to the registration provisions are currently active.

The determination of status under the *Indian Act* is both a complex topic and a live issue. Many Canadians may find the matter merely confusing, but for Aboriginal people it is critical. Through the federal government and provincial agencies, a wide range of programs and services are available to Status Indians that are not available to non-registered individuals; status determines eligibility for living on reserves, eligibility for tax exemption, and access to health care and education. In addition to these tangible benefits, being officially registered is for many individuals with Aboriginal ancestry an important part of identification with their family and with the larger community.

Birth and Death Rates

Like the birth rate for Canada as a whole, the birth rate for Aboriginal populations is declining over time. Despite this, the Aboriginal birth rate is still 1.5 times that of the non-Aboriginal population. As a result, the Aboriginal population is younger on average than the non-Aboriginal population. In fact, the median age (the point where exactly half the population is older and the other half younger) is 27 years for Aboriginal people, compared with 40 years for the non-Aboriginal population. The Inuit population is younger still, with a median age of 22 years. The Métis population, which is the fastest growing of all, has a median age of 30 years (Statistics Canada, 2006a).

Life expectancy for Aboriginal people, according to the 2006 census (Statistics Canada, 2006a), still lags behind that of the general population. On average, Aboriginal people's lives are approximately 7 years shorter than the lives of their non-Aboriginal counterparts, for both sexes. Seniors represent only 5 percent of both the Métis and the Aboriginal identity group, compared with the 13 percent they represent in the non-Aboriginal population. A number of issues that affect the mortality rate of Aboriginal people will be discussed later in this chapter.

POPULATION DISTRIBUTION

Geographical Distribution

According to the 2006 census (Statistics Canada, 2006a), 80 percent of Aboriginal people live in Ontario, Manitoba, Saskatchewan, Alberta, and British Columbia. The next greatest number live in Quebec. The Western provinces and the Territories have the greatest ratio of Aboriginal people to the total population. For example, the 24,920 Aboriginal people (mostly Inuit) in Nunavut make up 85 percent of Nunavut's population. Figure 10.4 shows the percentage of the total population that Aboriginal people represent, in Canada and in the respective provinces and territories.

Figure 10.4   Percentage of Aboriginal People in the Population, Canada, Provinces, and Territories, 2006

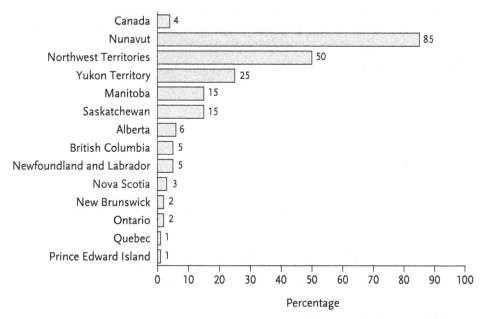

Source: Statistics Canada (2008a, p. 11). http://www12.statcan.gc.ca/english/census06/analysis/aboriginal/pdf/97-558-XIE2006001.pdf.

Urban/Rural Distribution

Another trend shown by the 2006 census is that the Aboriginal population overall is becoming increasingly urban. Census figures indicate (Statistics Canada, 2006a) that 54 percent of Aboriginal people live in urban centres, including large cities and smaller urban centres. This is an increase from the 50 percent who lived in urban centres a decade ago (Statistics Canada, 2006a). Even though a large percentage of Aboriginal people live in urban centres, they do not make up a very large percentage of the populations in these places. For example, in Winnipeg, where more Aboriginal people (68,380) reside than in any other Canadian city, they account for only 10 percent of the population. The cities with the next largest Aboriginal populations are Edmonton (52,100 people, or 5 percent of the city's population), Vancouver (40,310 people, which is 2 percent of the population), Toronto (26,500, or 0.5 percent of the population), Calgary (26,575, or 2 percent of its population), Saskatoon (21,535 Aboriginal people, which is 9 percent of its population) and Regina (17,105, also about 9 percent of its population).

Among Aboriginal respondents to the 2006 census, First Nations people are most likely to be urban dwellers, though this figure has declined somewhat since 1996. Métis are increasingly living in cities, and the Inuit remain the least likely to live in large urban centres (Statistics Canada, 2006a). As noted previously, because the Aboriginal population is more mobile than the non-Aboriginal population, these statistics change frequently.

The trend toward urbanization among Aboriginal people goes back over four decades. In 1966, only 19.5 percent of status Aboriginal people lived off-reserve. In 1986, that percentage increased to 31.9 percent. By 2001, 42.5 percent of status Aboriginal people lived off-reserve. The 2006 statistics reflect both status and non-status First Nation, Métis, and Inuit, 54 percent of whom live off-reserve.

A number of factors influence the decision to migrate to urban centres. Population increases on reserves can lead to overcrowding, lack of housing, and unemployment, which can cause individuals to look elsewhere for opportunity. Individuals may move to an urban centre to enter the labour market and/or to acquire education not readily available on a reserve. Individuals are more likely to migrate to an urban centre if there is one in close proximity to their reserve.

Challenges for Urban Aboriginals

One of the challenges facing Aboriginal migrants to urban centres is the ongoing jurisdictional disputes as to which level of government has legislative authority and responsibility for them. The federal government acknowledges its responsibility for on-reserve registered First Nations people; however, the responsibility to provide services for other Aboriginal people is often subject to disputes between provincial, municipal, and federal governments. This often leads to a scarcity of services for Aboriginal people living in urban areas.

One analysis (Frideres & Gadacz, 2008, p. 170) has shown that urban Aboriginal people, compared with their non-Aboriginal counterparts,

- are more likely to have low levels of education,
- have low labour force participation rates,

- have high unemployment rates,
- have low income levels,
- have high rates of homelessness and greater housing needs,
- are overrepresented in the criminal justice system,
- have poor health status (particularly in the areas of suicide, HIV, AIDS, diabetes, and substance abuse), and
- are more than twice as likely to be members of lone-parent families and to experience domestic violence.

Currently in Ontario, some programs for urban-dwelling Aboriginal people are offered though the Ontario Federation of Indian Friendship Centres (OFIFC). There are 29 of these Friendship Centres, located in cities across Ontario; they offer programs to support education, economic development, cultural awareness, and youth initiatives for urban Aboriginal people. The goal is to encourage equal access to services and full participation in Canadian society for these populations. The OFIFC is funded by various levels of government; the level depends on the particular programs and services operated by each individual centre.

EDUCATION

The strong causal connection between education, participation in the labour market, and income has been well established by social science. Education is also connected to physical and mental health and to reduced criminal activity. There is also a generational spillover: the parents' educational level is connected to the educational attainment of their children. Aboriginal people in Canada have had persistently low academic achievement relative to the general population. This has perpetuated their economic disadvantage.

Delivery and Funding

There are a number of paths to education for Aboriginal people in Canada. There are First Nations–managed (that is, band-operated) schools, which are predominantly on First Nations reserves across Canada and serve mostly First Nations students living on reserves. There are 518 such schools. They are funded by the federal government and managed by First Nations bands. The degree of control that the band has over education budget, curriculum, and staffing differs according to reserve and often depends on the numbers of students and staff involved. The goal for Aboriginal people is to have the band exercise complete control over the education process, a goal that many bands have achieved (Laboucane, 2010, p. 18).

In 1988, The federal government created a "Band Operated Funding Formula" that sets out budgets for the operation of the schools. The formula, which is based on the number of students in the school multiplied by the cost of educational delivery, mirrors a similar funding formula that exists for the provincial school system throughout the rest of Canada. But there has been tremendous growth in Aboriginal communities, and the government has not kept pace in funding either children who attend on-reserve schools or those who attend provincially run schools off-reserve. Provincial schools are paid more than double what on-reserve schools are paid for student tuition. In 2006–7, the support provided to Aboriginal students by the Elementary/Secondary Education Program was on average *$2,000 less per student* than the amount provided to provincial students (Laboucane, 2010, p. 18). Some estimates of the funding gap indicate the amount may in fact be much greater (VanEvery-Albert, 2004, pp. 18–19). Teachers in band-operated schools are paid less than teachers in provincial schools. A Chiefs of Ontario report showed that the Ontario teacher's annual salary classed at year 5 level 5 on the grid was $54,079. First Nations teachers at the same level in band-operated schools had an average income of $46,179 (VanEvery-Albert, 2004, p. 7). This may account for some of the funding shortfall, since salaries are a large part of education budgets. Robert Laboucane (2010, p. 21) paints a grim picture of reserve schools:

> There is no funding for on reserve school libraries or books. Schools are unable to provide competitive salaries for teachers on reserves. There is no funding for vocational training in secondary schools on reserves. There is no funding for extra-curricular sports and recreation activities on reserves.

Post-secondary education for Aboriginal students is underfunded, too. In 2010–11, INAC's budget was $400 million for approximately 27,000 First Nations post-secondary students. In general, the number of First Nations students eligible for post-secondary education exceeds the budget, so applicants are turned away. In 2009, over 5,000 prospective students were denied funding (Laboucane, 2010, p. 18).

Of the 120,400 on-reserve students enrolled in kindergarten, elementary, and secondary schools in 2003–4, 60 percent were in First Nations–managed schools, while slightly less than 40 percent were in provincial/private schools (INAC, 2005). (These statistics exclude Nunavut, Northwest Territories, Atlantic Canada, and Quebec.) While 85 percent of INAC-funded students attended band-operated schools from kindergarten through to grade 5, this percent decreased sharply to only 45 percent by grade 12 (INAC, 2005). This decrease is largely due to the fact that secondary schools are often unavailable in First Nations communities, so students are transferred to the provincial system for secondary school.

Achievement Rates: A Comparison

There are clear differences in educational achievement rates between students who are educated on-reserve and those who attend provincial schools off-reserve. Within the provincial system, there are differences in achievement rates between Aboriginal students and their non-Aboriginal counterparts. Finally, there are differences among the achievement rates of First Nations, Métis, and Inuit students, both overall and when differences in location are factored in.

According to the 2006 census, there were 78,325 First Nations children living off-reserve between the ages of 6 and 14, representing 2 percent of all Canadian children in this age group. According to research, the parents of 90 percent of off-reserve First Nations children felt that the school provided enough information on their child's academic progress, behaviour, and attendance (Laboucane, 2010, p. 21). They also found the level of discipline, quality of teaching, and availability of extracurricular activities satisfactory.

In general, students who live and attend school off-reserve come from higher-income homes, which is one of the factors contributing to their higher academic achievement (see the discussion in the next section). However, 41 percent of First Nations youth who live off-reserve do not complete high school; interestingly, this figure is the same as the percentage of off-reserve students who live in single-parent families (another factor correlated with achievement). For First Nations youth living on-reserve, 58 percent do not complete high school. There has been no measurable increase in the high school completion rate for on-reserve students over the past 15 years (Laboucane, 2010, p. 21).

Differences also exist in post-secondary educational achievement among Aboriginal groups. For Inuit people, although 51 percent had less than a high school diploma, 36 percent had either a post-secondary diploma or degree: 17 percent with a college diploma, 13 percent with a trade certificate, and 4 percent with a university degree (Statistics Canada, 2008b). For the Inuit, the rates of educational achievement vary widely depending on the region.

Half of the Métis population has completed post-secondary education; 21 percent have a college diploma, 16 percent have a trade certificate, and 9 percent have a university degree. In the prairie provinces and New Brunswick, academic achievement for the Métis fell below the national average for this Aboriginal population (Statistics Canada, 2008b).

Collectively, according to the 2006 census, 42 percent of Aboriginal people completed a post-secondary education, compared with 61 percent of people in the non-Aboriginal population (Statistics Canada, 2006a). These numbers were lower for Aboriginal people living on-reserve (35 percent) than for Aboriginal people living off-reserve (46 percent).

Factors Correlated with Success and Failure

A number of studies have been done to determine why Aboriginal students perform as they do in the school system. These studies, along with more general research into the sources of academic achievement, confirm the role played by socio-economic status, parental education level, household living arrangements, and household income in determining student success.

The 2006 Aboriginal Peoples Survey (Statistics Canada, 2007b) has identified a number of factors that are positively correlated with perceived academic achievement. (Recall that this survey considers only off-reserve, status, and non-status Aboriginal people—in other words, those most likely to use their respective provincial schools rather than band-operated schools.) These factors included the following:

- getting along with peers and teachers,
- having parents who were satisfied with school practices,
- reading books every day,
- playing sports or extracurricular activities at least once a week, and
- living in a household with the highest income quintile.

The same survey identified a number of factors that correlated negatively with perceived academic achievement. These included the following:

- having missed school for a period of two or more weeks in a row,
- having been diagnosed with a learning disability, or
- having parents who attended a residential school.

Overall, studies show that students with the greatest difficulty in schools are those who come from a long history of discrimination, subjugation, and prejudice (Laboucane, 2010, p. 21).

In Canada, British Columbia is the only province to publish standardized test results by various characteristics of schools and students, including Aboriginal identity. In British Columbia there are 60,000 self-identified Aboriginal students in the provincial school system; they make up approximately 10 percent of the school population (Richards, Vining, & Weimer, 2010, p. 48) A study was conducted to assess Aboriginal performance in the grade 4 and 7 standardized tests that assess the foundational skills of reading, writing, and numeracy. The study, focused on the period spanning the 2001–2 and 2005–6 school years, showed that a sizable gap exists by grade 4 between Aboriginal and non-Aboriginal student performance, and that this gap widens by grade 7 (Richards, Vining, & Weimer, 2010, p. 54).

In the BC study, the school catchment areas from which the results were drawn were measured in terms of socio-economic status. The improvement in test scores remained fairly constant for both Aboriginal and non-Aboriginal students when the catchment area was in the highest income areas. Furthermore, the number of Aboriginal students in the school was measured in relation to achievement levels, and it was found that a higher Aboriginal student count in a school produced *lower* overall academic achievement for Aboriginal students.

The BC study also looked for common denominators in the more successful districts, and it was found (Richards, Vining, & Weimer, 2010, p. 63) that these districts

- had school administrators and teachers who more consistently emphasized Aboriginal educational success as a long-term priority,
- engaged Aboriginal leaders from the broader community with greater success,
- made more consistent use of objective data on Aboriginal student performance,
- had a reputation for following through on policy implementation.

Clearly, this study has some implications for BC school system policy changes.

Generally speaking, the statistics indicate that the educational system is failing Aboriginal students and failing Canada in the process. According to the Canadian Centre for the Study of Living Standards, Canada's economy would increase by $71.1 billion if Aboriginal people achieved the same educational levels as other Canadians (Laboucane, 2010, p. 18). Among the various factors contributing to the under-achievement of Aboriginal students, an impoverished sense of identity is surely one. Certain factors contribute to such impoverishment: curricula that exclude

Aboriginal children's history, cultures, languages, and contributions to Canada; and educators' lack of knowledge about Aboriginal culture and history.

INCOME AND LABOUR MARKET PARTICIPATION

In the years between the 2001 and 2006 censuses, the number of Aboriginal people of working age (that is, between the ages of 15 and 64 years) increased by 25 percent; for the general Canadian population, the increase was only 6 percent. The 2006 census enumerated 767,420 Aboriginal individuals of working age, of which 512,365 participated in the labour force (Aboriginal Affairs and Northern Development Canada, 2010a). Although the Aboriginal employment rate (for individuals of working age) increased from 58 percent to 63 percent between 2001 and 2006, this rate is still much lower than the 76 percent employment rate for non-Aboriginals. In addition, although the Aboriginal unemployment rate has decreased since 2001, in 2006 the unemployment rate for Aboriginal people of working age was almost three times that of non-Aboriginals (13 percent compared with 5 percent) and was higher than the national rate in every region.

Educational achievement levels are linked to employment rates and income levels. For all Canadians, those with 8 or fewer years of education had only a 24.5 percent labour market participation rate. Canadians with some high school education had a 51.2 percent labour market participation rate, and those who graduated from high school had a 69.5 percent labour market participation rate in 2006. Canadians who held a post-secondary certificate had a 76.6 percent participation rate, and those with university degrees had an 80 percent participation rate (Statistics Canada, 2008b).

Figure 10.5 shows the employment rate among First Nations people in various categories for the 2001 and 2006 census years, as well as the employment rate for

Figure 10.5   Employment Rates Among First Nations People Aged 25 to 54, by Registered Indian Status, Living On and Off Reserve, Canada, 2001 and 2006

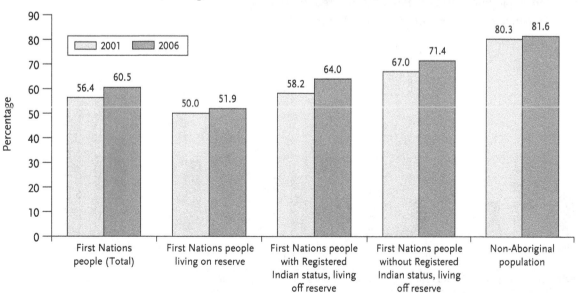

Source: Statistics Canada, Census of Population, 2001 and 2006. http://www.statcan.gc.ca/pub/11-008-x/2009001/c-g/10864/c-g001-eng.htm.

the non-Aboriginal population. Figure 10.6 shows the unemployment rate across several provinces for North American Indians, Métis, Aboriginal, and non-Aboriginal respondents.

The statistics above are taken from the 2006 census and do not reflect the 2008 economic downturn. It appears that Aboriginal people have been hardest hit by the current recession, with employment rates declining more steeply for the Aboriginal population than for the non-Aboriginal population (Statistics Canada, 2010). The unemployment rate in Canada for Aboriginal people increased from 10.4 percent in 2008 to 13.9 percent in 2009, while the rate for non-Aboriginal people rose from 6.0 percent to 8.1 percent. The manufacturing sector has been hardest hit in this recession, with an 8 percent employment decline in 2009 from 2008; however, manufacturing employment fell for Aboriginal people by 30 percent in the same year. In Alberta, the employment rate fell in 2008, at the start of the recession, from 75.1 percent to 65.1 percent, a steep decline for the province. The decline for Aboriginal people was twice that.

As mentioned above, educational attainment is related to employability, and it is also related to income levels. This is true for all Canadians. The 2006 census (Statistics Canada, 2006b) shows that Canadians who were employed full-time and who had less than a high school education had annual income levels of $32,029. Canadians with a high school education made $37,403. Those with trades or apprenticeships made $39,996, and those with a college education earned $42,937. Canadians with some university education earned $47,253, while those with a bachelor degree earned $56,048. The correlation between income and education levels is clear. Because Aboriginal people's educational levels lag behind, so do their income levels—on average, by about $7,500 per year, according to the 2006 census (Statistics Canada, 2008b). The gap between Aboriginal and non-Aboriginal education, employment, and income levels is closing, but slowly. Investment in Aboriginal education will accelerate this process.

Figure 10.6   Unemployment Rate of Population Aged 25 to 54 by Province or Region and Aboriginal Identity, 2007

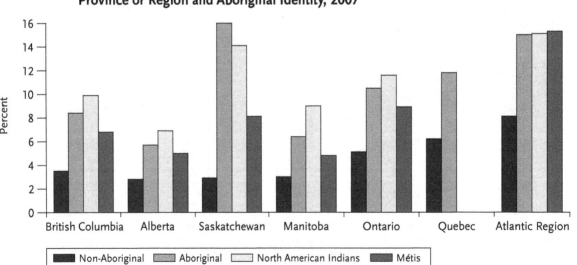

Source: Statistics Canada (2008b). http://www.statcan.gc.ca/pub/71-588-x/2008001/ct002-eng.htm.

The labour force as a whole is important to Canada's economic future. Precisely because the Aboriginal population is younger on average and its growth rate higher than the national average, it is an important resource for Canada's economic future. Key statistics in this regard include the following (Hull, 2008):

- Between 2001 and 2026, the number of Aboriginal youth coming of age to enter the labour market will exceed 600,000.
- The 15–29 age group in the Aboriginal population is projected to grow by 37 percent, compared with only 6 percent for this age group in the general Canadian population.
- By 2026, in Saskatchewan, 36 percent of the population between the ages of 15 and 29 is expected to be Aboriginal; in Manitoba, the figure is expected to be 28 percent.

According to a medium growth rate projection, the Aboriginal population will, by 2026, increase from its current 4 percent of Canada's population to 4.6 percent (Sharpe & Arsenault, 2010, p. 4). Because the Aboriginal population is much younger than the rest of the population, it will be an increasing presence in the labour force as the aging population retires. If the current education (and, therefore, the employment) gap closes between the non-Aboriginal and Aboriginal populations, the latter will account for 19.9 percent of labour force growth between 2006 and 2026 (Sharpe & Arsenault, 2010, p. 4). Conversely, if the education gap remains as it is or becomes wider, the result, given the projected increase in the Aboriginal population, will be a higher social assistance dependency rate for that population and a negative economic effect for Canada as a whole.

The increased Aboriginal population will have the greatest effect in the Western provinces, as suggested by the figures above. In Manitoba, Aboriginal people are expected to account for 50 percent of the labour force growth and employment growth between 2006 and 2026 (Richards, Vining, & Weimer, 2010; Sharpe & Arsenault, 2010, p. 23). In Saskatchewan, the decrease in the non-Aboriginal labour force (due to the aging population) between 2006 and 2026 means that Aboriginal people are expected to account for more than 100 percent of all labour force and employment growth (Sharpe & Arsenault, 2010, p. 16). Clearly, investing in an educated and skilled Aboriginal workforce is of paramount importance, in these two provinces and across the country.

HEALTH

As with education and employment, Aboriginal people suffer from a health gap; they are afflicted by certain illnesses more than the general population is, and overall life expectancy for Aboriginal people is seven years less than the general population's. The causes of death differ by age category.

Delivery of Services

Before discussing Aboriginal people's health issues, we need to discuss how health services are provided to them. Health care is generally a provincial responsibility, but for status Aboriginal people living on-reserve and for the Inuit in the North, it is a federal responsibility covered by Health Canada. For the rest of the Aboriginal population—those living off-reserve, whether status or non-status—it is provided by the province. Federal funding for health services on reserves flows through the band. The federal funding formula for health-care services and the itemized list of what is covered differ substantially from the provincial system.

Because hospitals and doctors bill the province for services, there has to be a way for the province to recoup from Health Canada the expenses it incurs for treating on-reserve status Aboriginal people. Different provinces have different policies concerning how this is done. Often, where the hospital or doctor prescribes or recommends a service not ordinarily covered by Health Canada, Health Canada must pre-approve the expenditure. The levels of coverage differ between the provincial and federal systems; Health Canada does not fund all of the services the provinces do. As with education, there is a funding gap for the services provided to Aboriginal people.

Because the provincial and federal systems are funded differently and have different operating budgets, disagreements sometimes arise over the financial obligations of service delivery. One such disagreement, central to events surrounding the death of five-year-old Jordan River Anderson in 2005, led to the passing of a private member's bill in the House of Commons known as Jordan's Principle. Jordan's story is about the inability of the federal and provincial governments to agree on who would cover the cost of his home care. While disagreements continued, Jordan remained in hospital, where he ultimately died as his family waited for a decision to be made. Jordan's story, and the tragic repercussions for his family, is the subject of Appendix 10.1.

The private member's bill, which passed in the House of Commons in 2007, proposed that, in the case of an on-reserve child who requires medical care, the level of government first contacted by the family, be it federal or provincial, should immediately pay to meet the child's medical needs, with the financial details to be worked out later. Although the bill has been passed, many provinces have yet to devise a concrete plan on how to implement it. The Assembly of First Nations asserts that there are currently 400 children tied up in disputes similar to the one in Jordan's case. It has been reported (Lett, 2008) that in the spring of 2008 there were 37 children with special needs in Norway House First Nation who were denied social and medical services because of jurisdictional disputes. By December 2008, there were promises from both the Indian Affairs ministers and Health ministers that by 2009 a formal cost-sharing agreement would be in place for delivery of services to families such as Jordan's. To date, no such formal agreement has been reached.

In order to be covered for health benefits provided by Health Canada under the Non-Insured Health Benefits (NIHB) Program, an individual must be either a registered Indian according to the *Indian Act*, an Inuk recognized by an Inuit land agreement, or the infant of a qualified parent. As well, he or she must have no access to any other public or private health plan. In 2010, 831,000 people of Aboriginal ancestry met these requirements (Health Canada, 2010). Although medical services are provided by all levels of government—provincial, municipal, and federal—the federal government, generally speaking, reimburses the other levels for services delivered to Aboriginal people recognized under the NIHB Program. All other people of Aboriginal ancestry are covered under their respective provincial or private systems.

On reserves, Health Canada also provides health promotion, nursing stations, transportation for health services, mental health and general health treatment, and many other services. Many First Nations and Inuit communities are taking more control over their own health services and programming; Health Canada is promoting the devolution—that is, the return—of administrative control over health-care responsibilities to the respective communities. In fact, by 2002, over 70 percent of First Nations and Inuit Communities had assumed some degree of responsibility for their community health programs. With new policies created in 2010, this process of devolution is set to continue.

Physical Health

Currently, the major health concerns facing Aboriginal people are diabetes, HIV/ AIDS, heart disease, tuberculosis, mental health issues, and suicide. All of these problems are significantly more prevalent among the Aboriginal population than among the general Canadian population.

Diabetes

The body of a person with diabetes, which is a chronic disease, either does not produce insulin (type 1 diabetes) or cannot properly use insulin (type 2 diabetes). Insulin is an essential hormone that regulates the amount of glucose in the blood. Those at greatest risk for developing type 2 diabetes are seniors, Aboriginal people, baby boomers, and people who are prone to obesity, such as those who lead a sedentary lifestyle.

Aboriginal people are three times more likely than the general population to be diagnosed with type 2 diabetes. Diabetes (both types) is three to five times more prevalent in Aboriginal populations than in the general population (Health Canada, 2002). The typical ages of onset for the disease are also much lower for Aboriginal people than for others, with a high incidence among their children. Diabetes has been diagnosed in Aboriginal children as young as five. The rates are highest for on-reserve populations, where 11 percent of adults have been diagnosed with diabetes compared with only 3 percent in the general population. During the same period, 6 percent of Métis and only 2 percent of Inuit were diagnosed with the disease.

In 2002, it was noted that rates of diabetes among the Inuit were lower than among the general population (Health Canada, 2002, p. 1). Since then, this statistic has changed dramatically. Recent research has determined (Egeland, 2010) that the Inuit are now diagnosed with diabetes at twice the rate of non-Aboriginal Canadians. This same report indicates that 75 percent of Northern Labrador Inuit are overweight or obese—conditions linked to diabetes and other diseases. Forty percent of those surveyed who were over 40 had high blood pressure, compared with 20 percent of non-Aboriginal Canadians in the same age category who had high blood pressure (Egeland, 2010). It is interesting to note that food insecurity—that is, concern about the affordability or availability of food—was highest among the Inuit, with 13 percent of families reporting severe food insecurity and 34 percent reporting moderate food insecurity, compared with the level of only 2.9 percent in the general population of Canada. Food insecurity among the Inuit is mostly a consequence of low incomes and the high cost of food in the regions where they live (Egeland, 2010).

To address the diabetes epidemic, Health Canada has overseen the Aboriginal Diabetes Initiative (ADI) since 1999. The ADI's primary purpose is to reduce the prevalence of type 2 diabetes by supporting health-promotion and disease-prevention activities and services, delivered by trained community diabetes workers and health service providers (Health Canada, 2011). The most recent budget, from 2010, granted the ADI $110 million over two years to fulfill its mandate.

It is now generally accepted that the increase in diabetes among Aboriginal people is related to their rapid transition from traditional lifestyles of hunting and fishing to the more sedentary lifestyles and diet of the general population. The ADI partners with Tribal Councils, First Nations organizations, Inuit community groups, and provincial and territorial governments to deliver a range of primary prevention, screening, and treatment programs for Aboriginal people. The ADI's aim is to implement strategies that are community based and culturally appropriate. The programs that ADI promotes vary by community and include walking clubs, weight-loss groups, diabetes workshops, fitness classes, community kitchens, community gardens, and healthier food policies in schools. For example, vending machines that sell sugar-sweetened soft drinks and high-sugar, high-fat snacks have been removed from many schools. The ADI also supports traditional activities such as drumming and dancing, canoeing, traditional food harvesting and preparation, and traditional games.

HIV/AIDS

As with many other health concerns, Aboriginal people are overrepresented in the Canadian HIV/AIDS epidemic. They have

- a lower onset age for HIV/AIDS than other ethnicities do;
- a higher rate of new HIV infections than the general population has, and a high percentage of infections related to injection drug use (IDU); and
- much higher rates of infection among women than is the case in the general population.

It has been reported (Public Health Agency of Canada, 2010) that Aboriginal people, who represented 3.8 percent of the Canadian population in the 2006 census, contracted fully 8.0 percent of all HIV infections in Canada—an estimated 4,300 to 6,100 cases. This represents a 24 percent increase over the 2005 numbers. With respect to new HIV infection rates, Aboriginal people accounted for approximately 12.5 percent of new infections in 2008, an increase over the 2005 figure of 10.5 percent. As these figures suggest, Aboriginal people are infected with HIV/AIDS at approximately 3.6 times the rate of the general population.

Figure 10.7 tracks the number of reported AIDS cases among Aboriginal people from 1998 to 2008, and represents this number as a percentage of the total AIDS cases reported for that year.

Injection drug use (IDU) represents a significant exposure category for the HIV epidemic in Canada. "Exposure category" refers to the way in which individuals who test positive for HIV have acquired the virus—for example, through sexual activity

Figure 10.7   Reported AIDS Cases Among Aboriginal People in Canada

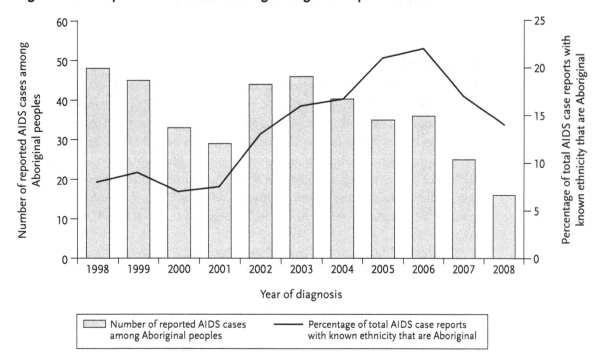

Note: Quebec AIDS data by ethnicity have not been available since June 30, 2003, and Ontario AIDS data by exposure category and ethnicity have not been available since the second half of 2005.

Source: Public Health Agency of Canada (2010, p. 3). http://www.phac-aspc.gc.ca/aids-sida/publication/epi/2010/pdf/EN_Chapter8_Web.pdf.

or through injecting drugs. Statistics concerning exposure categories reveal that the HIV epidemic in Canada is complex in its sources, with different ethnicities acquiring the virus via different modes of transmission. For Aboriginal people, IDU is a particularly important risk factor for HIV/AIDS. In 2008, the proportion of new HIV infections among those who inject drugs in the Aboriginal population was 66 percent, while the percentage among the non-Aboriginal IDU population was 17 percent. IDU accounts for more HIV infections and cases of AIDS among Aboriginal women than it does among Aboriginal men—from 1979 to 2008, approximately double the number (Public Health Agency of Canada, 2010).

The incidence of HIV/AIDS among young Aboriginal people is a growing concern; positive HIV test reports and reported AIDS diagnoses are, in general, seen in the Aboriginal population at younger ages than is the case with the general population. From 1998 to the end of 2008, nearly a third of the positive HIV test results among Aboriginal people were for individuals aged 15–29 (32.6 percent of people diagnosed). Among other ethnicities, the rate was 20.5 percent (Public Health Agency of Canada, 2010).

Females are disproportionately represented in the HIV/AIDS epidemic among Aboriginal people. Between 1979 and 2008, the percentage of females among the reported cases of Aboriginal people with AIDS was 29.0 percent; in the non-Aboriginal population for this same period, the percentage of women was 9.1 percent. In every year between 2001 and 2008, females have represented above 30.0 percent of reported AIDS cases among Aboriginal people. From 1998 to 2008, women represented 48.8 percent of all positive HIV test reports among Aboriginal people, compared with 20.6 percent of reports among other ethnicities (Public Health Agency of Canada, 2010).

Tuberculosis

The rates of tuberculosis infection for First Nations people are 8–10 times higher than for the non-Aboriginal population (Health Canada, 2006). It is most prevalent among individuals aged 15 to 44. The rates of infection vary by community, but the highest rates are in British Columbia, Saskatchewan, Manitoba, Alberta, and northwestern Ontario. Risk factors associated with the contraction of TB include HIV and diabetes as well as substance abuse, poor nutrition, and other factors that may weaken the immune system. Between 1990 and 2000, TB contributed to the death of First Nations people in only 4.1 percent of cases, generally only in older populations.

Overcrowded living conditions increase the rate of person-to-person transmission of TB. Living density among the general population of Canada is 0.4 persons per room (Health Canada, 2006). For First Nations people who live on-reserve, the living density is, on average, 0.7 persons per room (Health Canada, 2006), but in many on-reserve communities the number is much higher. The First Nations communities that, between 1996 and 2000, had the highest incidence of TB also had the highest living densities. TB is also more common in remote reserves, probably because these communities have restricted access to health professionals who can diagnose the disease early and restrict its rate of spread.

Tuberculosis is an even more pressing issue for the Inuit, whose infection rate was 32 times the national average in 2008 (Zarate, 2010). This statistic is related to the current problem in the Inuit community with severe overcrowding due to housing shortages.

Mental Health: Depression and Suicide

Aboriginal populations in Canada face unique challenges in the area of mental health. Studies show that First Nations people experience depression at twice the rate of the average Canadian and that they more frequently report that the depression interferes with the activities of daily life (Kahn, 2008). The levels of reported depression among the Inuit are very low, but their suicide rate is very high. Aboriginal people seek professional help in the form of treatment or counselling at twice the rate of the general Canadian population.

First Nations and Inuit communities experience higher rates of suicide, overall, than other communities in Canada do (see Figure 10.8). The rate varies from community to community, with some First Nations communities reporting no suicides or suicide attempts for years at a time, while others have annual suicide rates that are 11 times the national average. Suicide rates are highest for young Aboriginal people aged 15–24; the rates for this age group are 5 to 7 times what they are for people of this age group in the general population. Because of the relative youth of suicide victims in the Aboriginal community, suicide accounts for the greatest number of potential years of life lost in Aboriginal populations in Canada. As with the non-Aboriginal population, rates of completed suicide are higher among Aboriginal males than among Aboriginal females (Kahn, 2008).

Figure 10.8   Suicide Rates for First Nations, Inuit, and the General Population

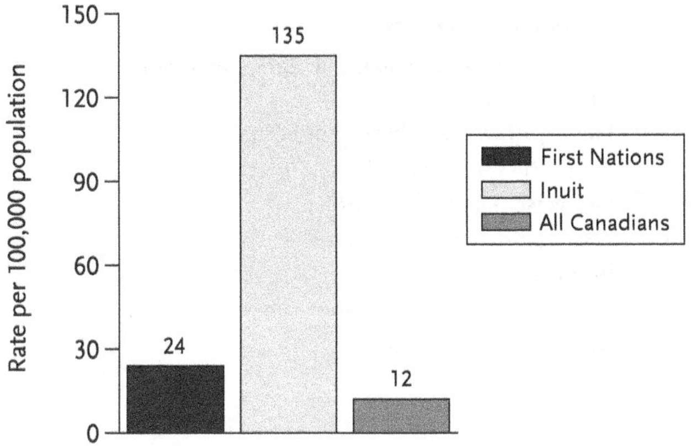

Source: Kahn (2008, pp. 6–7). http://heretohelp.bc.ca/publications/aboriginal-people/bck/3.

Research indicates (National Aboriginal Health Organization, 2003) that 31 percent of First Nations adults reported having had suicidal thoughts, and 16 percent had attempted suicide at some point in their lives. Thirty-nine percent of girls aged 12–17 and 17 percent of boys in the same age bracket have considered suicide. Young people with a close family member who had committed suicide in the last 12 months were more than twice as likely to report having had suicidal thoughts. A 2004 health survey (Anctil, 2008) suggested that 20 percent of Inuit respondents had made a suicide attempt in their lifetime and that 1 percent had done so in the last year. Having a parent who attended a residential school increased the odds from 18 percent to 26 percent that a youth would have thoughts about suicide (Public Health Agency of Canada, 2006, p. 166).

Studies have identified suicide risk factors and protective factors both at the individual and at the community levels (see Table 10.4). Anything that contributes to the risk of suicide is called a risk factor; any process that reduces the risk is referred to as a protective factor. Examining individual First Nations or Inuit communities with a view to these factors helps us to understand their suicide rates.

Many suicide prevention programs have been created and used in First Nations and Inuit communities. These programs aim at maximizing protective factors and minimizing risk factors. In keeping with the collectivist emphasis of first Nations and Inuit culture, prevention programs must address the entire community and the family as well as the individual. For an excellent overview of the programs currently available, visit the Honouring Life Network online (www.honouringlife.ca). Some of these programs, such as the Healthy Aboriginal Network (www.thehealthyaboriginal.net), have focused on creating literature about mental health issues that is accessible to Aboriginal youth. This literature, by using comic book style presentations and engaging stories that include recognizable characters and references to Aboriginal culture, is designed both to inspire its readers and to provide talking points for a dialogue about suicide.

First Nations communities, academic centres, and medical researchers have formed broad-based partnerships in the hopes of developing effective models of treatment for communities and training methodologies for community and health workers. One such team, the Aboriginal Mental Health Research Team, combines

Table 10.4   Suicide: Risk Factors and Protective Factors at the Community and Individual Levels

Community/social risk factors	Individual risk factors
Historical trauma and loss	Mood or other psychiatric disorder, including depression
Lack of meaningful activity or work available in the community	History of abuse (physical or sexual)
Interpersonal conflict and crisis within the community	Family history of suicide
Suicide common in community (clusters)	Hopelessness and pessimism
Use/abuse of alcohol and other substances prevalent in the community	Poor coping skills
Community social isolation	Impulsivity
Poverty	Influence of alcohol or other substances
Lack of community control over social services and finances	Access to lethal means

Protective factors

Perception of family connectedness
Intergenerational connectedness throughout the community
Emotional well-being
School/community involvement
Academic success or meaningful work
Spiritual connection and cultural continuity

Source: Kirmayer, Fraser, Fauras, & Whitley (2010). http://www.namhr.ca/pdfs/Suicide-Prevention.pdf.

the resources of the Nunavik Regional Board of Health and Social Services, the Cree Board of Health and Social Services, the Native Friendship Centre of Montreal (NFCM), the Native Women's Shelter of Montreal (NWSM), Waseskun House, and the Aboriginal Healing Foundation (AHF). As well, it involves researchers from the Culture & Mental Health Research Unit of the Jewish General Hospital Department of Psychiatry; the Addictions Research Unit of the Montreal General Hospital; the McGill University Departments of Psychiatry, Social Work, and Social Studies of Medicine; and the Departments of Anthropology at York University and Memorial University in Newfoundland.

Substance Abuse and Addiction

According to a survey conducted by Health Canada in 2003, 73 percent of First Nations and Inuit people consider alcohol a problem in their community, and 59 percent also report drug abuse as a problem (National Aboriginal Health Organization, 2003). In a survey, 1 in 5 Aboriginal youths reported having used solvents. Of those, 1 in 3 were under the age of 15. The rate of alcohol-related deaths in the Aboriginal population is twice what it is in the non-Aboriginal population, and death due to illicit drugs is three times the rate in Aboriginal populations. The rate of incarceration for Aboriginal youth is 8 times what it is for non-Aboriginal youth in Canada. Of those incarcerated youth, 8 in 10 had a substance abuse problem (Chansonneuve, 2007, p. 25).

Surveys of people living in First Nations communities indicate that 75 percent of those surveyed think alcohol is a problem in their community. Thirty-three percent indicate alcohol is a problem in their own family and 25 percent indicate that they have a personal problem with alcohol (Kahn, 2008). This is interesting, because fewer First Nations and Inuit people actually drink alcohol than do people in the general population: 66 percent of those living on reserve report consuming alcohol as compared with 76 percent of the general population. What is clear is that those First Nations and Inuit who do consume alcohol consume it in quantities that present problems for themselves and their communities (Kahn, 2008).

Health Canada funds the National Native Alcohol and Drug Abuse Program and has done so since the 1970s. In recent years, Aboriginal people themselves have taken control of much of this initiative and programming. There are 52 residential treatment centres across the country, equipped to treat Aboriginal people in culturally appropriate programs. This program also focuses on prevention, intervention, and aftercare.

Once again, it is important to remember that all Aboriginal communities are different. Some have few problems with alcohol and substance abuse, while others have severe problems. Communities that are in crisis need to be given culturally appropriate assistance and treatments.

LIVING CONDITIONS

Despite the major migration of Aboriginal people to urban centres, housing remains an issue on reserves. According to the 2006 census, 25 percent of First Nations people living on-reserve live in overcrowded conditions, which is defined as having more than one person per room in the residence. This situation is improving; the figure has declined from its level of 33 percent in 1996. Across Canada, the percentage of First Nations people living in crowded conditions in urban centres was only 7 percent. In Saskatchewan, however, this figure is 15 percent; in Manitoba, 10 percent; and in the Northwest Territories, 9 percent (Statistics Canada, 2006a).

The 2006 census indicates that, overall, First Nations people are 4 times more likely than non-Aboriginal people to live in houses in need of major repairs. Houses in poor condition are most common on reserves, where 44 percent of First Nations homes were in need of major repairs; this number has risen from 36 percent in the past decade. Poor housing conditions in the prairie provinces have increased: 54 percent of on-reserve housing in Saskatchewan is in need of major repair; 53 percent, in Manitoba; and 52 percent in Alberta.

For the Métis, the census shows that only 14 percent live in homes in need of major repairs and are only twice as likely as the non-Aboriginal population to live in crowded conditions. Once again, the prairie provinces are the most problematic for housing conditions, for the Métis as for the other Aboriginal populations.

In March 2010, the Inuit reported that 49 percent of their people in Nunavik are living in overcrowded conditions. The problem is made worse by the short lifespan of government housing, which is built to last only 15 years, in a region where weather conditions are extremely hard on the existing structures. In March of 2010, the federal and Quebec governments announced a five-year plan to build 300 houses to meet the housing need. However, the Inuit communities themselves see a need for at least 1,000 new houses (CBC News, 2010)

SOCIAL ASSISTANCE/ECONOMIC RENEWAL

Income assistance is common for First Nations people, particularly those living on-reserve, where there are few economic opportunities. According to Indian and Northern Affairs Canada (2005, p. 66), over 90 percent of First Nations communities in 2003–4 administered their own income assistance programs. Furthermore, the statistics show a slight decline in the number of First Nations people receiving income assistance.

Once again, it is important to realize that every Aboriginal community is unique. Needs for income assistance vary tremendously between communities. For example, Indian and Northern Affairs Canada data for the far north, including Yukon, Northwest Territories, and Nunavut, show that only 50 percent of the Aboriginal population had employment in 2001 compared with 90 percent of non-Aboriginal people in the same regions. In this case, the need for income assistance and government services is very high. In other areas of the country, such as southern Ontario, Aboriginal people have had relative success in education and in the labour market, and this reduces the need for assistance.

Ultimately, economic development on reserves is one of the best methods of addressing the social ills that exist there. However, there are barriers to such development. Under legislation such as the *Indian Act*, the *Indian Oil and Gas Act*, and the *First Nations Land Management Act*, federal organizations still have considerable responsibility and control over First Nations economic development. First Nations communities report that although the federal government has business-development programs and accepts proposals from First Nations communities, these communities find it difficult to meet the set criteria and thereby access the federal funding. First Nations communities see access to natural resources in the land as an important part of economic development, but they are having difficulty accessing those resources. Many of the resources are on lands that are currently under claim and are therefore inaccessible until a resolution is reached.

First Nations people have difficulty accessing capital to invest in economic development. Many do not have large investment funds, and, owing to the nature of communal ownership and to the *Indian Act*, they cannot use reserved land to secure loans for capital ventures. In the past, banks and other capital lending institutions have been reluctant to learn about and accommodate their policies to First Nations organizations, which have unique legal status. First Nations people have found that their funding proposals are often rejected by federal officials, who view these proposals as high-risk. First Nations people have suggested, too, that approval for the funding of prospective Aboriginal businesses does not move at the speed of non-Aboriginal business funding. At times, gaining funding approval can take years.

The *Indian Act* processes can be cumbersome, and the processes required by resource management are complex. For example, royalty payments to Aboriginal people from resource development on reserved lands are not paid to the band; they go to Indian and Northern Affairs Canada, to be held in trust accounts. To access the money, the band must make application to the minister concerned and detail the intentions of how the money will be spent. This requirement, intended to ensure that the Crown meets its fiduciary duty to First Nations, is a complex system that can cause delays in accessing capital. To bypass the red tape involved in accessing government economic development programs, some First Nations are looking to partner with the non-Aboriginal business communities (see Appendix 10.2).

One of the greatest obstacles to the economic development of Aboriginal society is the lack of land. Aboriginal people are trying to boost their economies; however, in a country whose economy is based on natural resources, it is difficult for First

Nations people to enter that economy when they have less than half of 1 percent of Canada's land mass. Resources that had supported First Nations people for thousands of years are now in the control and possession of private industry and governments that are not willing to allow First Nations to share in them. A 2005 decision by the Supreme Court of Canada denied Aboriginal people in Eastern Canada the right to access Crown land for logging to increase their presence in the logging industry. First Nations have privileges for logging on 3 percent of Crown land, with the remainder leased by the Crown to private industry. The Supreme Court ruled that logging for profit was not part of pre-contact Aboriginal economy and that therefore the Aboriginal people concerned had no right to access the industry.

Separating Aboriginal people from their land and its resources demoralizes them and entrenches them in Canada's economy as wage labourers for the dominant culture and for Canada's private business interests. Access to land and resources will be the primary focus of the next chapter.

EXERCISE 2

As a class, consider four social areas in which Aboriginal people experience lower quality of life than non-Aboriginal people, and link these deficits to historical events.

Discuss opportunities for economic development on reserves—initiatives that could create jobs and reduce the community's dependence on social assistance. Consider the obstacles and determine ways to overcome them.

Discuss the potential benefits and possible pitfalls of building casinos on reserves.

LANGUAGE

In the 2006 census, over 60 different Aboriginal languages were recorded as being spoken by First Nations people in Canada. In 2006, approximately 29 percent of First Nations respondents could speak an Aboriginal language well enough to carry on a conversation—roughly the same as in 2001, when the figure was 30 percent. In general, the percentage of individuals with knowledge of an Aboriginal language is far greater for First Nations people living on-reserve than for those living off-reserve. For off-reserve respondents, those with registered Indian status were more likely to have knowledge of an Aboriginal language than non-status Indians. While 51 percent of respondents living on-reserve could converse in an Aboriginal language, only 12 percent of those living off-reserve could do so. Of those living off-reserve, 17 percent of those with registered Indian status were conversant in a First Nations language compared with only 2 percent of those without such status who were conversant in a First Nations language. Fewer First Nations people are living on-reserve than are living off-reserve: in 2006, 40 percent as compared with 60 percent. The latter figure is up slightly from the 58 percent of 1996.

According to the 2006 census, the percentage of individuals who know a First Nations language was significantly greater for those aged 45 and over—and especially for individuals aged 65 and over—than for younger individuals. In 2006,

50 percent of respondents aged 65 to 74 years could converse in an Aboriginal language, and 52 percent of those aged 75 and over could do so. Again, the percentages were significantly higher for respondents living on-reserve (79 percent for respondents aged 65 to 74; 83 percent for those aged 75 and over) than for those living off-reserve (26 percent for respondents aged 65 to 74, and 24 percent for those aged 75 and over). In contrast, only 21 percent of respondents aged 14 and under could converse in an Aboriginal language, with higher numbers, once again, for on-reserve respondents than for off-reserve ones (39 percent as opposed to 6 percent). Overall, however, the percentages of young First Nations people with knowledge of an Aboriginal language remained approximately the same in the 2006 census as in the 2001 census. Table 10.5 illustrates the percentages within various age categories for the 2001 and 2006 censuses, and compares rates for respondents living both on- and off-reserve.

In the 2006 census, 25 percent of First Nations people reported having an Aboriginal mother tongue, roughly the same as in 1996 and 2001. But this represents a significant decrease overall since the 1940s. In 1941, English was the first language of less than 10 percent of Aboriginal people; in 1971, it was the first language of approximately 54 percent; in 1991, of 60.4 percent. For particular Aboriginal languages in the 2006 census, the number of individuals who could speak the language was often greater than the number who reported it as their mother tongue. This may be due to First Nations people learning Aboriginal languages as a second language. In the 2001 Aboriginal Peoples Survey, two out of three First Nations people reported that they felt that keeping, learning, or relearning their Aboriginal language was somewhat or very important (Statistics Canada, 2007a).

With regard to particular Aboriginal languages, some languages show, since 2001, an increase both in the number of respondents for whom the language is a mother

Table 10.5   Percentage of First Nations People Who Have Knowledge[1] of an Aboriginal Language, by Age Groups, Canada, 2001 and 2006[2]

	First Nations people					
	2001			2006		
Age groups	Total	On reserve	Off reserve	Total	On reserve	Off reserve
	percent			*percent*		
Total all ages	30	50	14	29	51	12
0 to 14 years	21	36	8	21	39	6
15 to 24 years	25	44	10	24	43	9
25 to 44 years	33	58	17	30	56	13
45 to 64 years	45	71	26	39	67	21
65 to 74 years	56	79	33	50	79	26
75 years and over	59	83	31	52	83	24

Notes:

1. "Knowledge" refers to languages in which the respondent can conduct a conversation.
2. Data have been adjusted to account for incompletely enumerated reserves in 2001 and 2006.

Source: Statistics Canada (2008a, p. 49). http://www12.statcan.gc.ca/english/census06/analysis/aboriginal/pdf/97-558-XIE2006001.pdf.

tongue and in the number of respondents who can converse in it. But many Aboriginal languages are in sharp decline and some analysts predict that many of them will very soon be lost. Indeed, in the case of certain First Nations languages, the number of individuals who speak them at home is alarmingly low. For example, the 2006 census recorded fewer than 150 individuals who speak Malecite and Chipewyan at home, 20 who speak Mohawk, and *zero* who speak Tlingit. The disappearance of First Nations languages has alarming implications for the persistence of their cultures.

Table 10.6 illustrates the Aboriginal language indicators for First Nations people and compares the results from 2001 and 2006. It shows the number of respondents who have a particular language as their mother tongue, and the number who can carry on a conversation in that language; in addition, the percentage change from 2001 to 2006 is shown. With regard to particular Aboriginal languages, Cree has by far the greatest number of speakers (87,285), followed by Ojibwa (30,255). Of all the languages and dialects recorded in the census, the long-term survival of these two First Nations languages, which have a relatively large base of speakers, can be considered more likely than the survival of others, such as Haida (Norris, 2007).

The percentage changes in Table 10.6 seem, at first glance, cause for hope about the survival of many Aboriginal languages. For example, the number of First Nations people who can converse in Carrier has increased by 18 percent since 2001.

Table 10.6   Aboriginal Languages Indicators for First Nations People, Canada, 2001 and 2006

Aboriginal languages	Aboriginal mother tongue[1]		Knowledge[2] of an Aboriginal language	
	2006	Percentage change from 2001 to 2006	2006	Percentage change from 2001 to 2006
Cree	76,460	10	87,285	7
Ojibway	24,410	−2	30,255	−2
Oji-Cree	11,605	18	12,435	20
Montagnais-Naskapi	10,470	8	11,080	10
Dene	8,495	9	9,250	8
Mi'kmaq	7,685	4	8,540	0
Siouan languages (Dakota/Sioux)	5,675	34	6,285	32
Atikamekw	5,140	11	5,320	12
Blackfoot	3,270	11	4,760	10
Salish languages	1,990	6	2,800	−1
Algonquin	2,020	10	2,560	12
Dogrib	2,055	10	2,540	17
Carrier	1,800	29	2,320	18
South Slave	1,575	15	2,160	7

Notes:

1. "Mother tongue" refers to the first language learned at home in childhood and still understood.
2. "Knowledge" refers to languages in which the respondent can conduct a conversation.

Source: Statistics Canada (2008a, p. 50). http://www12.statcan.gc.ca/english/census06/analysis/aboriginal/pdf/97-558-XIE2006001.pdf.

But these numbers should be viewed with an eye to long-term trends. In the case of Carrier, for example, the number of speakers declined by 29.3 percent, from 2,830 speakers to 2,000, between 1996 and 2001. By 2006, the number of speakers was back up to 2,320 (or 18 percent), which seems encouraging. But we need to keep in mind that the 2006 number is still lower than the number of speakers reported in the 1996 census (2,830). Nevertheless, in the case of Aboriginal languages that already had large numbers of speakers, the number of speakers has increased overall from 2001 to 2006.

Table 10.6, however, does not report on all First Nations languages, and some of those that are not included have seen significant declines since 2001. From 2001 to 2006, for example, the numbers of people speaking Haida, Tlingit, and Malecite declined by 31 percent, 30 percent, and 30 percent, respectively. Ojibwa saw only a small decline in percentage terms between 2001 and 2006 (2 percent). But, because of the large number of Ojibwa speakers, this apparently small percentage decline represents a loss of 600 speakers.

A 2007 study has shown that the continuation or retention of language is a factor in the well-being of individuals and communities (Hallett, Chandler, & Lalonde, 2007). This study tracked youth suicide rates in Aboriginal communities in British Columbia, and found that bands in which a majority of members could converse in an Aboriginal language experienced low to non-existent rates of youth suicide. Youth suicide rates were *six times greater* for bands in which less than half of the members could converse in an Aboriginal language. In sum, the study shows that "indigenous language use, as a marker of cultural persistence, is a strong predictor of health and wellbeing in Canada's Aboriginal communities" (Hallett et al., 2007, p. 398).

CONCLUSION

As stated in the introduction, Aboriginal people were not waiting on the shores of Canada for the white man to arrive with a welfare cheque; the dispossession of the Aboriginal peoples in this country has been a long process. They have been an *administrated* people for the last 150 years—subject to the power of the state, which has shaped them and brought them to their current pass. Low educational achievement, high unemployment rates, poor physical and mental health, substance abuse, and poverty continue to be prevalent in Aboriginal communities in Canada.

Canada has much to gain by working with Aboriginal communities to create a better future, and the consequences of inaction could be severe. The Aboriginal population is the fastest-growing segment of the Canadian population, so it is urgent that we invest now in Aboriginal education and economic development. Without economic development, social assistance is the only option for Aboriginal on-reserve communities. With no employment, the community becomes demoralized and lacks purpose, and this leads—as the case of Grassy Narrows has shown—to social problems, such as alcohol and substance abuse, poor mental health, and suicide. Without education, many Aboriginal people will seek employment in large urban centres, where many of them will end up in the ranks of the working poor and marginally employed.

It has been argued (Chandler et al., 2003) that a sense of "continuity, or persistent identity" is the key to a people's ability to thrive. In other words, anything that threatens the continuation of personal or cultural identity likewise threatens the well-being of individuals and communities. For Canada's Aboriginal communities, a sense of cultural continuity is linked to the following: community control over the delivery of health, education, child protection, and policing services; the achievement of a degree of self-governance; secure access to traditional lands; and the construction of facilities for preserving cultural artifacts and traditions. There is a positive correlation between the presence of these factors in an Aboriginal community and the well-being of its members.

Since the 1969s White Paper, which proposed eliminating the status of First Nations people as well as their title to their traditional territories, Canada has seemed prepared to relinquish some of its control over Aboriginal people. The latter have welcomed the opportunity to assert control over community infrastructure such as education, housing, delivery of social services, health, policing, and other areas of community life. Statistics indicate that the quality of life is improving with this new control, but much still needs to be done.

GROUP DISCUSSION

In *Surviving as Indians*, Professor Menno Boldt (1993, p. i) defines *justice* in terms of "the survival and well-being of Indians as *Indians*, that is, defined by their traditional principles and philosophies." Boldt highlights the following five imperatives:

1. Moral justice for Indians.
2. Canadian policies that treat the needs, aspirations, interests, and rights of Indians as equal to those of Canadians.
3. Indian leadership committed to returning Indian government to the people.
4. The revitalization of Indian cultures, languages, and social systems within a framework of traditional philosophies and principles.
5. Economic self-sufficiency and independence through employment in the Canadian labour force.

Based on what you have read in this chapter, how does the reality of Aboriginal people in Canada correspond to Boldt's imperatives? Do you see positive developments in certain areas?

Where does Canada currently stand in relation to Boldt's definition of "justice"?

REFERENCES

Aboriginal Affairs and Northern Development Canada. (2010a). Fact sheet: 2006 census Aboriginal demographics. http://www.aadnc-aandc.gc.ca/eng/1100100016377.

Aboriginal Affairs and Northern Development Canada. (2010b). How do the new legislative changes to the *Indian Act* affect me? http://www.aadncaandc.gc.ca/eng/1100100032501.

Anctil, M. (2008). Survey highlights. *Nunavik Inuit health survey 2004: Qanuippitaa? How are we?* Quebec: Institut national de santé publique du Québec (INSPQ) and Nunavik Regional Board of Health and Social Services (NRBHSS). http://www.inspq.qc.ca/pdf/publications/774_ESISurveyHighlights.pdf.

Assembly of First Nations. (2005, June 28). Bill C-31 twenty years later: AFN national chief calls for First Nations control of First Nations citizenship [Press release]. http://www.liveleak.com/view?i=033_1219811209.

Blackstock, C. (2009). Jordan's story: How one boy inspired a world of change. *Canadian supplement to* The state of the world's children 2009: *Aboriginal children's health: Leaving no child behind.* Toronto: Unicef Canada.

Boldt, M. (1993). *Surviving as Indians: The challenge of self-government.* Toronto: University of Toronto Press.

CBC News. (2010, March 18). Nunavik housing shortage a "crisis": Inuit. http://www.cbc.ca/news/canada/north/story/2010/03/18/ quebec-inuit-housing-shortage.html.

Chandler, M.J., Lalonde, C.E., Sokol, B.W., & Hallett, D. (2003). Personal persistence, identity development, and suicide: A study of Native and non-Native North American adolescents. *Monographs of the Society for Research in Child Development, 68*(2), Serial No. 273. http://web.uvic.ca/~lalonde/ manuscripts/2003-Monograph.pdf.

Chansonneuve, D. (2007). *Addictive behaviours among Aboriginal people in Canada.* Ottawa: Aboriginal Healing Foundation. http://www.ahf.ca/downloads/ addictive-behaviours.pdf.

Curry, B. (2011, April 10). A new development model gains steam in Aboriginal communities. *The Globe and Mail.* http://www.theglobeandmail.com/news/ national/time-to-lead/a-new-development-model-gains-steam-in -aboriginal-communities/article1979303/.

Egeland, G. (2010). *Inuit health survey 2007–2008: Inuvialuit settlement region.* Ste-Anne-de-Bellevue, QC: Centre for Indigenous Peoples' Nutrition and Environment, McGill University.

Frideres, J.S., & Gadacz, R.R. (2008). *Aboriginal peoples in Canada: Contemporary conflicts* (8th ed.). Toronto: Pearson.

Geddes, C., Doxtater, M., & Krepakevich, M. (1997). *No turning back: The Royal Commission on Aboriginal Peoples.* Montreal: National Film Board of Canada.

Hallett, D., Chandler, M.J., & Lalonde, C.E. (2007). Aboriginal language knowledge and youth suicide. *Cognitive Development, 22,* 392–399. http://web.uvic.ca/ psyc/lalonde/manuscripts/2007CogDevt.pdf.

Health Canada. (2002). First Nations, Inuit and Aboriginal health: Aboriginal diabetes initiative (ADI) evaluation framework. http://www.hc-sc.gc.ca/ fniah-spnia/pubs/diseases-maladies/_diabete/2002_frame-cadre-eval/ index-eng.php.

Health Canada. (2006). First Nations, Inuit and Aboriginal health: Tuberculosis in First Nations communities. http://www.hc-sc.gc.ca/fniah-spnia/ diseases-maladies/tuberculos/tb_fni-pni_commun-eng.php.

Health Canada. (2010). First Nations, Inuit and Aboriginal health: Non-Insured Health Benefits Program annual report 2008/2009. http://www.hc-sc.gc.ca/fniah-spnia/pubs/nihb-ssna/2009_rpt/index-eng.php#sec2.

Health Canada. (2011). First Nations, Inuit and Aboriginal health: Diabetes. http://www.hc-sc.gc.ca/fniah-spnia/diseases-maladies/diabete/index-eng.php.

Hull, J. (2008). Aboriginal youth in the Canadian labour market. *Horizons, 10*(1), 40–44. http://www.horizons.gc.ca/doclib/Horizons_Vol10Num1_final_e.pdf.

Hurley, M.C., & Simeone, T. (2010, March 18). Legislative summary of Bill C-3: Gender equity in *Indian Registration Act*. Ottawa: Parliamentary Information and Research Service, Library of Parliament. http://www.parl.gc.ca/About/Parliament/LegislativeSummaries/bills_ls.asp?Language=e&ls=C3&Mode=1&Parl=40&Ses=3&source=library_prb.

Indian and Northern Affairs Canada. (2005). *Basic departmental data 2004*. Ottawa: Minister of Public Works and Government Services Canada. http://dsp-psd.pwgsc.gc.ca/collection_2008/inac-ainc/R12-7-2004E.pdf.

Indian and Northern Affairs Canada. (2009). Discussion paper: Changes to the *Indian Act* affecting Indian registration and band membership—*McIvor v. Canada*. http://www.aadnc-aandc.gc.ca/DAM/DAM-INTER-HQ/STAGING/texte-text/mci_1100100032488_eng.pdf.

Kahn, S. (2008). Aboriginal mental health: The statistical reality. *Visions: BC's Mental Health and Addictions Journal, 5*(1), 6–7. http://heretohelp.bc.ca/publications/aboriginal-people/bck/3.

Kirmayer, L.J., Fraser, S.-L., Fauras, V., & Whitley, R. (2010). Current approaches to Aboriginal youth suicide prevention. Canadian Mental Health Research Unit working paper #14. Montreal: Jewish General Hospital. http://www.namhr.ca/pdfs/Suicide-Prevention.pdf.

Laboucane, R. (2010, October). Canada's Aboriginal education crisis. *Windspeaker, 28*(7), 18–19. http://www.ammsa.com/publications/windspeaker/canada%E2%80%99s-aboriginal-education-crisis-column.

Lett, D. (2008). Whatever happened to Jordan's principle? *Canadian Medical Association Journal, 178*(12), 1534–1535. http://www.cmaj.ca/content/178/12/1534.2.full.

National Aboriginal Health Organization. (2003). *First Nations regional longitudinal health survey 2002/2003*. Ottawa: Assembly of First Nations/First Nations Information Governance Committee. http://www.rhs-ers.ca.

Norris, M.J. (2007). Aboriginal languages in Canada: Emerging trends and perspectives on second language acquisition. *Canadian Social Trends*, no. 83, Statistics Canada, catalogue no. 11-008.

Public Health Agency of Canada. (2006). *The human face of mental health and mental illness in Canada 2006*. Ottawa: Minister of Public Works and Government Services Canada. http://www.phac-aspc.gc.ca/publicat/human-humain06/pdf/human_face_e.pdf.

Public Health Agency of Canada. (2010). HIV/AIDS among Aboriginal people in Canada. *HIV/AIDS Epi Updates—July 2010.* http://www.phac-aspc.gc.ca/aids-sida/publication/epi/2010/pdf/EN_Chapter8_Web.pdf.

Richards, J.G., Vining, A.R., & Weimer, D.L. (2010, February). Aboriginal performance on standardized tests: Evidence and analysis from provincial schools in British Columbia. *Policy Studies Journal, 38*(1), 47–67.

Sharpe, A., & Arsenault, J.-F. (2010, December). Investing in Aboriginal education in Canada: An economic perspective. *CPRN research report.* Ottawa: Canadian Policy Research Networks. http://www.cprn.org/documents/51980_EN.pdf.

Shkilnyk, A. (1985). *A poison stronger than love: The destruction of an Ojibwa community.* New Haven, CT: Yale University Press.

Statistics Canada. (2006a). 2006 census: Aboriginal peoples in Canada in 2006: Inuit, Métis and First Nations, 2006 census: Findings. http://www12.statcan.ca/census-recensement/2006/as-sa/97-558/index-eng.cfm.

Statistics Canada. (2006b). Earnings and incomes of Canadians over the past quarter century, 2006 census: earnings [Higher education: Gateway to higher earnings]. http://www12.statcan.gc.ca/census-recensement/2006/as-sa/97-563/p8-eng.cfm.

Statistics Canada. (2007a). Aboriginal peoples survey 2001. http://www.statcan.gc.ca/aboriginal/aps/5801796-eng.htm.

Statistics Canada. (2007b). Aboriginal peoples survey 2006. http://www.statcan.gc.ca/aboriginal/aps/5801794-eng.htm.

Statistics Canada. (2008a). *Aboriginal peoples in Canada in 2006: Inuit, Métis and First Nations, 2006 census.* Catalogue no. 97-558-XIE. Ottawa: Statistics Canada. http://www12.statcan.gc.ca/english/census06/analysis/aboriginal/pdf/97-558-XIE2006001.pdf.

Statistics Canada. (2008b). Aboriginal people living off-reserve and the labour market: Estimates from the labour force survey, 2007. http://www.statcan.gc.ca/pub/71-588-x/71-588-x2008001-eng.htm.

Statistics Canada. (2010, May 13). Study: Aboriginal labour market update. *The Daily.* http://www.statcan.gc.ca/daily-quotidien/100513/dq100513b-eng.htm.

VanEvery-Albert, C. (2004). A review of the band operated funding formula. http://chiefs-of-ontario.org/Assets/A%20Review%20of%20the%20Band%20Operated%20Funding%20Formula.pdf.

Zarate, G. (2010, March 10). Inuit TB infection rate 32 times above national average in 2008. *Nunatsiaq Online.* http://www.nunatsiaqonline.ca/stories/article/9879_inuit_org_wants_tuberculosis_strategy/.

REVIEW QUESTIONS

TRUE OR FALSE?

_____ 1. The federal government relocated the Ojibwa of Grassy Narrows in 1963 because it wanted to end the isolation that had helped this community resist assimilation.

_____ 2. Most Aboriginal communities have been relocated from their original territories.

_____ 3. With the 1951 changes to the *Indian Act*, Indian women who "married out" no longer lost their Indian status.

_____ 4. The *Canadian Charter of Rights and Freedoms* has had little effect on Canada's registered Indian population.

_____ 5. Government funding of on-reserve schools has kept pace with the rapid growth in Aboriginal communities.

_____ 6. By 2026, over one-third of Saskatchewan's population between the ages of 15 and 29 is expected to be Aboriginal.

_____ 7. The passing of Jordan's Principle in the House of Commons in 2007 put an end to jurisdictional disputes over the funding of government services to on-reserve Aboriginal children.

_____ 8. The increase in diabetes among Aboriginal people is partly related to their rapid transition from traditional lifestyles of hunting and fishing to a more sedentary lifestyle.

_____ 9. The proportion of people in the Aboriginal population who drink alcohol is smaller than the proportion of people in the general population who do so.

_____ 10. All Aboriginal languages are in sharp decline and will soon be lost.

MULTIPLE CHOICE

1. Which of the following calamities came to the people of Grassy Narrows in the 1960s?
   (a) HIV/AIDS
   (b) competition in the wild rice market from non-Aboriginal farmers
   (c) the *Indian Act*
   (d) mercury poisoning from a pulp and paper mill

2. Among the people in Canada reporting Aboriginal ancestry, the fastest growing population is
   (a) Cree
   (b) Inuit
   (c) Métis
   (d) Indian

3. The growth rate of Canada's Aboriginal population is significantly affected by which of the following factors?

    (a) the birth rate

    (b) the death rate

    (c) the rate at which individuals lose or gain status

    (d) all of the above

4. Which of the following Canadian cities has the largest population of Aboriginal people?

    (a) Kenora

    (b) Montreal

    (c) Winnipeg

    (d) Vancouver

5. Which of the following factors is negatively correlated with academic achievement?

    (a) playing sports every day

    (b) living in a household with a high income

    (c) strong social skills

    (d) none of the above

6. For status Aboriginal people living on-reserve and for the Inuit, health care is

    (a) a provincial responsibility

    (b) a community responsibility

    (c) a federal responsibility covered by Health Canada

    (d) none of the above

7. Compared with people in the general population, how likely are Aboriginal people to be diagnosed with type 2 diabetes?

    (a) no more likely

    (b) twice as likely

    (c) less likely

    (d) three times as likely

8. Which of the following Aboriginal populations has an infection rate for tuberculosis that is 32 times the national average?

    (a) the Métis

    (b) those who live in cities

    (c) the Inuit

    (d) the Ojibwa of Grassy Narrows

9. One path to economic development for Aboriginal communities is to access the natural resources in the land, but they are having trouble doing so because

    (a) the equipment required is expensive

    (b) the resources are on lands that are currently under claim

    (c) the resources have been used up

    (d) it goes against their conservationist beliefs

10. Which of the following is thought to contribute to Aboriginal communities' sense of continuity and their ultimate well-being?

    (a) facilities for preserving cultural artifacts and traditions

    (b) a degree of self-governance

    (c) secure access to traditional lands

    (d) all of the above

APPENDIX 10.1

JORDAN'S STORY: HOW ONE BOY INSPIRED A WORLD OF CHANGE

JURISDICTIONAL DISPUTES AND THE DENIAL OF GOVERNMENT SERVICES

Jordan was born in 1999 to a large family in Norway House Cree Nation, Manitoba. ... He was born with complex medical needs and remained in a Winnipeg hospital for the first two years of his life while his medical condition stabilized. While Jordan's mother, Virginia, stayed with him in Winnipeg, his father, Ernest, returned to Norway House First Nation in northern Manitoba to look after the couple's other children. ... Shortly after Jordan's second birthday, his doctors agreed that he was ready to go home. But Jordan never made it. ...

Provincial and federal governments do not always agree on which level of government is responsible for the payment of government services for First Nations children living on-reserve, services that are routinely available to other children. When one of these jurisdictional disputes occurred, the typical practice of both levels of government was to deny or delay the provision of services to the child until the payment issue could be sorted out. ...

For Jordan, this amounted to provincial and federal bureaucrats arguing over every item related to his at-home care—while he stayed in hospital at about twice the cost. ...

Jordan died while waiting for a resolution. He was only five, and he had never spent a day in his family's home.

We can say that two lives were lost as a result of this jurisdictional dispute. Jordan's mother, Virginia, did not have a history of substance abuse prior to Jordan's hospitalization, but the heartbreak of seeing her young son remain needlessly in hospital, and enduring the long separation from her husband and other children, likely contributed to Virginia's subsequent slide into substance abuse. Just months after Jordan passed away, Virginia died in a Winnipeg bus shelter. ...

A GROUNDSWELL OF ADVOCACY FOR CHANGE

Buoyed by the strength of his son's spirit, Ernest Anderson vowed this type of discrimination would never happen to another First Nations child in Canada. Those touched by Jordan and the Anderson family were galvanized by the compelling need for change, but uncertain about how to address federal and provincial government policies to make Ernest's dream come true. There was no money and only a small group of Jordan's Principle supporters at the beginning, but all knew Ernest was right, and they were determined to succeed.

When Jordan passed away in 2005, the First Nations Child and Family Caring Society of Canada was conducting a research project on First Nations child welfare, which provided a platform to study the incidence of jurisdictional disputes affecting First Nations children. This study ... suggested that each year, thousands of First Nations children were being denied on the basis of their race and residency the government services that are routinely available to other children.

Just as these findings were coming to light in June 2005, UNICEF Canada hosted the North American consultation on violence against children, during which Jordan's

Principle to resolve jurisdictional disputes was announced for the first time. Simply put, Jordan's Principle puts the child's interests first in any jurisdictional dispute within and between federal and provincial/territorial governments. When a dispute arises around the provision or payment of government services (such as health care, education, child welfare, recreation, and other services normally enjoyed by all Canadian children) to a status Indian or Inuit child, Jordan's Principle requires that the government of first contact pays the bill immediately—and then resolves the payment issue later. ...

In 2005, all of the provinces/territories and the federal government were notified of Jordan's Principle and asked to take immediate steps to implement it. ...

Although the federal government and provinces/territories were slow to act, hundreds of Canadians and Canadian organizations stepped forward to support an online declaration for Jordan's Principle, calling on governments to move quickly to adopt and implement the principle. ... By the time Jordan's Principle came for a vote in the House of Commons, more than 1,400 Canadians and organizations had officially registered their support.

Ernest Anderson and his daughter Jerlene, along with other families from Norway House Cree Nation who were also affected by jurisdictional disputes, flew to Ottawa to watch the vote take place. At 5:30 p.m. on December 12, 2007, members of Parliament stood in unanimous support of Private Members' Motion-296 supporting Jordan's Principle and followed with a standing ovation for the Anderson family and all those who supported Jordan's message. It was, by all accounts, a wonderful day, but, as Ernest Anderson warned, the good that was accomplished in Jordan's name that day would be little more than a victory in name only if Canada and the provinces/territories did not immediately move to implement Jordan's Principle. The result? The federal government decided to strike a working committee to discuss implementation.

GATHERING PROVINCIAL/TERRITORIAL GOVERNMENT SUPPORT FOR JORDAN'S PRINCIPLE

On January 24, 2008, British Columbia Premier Gordon Campbell announced that B.C. could become the first province to endorse Jordan's Principle. ... More recently, the government of Ontario announced its support for Jordan's Principle and although it plans to begin implementation for children with special needs, it has acknowledged the need to apply Jordan's Principle across health and social programmes in the province.

Meanwhile, jurisdictional disputes continue to negatively affect the lives and health of First Nations children. As of May 2008, as the governments of Manitoba and Canada engaged in a jurisdictional dispute concerning payment for children's special-needs care, 37 children in Norway House Cree Nation faced unnecessary placement in foster care. Norway House Cree Nation used their own revenue to provide the life-saving and wellness services these children needed, while the governments continued to argue that they lacked sufficient funds. ...

JORDAN'S LASTING LEGACY

Jordan's Principle is now the most widely supported child policy movement in recent Canadian history. It is an example of what can be accomplished when a group of committed people stand up against injustice for the best interests of children, leveraging their networks and talents to bring about change, even without financial resources. However, the question remains: Why won't Canada vigorously and fully implement Jordan's Principle without delay? We must have an immediate answer: First Nations children are dying, and their best interests and safety are being jeopardized while waiting for governments to do the right thing.

Source: Blackstock, C. (2009). Jordan's story: How one boy inspired a world of change. *Canadian supplement to* The State of the world's children 2009: *Aboriginal children's health: Leaving no child behind.* Toronto: Unicef Canada.

APPENDIX 10.2

A NEW DEVELOPMENT MODEL GAINS STEAM IN ABORIGINAL COMMUNITIES

Rejecting the advice of government bureaucrats, Ken Noble decided to think big.

A member of Henvey Inlet First Nation, he led direct talks with developers—bypassing Ottawa and other "economic development" officials—to find out what type of project might work for his reserve near Parry Sound, Ont.

"We just really listened to the industry and paid attention to what a developer required," he said. "We didn't apply to any government."

The message to Mr. Noble, whose community sits on 20,000 windswept acres on the northeast shore of Georgian Bay, was to go big. It did—and in February, the Ontario government approved a proposal to build a $1-billion wind farm that will generate 300 megawatts of electricity—enough to supply 70,000 homes.

The project involves $700-million in debt financing from Canada's five big banks, as well as foreign lenders. Mr. Noble estimates that, when the turbines are up and running in 2015, the band will receive $25-million in annual revenues, of which about $15-million will go toward paying off the debt.

"We're getting into an industry and a project that's making more money than we ever dreamed possible," said Mr. Noble, president of Nigig Power Corporation, an energy company run by the band. "It means we'll shut down our welfare department."

The widespread problems of substance abuse, despair and suicide in Canada's native communities are well documented. Less well known are the small pockets of economic success that show how some communities—even those far from urban centres—can thrive under the right circumstances.

Big success stories remain rare, but first nations are increasingly trying to work with the business community to change that. Their optimism is tempered with frustration that federal parties aren't seized with efforts to spread this economic activity more broadly.

Many business leaders—more accustomed to conflict when it comes to projects that involve native Canadians—are going out of their way to smooth relations. Mining, forestry and energy still provoke battles, but experience is leading to more enlightened resource deals that go beyond the traditional model, which sees a company simply handing out royalty cheques.

The Churchill Falls development project has yet to receive final approval from the Labrador Innu, but is considered an example of this new approach: It promises the Innu an annual $2-million in royalties, but the government of Newfoundland and Labrador and Nalcor Energy also pledge to provide jobs, training and $400-million in business contracts.

Even if Churchill Falls doesn't go ahead, the Innu have already seen increased employment and training in recent years because of a 2002 deal with the Voisey Bay Nickel Mine.

"I think there's been a significant change," said Grand Chief Joseph Riche, whose community attracted national attention more than a decade ago with images of despair and gas-sniffing children.

WHAT'S HAPPENING

To succeed, communities often must find a way around a key hurdle: the fact that property on reserves is communal. This means that people have no collateral to offer when they want a personal or business loan.

Long-term leases between first nations and their members are starting to fill that void. Banks increasingly recognize them as a form of security, and offer special on-reserve mortgages. Some native leaders and academics are pushing to tackle the land issue head-on, prompting strong debate as to whether the 19th-century *Indian Act*'s restrictions should be scrapped entirely in favour of full private property.

First nations still block some projects with protests and barricades, but corporations increasingly realize the futility of battling aboriginals in courts of justice and public opinion. It is virtually impossible to be in the natural resources business in Canada without dealing with natives, and companies now try much harder to build positive relations.

Ontario's *Green Energy Act*—a controversial 2009 law that critics warn will drive up consumer prices—is turning into a good news story for many communities. Provincial programs pay energy producers a higher fee per kilowatt if they are at least 10-per-cent aboriginal-owned. Henvey Inlet is one of 16 aboriginal groups to sign power-generation deals. Many others are in the works.

In British Columbia, Chief Clarence Louie has received lots of attention for the dramatic turnaround he engineered for the Osoyoos Indian Band in the Okanagan Valley, creating many jobs with a winery, golf resort and other real-estate ventures.

The major banks are trying harder to deal with the complicated web of rules that block natives from access to capital. As national chief of the Assembly of First Nations, Phil Fontaine once led the AFN's "day of action" protests; today he is a senior adviser with the Royal Bank of Canada, overseeing regional aboriginal banking projects.

"We do have a ways to go, but we are making some progress," RBC president Gordon Nixon said in an interview, pointing to his bank's growing number of loans to aboriginal clients.

WHAT'S WORKING

Rulings by the Supreme Court of Canada have drilled home the message that companies and governments have a duty to consult first nations on projects that touch on their traditional territories. Last November, the federal government ended its objections and endorsed the United Nations Declaration on the Rights of Indigenous Peoples, which goes one step further to state that exploiting resources on their land requires the "free and informed consent" of indigenous peoples.

For business, that means it's better to forgo the legal battles and try to strike a deal.

Sharing their experiences, first nations are also finding creative ways to get around the red tape of the *Indian Act*, which forces them constantly to seek Ottawa's approval. A string of relatively recent laws allowing communities to opt out of certain sections of the *Indian Act*—such as the *First Nations Land Management Act*—offers more freedom to do business.

How to Spread the Success

A stronger focus on education and training is widely viewed as a priority. The high-school dropout rate on reserves is over 60 per cent, and schools are strapped for cash.

"The underfunding by the federal government is just immoral," said former prime minister Paul Martin, whose 2005 Kelowna Accord with aboriginals was not implemented when the Conservatives took office.

Since leaving politics, Mr. Martin has launched a $50-million venture-capital fund (including $2.5-million of his own money) that brings some of Canada's biggest companies together to support aboriginal businesses, as well as apprenticeships and business curriculums for aboriginal students.

In an interview, he said that more education funding is the key, but tax breaks for "social enterprise" investments also would make a big difference. They would encourage investment in companies that make money but also perform a social good, such as curbing aboriginal unemployment.

Communities with resource deals in the works are already training residents for the jobs that will come, whether they be in catering, construction or something more skilled, such as environmental testing. This summer, the AFN is hoping to announce a new institute, involving universities and the private sector, that would help first nations with legal advice and on-site training to take advantage of resource jobs—and produce more success stories like the one at Henvey Inlet.

Shawn Atleo, now the AFN's national chief, is a vocal advocate for more education funding and moving "beyond" the *Indian Act* to tackle the legal hurdles to development. He says government funding for the basics such as education, water and housing pay off in the long run because it allows communities to take advantage of the economic activity around them—ultimately becoming self-sufficient. Yet he said he's frustrated so far by how little talk there is in the campaign when it comes to addressing these issues.

"It really feels like, once again, first nations are like the forgotten population," he said. "Unless we have some real leadership, some courage from the federal level, this will continue to be something that confounds Canadians and federal governments."

Source: Curry, B. (2011, April 10). A new development model gains steam in Aboriginal communities. *The Globe and Mail*. http://www.theglobeandmail.com/news/national/time-to-lead/a-new-development-model-gains-steam-in-aboriginal-communities/article1979303/.

Current Issues Over Land

11

INTRODUCTION

On Thursday, November 27, 2003, the *National Post* reported that 50 percent of Canadians believe that land claims made by Aboriginal people in Canada are not valid (Curry, 2003). The journalist's source of information was the Centre for Research and Information on Canada, which conducted a poll to gauge the public's readiness to move forward on recommendations made by the Royal Commission on Aboriginal Peoples concerning the enlargement of Aboriginal people's land base in Canada. Aboriginal-held territory at the time made up less than one-half of 1 percent of the Canadian land mass (Coon Come, 2003). Today, almost a decade later, the Canadian public still seems relatively uninformed about land claims and the legal processes involved in resolving them. Being uninformed can give rise to fear and resistance in the public.

Members of police services are no different in this respect from other members of the public; without special training in the subject, their understanding of Aboriginal land claims is limited. And yet it is their responsibility to keep the peace when land claims issues arise in the form of roadblocks or peaceful (and sometimes not so peaceful) reclamations. Provincial and federal governments have sometimes—for example, in the case of the Ipperwash incident (see Appendix 11.1)—used police as an enforcement arm in resolving both land and resource disputes with Aboriginal people. The results of this have been disastrous for both officers and Aboriginal people, ending in severely strained relationships between the two.

Police services today are seeing the need to ensure that their officers have a broader understanding of the legal landscape that surrounds land claims. If an officer believes that Aboriginal protestors have no legal grounds for their actions or their grievances, he or she will have trouble maintaining an objective and unbiased approach to peacekeeping. This chapter will outline the legal background of Aboriginal land and resources claims in Canada. This will involve reviewing the constitutional rights granted to Aboriginal people and the case law that has evolved to define those rights.

CHAPTER OBJECTIVES

After completing this chapter, you should be able to:

- Connect contemporary land claims to historical treaties and case law.

- See how access to land and resources is essential to Aboriginal self-determination and independence.

- Understand the present-day process of defining Aboriginal rights to land and resources.

- See how police services can benefit from understanding the background and context of Aboriginal land claims.

- Describe the particular issues in some specific land claims cases.

BACKGROUND

The *British North America Act* of 1867 established the legislative powers of the government in Canada, dividing them between the federal government and the provinces. Under s. 91(24) of the Act, jurisdiction and governance over territories reserved for Aboriginal people were given to the federal government of Canada. Aboriginal nations were not party to the creation of this Act, nor were they consulted about it. Nine years after the implementation of the BNA Act, previous policies regarding Aboriginal people were consolidated in the *Indian Act*, an oppressive statute designed to strip away the governing rights of Indian nations. The government also used the *Indian Act* to force relocations and land seizures upon Aboriginal people. As the land base of Aboriginal people dwindled, their level of poverty increased and their dependence on the government deepened. In a country whose economy was, and is, based on the harvest and export of natural resources, Aboriginal people, now divested of land, would become the poorest group in the country.

Most Aboriginal communities in Canada today are economically dependent on the federal government for support, much to their own dismay. Economic independence for these communities depends on their gaining access to the harvest of natural resources on lands which, though outside their small reserves, are areas that are part of their traditional territory—that is, areas to which they have been granted access under the Constitution. Until recently, the government of Canada, in collusion with large corporations, has been successful in using legislative means to shut out Aboriginal people from those lucrative harvests and trap them in a position of dependency.

HISTORICAL CASE LAW

One of the first cases concerning the land claims of Aboriginal people in Canada was *St. Catherine's Milling & Lumber Company v. The Queen* (1888). It set a precedent for the land claims of all Aboriginal nations in Canada. Aboriginal people were not represented and were not even involved in this litigation process.

The Ojibwa people in northern Ontario entered into Treaty No. 3 with the federal government of Canada in 1873. Shortly thereafter, Sir John A. Macdonald, acting in his capacity as prime minister of Canada and superintendent of Indian Affairs, issued a timbering licence to St. Catherine's Milling and Lumber Company (an interest with which he is alleged to have been closely connected) (Monture-Angus, 1999, p. 68). The company had cut 2 million feet of lumber when Ontario filed for an injunction to prevent both further cutting of the lumber and its removal. Ontario asserted that the province, not the federal government, was entitled to licensing fees and royalties for timber, since Treaty No. 3 areas fell within the boundaries of Ontario. The province cited s. 109 of the BNA Act as its authority. Section 109 of the Act reads as follows:

> All Lands, Mines, Minerals, and Royalties belonging to the several Provinces of Canada, Nova Scotia, and New Brunswick at the Union, and all Sums then due or payable for such Lands, Mines, Minerals, or Royalties, shall belong to the several Provinces of Ontario, Quebec, Nova Scotia, and New Brunswick in which the same are situate or arise, subject to any Trusts existing in respect thereof, and to any Interest other than that of the Province in the same.

The federal government was the defendant in this case. Its argument was that the Indians had owned the land and had passed that ownership on to the federal government through Treaty No. 3; therefore, the federal government owned the land and the resources within it despite the fact that it lay within Ontario's provincial boundaries. The federal government cited s. 91(24) of the BNA Act, which states that the responsibility for "Indians, and Lands reserved for the Indians" falls to the federal government. Ontario argued, successfully, that Indian title to land did not constitute full ownership since Indians had no concept of property rights as recognized in British law. Ontario argued that the Crown had title to all lands of North America and that any rights to land asserted by Indians were granted by the generosity of the Crown. This, of course, is inconsistent with both the *Royal Proclamation of 1763* and the treaties themselves. Nevertheless, the result of the decision was that Indian title in the land was defined as less than full title. It was held that Indian interest in the land was mere "personal and usufructuary right"; in other words, Aboriginal people's right to use the land was held at the pleasure of the Crown, which had the power to take that right away at any time.

Since this decision was made by the Judicial Committee of the Privy Council in England, the highest court in the land, it became binding on all future land issues involving Indian title to land. It is one of those precedents in the Canadian court structure that has been a huge obstacle to anyone attempting to move forward in Aboriginal rights cases (Monture-Angus, 1999, p. 67), and it was followed for almost a century, until the *Calder* case in 1973. During the hundred years separating these two cases, the movement toward Aboriginal land and resource rights was also hindered by provisions placed in the *Indian Act* in 1927, which prohibited Aboriginal nations from hiring lawyers or pursuing claims to land. These provisions were not repealed until 1951.

The *Calder* case began in 1971, when four Nisga'a communities in British Columbia's Nass Valley brought their case to the Supreme Court of Canada, asserting their claim to traditional territory that was outside the reserve created for them by the federal government. The communities based their claim on the fact that they had never entered into any treaties and had never relinquished their lands to either the federal government or the province of British Columbia. They and their ancestors had in fact occupied the land since time immemorial, and they had never agreed to relinquish any land or resources. The Supreme Court was split three to three on whether the claim to the land was valid (the seventh judge dismissed the case on a technicality). In his decision, Justice Judson stated:

> [T]he fact is that when the settlers came, the Indians were there, organized in societies and occupying the land as their forefathers had done for centuries. This is what Indian title means and it does not help one in the solution of this problem to call it a "personal or usufructuary right." What they are asserting in this action is that they had a right to continue to live on their lands as their forefathers had lived and that this right has never been lawfully extinguished. (*Calder et al. v. Attorney General of British Columbia*, 1973, p. 328, quoted in Monture-Angus, 1999, pp. 75–76)

Justice Hall discussed the process of extinguishment further. He stated that should the Crown claim to have extinguished Aboriginal title to land, it must do so in a clear and plain manner; it cannot rely on implied extinguishment. The most significant part of this judgment is that all six of the judges agreed that

- Aboriginal title to land existed, as defined by British law, prior to and at the time of colonization; and,
- the Crown must act in a clear and plain way to extinguish that title ("Calder case," n.d.).

Although the *Calder* case did not provide a clear test of extinguishment—this did not come till the case of *Sparrow*, in 1990—it did force the federal government to work toward settling Aboriginal claims in regions of the country where treaties had not extinguished Aboriginal title. This was something Aboriginal activists had long wanted; since the 1951 revision of the *Indian Act*, which had repealed the prohibition against the Aboriginal pursuit of land claims, they had been pressing the government, to no avail, to create a process for settling land claims.

Another case that significantly affected Aboriginal land and resource claims in Canada was *Guerin v. The Queen* (1984). Prior to the verdict in *Guerin*, the Department of Indian Affairs had a *moral duty* to act in the best interest of Aboriginal nations in the administration of reserve lands and resources. But this duty, known as a *fiduciary duty*—in other words, the duty to act in the best interest of another—was not recognized in law. Accordingly, the department had limited accountability to the Aboriginal people it administrated; it was accountable only to the federal government, whose interests were opposed to those of the Aboriginal people, particularly in financial matters.

In *Guerin*, the Musqueam Indian Reserve had agreed to lease 66 hectares of reserve land in the city of Vancouver to the Shaugnessy Golf Club in 1955. In keeping with the *Royal Proclamation of 1763*, which provides that Indian land is "alienable"—in other words, can be surrendered or leased—only to the Crown, the band was required to surrender the 66 hectares to the Crown before the lease could take place. In a meeting, the band and the Indian agent agreed upon the terms of the lease to be put in place with the golf club. However, these terms were misrepresented to the band. The land was surrendered and the Crown entered into a lease agreement with the golf club on terms that were unfavourable to the band and inconsistent with what it had agreed to. The band attempted to grieve this action to no avail. The band was unable even to procure a copy of the lease agreement, which it had never received at the time the land was transferred, until 1970. When the band obtained a copy of the lease, it attempted to sue the Crown for damages. The case made its way to the Supreme Court of Canada, which issued its decision in 1984. At the heart of the argument was the Crown's responsibility to act in the best interest of the band. The Crown argued that the responsibility amounted to a "political trust" enforceable by Parliament but not to a "true trust" enforceable by the courts. The Crown was unsuccessful in its argument, and the SCC ruled as follows (*Guerin v. The Queen*, 1984, p. 376) in its final verdict:

> An Indian Band is prohibited from directly transferring its interest to a third party. Any sale or lease of land can only be carried out after a surrender has taken place, with the Crown then acting on the Band's behalf. The Crown first took this responsibility upon itself in the Royal Proclamation of 1763. It is still recognized in the surrender provisions of the *Indian Act*. The surrender requirement, and the responsibility it entails, are the source of a distinct fiduciary obligation owed by the Crown to the Indians.

Justice Dickson also stated the following:

After the Crown's agents had induced the Band to surrender its land on the understanding that the land would be leased on certain terms, it would be un-conscionable to permit the Crown simply to ignore these terms. Equity will not countenance unconscionable behaviour in a fiduciary whose duty is that of utmost loyalty to his principal. (*Guerin v. The Queen*, 1984, pp. 336–337)

There have been many cases like *Guerin*—that is, cases that bring into doubt the Crown's responsible administration of band resources and band land. *Guerin* set a precedent; the government would be held responsible for mismanagement. In the *Guerin* case, the band was awarded $10 million in restitution. The sum of the settle-ment was based on what the lease value of the land would have been to that point had the band never surrendered the land to the government to facilitate the un-favourable lease (Henderson, 1996). The settlement of the case came at the end of a long, slow process. There were a number of appeals; the final decision was ren-dered a full 14 years after the band first obtained a copy of the lease and the Crown's misdealings were seen in their full extent. This was 29 years after the original proposed lease.

CONSTITUTION

During the litigation of the *Guerin* case, the Canadian Constitution was patriated. Prior to the patriation of the Constitution, Aboriginal activists had appealed to international powers and to governments in Canada and Europe for the inclusion of Aboriginal rights within the Constitution. Their work culminated in the inclu-sion of s. 35 of the *Constitution Act, 1982*, which states the following:

35(1) The existing aboriginal and treaty rights of the aboriginal peoples of Canada are hereby recognized and affirmed.

(2) In this Act, "aboriginal peoples of Canada" includes the Indian, Inuit and Métis peoples of Canada.

(3) For greater certainty, in subsection (1) "treaty rights" includes rights that now exist by way of land claims agreements or may be so acquired.

(4) Notwithstanding any other provision of this Act, the aboriginal and treaty rights referred to in subsection (1) are guaranteed equally to male and female persons.

Since the introduction of this provision in 1982, Canadian courts have been trying to clarify the extent of Aboriginal rights in this country. It is important to note the wording of the section; the *existing* rights of Aboriginal people are *recognized and affirmed*. This section does not provide any new rights for Aboriginal people in Canada. Of course, Aboriginal rights existed in common law in Canada prior to the enactment of the Constitution. The source of those common law rights was the Aboriginal people's original occupation of land and their social and political organ-ization, which existed prior to Canada's assertion of sovereignty. Some of those rights were expressly terminated by the Crown through treaty, but many were not. Some Aboriginal rights were established through the treaty process. Section 35 of the Constitution, rather than creating new rights, elevates the rights that existed already, through common law and treaty, to constitutional status. This restricts the right of the Crown to modify or extinguish Aboriginal rights (Bell & Paterson, 2003, p. 108).

Section 35 provided protection for Aboriginal rights but did not simplify the process of defining what an Aboriginal right is or is not. So—what is protected under s. 35 of the Constitution? Aboriginal people have been taking their cases to court continually over the years to have the courts define these rights.

EXERCISE 1

Aboriginal activist, author, and lawyer Ardith Walkem (2003, p. 198) has written the following about the purpose of Aboriginal people's battle for rights in the Canadian courts:

> When Indigenous Peoples speak of Aboriginal Title and Rights, it is a much broader conception than that which has evolved under Canadian Law. Indigenous Peoples are not seeking to have distinct practices protected, nor title recognized to small parcels of land. The reason that Indigenous Peoples engage in the court process stems from a simple desire and imperative: Our continued existence as peoples and maintenance of our ability to continue to exist and thrive on the territories on which the Creator placed us and according to the laws which bind us to the lands and waters and govern the relationships between all living things and the spiritual beings that also live within and through the lands and waters. These elements, at a minimum, embrace the fundamental aspects of Indigenous Peoples' aspirations:
>
> 1. Territory (both land and water) and recognition of our responsibility to manage, protect and benefit from that territory.
> 2. Recognition of the laws, traditions, languages and cultures of Indigenous peoples which flow, and are intricately tied to, our territories, and
> 3. Recognition of a right to self determination which ensures that we are able to survive into the future governed by, and accountable to, our own laws.

With reference to Walkem's description above, discuss the importance and role of land within an Aboriginal and a non-Aboriginal framework, including its connection to identity and survival.

The right to self-determination is one of the fundamental aspirations of Aboriginal people, and being able to achieve this requires a certain degree of independence from the control of the Canadian government. This independence will require a degree of economic self-sufficiency, which means, in turn, that Aboriginal people must rebuild their economies to thrive in today's world. Such rebuilding will require both land and control over resources of the land.

Many of the cases that have been brought before the Supreme Court involve rights to the harvest of natural resources—hunting and fishing rights, for example, as in *R v. Sparrow* (1990). Mr. Sparrow is a Salish and lives on the Musqueam Indian Reserve, which is located within Vancouver's city limits. He fishes commercially and for food. In May 1984, he was charged with using a drift net that was longer than British Columbia fishing regulations allowed. Mr. Sparrow did not dispute the facts at issue in the case but argued that he had an Aboriginal right to fish in the area, as his forefathers had for generations, and that this right was protected under s. 35 of the Constitution. An *Aboriginal right* to fish in the area—so Mr. Sparrow's argument went—meant that he was not bound by the British Columbia fishing regulations applicable to non-Aboriginal fishermen. Mr. Sparrow did not decide lightly to embark upon this case; he was aware that the outcome would affect Aboriginal fishing rights across Canada. He was supported in his decision by the band. Its members were being charged more and more frequently under the fishing regulations, and relations between the band and the Department of Fisheries were growing hostile. Sparrow's decision to embark on the case was in the interest of his community, not simply himself (Monture-Angus, 1999, pp. 88–89).

Mr. Sparrow's case was heard by the Supreme Court of Canada in 1990. In reviewing the case, the Court recognized that the main issue was whether Parliament had the right to regulate Aboriginal fishing in light of s. 35 of the Constitution. The first matter to be decided was whether the rights of the Salish to fish were "recognized and affirmed" in the Constitution at the time of its patriation in 1982. The Crown's position was that the right claimed by Sparrow was extinguished prior to 1982 amid the myriad provincial fishing regulations enacted over time in British Columbia. The Crown was unsuccessful in its argument due to the precedent set by the *Calder* case in 1973, where the Court stated that the Crown must articulate in a plain and clear manner its intent to extinguish an Aboriginal right and cannot rely on implied extinguishment. Justices Dickson and La Forest stated the following in the *Sparrow* case: "The test of extinguishment to be adopted, in our opinion, is that the Sovereign's intention must be clear and plain if it is to extinguish an aboriginal right" (*R v. Sparrow*, 1990, p. 1099).

The Supreme Court found that the enactment of provincial regulations prior to 1982—the rationale for extinguishment cited by the Crown in the *Sparrow* case—is implied extinguishment only and does not meet the test for extinguishment. On this basis, the Supreme Court concluded that Mr. Sparrow's right to fish was constitutionally entrenched in 1982.

Since the Constitution is the supreme law of the land, statutes cannot be enacted to alter rights guaranteed in it. However, the Supreme Court in *Sparrow* recognized that the rights of Aboriginal people to the fisheries are not absolute. In *Sparrow*, the Supreme Court set out a two-part test for determining whether infringement on an Aboriginal people's constitutional right to fish is justified. The first part of the test asks whether the Crown has "compelling and substantial objectives" for infringement—for example, the protection of the resources in order to ensure the continuation of the right. The second part of the test requires that any legislation aiming to limit Aboriginal people's constitutional rights to fisheries must be consistent with the Crown's fiduciary obligation to Aboriginal people. Other compelling objectives may involve balancing the constitutional rights of Aboriginal people to the fisheries with the rights of non-Aboriginal peoples to the fisheries. In the latter circumstance, the test of fiduciary duty would come first.

The judgment rendered in *Sparrow* was seen as a victory for Aboriginal people, whose aim in establishing a right to the resource was not to exclude non-Aboriginal access but to increase their own economic self-sufficiency. Ultimately, of course, this victory was significantly limited by the power the decision gave the Crown to limit Aboriginal access through the two-part test. Still, the onus was now on the Crown to justify infringement, including minimal infringement. If the rights were infringed for justifiable reasons, this must be established through a process of negotiation. Bell and Paterson (2003, p. 107) offer a concise summary of the litigation process used to determine what Aboriginal rights are constitutionally protected:

1. identification of the nature and content of the right;
2. determining whether the right is an "existing right" recognized and affirmed by section 35 (or whether it has been lawfully extinguished prior to the enactment of Section 35);
3. determination of whether federal or provincial legislation constitutes a prima facie infringement with the exercising of an existing Aboriginal right; and
4. analysis of the legitimacy of justification for government interference.

The *Sparrow* decision shows how a common law Aboriginal right to fish becomes protected under the Constitution. Later, in *R v. Badger* (1996), the Supreme Court clarified that rights set out in treaties must be protected in the same manner. This will have far-reaching consequences; many of the 500 plus treaties give Aboriginal people the right to hunt and fish without interference by the Crown, and many treaties give them hunting and fishing rights over territories ceded in the treaties that are now Crown land or over territories in which interest has been vested in third parties due to grants by the Crown. The same two-part test set out in *Sparrow* must be applied to infringement of an Aboriginal right that is set out in a treaty.

There have been a number of cases since *Sparrow* that elaborate upon the two-part test. The *R v. Van der Peet* case settled by the Supreme Court of Canada in 1996 offers a new twist to the *Sparrow* two-part test. Dorothy Van der Peet was charged for violating the British Columbia fishing regulations, which prohibited the sale and barter of fish. Van der Peet was a member of the Sto:lo First Nation. She sold 10 salmon for $50 to a non-Aboriginal person. In this case, the Supreme Court set new criteria for characterizing and interpreting Aboriginal rights. It narrowed the definition of what could be considered an Aboriginal right to a right that existed pre-contact. It held that a right is not an Aboriginal right if it exists because of European influence. In this case, the Supreme Court held that the pre-contact activity of exchanging fish among nations or people did not correspond to an unlimited commercial right to fish for contemporary Aboriginal people; it corresponded to a right to fish for livelihood. According to the principle in *Van der Peet*, contemporary Aboriginal rights must in some cases be grounded in pre-contact activities. This decision would set a precedent for the battle between mainstream Canada and Aboriginal people over the latter's right to access the forestry industry, Canada's greatest export and source of wealth. The Supreme Court would later rely on the *Van der Peet* decision to disallow Aboriginal people increased commercial access to the forestry industry, on the basis that logging is not an activity in which they engaged pre-contact.

ABORIGINAL TITLE TO LAND

The *Delgamuukw v. British Columbia* case (1997) began its journey through the Canadian court system in the early 1980s. It developed in the following way. The Gitksan and Wet'suwet'en people sought to force the province of British Columbia to recognize Aboriginal title over the two bands' traditional territory, which they had never ceded to the province or federal government through treaty or any other means. The area encompasses approximately 58,000 square kilometres in north-central British Columbia. The province asserted that Aboriginal title to land in British Columbia had been extinguished in 1871, upon the incorporation of the province into the Dominion of Canada. This case was decided by the Supreme Court in 1997.

This case set precedents for Aboriginal rights, including Aboriginal title to land, and for Crown sovereignty, which the courts assert can coexist with Aboriginal rights.

The BC Crown argued the following:

1. Aboriginal peoples were so low on the scale of social organization that their lands can be treated as vacant and unoccupied for the purpose of issuing Crown grants pursuant to laws enacted by settler governments without regard to the prior occupation of Aboriginal peoples (Mandell, 2003, p. 166).

2. Colonial land legislation before Confederation extinguished Aboriginal peoples' relations to the land; once the colony (soon to become a province) enacted legislation regulating Aboriginal peoples' rights to the land and resources, their rights were extinguished by implied extinguishment and by the powers vested in the colony/province (Youngblood Henderson, 1999).

3. The creation of land grants by British Columbia to settlers extinguished the Aboriginal tenure because Aboriginal people were precluded from sustaining their relationship with the land; once settlers were granted land and began occupying it, Aboriginal people's relationship to the land was broken. The existence of third-party interests displaces Aboriginal use, right, and title (Youngblood Henderson, 1999; Mandell, 2003).

4. The establishment of federal Indian reserves in British Columbia extinguished Aboriginal tenure because Aboriginal people "abandoned" their territory (Youngblood Henderson, 1999). An underlying assertion of this argument is that the benefits of colonization, such as "civilization" and "Christianity," were compensation enough for voluntarily vacating traditional lands (Mandell, 2003).

5. Section 88 of the *Indian Act* allowed provincial laws of general application to apply as well to Indians, extinguishing Aboriginal title and rights (Youngblood Henderson, 1999).

6. Aboriginal title and rights vanish with the passage of time (Mandell, 2003, p. 169).

The above arguments, made by the Crown to assert the absence of Aboriginal title over the land, are the same ones put forward initially by many students who are studying land claims for the first time. It is important to understand that the Supreme Court heard—and rejected—all of these arguments in the *Delgamuukw* decision. Arguments 2 to 5 rest on the assumption that the colony or province of British Columbia has the power to extinguish Aboriginal title to land. The Court ruled that the province never had the constitutional authority to extinguish Aboriginal title, and since that title has never been extinguished, it is protected under s. 35 of the Constitution.

The Court did not recognize the passage of time as extinguishing title or rights, nor did it recognize the argument that Aboriginal people, because "uncivilized," were not a people capable of holding territory.

In its decision, the Court identified three components of Aboriginal title:

1. That it encompasses the right to exclusive use and occupancy of the land.
2. That it gives Aboriginal people the right to choose what uses the land can be put to, with the limitation that the land cannot be altered so as to destroy its capacity to sustain future generations of Aboriginal people.
3. That the lands held pursuant to Aboriginal title have an economic component.

The first component of the Supreme Court's ruling in *Delgamuukw* displaced the *St. Catherine's* ruling of 1888, which had stated that Aboriginal interest in the land was merely "personal and usufructuary"—that is, held at the pleasure of the Crown. It elevates the Aboriginal interest in the land to exclusive use and occupancy. The second component of the ruling states that Aboriginal people must be consulted over decisions pertaining to the uses of the land held under Aboriginal title. In other words, holding title to land gives Aboriginal people mineral rights and rights to make decisions over resource harvesting and development. The third part of the Court's ruling in *Delgamuukw*, by which the economic component of the land's value is recognized, suggests that the fiduciary responsibility of the Crown must be scrutinized in the dealings with Aboriginal land, and that Aboriginal people must benefit from the lands and resources. The Supreme Court also established a test for infringement on the rights inherent in Aboriginal title. It specified that the Crown must provide justifications for infringement and that compensation must be paid for the infringement based on the nature of the infringement, in recognition of the economic component of Aboriginal land title.

As in all cases involving Aboriginal rights, a move forward would not be complete without a limitation being placed on it. The *Delgamuukw* decision set a two-part test for determining whether infringement on Aboriginal title is justified. The first requirement is that the infringement be for a valid legislative directive. The Supreme Court definition of these "valid legislative directives" was very broad; it included the following:

1. the development of agricultural, forestry, mining, and hydroelectric power;
2. the general economic development of the province;
3. the protection of the environment or endangered species;
4. the building of infrastructure; and
5. the settlement of foreign populations to support those aims (McDonald, 2003, p. 231).

The second part of the test for justifiable infringement asks whether the infringement is consistent with the fiduciary responsibility of the Crown to Aboriginal people. It makes it mandatory for the government to consult with Aboriginal people before reaching a decision about infringement and compensation. This consultation process has not always gone smoothly, and the breakdowns can lead to serious and sometimes dangerous confrontations. For an example of such a breakdown, we will look briefly at the East Coast lobster fisheries dispute between the Crown and the Mi'kmaq.

RECENT CASE STUDY

Originally, the Mi'kmaq were partners in the Wabanaki Confederacy, which comprised five nations: the Mi'kmaq, the Passamaquoddy, the Penobscot, the Maliseet, and the Abenaki. The traditional territory of this group included Atlantic Canada, Maine, and parts of Quebec. Post-contact, the Mi'kmaq were aligned with the French but made treaties with the British after France was forced to cede its territories in Acadia to the British. Settlers and the original inhabitants of the territory signed a series of treaties, beginning in 1725, to establish peace. These treaties gave the Mi'kmaq the right to fish and hunt the territory as they had always done. The treaties did not contain any provisions about transferring the land's ownership. Renewed in 1749, 1752, 1760, 1761, and 1794, this series of treaties was characterized as a covenant chain, with each treaty connected and linked to the others. The highlights of those treaties were as follows:

> British laws would be a great hedge about the Mi'kmaq property and rights. Mi'kmaq could traffic and barter or exchange commodities in any manner with managers of truckhouses (trading posts). Mi'kmaq would receive gifts in the form of goods on the First day of each October and the nation to nation relationship between the British and the Mi'kmaq would be respected and the Mi'kmaq way of life would be preserved. (Knockwood, 2003, p. 47)

Following this chain of treaties, the BNA Act was instated, followed by the *Indian Act*, which essentially denied the treaty rights of the Mi'kmaq. Following this, a myriad of federal and provincial laws was enacted to regulate and limit the Mi'kmaq rights to fish and hunt. Nevertheless, the Mi'kmaq continued to press for the recognition of the treaties and continued to hunt and fish outside the regulations that were unilaterally imposed. In 1928, Mi'kmaq Gabriel Sylliboy was charged for hunting out of season. He was found guilty when the trial judge asserted that the treaty protection did not extend to Mi'kmaq outside the small band of the Shubenacadie, and since Sylliboy was not a member of that specific band, he had no protection under the treaty. Furthermore, the judge ruled that even if Sylliboy were a member of that small band, he would still be found guilty on the following grounds: when the treaty was signed in 1752, the Mi'kmaq were not an independent power legally capable of entering into a treaty. One must question the logic of this statement. Why would the British negotiate a treaty with a group whom they did not recognize as having the legal capacity to enter into a treaty?

The precedent was set; in a subsequent case, *Francis v. The Queen* in 1969, Justice Richard of the New Brunswick Magistrate's Court convicted Martin Francis of fishing without a licence (Knockwood, 2003, p. 52). Francis asserted that the treaties set out his right to fish. Although the judge was sympathetic to the issues, he found it his "painful duty" to convict because, he said, previous case law meant that the law did not recognize the treaty.

A number of cases ensued involving the Mi'kmaq, who, seemingly undaunted, continued to battle in the courts to assert their rights. The first case that followed the constitutional provisions enshrined in s. 35 was *Simon v. The Queen*, in 1985. The *Sylliboy* decision, stating that the Mi'kmaq were not capable of entering into treaties, was overturned. Mr. Simon, charged with hunting infractions, was not convicted. The basis given by the Supreme Court for his acquittal was that the treaty of 1752 was a valid treaty which the Mi'kmaq had legitimately entered into and which ought to protect them against infringements on their hunting rights. The Supreme Court also found that the right was not an "absolute right" and was subject to federal regulation. Nevertheless, this was a victory, as it was the first time the Mi'kmaq treaties had been recognized, affording them protection under s. 35.

The last related decision of the Supreme Court came in 1999, in the case of *R v. Marshall*. Donald Marshall Jr., a Mi'kmaq fisherman, was charged with violating federal fishing regulations by selling eels without a licence, by fishing without a licence, and by fishing during the closed season with the use of illegal nets. Marshall had caught 463 pounds of eels that he sold for $787.10 (*R v. Marshall*, 1999, para. 4; Donham, 2003, p. 366). Entered into evidence for the defence were minutes from the treaty negotiations from 1760–61. Those minutes included requests from the Mi'kmaq for truckhouses in which to sell their peltries (animal skins), and agreements by which the Mi'kmaq could barter and trade their catches and hunting spoils with the managers of the truckhouses for "necessaries." In 1999, the Supreme Court interpreted this as the Mi'kmaq having retained not only their right to harvest resources but also the right to sell and trade to their best advantage. The Court interpreted "necessaries" to mean "a modest livelihood." The Court, as in other cases previously discussed, did not give the Aboriginal group the right to an unlimited commercial harvest; it provided that federal regulations might restrict the Aboriginal right if the resource needed to be protected. In keeping with the *Delgamuukw* decision, it was agreed that decisions about restricting or impinging on Aboriginal rights must involve negotiation with the Mi'kmaq, as well as close attention to the Crown's performance of its fiduciary duty.

Approximately 40 Mi'kmaq boats took to the water to celebrate the recognition of their rights and began to fish lobster. The same waters were home to some 2,893 non-Aboriginal lobster boats. The backlash by non-Aboriginal fishers, particularly commercial fishers, was fierce. They lobbied the government to re-open the *Marshall* case and insisted that the conservation of lobster fisheries was at stake. Violence broke out in some communities between Aboriginal and non-Aboriginal fishers. The Department of Fisheries quickly pressured Mi'kmaq and other bands to sign agreements limiting their newly recognized rights to fish. Twenty-seven bands signed agreements with the department within a year. Bands at Indian Brook and Burnt Church refused to sign, and continued to fish and develop their own conservation plan. They were portrayed in the media as renegades, adamant and unreasonable in their determination to fish illegally. The media failed to point out that the quantity of Aboriginal traps was in fact less than 0.2 percent of the non-Aboriginal traps (Donham, 2003, p. 371).

As Aboriginal traps were destroyed by angry non-Aboriginal fishers, and violence broke out, the RCMP was called upon to keep the peace and the Department of Fisheries was sent in to save the lobsters from Aboriginal fishers who, according to the media, were about to drive the lobsters to extinction. The Department of Fisheries arrested Mi'kmaq fishers and participated in sinking several of their vessels (Obomsawin, 2002). The RCMP did what it could to keep the peace. By 2002, the Mi'kmaq had acquiesced and signed agreements to severely limit their take of the resource. Ten Mi'kmaq fishers had been arrested for fishing violations and for further criminal offences related to resisting Department of Fisheries officers' arrests. The conflict is not over; the Mi'kmaq continue to attempt to inch their way into the commercial fishing business.

What all of this means is that one of the poorest Aboriginal groups on the East Coast, and a group with the greatest right—according to the Supreme Court of Canada—to resource harvesting, has been assigned a negligible amount of the harvest. The Supreme Court decision rendered in *Marshall* was intended to increase Mi'kmaq access to the fishery and to provide economic hope for the community. It would appear, however, that non-Aboriginal commercial fishers are not prepared to share the resource.

WORKING TOGETHER

Thus far we have examined the litigious and adversarial nature of defining Aboriginal rights to land and resources. Because our system is based on Western European legal structures, it is adversarial in nature. However, there are other ways of defining rights and reaching mutually acceptable agreements about resource sharing and management. Because pursuing land claims through litigation is so slow and costly, it often happens that development continues on the contested lands until, by the time settlements are reached, the land's resources are already harvested or the land is permanently altered by, for example, mining or oil or gas exploration.

One of the new approaches to land claims is co-management. Co-management is a more inclusive and consensus-based approach to resource harvesting and development; it involves government and private industry sharing decision-making power with non-traditional actors—environmental groups, Aboriginal groups, and local users of the resources—in the process of resource management. Co-management stresses resolving conflict through negotiation rather than litigation (Campbell, 1996). It has been implemented in areas where Aboriginal rights to lands have not been extinguished and seems to have been most successful in more remote areas where settlement and the harvesting of resources are just beginning to occur.

As discussed earlier in this chapter, particularly in the *St. Catherine's Milling* case, the protection of Aboriginal treaty rights, such as hunting and fishing, is seen as the responsibility of the federal government. However, the management of natural resources is seen as a provincial responsibility. Confusion can result when Aboriginal people choose to exercise on provincial Crown land their treaty rights to natural resources. Whether they are permitted to do so depends on how developed that provincial land is.

Concepts of co-management fit well with the Supreme Court ruling in *Delgamuukw*, particularly the second component of the ruling, which set out the right of Aboriginal people to determine the uses to which the land can be put. The process of co-management is a good answer to that component of the ruling, which made sincere negotiations over land usage mandatory.

Current co-management schemes vary in the degree of control they allow Aboriginal people in the management of resources. Provincial governments sometimes call their proposals "co-management" when what they are actually doing is informing Aboriginal people about decisions already made with regard to the contested territories; they are not consulting with them on how to minimize the harmful effects to their communities. This kind of process is inconsistent with the true spirit of co-management. Even with real co-management, the degree of control allowed Aboriginal people tends to vary; it can range from cooperation, to communication with advisory committees, to participation on management boards, all the way to partnership and community control. Ideally, the co-management process means a partnership of equals and completely joint decision making. This requires commitment and a delicate balance of interests.

LAND CLAIMS

comprehensive land claims
claims to territory that are not covered by treaty or land cession agreements

Land claims are divided into two categories, comprehensive land claims and specific land claims. **Comprehensive land claims** affect land that has not been covered by treaty, meaning approximately 50 percent of Canada's land mass. Since a treaty involving that land was not entered into, Aboriginal people have an interest in any land that, as per *Delgamuukw*, has a distinct economic nature. Treaties are not a thing of the past; the processes through which these contemporary claims are settled constitute modern-day treaties. Settlement of them can involve terms and conditions touching on a variety of matters, including money, land, forms of local government, rights to wildlife, the protection of Aboriginal language and culture, and the joint management of lands and resources. These modern treaties set out conditions concerning resource allocations, structures for self-government, and many other matters related to economic interests in the land. Government negotiators often offer an increase in the existing Aboriginal land base in return for the extinguishment of Aboriginal title over an even larger portion of land. Such exchanges are highly controversial for Aboriginal people, since the extinguishment of rights over territory is precisely what they are fighting against. As previously discussed, Aboriginal people have a special sense of their connection to the land.

Recent negotiations have led to portions of urban land being added to reserve holdings. The Manitoba Treaty Land Entitlement Framework Agreement, signed in 1997 by Canada, Manitoba, and Aboriginal representatives, was an agreement that land should be added to Aboriginal peoples' reserved land base to compensate for land improperly expropriated from them. The land was to come from Crown holdings. But the agreement allowed for the purchase of private land, on a willing buyer–seller basis, by Aboriginal groups who do not have sufficient Crown land to choose from in their immediate vicinity, with the federal government supplying $76 million for this purpose (Treaty Land Entitlement Committee of Manitoba Inc., n.d.). Purchases of this sort have gone forward in a number of Western agreements. In some cases, Aboriginal bands have used settlement money to purchase properties in urban centres to provide housing for urban Aboriginal people, and they have started economic ventures in traditionally non-Aboriginal areas where proximity to urban centres increases their chances of business success.

specific land claims
claims that relate to specific misdealings of the Crown with relation to land or resources

Specific land claims are based on lawful obligation and involve claims related to the management of Aboriginal lands and assets. With specific claims, the main issues are the loss of established band lands and of natural resources in that land as a result of unilateral action by the Crown. The *Guerin* case discussed earlier in this chapter is an example of a specific land claim.

EXERCISE 2

The average amount of time taken to resolve a specific claim is 13 years, but many claims take much longer. Discuss some of the consequences of this for the Aboriginal groups involved, for non-Aboriginals, and for the larger Canadian society.

Each claim is distinct, reflecting the particular needs and history of each area. Take, for example, the claim put forward in 1988 by the Golden Lake Algonquin (Steckley & Cummins, 2001a). This claim is still under negotiation 30 years after the process began, and remains a long way from settlement. The Golden Lake Algonquin live 140 kilometres west of Algonquin Park, Ontario. They have never surrendered their rights to the land and have never signed a treaty. The government originally signed a treaty with a band of Ottawa Aboriginals who spent a few years in the Algonquin area around 1680 but did not claim the area, at the time, as their traditional territory. The Algonquin, whose traditional territory the area was, were overlooked in the treaty process. This is not unusual and has happened to different Aboriginal groups in Canada—the Lubicon Cree in Alberta, for example, and the Temagami Anicinabe in northern Ontario.

The Golden Lake Algonquin have been asserting their claim to the land since 1772, when they petitioned the government to recognize their title. Sir William Johnson assured the Algonquin that their title was protected under the *Royal Proclamation*—despite the fact that, at the time, they were being overwhelmed by white settlement. The government, after promising several times to keep settlers off the land, abruptly announced in 1836 that the Algonquin had already surrendered the land to the Crown under treaty and had been compensated accordingly. The 1845 Bagot Commission, which investigated the uncompensated alienation of Aboriginals from their lands, looked at the Algonquin situation and recommended that the Algonquin be compensated for their land and that a tract of land be set aside for them. This recommendation was not followed.

In 1857, hemmed in by settlers on all sides, five Algonquin families petitioned the government for reserve land. Six years later, they were granted 631 hectares of land on which to live. Soon, other families joined the group and the population grew to the point that the established acreage could not sustain them. Algonquin Provincial Park was created in 1893 from Crown land that was for sale for settlement. Other groups of Algonquin were living in the area that would become the provincial park, and they petitioned the government to set aside lands for them, given that they had been displaced by the creation of the park. The government advised them to join the Golden Lake group on the area already set aside. (The government wished to avoid creating more reserves because it believed that real estate would drop if there were too many Indians in the area.) The Algonquin continued to petition the government, insisting that they had neither surrendered their land nor been compensated for its loss; furthermore, they had been told—and had believed—that their title to the land was protected under the *Royal Proclamation*. Their petitions were ignored.

In the mid-1980s, a Provincial Court judge agreed with the Algonquin that they had not ceded their traditional land and that therefore their title to the land was protected under the *Royal Proclamation*. The Supreme Court of Ontario overturned that decision; regardless, the Algonquin entered a claim that involved 8.8 million hectares, which included most of the park and much of the surrounding area, including small municipalities.

The Algonquin wished to reclaim unoccupied Crown land only, not private, commercial, or municipal lands. Four subjects were brought forward in this claim: land, natural resources, self-government, and compensation for the loss. The province began the negotiation process in response to the claim, but the public was outraged. The loss of the park and of Crown land meant that there was no room for non-Aboriginal communities to expand.

By 1991, the two sides reached an interim agreement outlining hunting and fishing rights in the area. This agreement gave the Algonquin rights within the park, much to the dismay of non-Aboriginal hunters. Today, a quarter century after the claim was first entered, no resolution has been reached with regard to the land or to the other resources. Negotiations are ongoing. A few years ago, the parties committed to trying to reach an "agreement-in-principle" by 2011. An agreement-in-principle is something sought for in all negotiations. It is an interim point in the process, not legally binding, but it determines the scope of the negotiation and determines what its goals are. An agreement-in-principle requires ratification by all negotiating parties. In the Algonquin case, according to reports (Ministry of Aboriginal Affairs, 2010), the agreement-in-principle between the province, the federal government, and the Algonquins would address the following:

- Crown land that could be transferred to Algonquin ownership;
- the nature of Algonquin rights to resources, including hunting and fishing rights;
- a financial payment to the Algonquin;
- a definition of the geographic area covered by the settlement agreement;
- criteria that a person must meet to qualify as an Algonquin within the settlement; and
- other matters, such as initiatives for economic development or Algonquin cultural initiatives.

Once an agreement-in-principle is officially approved by all three parties, work will begin on the detailed legal wording of a final agreement. In the case of the Algonquin land claim, the final agreement will be a modern treaty, which means it will be ratified by special legislation protected under the Canadian Constitution.

The considerable time it takes to negotiate a claim is obviously a major problem. Proposals have been put forward to speed the process along, but it remains painfully slow. Many claims have taken or will take much longer than the Algonquin's. Most claims are negotiated without protests or violence; however, when the negotiations break down, Aboriginal people sometimes take action in the form of protests and/or setting up blockades. This most often happens when resource harvesting or development is occurring at a rapid rate on contested land. Aboriginal groups cannot afford to wait 20, 30, or 50 years while their claim makes its way through stages of research and negotiation. If they wait too long, there will be nothing left to negotiate for. These protests and/or blockades have the potential for violence: investors and construction or forestry crews become angry with the work stoppage, and Aboriginal people become frustrated at the idea that their petitions are being ignored.

For specific claims, which are far easier to resolve than comprehensive claims, the resolution process has taken 13 years on average. In October 2008, the government passed the *Specific Claims Tribunal Act* (SCTA), which set a limit on how long a claim could remain outstanding. The Act was given the slogan "Justice at Last" and was approved by the National Assembly of First Nations. It was meant to increase impartiality and fairness, provide greater transparency, result in faster processing of claims, and provide better access to mediation. The SCTA imposes a three-year time limit on Canada's responding to a First Nations specific claim that has either been rejected by the minister or not been settled through negotiation (Assembly of First Nations, 2011). As we approach the third year since its enactment, however, the Act has not produced the results hoped for by Aboriginal leaders. Aboriginal Affairs and Northern Development Canada (AANDC) reports (2011) that the SCTA has resulted in 445 specific claims being successfully addressed since 2007. However, the three-year deadline for negotiation (October 16, 2011) is now past, and claims not successfully negotiated must start their way to the new Specific Claims Tribunal. The Tribunal opened in June 2011, after a delay in appointing judges and developing rules and procedural guidelines. In a report published by the Union of BC Indian Chiefs (2011), it was asserted that since the opening of the Tribunal they are being forced into take-it-or-leave-it offers from the government, on claims that have spent years under negotiation. They perceive that Canada has stopped negotiating in good faith and is intent on transferring the many outstanding specific claims to the newly created Tribunal, which will quickly become overwhelmed. Jim Rankin of the *Toronto Star* reported in July 2011 that, nationally, there were 471 specific claims in progress and 142 in active negotiations. The report stated that almost 1,000 have been concluded—a number that includes those that have been closed or rejected as well as the 349 that have been settled through negotiations (Rankin, 2011). Time will tell if the newly created Specific Claims Tribunal is able to handle the volume of claims that will now come its way.

ONTARIO

Generally, there are three kinds of land claims in Ontario.

(1) **Claims relating to the fulfillment of terms of treaties**. These claims are usually the result of disagreements between the Crown and First Nations about the size and location of the reserves that were set aside in accordance with the treaties. These claims may also involve the wording of treaties and the understanding of the parties at the time of treaty signing. Claims can also arise as a result of events that occurred after the treaty signing, such as the flooding of reserve land for hydro-electric power and the expropriation of reserve land for public purposes such as highways, infrastructure, or military building without compensation. The Ipperwash land dispute falls into this category. (See Appendix 11.1 for details.)

(2) **Claims arising from the surrender for sale of reserve land**. These occur when an Aboriginal community seeks compensation for, or the return of, land that had been surrendered to the Crown for sale for the benefit of the band. These surrenders did take place, and the funds generated from the sale of land were to be set aside

claims relating to the fulfillment of terms of treaties
claims that are usually a result of disagreement between the Crown and First Nations about the size and location of reserves set aside by treaties

claims arising from the surrender for sale of reserve land
claims occurring when First Nations seek compensation for, or the return of, land that had been surrendered to the Crown for sale for the benefit of the band

for the sole benefit of the band. In many cases, however, the band did not receive these funds, or the land remained unsold and the band was not compensated.

claims arising from Aboriginal title
claims based on the allegation that lands traditionally used and occupied by Aboriginal people were never surrendered to the Crown by Aboriginal people

(3) **Claims arising from Aboriginal title**. There are few of these claims in Ontario, since most of the province is covered by treaty; however, other large areas of Canada are not covered by treaty. These claims are based on the allegation that lands traditionally used and occupied by Aboriginal people were never surrendered to the Crown by Aboriginal people. The Golden Lake Algonquin claim is an example of this type of claim in Ontario.

When it comes to negotiating land claims, the Ontario government has adopted the following policy:

> Ontario will not expropriate private property to reach a land claim settlement. However, when it would help to reach a settlement, Ontario may agree to buy land from an owner who wants to sell, in order to include it in a claim settlement.
>
> During negotiations, Ontario considers how Crown lands are being used. Potential impacts on current uses are reduced as much as possible. For example, the province will not cancel Crown land leases, easements, mining claims, timber allocations, and other licences and permits during their term. (Ontario Ministry of Aboriginal Affairs, 2011)

In other words, Ontario residents need not fear a loss of land or loss of economic revenue as a result of a land claims negotiation or settlement. If a settlement indicates that acreage should be added to reserve holdings, the Crown would seek to negotiate the transfer of Crown land or would seek to purchase land from a willing seller.

Caledonia Land Claim

One well-known Ontario land claim involves the Six Nations of the Grand River, near Brantford, in what is now Caledonia. The history of this claim dates back to 1784, when Britain allowed the Six Nations to "take possession of and settle" approximately 385,000 hectares of land along the Grand River as a reward for their loyalty during the American Revolution. In 1792, the grant was reduced to 111,000 hectares by Lieutenant Governor John Graves Simcoe, and over the next two hundred years, much of the land was the subject of various transactions, with portions sold, leased to the Crown and then sold to third parties, surrendered (although this has been disputed), and set aside for a reserve.

In 1992, another element was added to the land's complex history when Henco Industries bought a company that owned about 40 hectares of land in the area. In 1995, Six Nations sued the Canadian and Ontario governments, asserting a land claim that included the land allegedly owned by Henco Industries. Ten years later, in July 2005, Henco registered plans for the Douglas Creek Estates subdivision with the province of Ontario and was granted title. In February 2006, when Henco began building homes on the land, a small group of Six Nations protestors moved onto the construction site and set up tents, a teepee, and a wooden building, and refused to leave. On March 10, Henco was granted a court order that required the protestors to leave the site by March 22, but they continued their occupation. During a pre-dawn raid by the OPP on April 20, which police stated was in response to "an escalation of activity," 16 people were arrested, and officers used pepper spray and Tasers against protesters. Protesters returned by 9 a.m. and blocked off the road using a dump truck and burning tires (CBC News, 2006a).

The initial protests were followed by counter-protests from some residents of Caledonia who were frustrated by the chaos and disruption of the protests; by the building and removal of barricades; and by general looting, vandalism, and violence. On May 19, the Ontario government announced an indefinite construction ban, and in mid-June the government bought out the disputed land for $12.3 million; the settlement was also to include compensation for the loss of future profits, to be determined later (CBC News, 2006a). Despite further judicial efforts to have the protestors removed, on August 27 the Ontario Court of Appeal ruled against ordering the protestors off the land.

In 2011, the government agreed to pay $20 million to compensate residents and business owners for the disruption caused by the protests. To resolve the claim, however, one must determine which part of the original land grant was surrendered by Six Nations legitimately, which part was kept, and which part was taken without Six Nations' consent (Darling, n.d.). Negotiations to settle the land claim are ongoing at the time of writing.

For more perspectives on the dispute, read Appendix 11.3.

EXERCISE 3

Caledonia offers examples of the competing interests and obligations involved in any dispute over land—in this case, those of Henco Industries, the Six Nations protestors, the residents of Caledonia, the government, the court, and the police. In a dispute like this, what do you think the first priority should be? How would you balance the other interests against the priority you identified? Comment on the way this balance was struck in the case of Caledonia.

CONCLUSION

The Mi'kmaq fishing crisis on the East Coast and, more recently, the dispute in Caledonia (see Appendix 11.3) are two of the many conflicts between Aboriginal protesters and police in Canada that have escalated into violence. Whenever these situations occur, the police are called to the front line to keep the peace. For police officers, the importance of maintaining a neutral position cannot be overstated. Understanding the issues will help police in this respect. Of course, it is not up to the police to actually *resolve* the larger issues. When some Caledonia residents called on police to remove the demonstrators from the land and thereby take a more forcible role in ending the crisis, the OPP commissioner, Julian Fantino, underscored the specific role of law enforcement in the dispute—namely, to "preserve the peace, deal with offences and bring those who transgress the laws of the land to justice" (CBC News, 2006b).

Of course, we all have biases; to state otherwise would be deceiving ourselves. And these inevitable biases may emerge under stressful conditions. When it comes to Aboriginal land and resources disputes, these biases are increasingly fed by the media. It is important to look behind the press coverage, behind the events that are unfolding moment by moment, and outside the traditional tactical box of policing. It is crucial to look at the issue at hand in its historical context to understand how emotionally charged these situations can be for all parties involved, Aboriginal and non-Aboriginal. It is the responsibility of police to ensure the safety of all persons involved and to maintain a neutral position.

After reading this chapter, it should be clear to you that Aboriginal land and resource claims have their foundations in law. The Supreme Court has clearly laid out the obligations of all parties with regard to negotiating claims to both resources and land. Problems arise, however, when governments, instead of meeting these legal obligations, allow the prospect of gaining income through development and commercial industry to take precedence.

KEY TERMS

claims arising from Aboriginal title
claims arising from the surrender for sale of reserve land
claims relating to the fulfillment of terms of treaties
comprehensive land claims
specific land claims

REFERENCES

Aboriginal Affairs and Northern Development Canada. (2011). Fact sheet—three-year time frames for negotiating specific claim settlements. http://www.aadnc-aandc.gc.ca/eng/1314235060601.

Amnesty International. (2005, December 19). It's time to comply: Canada's record of unimplemented UN human rights recommendations. http://www.amnesty.ca/resource_centre/reports/view.php?load=arcview&article=3131&c=Resource+Centre+Reports.

Assembly of First Nations. (2011, June 1). AFN congratulates Specific Claims Tribunal on commencement of operations. http://www.afn.ca/index.php/en/news-media/latest-news/afn-congratulates-specific-claims-tribunal-on-commencement-of-operatio.

Badger, R v. (1996). [1996] 1 SCR 771.

Bell, C., & Paterson, R. (2003). Aboriginal rights to repatriation of cultural property in Canada. In A. Walkem & H. Bruce (Eds.), Box of treasures or empty box? Twenty years of section 35 (pp. 104–154). Penticton, BC: Theytus Books.

The Calder case: A split decision. (n.d.). http://www.kermode.net/nisgaa/story/calder.html.

Calder et al. v. Attorney-General of British Columbia. (1973). [1973] SCR 313.

Campbell, Tracy. (1996, March). Co-management of Aboriginal resources. Information North, 22(1). Arctic Institute of North America. http://arcticcircle.uconn.edu/NatResources/comanagement.html.

CBC News. (2006a). Indepth: Caledonia land claim, historical timeline. CBC.ca. http://www.cbc.ca/news/background/caledonia-landclaim/index.html.

CBC News. (2006b). OPP's job to "preserve the peace" in Caledonia: Top cop. CBC.ca. http://www.cbc.ca/news/canada/toronto/story/2006/10/30/fantino-firstday.html.

Churchill, W. (1992). *Last stand at Lubicon Lake: Struggle for the land.* Toronto: Between the Lines.

Coon Come, M. (2003, April 18). Remarks of National Chief Matthew Coon Come, Commonwealth Policy Studies Unit London. http://www.cpsu.org.uk/downloads/MatthewC.pdf.

Curry, B. (2003, November 27). Half of Canadians disbelieve land claims, National survey: Atlantic Canada most opposed to special rights for Aboriginals. CanWest News Service. http://groups.yahoo.com/group/protecting _knowledge/message/7089.

Darling, G. (n.d.). Land claims and the Six Nations in Caledonia Ontario. University of Alberta: Centre for Constitutional Studies. http://www.law.ualberta.ca/centres/ccs/issues/landclaimsandthesixnationsincaledoniaontario.php.

Delgamuukw v. British Columbia. (1997). [1997] 3 SCR 1010.

Donham, P.B. (2003). Fishery: Lobster wars. In R. Anderson & R. Bone (Eds.), *Natural resources and Aboriginal people in Canada: Readings, cases and commentary.* Concord, ON: Captus Press.

Francis v. The Queen. (1969). [1969] 1 NBR (2d) 886.

Friends of the Lubicon. (2006). United Nations holds Canada in continuing violation of Lubicon human rights. http://www.tao.ca/~fol/pa/humanr.htm.

Gibson, G., Higgs, E., & Hrudey, S. (1998). Sour gas, bitter relations. *Alternatives Journal: Environmental Thought, Policy and Action, 24*(2).

Goldi, J., & Goldi, J. (Producers). (2004). *Ipperwash: A Canadian tragedy.* [Motion picture].

Guerin v. The Queen. (1984). [1984] 2 SCR 335.

Henderson, B. (1996). Guerin v. The Queen [A brief introduction to Aboriginal law in Canada]. Welcome to my Virtual Law Office. http://www.bloorstreet.com/200block/rguerin.htm.

Knockwood, C. (2003). The Mi'kmaq-Canadian treaty relationship: A 277-year journey of rediscovery. In A. Walkem & H. Bruce (Eds.), *Box of treasures or empty box? Twenty years of section 35* (pp. 43–60). Penticton, BC: Theytus Books.

Mandell, L. (2003). Offerings to an emerging future. In A. Walkem & H. Bruce (Eds.), *Box of treasures or empty box? Twenty years of section 35.* Penticton, BC: Theytus Books.

Marshall, R v. (1999). [1999] 3 SCR 533.

McDonald, M. (2003). Aboriginal forestry in Canada. In R. Anderson & R. Bone (Eds.), *Natural resources and Aboriginal people in Canada. Readings, cases and commentary.* Concord, ON: Captus Press.

Ministry of Aboriginal Affairs. (2010, September). Algonquin land claim update. http://www.aboriginalaffairs.gov.on.ca/english/negotiate/algonquin/algonquin_land_claim_update_sept2010.pdf.

Monture-Angus, P. (1999). *Journeying forward: Dreaming First Nations independence.* Halifax: Fernwood Publishing.

Nolan, D. (2011, February 26). Five years later, people on both sides are making efforts. *The Hamilton Spectator.* http://www.thespec.com/news/local/article/493511--caledonia-five-years-later-people-on-both-sides-are-making-efforts.

Obomsawin, A. (2002). *Is the Crown at war with us?* [Motion picture.] National Film Board of Canada.

Ontario Ministry of Aboriginal Affairs. (2006). Shared objectives. http://www.aboriginalaffairs.gov.on.ca/english/negotiate/algonquin/objectives.asp.

Ontario Ministry of Aboriginal Affairs. (2011). Ontario's approach to land claim negotiations. http://www.aboriginalaffairs.gov.on.ca/english/negotiate/aboutclaims/approach.asp#framework.

Radford, T., & Schreiber, D. (2001). *Honour of the Crown.* [Motion picture.] National Film Board of Canada.

Rankin, Jim. (2011, July 31). Justice on a deadline for native land claim deals. *Toronto Star.* http://www.thestar.com/news/insight/article/1032529--justice-on-a-deadline-for-native-land-claim-deals.

Royal Proclamation of 1763. (1970). RSC 1970, App. II, No. 1.

Simon v. The Queen. (1985). [1985] 2 SCR 387.

Sparrow, R v. (1990). [1990] 1 SCR 1075.

Specific Claims Tribunal Act. (2008). SC 2008, c. 22.

St. Catherine's Milling & Lumber Company v. The Queen. (1888). 14 App. Cas. 46 (PC).

Steckley, J., & Cummins, B. (2001a). The Golden Lake Algonquin and Algonquin Park: Missed by treaty. In *Full circle: Canada's First Nations* (chap. 14). Toronto: Prentice Hall.

Steckley, J., & Cummins, B. (2001b). Social issues: The Dudley George story. In *Full circle: Canada's First Nations* (chap. 20). Toronto: Prentice Hall.

Sylliboy, R v. (1929). [1929] 1 DLR 307.

Treaty Land Entitlement Committee of Manitoba Inc. (n.d.). http://www.tlec.ca/Home.page.

Union of BC Indian Chiefs. (2011). Canada's undermining of the specific claims process—a summary and analysis. http://www.ubcic.bc.ca/News_Releases/UBCICNews07261101.html#axzz1br1zzJj8.

Van der Peet, R v. (1996). [1996] 2 SCR 507.

Walkem, A. (2003). Constructing the constitutional box: The Supreme Court's section 35(1) reasoning. In A. Walkem & H. Bruce (Eds.), *Box of treasures or empty box? Twenty years of section 35* (pp. 196–222). Penticton, BC: Theytus Books.

Youngblood Henderson, J. (1999). Impact of Delgamuukw guidelines in Atlantic Canada. Cape Breton University. http://www.cbu.ca/mrc/impact-delgamuukw.

REVIEW QUESTIONS

TRUE OR FALSE?

_____ 1. *St. Catherine's Milling & Lumber Company v. The Queen* concerned a dispute between the Ojibwa people and Ontario over logging leases.

_____ 2. Section 91(24) of the *British North America Act* gave jurisdiction over Indians and lands reserved for Indians to the provincial governments.

_____ 3. In the case of *Guerin v. The Queen*, the Supreme Court ruled that the Crown's responsibility was only a "political trust" rather than a true trust and that therefore the Crown was not accountable for the $10 million that had gone missing through the leasing of land to the golf club.

_____ 4. Section 35 of the *Constitution Act, 1982* created entirely new rights for Aboriginal people, which had never existed in law before.

_____ 5. In *Delgamuukw*, the Supreme Court ruled that the Crown can never infringe on an Aboriginal right in any circumstances.

_____ 6. Of the six arguments put forward by the Crown in the *Delgamuukw* case, the Crown was successful with the argument that a third-party interest in unceded Aboriginal land displaces Aboriginal title.

_____ 7. In the *Marshall* case of 1999, the Court gave an unlimited right to the Mi'kmaq to fish, which led to the lobster-fishing dispute in the Maritimes.

_____ 8. The *Calder* case, in which four Nisga'a communities asserted rights over traditional territory outside the reserve created by the federal government, is an example of a specific land claim.

_____ 9. With reference to the *Sparrow* case, it has been found that the enactment of provincial fishing regulations is evidence of clear and plain extinguishment of an Aboriginal right.

_____ 10. The management of natural resources is a provincial responsibility.

MULTIPLE CHOICE

1. In the case of *R v. Sparrow*, a two-part test for limiting an Aboriginal right was created. The first part of that test says that the Crown must have a compelling and substantial objective if it is to limit an Aboriginal right. An example of this is

   (a) protection of a resource

   (b) protection of the economy

   (c) obtaining votes

   (d) there is no such thing as a compelling or substantial object

2. The 1888 *St. Catherine's Milling* case set the precedent for the definition of Aboriginal title to land for ___ years.

   (a) 10

   (b) 30

   (c) 50

   (d) 100

3. In the *St. Catherine's Milling* case, the Court came to the conclusion that Aboriginal groups had "personal and usufructuary right" to land, which means

   (a) the right to use the land at the pleasure of the Crown, so that the Crown has the authority to remove the right at any time

   (b) the right to use the land but never own it

   (c) the right to sole possession of the land

   (d) no rights to the land whatsoever

4. In the *Calder* case, the decision over whether or not Indian title to land can be extinguished without treaty resulted in the setting of a standard by which such extinguishment can occur. Which of the following defines that standard?

   (a) by implication through other laws

   (b) by a failure to occupy the land

   (c) in a clear and plain way

   (d) by assumption

5. In the *Sparrow* case, the Crown set out a two-part test for limiting an Aboriginal right. The first part was that the Crown must have a compelling and substantial objective, and the second part was that

   (a) the limit must be fair

   (b) the limit must be consistent with the Crown's fiduciary responsibility to Aboriginal peoples

   (c) the limit must protect the Canadian economy

   (d) the limit must be temporary

6. The framework of the litigation process to determine an Aboriginal right has four steps. Which of the following is not one of those steps?

   (a) identification of the nature and content of the right

   (b) determining whether the right is an "existing right" recognized and affirmed in s. 35 of the *Constitution Act, 1982* (or whether it was extinguished prior to the constitution)

   (c) determination of whether the provincial or federal legislation or regulation interferes with the right

   (d) paying out for loss of the right

7. A comprehensive land claim is
   (a) a claim to an entire province
   (b) a claim to territory that is not covered by treaty or land cession agreements
   (c) a claim to resources but not to land
   (d) a claim to privately and individually owned land

8. Co-management of land and resources has been implemented in some areas where Aboriginal rights have not been extinguished. Co-management effectively is
   (a) the inclusion of non-traditional groups such as environmentalist groups, Aboriginal groups, and industry in decision making over resources
   (b) the division of management over resources strictly between federal and provincial governments
   (c) the division of responsibility for the area among a vast number of government agencies
   (d) the granting of exclusive authority to Aboriginal groups to manage the area

9. A specific land claim is
   (a) a claim that relates to a specific surveyed parcel of land
   (b) a claim that relates to specific misdealings of the Crown with relation to land or resources
   (c) a claim that results because Aboriginal title was never extinguished by treaty
   (d) a claim that cannot be legitimized

10. Which of the following is not one of the three types of land claims active in Ontario?
    (a) claims relating to the fulfillment of terms of treaties
    (b) claims arising from the surrender for sale of reserved lands
    (c) claims arising from Aboriginal title
    (d) claims of abuse

APPENDIX 11.1

THE DUDLEY GEORGE STORY

During the American Revolution and the War of 1812, the Anicinabe, originally from northern Ontario, were allies with the British. They settled in southern Ontario following the wars and became known as the Chippewa. The government of the Chippewa signed a treaty in 1825 that created four reserves: Sarnia, Walpole Island, Kettle Point, and Stoney Point. In 1928, the provincial government pressured the Stoney Point people to sell 152 hectares of prime waterfront land to private interests. Although they were against the idea of selling their land, the band had little control. Indian Affairs, through the oppressive *Indian Act*, sold the land without the band's permission. A large part of that land was reserved to create the Ipperwash Provincial Park in 1936. The Stoney Point people were unhappy about the sale and unhappier still when their burial site was disturbed in the creation of the park.

In 1942, the federal government asked the Stoney Point people to relinquish what remained of their land so that a military base could be built to support the war efforts. (Many of the Stoney Point men were, in fact, overseas serving as soldiers.) The federal government offered $23 per acre for 2,211 acres of land (895 hectares). The Stoney Point people voted on the offer and declined. Invoking the *War Measures Act*, the federal government expropriated the land regardless. The Stoney Point people were paid the said amount and were promised that the land would be returned to them at the end of the war, provided the military had no further need for it. The Stoney Point people were forced to leave and live with their neighbours at Kettle Point.

At the end of the war, the Stoney Point people requested to enter into negotiations for the return of their land. The armed forces continued, however, to make peacetime use of the land as a cadet training camp and therefore did not return the land. In 1981, 36 years after the end of the war, the federal government agreed to pay the Stoney Point band $2.4 million in compensation for the 40-year use of the land and agreed to return the land pending an environmental assessment. The cost of cleaning the area environmentally was expected to be high because of the way it was used by the military. The Department of National Defence then decided that it did not want to relinquish the land. The department promised to review the requirements for the training camp every three years; if the training camp was deemed unnecessary, the department would turn it over to the Stoney Point people.

A recommendation was put forward in 1992 by the Standing Committee on Aboriginal People that the federal government return the land. The committee insisted that the government's reasons for failing to relinquish the land were "without substance." The recommendation was not followed. In May 1993, the Stoney Point people, bringing tents and trailers, moved onto the military property. They maintained a tenuous relationship with the military they were living alongside. In September of that same year, they walked for three weeks to Ottawa to insist that action be taken to return the land. No action was forthcoming.

On September 4, 1995, Aboriginal protestors moved into the adjacent provincial park after it had closed for the season. One of the contentious issues about the park was the burial ground, which the Stoney Point people had requested be protected and fenced off. This had never been done despite clear archeological records of the existence and location of the burial ground. The Harris government would deny that a burial ground was even located in the park; the government was subsequently proven wrong.

Newly elected Premier Mike Harris held an emergency meeting the day following the occupation. OPP Inspector Ron Fox was at that meeting. It was alleged that Premier Mike Harris insisted that the protestors be removed from the park. This allegation appears to have been substantiated: years later, at the 2006 inquiry into the incident, on a tape-recorded conversation from 1995 between Fox and OPP Inspector John Carson, made directly following the emergency meeting, Fox can be heard saying the following: "No question they don't give a shit about Indians"; and "They just want us to kick ass." During the course of the inquiry Mike Harris would deny saying, "Get the fucking Indians out of the park." Various people present at the meeting would testify that they heard Mike Harris say this; others would testify that he did not. Regardless, after four days of testimony at the inquiry, Harris stated that he would not make any changes in the way he had handled the Ipperwash incident.

Following the September 5, 1995 meeting, the OPP prepared themselves for the altercation they expected. They ordered night-vision goggles, gas masks, and helicopters, and brought in 250 officers from across the province. The OPP had received intelligence information that the protestors were unarmed.

On September 6, the order was given to the OPP to get the protestors out of the park. After dark, the OPP advanced on the 30 unarmed protestors in the park. Sergeant Kenneth Deane, a sniper for the Tactics and Rescue unit, then shot Aboriginal protestor Dudley George, who later died from his injuries. Deane would testify that he witnessed a muzzle flash and saw George with a rifle. The investigation would reveal that there was no rifle and that George was unarmed at the time of the shooting. The police did not call an ambulance for George; the protestors attempted to call for one but were arrested. George was driven to the hospital by family members; a car breakdown en route delayed medical treatment even further. George's family members were arrested at the hospital; it was too late to save George, who died from his wound.

Kenneth Deane was charged and found guilty of criminal negligence causing death. He was sentenced to two years less a day to be served in the community plus 180 community service hours. He appealed his conviction unsuccessfully. Deane did not testify at the 2006 inquiry because he died in a car accident before it took place.

The Aboriginal protestors were arrested and faced 62 charges, most of which were dropped. Charges that stemmed from their entry into the park were dismissed because it was decided that they had colour of right to the park—that is, interest in the property—because the burial ground, previously alleged to be non-existent, was now acknowledged to be there.

Aboriginal rights groups immediately demanded an inquiry into the incident. The Conservative government refused, and it was not until the election of a new government in 2003 that an announcement was made that an inquiry would begin.

Following the announcement of the inquiry, the CBC received OPP surveillance tapes that were aired on the news. The tapes show OPP officers at the scene just prior to the shooting making racist comments about the protestors. These tapes brought the OPP's actions and motives into question.

The inquiry's report, released May 31, 2007, ruled that the OPP, the government of former Ontario premier Mike Harris, and the federal government all bear responsibility for events that led to Dudley George's death. Both federal and provincial governments had more than 50 years to resolve these issues and chose not to. This choice led to a violent confrontation between police and Aboriginal protestors that culminated in the death of Dudley George. This tragedy could certainly have been avoided. Police services in Canada would be wise to study and learn from these events to ensure that they are not repeated in the future, as confrontations involving Aboriginal land and resources are likely to occur for decades to come.

In December 2007, the Ontario government announced that it would return the 56-hectare Ipperwash Provincial Park to the Chippewas of the Kettle and Stoney Creek First Nation, after a period of co-control between the Chippewas and the government. On May 28, 2009, the province officially signed over control of Ipperwash Park to the Chippewas.

Sources: Goldi & Goldi (2004); Steckley & Cummins (2001b).

APPENDIX 11.2

THE LUBICON CREE

The Lubicon Cree were traditionally hunters and gatherers. From time immemorial, they had lived in a 10,000 square kilometre area surrounding Lubicon Lake in northern Alberta. In 1899, a delegation from the Canadian government travelled through northern Alberta to secure for Treaty No. 8 the signatures of bands occupying the area. However, treaty commissioners failed to contact a number of small bands scattered throughout the vast territory covered by the treaty. The Lubicon was one of those bands; members did not hear of the treaty until 1912. The band never signed a treaty, nor did they ever cede or relinquish rights to their traditional territory.

Under the provisions of Treaty No. 8, each band was to receive a "reserved" land, the acreage depending on the population of the band, and each member was to receive an annuity in payment for the alienation of the land. Bands that were not notified of the treaty could go to designated locations and be added to the pay list for annuities. When the Lubicon band members were notified of the treaty by other bands, they made their way to Whitefish Lake and received an annuity there. Government officials then added the Lubicon names to the band list at Whitefish Lake, although the Lubicon group had no connection to that band and were a separate and individual band as they had always been.

In 1935, the Indian Department sent notice to the Lubicon band that they were living off their designated reserve, and must relocate to live at Whitefish Lake. The Lubicon protested that they had never lived there and were a separate and distinct band that resided at Lubicon Lake; they requested that they be declared a band by the Indian Department. The department investigated, concluded that the Lubicon were indeed a separate and distinct band, and approved the creation of a new reserve at Lubicon Lake. In 1940, that reserve was surveyed by the department according to the population of the band at the time, which was set by the Indian agent at 127 members. At 52 hectares per person, the reserve was surveyed for 6,500 hectares.

Prior to the completion of the deal in 1942, Indian Affairs official Malcolm Mc-Crimmon was sent to northern Alberta to see that the pay lists for annuities for Indians were in order. Because Second World War expenses were mounting, the federal government was looking to reduce expenditures elsewhere and the Indian Department seemed a logical place to cut costs. McCrimmon rewrote the rules for addition to treaty annuity lists and eliminated all members who joined after 1912. He insisted that birth records be provided to prove that only pure-blood Indians were on the lists—but this was in a remote area where children were born at home and it was common to have no birth record. McCrimmon eliminated 700 names from the annuity pay list, including 90 members of the Lubicon Cree band. He then argued against the establishment of a reserve for the Lubicon, saying that there were insufficient members of the band to warrant one. As a result, the Indian Department postponed the creation of a reserve indefinitely.

The Lubicon continued to live at Lubicon Lake, but a renewed interest in the area occurred in 1950 when Alberta Lands and Forest Division received inquiries from a large mining corporation regarding the Lubicon area. The company wanted the provincial government to open it for exploration. The province of Alberta requested that the Indian Department relocate the proposed reserve for the Lubicon to a "less isolated area." However, the federal government failed to respond to the province, which was anxious to lease the land. The province eventually sent a letter with an ultimatum, that the federal government respond within 30 days or the province would deem the proposed reserve not to exist. The federal government failed to respond. Alberta then requested that Indian Affairs strike the band from the record as an official band. The federal government could not comply with this request because it had declared the Lubicon a distinct band in 1939 even though it had failed to finalize a reserve for the band. Alberta insisted that the Lubicon band be reduced through enfranchisement where possible, and the remainder of the band relocated to live with the Whitefish band. The two levels of government could not come to an agreement on how to resolve this issue.

In 1971, Alberta secured oil company financing to build an all-weather road into Lubicon territory for the purposes of exploration. The Lubicon lobbied the government to stop the encroachment of corporations, insisting on their right to their traditional territory. The Alberta government insisted that the Lubicon were squatters on provincial Crown lands with no land rights to negotiate. In 1975, as developers began exploration, the Lubicon filed a caveat under provincial law to place would-be developers on notice that title to the land was contested. The provincial government asked for a postponement of the caveat and rewrote legislation under Bill 29 to end grounds for Lubicon legal action.

In 1979 the all-weather road was completed and people poured into the area, severely disrupting the Lubicon way of life. In 1980, the Lubicon appealed to the federal government to provide them with financial assistance to seek an injunction to stop development until a resolution could be reached over the land title issues. The federal government denied the request. In 1981 Alberta declared the main settlement area of the Lubicon a hamlet, subdivided the area into 0.8 hectare lots, and proposed to lease or gift the lots to individual band members. The Lubicon were very concerned about how this "land tenure program" would affect their land claim and petitioned the federal government to look into the matter.

The minister of Indian Affairs discovered that the land in question could no longer be subject to a land claim because as a hamlet it was no longer classed as provincial Crown land.

In 1982, with the federal and provincial governments still unable to reach an agreement over the land allocation, the Lubicon filed a second legal action before the Alberta Court of Queen's Bench requesting the retention of Aboriginal rights over their traditional area, which would void the leases provided by the province to oil companies. The band requested an immediate injunction to stop development until the land issues could be resolved. The concluding arguments in the case were heard on December 2, 1982, but the Court postponed the delivery of its verdict until March 1983. At that time an injunction to stop development was received—too late. The companies had simply accelerated their exploration through the winter, and the area became irreversibly altered environmentally.

By 1983, 400 oil wells had been drilled within 15 kilometres of the Lubicon's main settlement. The typical trapper's income was reduced from $5,000 per year to $400, and the number of moose killed for food plummeted from 200 to 19. The Lubicon experienced a rash of suicides and rising alcoholism within the community. Welfare dependence in the community increased from 5 percent to 90 percent. The extreme poverty and a tuberculosis outbreak affecting one-third of the community demoralized the band even further.

Following the injunction, the companies returned to court to argue that the injunction was unnecessary since the drilling was already complete and the pumping process put in place would not cause any further environmental degradation. By 1987, it was estimated conservatively that oil and gas revenues from the area were in excess of $500 million per year.

In 1984, after the Supreme Court of Canada refused to hear their case, the Lubicon appealed to the United Nations Human Rights Commission. The United Nations conducted a study of the situation and concluded in 1987 that the Lubicon could not possibly achieve political redress in Canada. The United Nations appealed to Canada to do no further harm to Lubicon territory until a hearing could be held on human rights violations. However, in 1988, Alberta announced that it had granted timber rights in the Lubicon territory to a Japanese company, Daishowa, which planned to cut 4,500 hectares of timber per day to produce 1,000 tonnes of pulp per day.

In response to the news of the lease, the Lubicon toured Europe prior to the 1988 Olympics seeking support from other countries. Then, at the winter Olympics in Calgary, they boycotted the Aboriginal art exhibition ("The Spirit Sings"), having discovered that its sponsors were the very oil companies that were undermining Aboriginal land claims in Canada. Their boycott was supported by human rights organizations around the world. Also in 1988, the Lubicon, fed up with the system, withdrew all cases from Canadian courts, declared themselves a sovereign nation, and blockaded all roads leading into their territory. The RCMP arrested 27 people involved in the blockades, and the province refused to negotiate with the Lubicon until the blockades were removed.

Concerned that the situation could escalate into violence, Alberta returned to the negotiating table. Alberta negotiated the Grimshaw Accord, which called for the creation of a reserved land base for the Lubicon people that included subsurface rights to the land. The federal government disagreed, offering a reserved land base with no subsurface rights. The subsurface rights were critical for the Lubicon, since mining and drilling are the only ways they can now sustain their people—the degradation of the land made their traditional economy impossible. The subsurface rights are not forthcoming.

In 1989, the federal government exploited divisions within the band. Facing extreme poverty, with no resolution in sight, some members of the band wavered in their support of the band governance body. The federal government met with a dissident group and agreed to create a new band called the Woodland Cree, insisting that they have rights to the contested area. The federal government presented the rejected offer from the Lubicon band to the Woodland band, offering them an additional $1,000 each to sign the agreement that did not include subsurface rights. The federal government offered the same deal to the Loon Lake Cree, and subsequently pressured the Lubicon to sign the same agreement without subsurface rights. The chief of the Lubicon band, Bernard Omniyak, says the agreement is "deficient in the area of providing economic stability for the future. In essence, the Canadian government has offered to build houses for the Lubicon and support us forever on welfare like animals in the zoo who are cared for and fed at an appointed time."

In 1990, the United Nations charged Canada with human rights violations under article 27 of the *International Covenant on Civil and Political Rights.* Canada did not answer to the charges, which stand today.

In 1991, the Lubicon organized an international boycott of Daishowa. In response, Daishowa agreed to stay out of Lubicon territory until the land issue was resolved; however, in 1994, Daishowa sued the organizers of the boycott for $5 million in compensation for lost business. The suit was unsuccessful.

In 1994 the Lubicon protested oil and gas corporation Unocal's plans to build a sour gas processing plant within 4 kilometres of the proposed reserve. Alberta's energy board failed to convene a hearing on the matter until after the plant was built. The plant went into operation in 1995.

Following the opening of the sour gas plant, Alberta proposed that the size of the proposed reserve be reduced from the original 243 square kilometres specified in the Grimshaw Accord; their rationale was that the population of the Lubicon band had decreased due to the creation of the Woodland Cree band and the transference of members to that group (Gibson, Higgs, & Hrudey, 1998).

In 2002, an agreement was finally reached between the federal and provincial governments and the Lubicon Cree over the construction of a new reserve, although subsurface rights were still undetermined. On November 1, 2005, the United Nations Human Rights Committee reaffirmed its earlier conclusion that Canada is violating article 1 of the *International Covenant on Civil and Political Rights* insofar as it is denying the Lubicon basic subsistence by destroying their traditional economy and way of life. Furthermore, Canada is in violation of article 27 of the Covenant insofar as it is participating in the destruction of the Lubicon's culture, language rights, and way of life by refusing to negotiate a reasonable resolution to their land claim. The committee reiterated its 1987 recommendation (for which there is support in Canadian case law, established by the 1997 *Delgamuukw* decision) that Canada should consult with the band before granting licences for economic exploitation of the disputed land and ensure that in no case such exploitation jeopardizes the rights recognized under the Covenant. Canada has not responded to the committee's findings. However, Amnesty International provided the following statement:

> One of the most glaring failures to implement UN level human rights recommendations is the situation of the Lubicon Cree in Alberta. In 1990, the Human Rights Committee issued a detailed report documenting serious violations of the rights of the Lubicon, stemming from a decades-old failure to enter into an agreement with the Lubicon regarding their land rights. The Committee called on the government to ensure a prompt and just settlement of the dispute. Fifteen years later, the dispute remains unresolved, the ability of the Lubicon to provide for themselves remains under threat, and there have been no negotiations between the government and the Lubicon for over two years. (Amnesty International, 2005; also see Friends of the Lubicon, 2006)

The issues regarding land rights have still not been resolved. The Lubicon band suffers economically and socially, and the resource that has brought economic wealth to the province of Alberta and Canada has led to economic collapse for the Lubicon. In 2009, the Alberta Government approved the extension of an oil pipeline through the contested territory, and 2,400 kilometres of pipeline now snake through the Lubicon's traditional land. In May 2011, an oil spill leaked an estimated 28,000 barrels of oil onto the Lubicon's traditional territory, approximately 30 kilometres from the site of their community's main town, contaminating the surrounding areas. While their land claim remains unresolved, the Lubicon are fighting not just for a resolution of their claim but for environmental protection for their community.

APPENDIX 11.3

CALEDONIA: FIVE YEARS LATER, PEOPLE ON BOTH SIDES ARE MAKING EFFORTS

Caledonia: It's a barren, rough-hewn piece of land on the outskirts of town that doesn't look out of place outside any rural Ontario town.

On a mid-February visit, it is covered with heavy patches of snow. It spreads out beside the Caledonia Baptist Church and a street of upscale homes.

But the peacefulness of the Argyle Street South land belies its role in the drama that has made Caledonia synonymous with Oka and Ipperwash.

A road leads into the field and branches into other roads; some are lined with lamp posts and fire hydrants. A model home and a trailer sit a block off Argyle, guarded by three dogs.

At the entrance, a visitor has to drive through an old hydro tower, chopped in half and which one assumes can be quickly pulled together like a gate to bar entry. An old shack sits nearby with a message on it: "This is Indian Land. This Land is Not for Sale."

It was five years ago—Feb. 28, 2006—when a group of Six Nations activists moved onto the Douglas Creek Estates subdivision over a land claims dispute. The standoff remains one of the longest in Canadian history.

The natives called it a reclamation and renamed the site Kanonhstaton (The Protected Place).

The province bought the land from developers Don and John Henning following a botched OPP raid and native barricades going up.

Natives claim the land was never surrendered, but Ottawa says it was, in 1844.

Cost to both Ottawa and Queen's Park has topped more than $81 million. That included $46 million, $21 million to the Hennings and seven builders and about $4 million in compensation to residents, businesses and the county.

Aboriginal Affairs Minister Chris Bentley, the fourth person to hold that job since 2006, says it is "absolutely" one of his most challenging files. He remains optimistic it can be resolved through negotiations and, though talks are stalled, is heartened by initiatives between citizens in Haldimand and Six Nations.

"It won't surprise you that the Minister of Aboriginal Affairs would always wish to find discussions as the route to these issues," Bentley said.

The standoff grew to encompass court injunctions, lawsuits, assaults, arsons, blockades, boycotts, a blackout, a state of emergency, rallies and thousands of police officers (3,000 of the force's 7,000 officers passed through in 2006). Police laid 162 charges against 69 people and the dispute pulled in such people as David Peterson, Barbara McDougall, David Crombie and Jane Stewart.

There were calls to bring in the Canadian army. Haldimand officials were told by provincial officials the army would not leave soldiers on the site. Residents along the 6th Line lost OPP service for four years. The dispute also led to native protests at projects in Hagersville, Cayuga, Dunnville and Brantford.

For the most part, Caledonia has returned to normal. There are no blockades or rallies against blockades.

Realtor Peter Vandendool says the real estate market is "as close to normal as it can be." He admits prices dropped for homes around DCE in the wake of the blockades, but once peace returned home sales began to rise again in 2008. In 2007, he sold a home backing on to DCE for $205,000. Last year, a similar sale brought in $240,000.

Vandendool uses the term "normal as it can be" because the big impact has been the halting of housing construction in Caledonia. He notes the Stirling Woods subdivision just has two new homes left for sale.

There were 188 home sales in Caledonia in 2005, compared with 167 in both 2006 and 2007. There were 198 home sales in 2010. The average price for a Caledonia home is $260,884, compared to $231,977 in 2006.

Businesses were hit by a boycott by some Six Nations members. Suzanne Athanasiou, president of the Caledonia chamber of commerce, said she has no hard figures, but anecdotally she said business from Six Nations residents is not back to pre-standoff days. She says, however, the recession could also be a factor.

Barber Don Smith lost a lot of his Six Nations customers at the height of the dispute, but says the majority have come back "As long as it stays peaceful, it's good," he says.

But bad feelings remain.

"No one wants anyone to forget," says Caledonia councillor Craig Grice. "No one is asking anyone to forgive, but, at the same time, everyone is trying to say 'Let's recognize what has happened, let's recognize what we can do to move forward.'"

Haldimand Mayor Ken Hewitt says residents remain frustrated, but he believes the animosity is for Ottawa and Queen's Park. Former mayor Marie Trainer, defeated last year by Hewitt, says "the tension is always there."

There's a Tim Hortons near the former Douglas Creek Estates. During the height of the dispute, it became a neutral spot for all participants.

Diane, who declines to give her last name, is enjoying a coffee with two friends. The 60-year-old woman has lived in Caledonia for 12 years. She did not take part in any of the rallies, but came to watch.

"It was like watching CNN on TV," she said. "It was something."

Diane says what happened remains an issue, but it's not talked about as much anymore. What riled her was that it was allowed to happen at all.

"I didn't think that could happen in Canada," she says. "There was the rule of law. ... If anyone else had done that they would have been thrown in jail."

Derek Taylor, 83, was visiting the town he and his wife moved to in 2000. They lived around the corner from DCE, but moved to Guelph just before Christmas because they couldn't stand the uncertainty.

"We feel disappointed the government and police didn't resolve it and still haven't," he said.

At a nearby table sits Mike, 56, a retired construction worker. He is from Six Nations. He heard the comments from his fellow coffee drinkers. He does not feel he should pull his punches, although he declines to give his last name.

"It was a political issue," he says. "It didn't involve the townspeople. The townspeople should never have got involved. I was called names ... I got a real bitter taste in my mouth."

Mike was working in Omaha, Nebraska, when DCE erupted. He quit his job and hurried back "because my people needed me." He spent a year performing duties on DCE and still plows snow there.

He said the problem is that non-natives do not know the history of Six Nations. They don't know Six Nations once controlled land all along the Grand River and now possess 5 per cent of their original holdings. Six Nations claims a lot of the land was taken under dubious circumstances.

The $20 million inquiry into the Ipperwash dispute indicated there should be a more measured than emotional, and negotiation rather than confrontation, reaction to land claims. Six Nations has filed 29 claims with Ottawa and only one has been resolved. About 10 land claims are settled each year between Ottawa and First Nations.

OPP Commissioner Chris Lewis questions whether police would ever launch another raid like it did on DCE in April 2006, but noted the force cannot ignore court injunctions like the one issued by Justice David Marshall against the protesters on behalf of the Hennings.

"We would still try and negotiate our way through it to avoid taking any physical action," he said.

Lewis said the OPP meet regularly with Confederacy chiefs to keep lines of communication open, deal with problems and get to know each other. He met with chiefs this past Wednesday to introduce them to new deputy commissioner Scott Tod. Likewise, Mayor Hewitt is meeting with Six Nations Chief Bill Montour to foster dialogue.

Law professor Michael Coyle, a specialist in land claims, says Canadians must realize native land claims will not go away. He said a lesson from Caledonia could be delays in resolving claims should be avoided.

"There was a judge in the Supreme Court of Canada who used to say, 'Conflicts, unlike good wine, rarely improve with aging," said Coyle, who prepared a fact-finder's report on Caledonia for Ottawa in early 2006.

Source: Nolan, D. (2011, February 26). Five years later, people on both sides are making efforts. *The Hamilton Spectator.* http://www.thespec.com/news/local/article/493511--caledonia-five-years-later-people-on-both-sides-are-making-efforts.

Aboriginal People and the Criminal Justice System

12

INTRODUCTION

The incarceration rate for Aboriginal people in Canada is high, as is their victimization rate. Both statistics have been linked to socio-economic issues and institutionalized discrimination. In this chapter we will examine the relationship between the criminal justice system and Aboriginal people in Canada, the advent of Aboriginal policing and alternative justice, the role of Correctional Service Canada in delivering services to Aboriginal people, and the unique challenges that Aboriginal people face within the justice system. This chapter addresses a variety of issues and should prompt discussion on how to improve the relationship between Aboriginal people and the criminal justice system.

CASE STUDY: HOBBEMA

Like Chapter 10, this one begins with a case study—in this instance, a description of the Hobbema reserve, taken from a CBC news article (2008, pp. 31–32). Just as Grassy Narrows is not representative of all Aboriginal communities, Hobbema is not typical of all reserves; it is an extreme case.

A Community Fights Gangs and Guns

Two-year-old Asia Saddleback was eating a bowl of soup at her family's kitchen table when a bullet ripped through the side of her house, striking her in the stomach. Asia was taken by air ambulance to an Edmonton hospital. The bullet hit her kidney and her spine, but the resilient girl survived—despite the fact that doctors were unable to remove the bullet. Within days, two teenage boys, one 15 and one 18, were charged in the drive-by attack. While it was clear the boys didn't intend to shoot Asia, police struggled to find out why they fired on the house in the first place. The incident horrified people living in Hobbema, and soon all of Canada would learn of the serious gang problem in the small Alberta town.

Descent into Chaos

The descent of Hobbema into chaos can be traced to a number of factors: substance abuse, shattered families, poverty, unemployment, and the erosion of

---

CHAPTER OBJECTIVES

After completing this chapter, you should be able to:

- Distinguish between Aboriginal and non-Aboriginal concepts of justice.

- Identify reasons for Aboriginal people's overrepresentation in the criminal justice system, both as victims and offenders.

- Recognize that Aboriginal communities have different needs with regards to policing and justice.

- Identify the internal changes that have been made to the justice system to address the unique challenges faced by Aboriginal people in that system.

Aboriginal traditions to name a few. Couple these socio-economic factors with evidence of systemic racism (much of which was revealed in the now defunct residential school system that openly tried to destroy Aboriginal culture over its 100-year history) and it becomes clear why First Nations communities are in what seems to be a state of perpetual crisis. Hobbema appears to be the current epicentre of this crisis, as an array of troubles have hit the town.

Hobbema, Alberta

Hobbema is a town of about 12,000 people located within a one-hour drive south of Edmonton. It is the home of four First Nations communities, including the Samson Cree reserve where Asia lives with her family. What might come as a surprise to most Canadians is that the RCMP office in Hobbema is arguably the busiest police detachment in all of Canada. They are dealing with a high volume of violent crime brought on by Hobbema's 13 gangs, who are fighting for drug turf in the town. In fact, Hobbema has the highest ratio of gang members in Canada, with 18.75 members for every 1,000 people living in the town (compared with Toronto's 1.15 members for every 1,000 people) (*Toronto Star*, July 20, 2008). Of all calls received by the RCMP, two-thirds of them come from the Samson Cree reserve. How did a town of 12,000 become a gang hub, producing so much violence in such a concentrated area?

Squandered Cash

One would think that Hobbema would be sitting pretty. Located on prime Alberta oil land, local residents have historically been the beneficiaries of royalty money collected by the federal government and redistributed to each citizen of the town. Instead of saving the money, most residents squandered the cash, going on shopping sprees—with more than a few spending their money on drugs, drinking, and gambling. Despite the fact that oil revenues on the reserve have been steadily declining, Aboriginal youth still manage to receive a large, lump sum royalty payment when they turn 18. Candace Saddleback, Asia's mother, received a cheque for $234,000 when she turned 18 and she has nothing left to show for it. This is common in Hobbema.

Gang Formation

The royalty cheques are one way that gangs are putting Hobbema's youth under their control. Drug dealers give kids under 18 free drugs for years on condition that they pay for the drugs when they get their royalty cheque when they turn 18. By the time the dealers come to collect, many of the youth are fully fledged gang members who willingly turn over their mountain of cash. With over half of Hobbema's population under the age of 18, gangs have no shortage of targets on which to set their sights. The gang life inevitably draws the attention of the police, and many of Hobbema's youth find themselves in young offenders' institutions or, after they turn 18, provincial and federal prisons. It is in prison that gang members get their real education. Surrounded by other professional criminals, novices enter incarceration ignorant and leave with skills that will serve them in their later criminal endeavours.

Once released, gang members return to their surrogate families—the gang itself—and Hobbema has no shortage of places for gang members to find a safe haven. With 13 known gangs in the town, many of which are on the Samson Cree reserve, the RCMP have their hands full keeping a lid on the high level of violence brought on by the gangs. Whether it's Redd Alert, the Alberta Warriors, the Indian Posse, or one of the up-and-coming gangs, Hobbema is a community held on the ropes by the two-punch combination of violence and intimidation.

Community Activism

In the meantime, the citizens of Hobbema have rallied together in response to the shooting of little Asia Saddleback. Abandoned homes are being torn down to prevent the gangs from turning them into crack houses. Graffiti, one of the main ways that gangs use to mark their turf and communicate their messages, is being painted over almost as soon as it goes up. In the summer of 2008, the RCMP declared a four-month gun amnesty, allowing gang members to turn in their weapons and ammunition without being charged with weapons offences. Despite these measures, Hobbema is still mired in gang violence, with almost daily reports of shots being fired and three gang-related shooting deaths in the summer of 2008.

Conclusion

Hobbema has become the flashpoint for communities rallying to keep gangs from taking over their neighbourhoods. The gangs didn't just show up one day and declare Hobbema to be their own. They established themselves over time, feeding on the general state of decay on the reserves and capitalizing on the oil money that many people were happy to party away. While lessons can be learned from Hobbema, it will be interesting to see if anyone is taking note.

Since the shooting of Asia Saddleback, the following acts of violence have occurred in Hobbema:

- July 27, 2008: Sixteen-year-old Billy Buffalo was killed in what is believed to be a gang-related shooting.
- August 1, 2008: A four-month gun amnesty was introduced in response to the shooting of Asia Saddleback.
- August 2, 2008: Dale Dechamps, 21, was found dead in a back alley on the Samson townsite.
- August 16, 2008: Delena Lefthand, 20, was killed when a bullet was fired through the wall of a home.
- April 30, 2010: A 22-year-old woman was wounded after shots were fired at her home in a suspected gang-related incident.
- December 10, 2010: Joseph Daniel Moonias, 28, was fatally stabbed, and a teenager charged in his murder.
- December 24, 2010: Preston Thom, 15, was shot dead as he and his little brother stood outside their home.
- July 11, 2011: Shots fired from outside a house killed five-year-old Ethan Yellowbird while he slept.
- September 6, 2011: Chelsea Yellowbird, Ethan's aunt, died after being shot in the neck at 3 a.m. in the backyard of the house, next door to the house where Ethan lived.

EXERCISE 1

Consider the case of Hobbema in the light of what you have learned so far in this text about the Aboriginal experience in Canada. Write a brief in-class essay (approximately 500 words) that attempts to explain, in broad terms, how the community has reached its current condition. Then discuss, as a class, possible strategies for intervention.

ABORIGINAL OVERREPRESENTATION IN THE CRIMINAL JUSTICE SYSTEM

Aboriginal people are overrepresented in the criminal justice system, both as perpetrators and as victims of crime. According to the Office of the Correctional Investigator (Mann, 2009), Aboriginal people, who make up almost 4 percent of Canada's population, account for 19.7 percent of federally sentenced offenders and 21 percent of provincial admissions to custody. Approximately 33 percent of women in federal custody are Aboriginal women, and nearly one-third of provincially sentenced offenders are Aboriginal (Statistics Canada, 2010a). In Saskatchewan, Aboriginal people make up 80 percent of those sentenced to Provincial custody; in Manitoba, the number is 68 percent, while in Alberta it is 39 percent (Perrault, 2009).

In addition to higher rates of incarceration, the report (Mann, 2009) notes that, compared with non-Aboriginal inmates, Aboriginal inmates

- are released later in their sentences,
- are overrepresented in solitary confinement,
- are more likely to have previous sentences, and
- are classified as higher risk and are more likely to reoffend.

Just as Aboriginal people are overrepresented among the accused in the justice system, they are also overrepresented among victims, especially victims of violent crime. The best measure of victimization comes from Statistics Canada's "General Social Survey—Victimization" (GSS), which collects information from a sample of Canadians in the provinces regarding their victimization in eight categories of crime in the last 12 months: sexual assault, robbery, assault, break and enter, theft of motor vehicle, theft of household property, vandalism, and theft of personal property (Statistics Canada, 2010b). The GSS also rates opinions and satisfaction with the criminal justice system in its various forms.

The GSS reports that, in 2009, 37 percent of Aboriginal people living in the provinces had been a victim of one of the identified eight types of crime in the past 12 months. This is 11 percent higher than for the non-Aboriginal population (Perrault, 2011).

Violent crime is divided into two areas: spousal violence and non-spousal violence. In 2009, 12 percent of Aboriginal people reported being the victim of non-spousal violence in the past 12 months. This is more than double the rate of the non-Aboriginal population. The most commonly reported violent crime was assault, where Aboriginal people were twice as likely to be victimized; however for sexual assault, Aboriginal people were three times more likely to be victimized (see Figure 12.1).

Figure 12.1   **Self-Reported Non-Spousal Violent Victimizations, Canada's Ten Provinces, 2009**

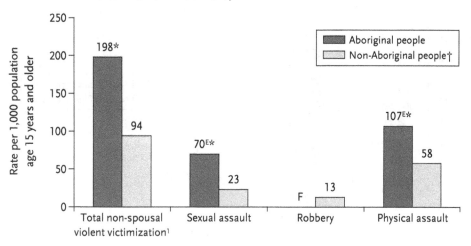

Type of victimization

Notes:

† reference category
* significantly different from reference category (p < 0.05)
F too unreliable to be published
1. Includes robbery and excludes all incidents of spousal sexual and physical assault. Includes incidents that occurred during the 12 months preceding the survey.

Source: Perrault (2011, p. 8). http://www.statcan.gc.ca/pub/85-002-x/2011001/article/11415-eng.pdf.

The Homicide Survey collects data on all reported homicides in Canada (Perrault, 2011, p. 8). In 50 percent of cases, the cultural identity of the accused is unknown. Nonetheless, between 2004 and 2009, police reported 330 homicides with an Aboriginal victim and 417 with an Aboriginal accused. Most of these homicides involved the use of alcohol or drugs. In 73 percent of these cases, the victim was under the influence of drugs or alcohol, as was the accused in 91 percent of these cases (Perrault, 2011, p. 8). Eighty-two percent of the accused were young males, with an average age of 24.

The GSS also collects data regarding socio-demographic factors in connection with violent victimization, such as age, marital status, and the lifestyle characteristics of victims (for example, alcohol and recreational drug use). A number of factors associated with a high risk of victimization were reported more frequently by Aboriginal people than by others. It was concluded (Perrault, 2011, p. 9) that, with these risk factors taken into account, Aboriginal people are 58 percent more likely to be victimized than are non-Aboriginal people.

Aboriginal people are also twice as likely as non-Aboriginal people to be the victims of spousal violence (Perrault, 2011, p. 10). Most of this violence is directed at women. For Aboriginal victims of spousal assault, the frequency and severity of the assaults were greater than for victims in the non-Aboriginal population (Perrault, 2011, pp. 10–11). Twice as many Aboriginal victims reported having been injured, and 48 percent (as opposed to 18 percent for non-Aboriginal victims) reported that they feared for their lives (see Figure 12.2).

Figure 12.2   Self-Reported Spousal Victimizations, in the Preceding Five Years, Canada's Ten Provinces, 2009

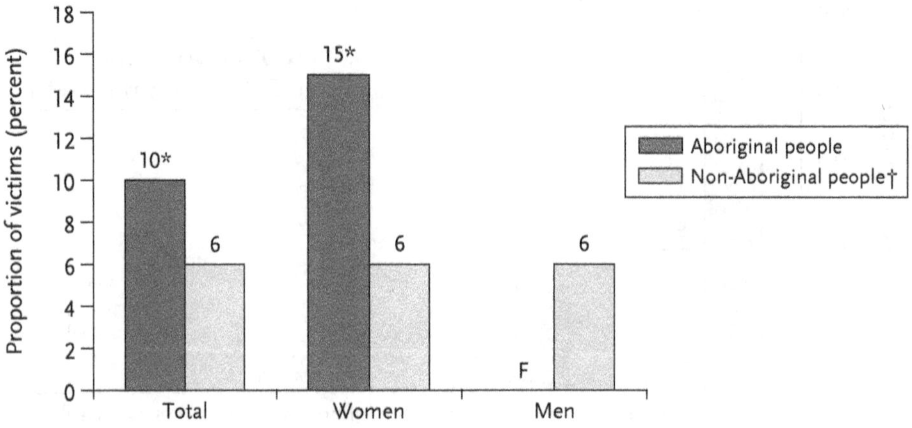

Notes:
† reference category
* significantly different from reference category (p < 0.05)
F too unreliable to be published

Source: Perrault (2011, p. 10). http://www.statcan.gc.ca/pub/85-002-x/2011001/article/11415-eng.pdf.

CAUSES OF OVERREPRESENTATION

According to Aristotle, "poverty is the mother of crime." If he is correct, then the overrepresentation of Aboriginal people in the criminal justice system is a natural consequence of the poverty and marginalization of Aboriginal people in Canada today, as discussed in Chapter 10. The failure of the system to address this over-representation is also connected to the vast difference between Aboriginal concepts of justice and European concepts of justice, Canada's system being constructed on the latter.

There is good reason to associate Aboriginal criminality with the effects of col-onization. Colonization has led to poverty and marginalization. Carole LaPrairie (2002) has sought to refine this general notion, asserting that if colonization and cultural conflict are the main source of Aboriginal criminality, there should be no variation across the country in the levels of Aboriginal overrepresentation, since all Aboriginal people suffered colonization.

LaPrairie looks at provincial differences in Aboriginal admissions to custody. The greatest overrepresentation, she notes, is in Alberta, where Aboriginal people are incarcerated at 9 times the rate of non-Aboriginals; in Saskatchewan, where they are incarcerated at 10 times the rate; and in Manitoba, at 7 times the rate. The rate of Aboriginal incarceration in federal institutions had increased from 11 to 17 percent in 2002, and the numbers have increased since then (Perrault, 2009). According to McGillivray and Comaskey (1999), the highest enrollment rates at residential schools were also in these provinces. This suggests that assimilation and colonialism are primary factors rather than contributing factors in the over-representation of Aboriginal criminality in Canada. To assist you in visualizing the severity of this overrepresentation, Figure 12.3 shows the Aboriginal and non-Aboriginal populations of Saskatchewan's prison system, using figures from the 2006 census.

Figure 12.3   Incarceration Rate on Census Day, by Age Groups, Saskatchewan, May 16, 2006

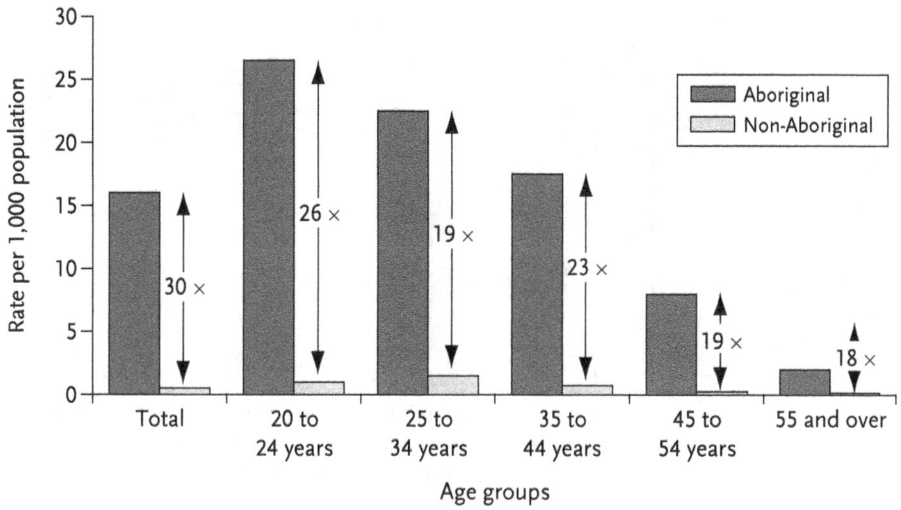

Source: Perrault (2009, July). http://www.statcan.gc.ca/pub/85-002-x/2009003/article/10903-eng.htm.

The crime statistics for urban Aboriginals, a fast-growing population, are higher than for Aboriginal people living on-reserve. According to the 2006 census, only 46 percent of Aboriginal people live on reserves. A 1992 study revealed that only 19 percent of federally sentenced Aboriginal offenders were from a reserve. In 1992, the Edmonton Inner City Violent Crime Task Force found that 50 to 60 percent of incarcerated Aboriginal offenders in Alberta come from urban areas (LaPrairie, 2002). LaPrairie conducted a study in 1992 and 2000 on urban Aboriginal crime in Winnipeg, and on the basis of this study she argued that high Aboriginal crime rates were related to disadvantaged living conditions. This hypothesis was tested again in 2008, by researchers Fitzgerald and Carrington (2008). Their results confirmed LaPrairie's earlier findings: the high level of police-reported Aboriginal crime is related to the characteristics of the neighbourhoods in which Aboriginal people tend to live—namely, neighbourhoods consisting of low incomes, unemployment, low academic achievement, and a high incidence of family breakdown.

Enforcement directives differ greatly between on-reserve policing and urban policing. Urban police are more likely than on-reserve police to resolve criminal behaviour by laying charges; they are less likely to seek other means of resolving a situation. As a result, a relatively high number of charges are laid against urban Aboriginal people. Many urban Aboriginal people suffer from low socio-economic status and marginalization, and are isolated in high-crime urban communities. This puts them doubly at risk—of being victimized, and of engaging in criminal activity themselves.

Figure 12.4 shows the employment and education status of the prison population aged 20 to 34 in Alberta on census day, 2006. The figures suggest that not having a high school diploma or a job contribute to the incarceration rate of Aboriginal adults of this age bracket. But even when education and employment deficits for Aboriginal people are factored out, the risk of incarceration is still higher for Aboriginal people than for non-Aboriginal ones. This points to the likelihood that other factors are

Figure 12.4 Incarceration Rate on Census Day, by Employment and Education Status, Population Aged 20 to 34, Alberta, May 16, 2006

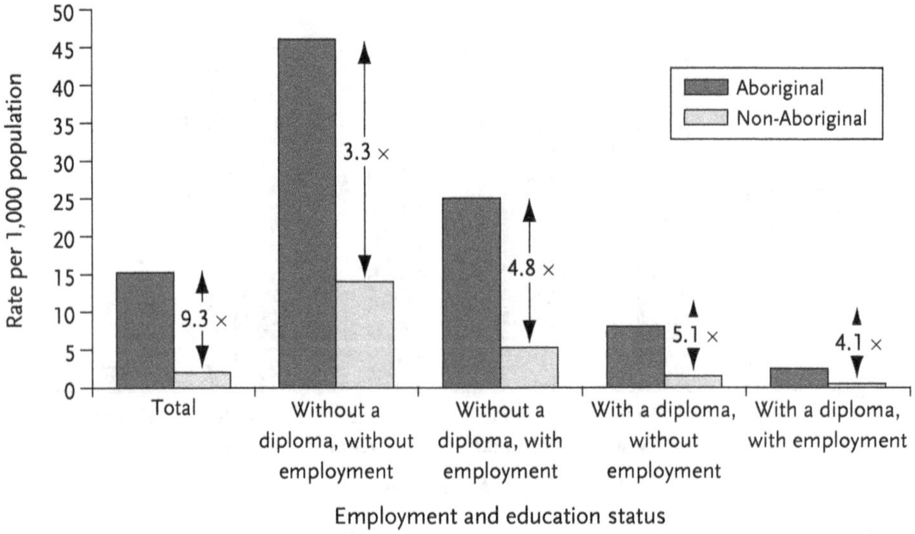

Source: Perrault (2009). http://www.statcan.gc.ca/pub/85-002-x/2009003/article/10903-eng.htm.

contributing to the high incarceration rate for Aboriginal people, factors such as income, housing, and the criminal justice process itself (Perrault, 2011).

Aboriginal people see the family as a central part of the social health of their communities. Other marginalized groups view the family similarly. The assimilation process enforced by the federal government severely disrupted family relationships in First Nations communities. Residential schools caused the greatest damage; the abuse left the children with serious emotional scars. Those who escaped the worst abuse still suffered loss of both language and family relationships. Some were unable to develop healthy relationships with their own children.

As the residential school system wound down in the 1960s, a new form of family dislocation occurred: the child welfare system. Cross-cultural adoptions and foster placements were so common that many communities lost almost an entire generation of children. Those adoptions rarely worked out; adoptive parents were often unprepared for the challenges of rearing an already troubled child whose problems were then compounded by discrimination (Wagamese, 1996). Communities reeling from the loss of their children continued to unravel (Fournier & Crey, 1997). In some penitentiaries, 95 percent of First Nations prisoners are victims of the child welfare system, having been separated from family, culture, and community through adoption, foster care, and, eventually, custody (Royal Commission on Aboriginal Peoples [RCAP], 1996a, p. 129). Figure 12.5 shows the statistics concerning involvement in the child welfare system for Aboriginal and non-Aboriginal inmates. In the Prairie Provinces, an attempt was made to quantify the number of inmates who had been through the child welfare system in relation to their non-Aboriginal counterparts. It was found that 50 percent of Aboriginal inmates had been through the system—twice the rate of non-Aboriginal inmates (Trevethan, Auger, & Moore, 2001).

Loss of land through the colonization process and economic collapse in Aboriginal communities led to extreme poverty and economic reliance on the Canadian

Figure 12.5   Inmate Involvement in the Child Welfare System

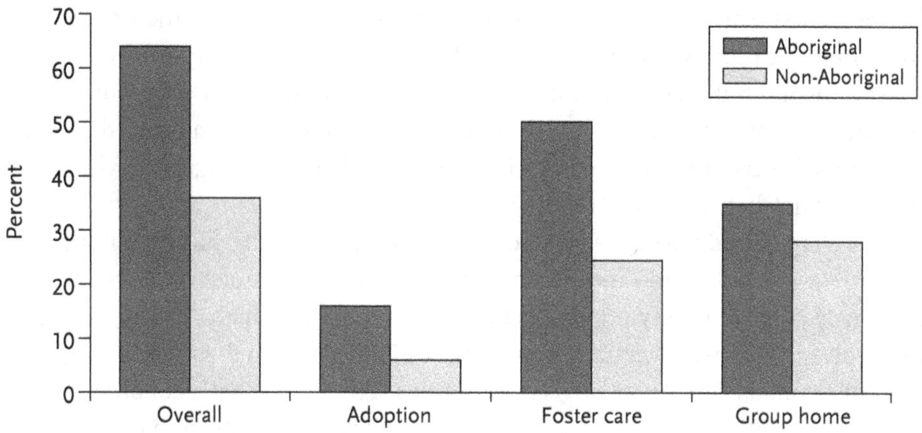

Source: Trevethan, Auger, & Moore (2001). http://www.csc-scc.gc.ca/text/rsrch/reports/r113/
r113-eng.shtml#Anchor-Figur-32166.

government. At the conclusion of the era of colonization—an era that arguably continues to this day—Aboriginal people endured "ill health, run-down and over-crowded housing, polluted water, inadequate schools, poverty and family breakdown/ violence at rates found more often in developing countries than in Canada" (RCAP, 1996b). These problems reinforce one another, creating a circle of disadvantage for Aboriginal people; swirling amidst this circle is the prevalence of alcohol and substance abuse (discussed below).

Joan Sangster (1999) examined the historical overrepresentation of Aboriginal women in custody at the Mercer Reformatory between 1920 and 1960. Her study of admissions records at the Mercer Reformatory in the 1950s indicated that 70 percent of Aboriginal women's admissions were for alcohol-related offences. Sangster (1999) writes, "When a middle aged woman, who lost all her eight siblings to disease and her father to alcoholism, told the Mercer doctor that her drinking is 'unfortunate but unchangeable' one can perhaps understand her tone of resignation." Sangster attributes three factors to the overrepresentation of Aboriginal women in the criminal justice system. The first is material and social dislocation due to colonization. The second is gender and race **paternalism**, which translates into loss of autonomy and therefore agency over one's own actions. The third is the cultural gap between indigenous ideas of justice rooted in healing and restoration and European ideas of justice rooted in crime and punishment. The three factors Sangster cites are rooted in the Aboriginal experience of colonization.

paternalism
a system in which a dominant person or institution assumes authority for supplying the needs and regulating the conduct of those under its control

Alcohol, Substance Abuse, and Criminality in Aboriginal Communities

In the past, alcohol problems in Aboriginal communities were examined from a biological perspective; problem drinking was seen as a weakness of race, and Aboriginal people were believed to have a genetic predisposition to alcoholism. Several studies in the 1970s disproved this theory, but it continues to surface today. The disease model of alcoholism gained popularity after the demise of genetic- or race-based theories. First Nations addiction workers quickly embraced this model, as it not only offered a reprieve from the victim blaming and racial bias intrinsic in the genetic theory, but also held out hope for treatment and recovery. More recent examinations of the disease model question its validity; they indicate that many problem drinkers are not alcoholics but binge drinkers who engage in violent behaviour (Thatcher, 2004, p. 21).

This chapter addresses the issue of alcohol because its use has a strongly positive correlation with crime and violence, particularly family violence. As mentioned previously, alcohol is very often a factor in homicides in which Aboriginal people are involved, whether as victims or as accused. There are two theories on the prevalence of alcoholism in Aboriginal communities. The first is that alcohol/substance abuse is a symptom of social problems such as poverty, ill health, and family breakdown. The second theory inverts the first: alcoholism is the primary factor in the ill health, family breakdown, and violence in Aboriginal communities (Whitehead & Hayes, 1998, pp. 6–7). All things considered, it seems most likely that alcoholism among Aboriginal people stems from their experience of colonization and the consequent social upheaval they endured.

For some Aboriginal communities, alcohol-related crime and family violence have been the norm. In her study of the Grassy Narrows reservation in 1984, Shkilnyk (1985, p. 25) wrote that "they reject the concept of guilt and punishment for behavior influenced by alcohol ... they are not condemned by members of their own community." In their examination of family violence, Anne McGillivray and Brenda Comaskey (1999, p. 13) noted that 75 to 80 percent of adult Aboriginal women in northern Ontario had been assaulted in an intimate relationship. Domestic violence was considered normal in many Aboriginal communities: "In the reserve just, like, everybody had black eyes, walking around, all the ladies, all black. I thought that's the life ... nobody don't say nothing" (quoted in McGillivray & Comaskey, 1999, p. 8).

In some Aboriginal communities, crimes committed under the influence of alcohol were generally deemed not to be criminal. Domestic violence was not seen as criminal or deviant; it was ordinary. It was a situation where denunciation and deterrence (s. 718 of the *Criminal Code*) as one of the aims of criminal sentencing in criminal law had become irrelevant. With domestic violence, there is a strong intergenerational correlation; that is, children who witness or experience abuse are more likely to become abusers. The intergenerational correlation likewise exists with alcohol and substance abuse; its onset takes the form of gas sniffing, which is a particular problem in more isolated and economically desperate Aboriginal communities. Gas sniffing has been reported in children as young as four years of age.

In 2009, Correctional Service Canada reported that substance abuse was a problem for 80 percent of adult male inmates, but for 95 percent of Aboriginal inmates. This cycle seems almost impossible to stop. Nonetheless, many Aboriginal communities are currently making serious efforts to confront these issues in their communities. Inuit communities in Nunangat, for example, have attempted to regulate alcohol in their communities, and others have done the same (see Figure 12.6). Other communities have prohibited alcohol altogether. Statistics for the years between 2006 and 2008 show that the prohibition of alcohol has significantly reduced the incidents of violent crime for these communities.

**Figure 12.6   Three-Year Mean Violent Crime Rates, Wet Versus Dry
Nunavut Communities, 1987–2005**

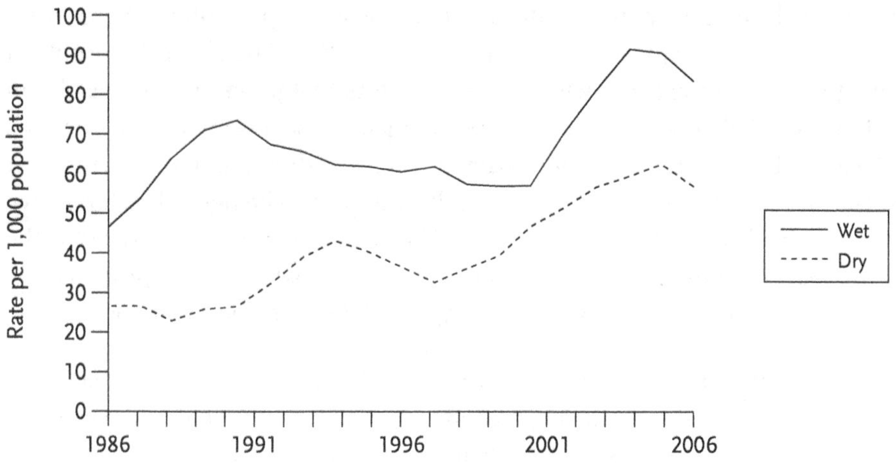

Source: Wood (2008). http://www.darrylwood.com/NunavutAlcoholViolence.pdf.

Systemic Problems

Much attention has been paid in the last two decades to the overrepresentation of Aboriginal people in the criminal justice system, including correctional facilities. Of grave concern are the matters of justice and economics. As we discussed in Chapter 10, the Aboriginal population is increasing at double the rate of the non-Aboriginal population in Canada (Statistics Canada, 2006). The demographic statistics for Aboriginal communities show an average age much younger than that for non-Aboriginal Canadians. For example, in Hobbema, more than half of the population is 18 or younger (Offman, 2008). Since youth is recognized to be a contributing factor in criminal behaviour (most who engage in criminal activity are 18–35), there is cause for serious concern about the Aboriginal population; the overrepresentation of Aboriginal people in the criminal justice system will increase unless significant interventions occur. Inaction could have serious financial repercussions, too. The cost of incarceration in a federal penitentiary is approximately $110,000 per year for males and $150,000 per year for females (Edmonton Public Library, 2010).

A number of studies have been undertaken with a view to establishing policy and action for intervention. One such study (Aboriginal Justice Implementation Commission [AJIC], 1991, p. 86) discovered the following to be the case:

- More than half of the inmates of Manitoba's jails are Aboriginal.
- Aboriginal accused are more likely to be denied bail than are non-Aboriginal accused.
- Aboriginal people spend more time in pre-trial detention than non-Aboriginal people do.
- Aboriginal accused are more likely to be charged with multiple offences than non-Aboriginal accused are.
- Lawyers spend less time with their Aboriginal clients than with their non-Aboriginal clients.
- Aboriginal offenders are more than twice as likely as non-Aboriginal offenders to be incarcerated.

systemic discrimination
the enforcement of laws and
the enforcement of policies
that are inherently prejudicial
to a group or culture

These 1991 findings supported the concept of systemic discrimination against Aboriginal people. **Systemic discrimination** is the enforcement of laws and the creation of policies that are inherently prejudicial to a group or culture. Sometimes treating all people as equals does not amount to justice. The clearest example of this inequality is in the sentencing process. Factors that judges must consider in providing custodial or non-custodial sentences include socio-economic factors such as education level, family situation, having a fixed address, and employment or prospects of employment. On the surface, these appear to be neutral factors; however, as you will recall from Chapter 10, Aboriginal people are most often the unemployed, the transient, and the poorly educated, making them prime candidates for custodial sentences. Manitoba's AJIC (1999) observed the following:

> Historically, the Justice system has discriminated against Aboriginal people by providing legal sanction for their oppression. This oppression of previous generations forced Aboriginal people into their current state of social and economic distress. Now, a seemingly neutral justice system discriminates against current generations of Aboriginal people ... of lower socio-economic status. This is no less racial discrimination; it is merely "laundered" racial discrimination. It is untenable to say that discrimination which builds upon the effects of racial discrimination is not racial discrimination itself. Past injustices cannot be ignored or built upon. ... These statistics [of overincarceration] are dramatic. There is something inherently wrong with a system that takes such harsh measures against an identifiable minority. It is also improbable that systemic discrimination has not played a major role in bringing this state of affairs into being.

Racial profiling in policing is a problem faced by many minority groups in Canada, and Aboriginal people are no exception. This overpolicing of their populations generates more charges against Aboriginal people. Aboriginal people are also overrepresented as victims of crime; nevertheless, in the past, police have at times given less consideration to Aboriginal victims of crime than to non-Aboriginal victims.

Consider also the conclusions of the Royal Commission on the Donald Marshall, Jr., Prosecution in 1989. Donald Marshall was falsely accused and convicted of murder, and spent 11 years in jail until witnesses heard the real murderer bragging about his deeds. The case was re-opened and Marshall was acquitted after witnesses in the original trial admitted giving false evidence. The Royal Commission on the Donald Marshall, Jr., Prosecution (1989) came to the following conclusion:

> Donald Marshall, Jr.'s status as a Native contributed to the miscarriage of justice that has plagued him since 1971. We believe that certain persons within the system would have been more rigorous in their duties, more careful, or more conscious of fairness if Marshall had been White.

Cultural Conflict and Alternative Justice

Besides systemic discrimination, the fact that Aboriginal people's traditional notions of justice differ from those of the dominant system is considered to be another cause of their overrepresentation in the criminal justice system. Before European contact, Aboriginal people did not have jails, police officers, or courts. Each group had its own methods of social control and its own manner of dealing with people who behaved outside what was accepted in the community. Disputes were resolved through mediation, with elders playing a primary role. The focus was on restoring harmony within the community. Offenders were encouraged to accept responsibility for their offence and to make amends to the victim and the community. All community members played a role in restoring the offender to a harmonious relationship within the community.

These were the broad principles of Aboriginal justice, though each community had distinct ways of handling it. The fact that systems of justice vary among communities raises a vexing question. Should we allow each group to structure its own system, based on traditional, pre-colonial methods of administering justice? Can and should pre-colonial systems be resurrected, and would they be successful in today's environment? Mary Ellen Turpel addresses this question in the RCAP report on justice issues (RCAP, 1996a, pp. 65–66):

> Can the pre-colonial regime ever be reconstructed? My own view is no, not except as a relic of the past. It cannot be resurrected because we have all been touched by imperialism and colonialism, and there is no simplistic escape to some pre-colonial history except a rhetorical one. In my view, we [Aboriginal people] need to regain control over criminal justice, indeed all justice matters, but in a thoroughly post-colonial fashion. ... One cannot erase the history of colonialism, but we must, as an imperative, undo it in a contemporary context. ... We have to accept that there are profound social and economic problems in Aboriginal communities today that never existed pre-colonization and even in the first few hundred years of interaction. Problems of alcohol and solvent abuse, family violence and sexual abuse, and youth crime—these are indications of a fundamental breakdown in the social order in Aboriginal communities of a magnitude never known before. A reform dialogue or proposals in the criminal justice field have to come to grips with this contemporary reality and not just retreat into a pre-colonial situation.

Aboriginal people are infusing different approaches into criminal justice programs directed at their communities. In the traditional Aboriginal justice system, authority is dispersed among many people, with consensus as a goal. This approach contrasts with the mainstream one, whereby sole authority for sentencing rests with one individual, such as a justice or a judge, and decision-making power is confined to the Crown, the defence attorney, and the justice. Another difference in the Aboriginal justice system is that Aboriginal women play a primary role in all stages of the process. Finally, when it comes to mediation or sentencing, the Aboriginal process considers a large web of relationships, far beyond the victims and offenders. This reflects the Aboriginal world view that all things are connected and nothing can be addressed in isolation (RCAP, 1996a). For a comparison of Canadian and traditional Aboriginal justice, see Table 12.1.

EXERCISE 2

Read Appendix 12.2. As a class, discuss the different conceptions of justice displayed in this community program.

Table 12.1 Canadian Versus Traditional Aboriginal Justice

Anglo-Canadian justice	Traditional Aboriginal justice
Laws formulated by elected representatives	Laws formulated by the community through tradition and consensus
Laws tied to man-made economy	Laws tied to the natural environment, only a few universally condemned actions
Protestant ethic and Christianity the moral foundation of law	Traditional Indian religions the foundations of codes of behavior
Personal offences seen as transgressions against the state as represented by the monarch	Personal offences seen as transgressions against the victim and his/her family; community threatened only when the public peace is threatened
Law administered by representatives of the state in the form of officially recognized or operated social institutions	Laws usually administered by the offended party, i.e., family, clan
Force and punishment used as methods of social control	Arbitration and ostracism usual peacekeeping methods
Individualistic basis for society and the use of the law to protect private property	Communal basis for society; no legal protection for private property; land held in trust by an individual and protected by the group

Source: Frideres & Gadacz (2005, p. 136).

PROPOSED SOLUTIONS

recidivism
the process of relapsing
into crime

According to a 2009 report released by the Office of the Correctional Investigator (Mann, 2009), Correctional Service Canada has not done enough to ensure that Aboriginal offenders receive sufficient access to culturally sensitive programming and services—factors which may reduce incarceration and **recidivism**. Ongoing problems include delays in the implementation of Aboriginal programming, a shortage of links to the Aboriginal community at the time of release, a shortage of Aboriginal elders within the prison system, and insufficient staff to deliver programming.

There are a number of proposed solutions to address the failure of Canada's mainstream criminal justice system. Patricia Monture-Angus (2000, p. 167) suggests creating one autonomous indigenous system. This has been recommended in most comprehensive studies and inquiries. Another option involves creating autonomous but government-funded Aboriginal agencies to work within the dominant system or, preferably, to integrate Aboriginal ideas and people into the dominant system (Monture-Angus, 2000, p. 167).

Creating an autonomous indigenous system has been recommended by academics, policy advisers, and both the Royal Commission and the AJIC of Manitoba. Programs similar to the one used in the Hollow Water community (see Appendix 12.2) hold great promise but they must have points of contact with the mainstream criminal justice system. For this reason, a two-track approach is recommended: reform of the non-Aboriginal system and creation of an Aboriginal system. These two efforts must occur simultaneously, with close attention to how they will work in partnership.

Autonomous government-funded agencies have been created to work within the dominant system. Examples of this include Aboriginal court liaison officers and corrections inmate liaison officers. These agencies will be discussed in the following sections.

The integration of Aboriginal ideas and people into the dominant system is happening currently as Aboriginal people gain entry into all levels of the system, as police officers, justices, lawyers, and correctional officers. Currently, however, Aboriginal people are underrepresented in all these areas.

The solutions generated in the past 15 years have been developed in consultation with First Nations political organizations. Some suggested solutions are as follows:

- Indigenizing existing criminal justice structures by increasing Aboriginal representation within the system. This includes the creation of a First Nations policing policy for Aboriginal-run police agencies on reserves, and other initiatives.

- Sentencing reforms, such as the creation of new sentencing directives, including s. 718.2(e) of the *Criminal Code* and the subsequent creation of alternative measures, sentencing circles, and diversion programs.

- Amendments to the *Corrections and Conditional Release Act* (including ss. 79 to 84), which recognize the needs of Aboriginal offenders.

- Implementing the Correctional Service Canada (CSC) Strategic Plan for Aboriginal Corrections, which provides for culturally appropriate rehabilitation programs in custody facilities (CSC, 2011).

Indigenization

Indigenization—that is, the incorporation of indigenous people as employees into the justice system—currently presents a number of challenges. First, as some academics have argued, the incorporation of a people does not guarantee the incorporation of their values and thought. The incorporation of Aboriginal police officers, court workers, lawyers, and judges does not change the adversarial nature of the judicial system, which is intrinsically opposed to indigenous values.

indigenization
the incorporation of indigenous people into a social system, such as the justice system

Policing

The evolution of First Nations policing began in 1969 when the Department of Indian Affairs and Northern Development (DIAND) encouraged bands to hire "band constables" to enforce band bylaws. In 1971, DIAND extended this authority, encouraging bands to hire "special constables." The authority of these officers was limited; they did not carry firearms and received very low pay. In 1973, a study by DIAND led to the prospect of employing Aboriginal people in a comprehensive policing role. One option was to establish autonomous police forces on reserves; another was to develop a special Aboriginal constable attached to existing police forces. The latter was the most common choice, with larger forces including Aboriginal contingents.

In 1991 the federal government announced a new on-reserve policing policy, making Aboriginal policing increasingly autonomous. First Nations reserve policing would now come under the authority of the Solicitor General. With the assistance of the Solicitor General's office, provincial, federal, and First Nations governments now come together to partner in agreements over police services that will meet the needs of each community. Agreements must be reached regarding cost sharing for the creation and maintenance of police services.

Under the federal government's First Nations policing policy, a number of forms of policing can exist. One is the First Nations-administered police service; for example, the Nishnawbe-Aski Police Service, which serves 46 Ojibwa and Cree communities. Another option is to have Aboriginal officers employed within a provincial or municipal service with dedicated responsibilities to Aboriginal communities, including urban Aboriginal communities—since, as we saw in Chapter 10, more than 50 percent of Aboriginal people now live in urban centres. A third model is a "developmental policing arrangement" whereby the special branch of Aboriginal officers within a non-Aboriginal-run police service work and train toward the creation of a First Nations-administered service. Today, 118 of the 134 Aboriginal communities in Ontario have their own police services, with additional support units provided by the OPP.

The First Nations policing policy generally has been deemed a success; however, there have been some criticisms. In 2000, a study was commissioned by the First Nations Chiefs of Police Association to survey police chiefs, police officers, civilian staff, and community stakeholders in connection with a number of issues affecting their First Nations Self-Administered Police Service. Ninety percent of community stakeholders felt that their local police service should have further Aboriginal awareness training, and 75 percent felt that recruit training did not reflect First Nations community values (Cummins & Steckley, 2003, p. 171). If this is the case in Aboriginal policing services, one can only imagine the inadequacies in non-Aboriginal policing agencies.

The Royal Commission on Aboriginal Peoples identified part of the problem as Aboriginal police agencies often being modelled on mainstream police agencies. Aboriginal communities must have more input into the structure, the function, and the mission statements of their police services. This can be accomplished only when control over policing and justice is connected to self-government. As discussed in Chapter 11, self-government requires an economic base.

Aboriginal Court Workers and Gladue Courts

Recently there has been an emphasis on recruiting Aboriginal people into all levels of the court system, including the appointment of Aboriginal justices of the peace and Aboriginal judges, particularly in areas of the country where there is a large Aboriginal population.

Most provinces also have an Aboriginal Courtworker Program funded through a cost-sharing initiative between the province and the federal government. The need for the program was identified in a number of studies of Aboriginal people in the justice system. One such inquiry in Toronto, in 1989, quoted a judge as saying, "Unfortunately, Indians are the ideal accused in the courts. They are quick to accept blame for their offences and they accept their punishment very passively.

In many ways they appear to be the victims of the system" (RCAP, 1996a, p. 97). Whether Aboriginal defendants' easy admissions of guilt are culturally based or based on an unfamiliarity with the criminal justice system is unclear; however, the courtworker program was initiated to address these specific issues. The program's purpose is to have the system feel less alienating for Aboriginal accused and to ensure they have a clear understanding of their rights as well as a person to advocate on their behalf as they make their way through the system. Low socio-economic status among Aboriginal people has, in the past, forced offenders to rely almost solely on the legal aid process, which may partly explain why Aboriginal accused spend less time with a lawyer and more time in pre-trial detention than do non-Aboriginal accused. Furthermore, if they spend less time with legal counsel, they are less likely to be informed of available alternative justice programs.

Aboriginal court workers are intimately familiar with the issues that are likely to bring Aboriginal offenders into court; they have a unique perspective on both Aboriginal and non-Aboriginal culture and can advocate for their clients to try to make the justice system work to their benefit.

Another initiative is the Gladue (Aboriginal Persons) Courts. The courts, which were first initiated by Toronto Aboriginal Legal Services, are named for the 1999 Supreme Court decision in *R v. Gladue*. In that case, an Aboriginal woman charged with manslaughter was not given access to sentencing reforms because she was urban dwelling, and the offence happened in a large urban centre. The Court found fault with this; the sentencing reforms had been aimed at all Aboriginal people. The *Gladue* decision marked the first time the Court interpreted the amended s. 718.2(e) of the *Criminal Code*, which reads:

> A court that imposes a sentence shall also take into consideration the following principles:
>   (e) all available sanctions other than imprisonment that are reasonable in the circumstances should be considered for all offenders, with particular attention to the circumstances of aboriginal offenders.

According to the Court, these amendments required a change in the way that judges should approach the sentencing process.

Prior to *Gladue*, various reports had pointed out the ways in which the Canadian justice system had failed the Aboriginal peoples of Canada, due primarily to "the fundamentally different world views of Aboriginal and non-Aboriginal people with respect to such elemental issues as the substantive content of justice and the process of achieving justice" (RCAP, 1996a, p. 309).

The first Gladue Court began functioning in October 2001, in Toronto. At the time of writing, there are three Gladue courts operating in Toronto and one in Sarnia. A Gladue Court is a court where all Crown attorneys, defence counsel, and judges have received supplemental training in the concepts of Aboriginal justice and in all of the alternative programs available to Aboriginal offenders. The court is available to all Aboriginal persons—status and non-status Indians, Métis, and Inuit—who wish to identify as such and have their matter heard in a Gladue Court. The accused is assigned a Gladue caseworker, who does extensive background investigation to determine what strategy would best ensure rehabilitation. In some cities, such as Brantford, Hamilton, Milton, and Kitchener-Waterloo, Aboriginal offenders can apply for a Gladue caseworker and a Gladue report will be prepared, but their cases will not be heard in a dedicated Gladue Court.

Gladue Courts accept guilty pleas, conduct remands and trials, sentence offenders, and carry out bail hearings. Judges consider the unique factors that may have contributed to the offender's being charged, and the sentencing procedures that may be appropriate, given the offender's Aboriginal heritage. This includes examining alternative justice processes such as restorative justice.

Cultural Awareness Training

Lately there has been a focus on the delivery of Aboriginal awareness training to non-Aboriginal employees of the criminal justice system. Studies in Aboriginal issues have been included in college courses for prospective police officers and correctional workers. Police-services and correctional staff now in the field have received training in Aboriginal issues and in the Aboriginal world view, so as to prevent miscommunications. This training is ongoing in most provinces and territories, although much work remains to be done.

Recommendations for this training were put forward in the 1996 RCAP report and endorsed by the First Nations Chiefs of Police Association's 2000 study. In 2007, as a result of Justice Linden's report on the Ipperwash Crisis, all OPP officers receive education in Aboriginal issues. OPP Crisis negotiators and Tactical Response Unit officers also receive additional training on Aboriginal issues, including history and legal and socio-economic issues. This training includes a one-week Aboriginal Awareness training program which includes Aboriginal elders and Aboriginal community partners in setting curricula.

Outside of Ontario, First Nations-administered police services are less common. The RCMP serves 634 Aboriginal communities across Canada. The RCMP reports that currently 67 percent of its detachments serve Aboriginal communities and more than 1,500 of its members are Aboriginal (Royal Canadian Mounted Police, 2011). The RCMP also provides its staff with training in Aboriginal perspectives to help them understand and to serve Aboriginal communities

Sentencing Reforms

As mentioned above, s. 718.2(e) of the *Criminal Code* states that "all available sanctions other than imprisonment that are reasonable in the circumstances should be considered for all offenders, with particular attention to the circumstances of aboriginal offenders." This provision, added in 1996, was intended to address the excessively high incarceration rate for Aboriginal people.

The wording of s. 718.2(e) states that sanctions other than incarceration must be available; these would include sentencing circles, alternative measures, and diversion programs. Since many offenders are in large urban centres, programs are required both on- and off-reserve. This is supported by the Supreme Court's decision in *R v. Gladue* in 1999, which states that urban Aboriginal people must be considered in accordance with this section even if they are not connected to a particular Aboriginal community. The alternatives created for sentencing by

s. 718.2(e) have been used widely by both Aboriginal and non-Aboriginal offenders, allowing for a more individualized and restorative approach to justice. There is concern, however, that these sentencing options, particularly conditional sentences, are being used more often as an extension of punitive power rather than as an alternative to incarceration. Twenty-eight thousand conditional sentences were ordered in the first two years of their existence, but prison populations have not been proportionately reduced (Roach & Rudin, 2000).

Alternative Measures

The alternative sentencing options under s. 718.2(e) include alternatives other than conditional sentences. Diversion programs are common for both Aboriginal and non-Aboriginal offenders, either pre-charge or post-charge. Diversion programs are used for a variety of criminal offences, particularly minor thefts. In a non-Aboriginal context, a diversion approach might involve the offender's being required, for example, to attend an education session or write letters of apology. In an Aboriginal context, cases more serious than minor theft may be subject to diversion, at the discretion of the Crown. The Crown may suspend the disposition of the case until the Aboriginal panel or deliberative body has settled on an appropriate resolution for the case. In the case of minor and non-violent offences, charges against the accused are then generally withdrawn, having been adequately dealt with by the community.

Sentencing circles and elders' panels are common alternative sentencing options. They are based on traditional Aboriginal justice structures and allow communities to have control over rehabilitation efforts for offenders. (Sentencing circles have also become commonplace for non-Aboriginal youth offenders under the *Youth Criminal Justice Act*, although they are known as "youth justice committees.") This initiative addresses the problem of having an outside person pass sentence over an Aboriginal person in an Aboriginal community; people who, as well as sharing their culture, know the accused and the victim and have relationships with their families have insight that an outsider may not possess and that may be difficult to translate into a pre-sentence report.

An elders' panel consists of elders or clan leaders who sit with the judge and provide advice regarding an appropriate sentence. In a sentencing circle, community members are invited to sit in a circle with the accused and a judge to decide the sentence. There are prerequisites for a sentencing circle. First, the accused must recognize his guilt and have a clear intention to rehabilitate and become a good citizen of his community. Second, the community must have a desire to intercede on behalf of one of its members. Third, the victim must also support the initiative.

Youth

All of these options are also available for youth sentencing. Although the absolute numbers of Aboriginal youth in custody decreased from 1,128 to 720 between 2000 and 2003, Aboriginal youth are still overrepresented in the criminal justice system (see Figures 12.7 and 12.8). In 2003, the non-Aboriginal incarceration rate for youth was 8.3 per 10,000; the rate for Aboriginal youth was 64.5 per 10,000. A greater

Figure 12.7   Incarceration Rates for Aboriginal and Non-Aboriginal Youth in Canada

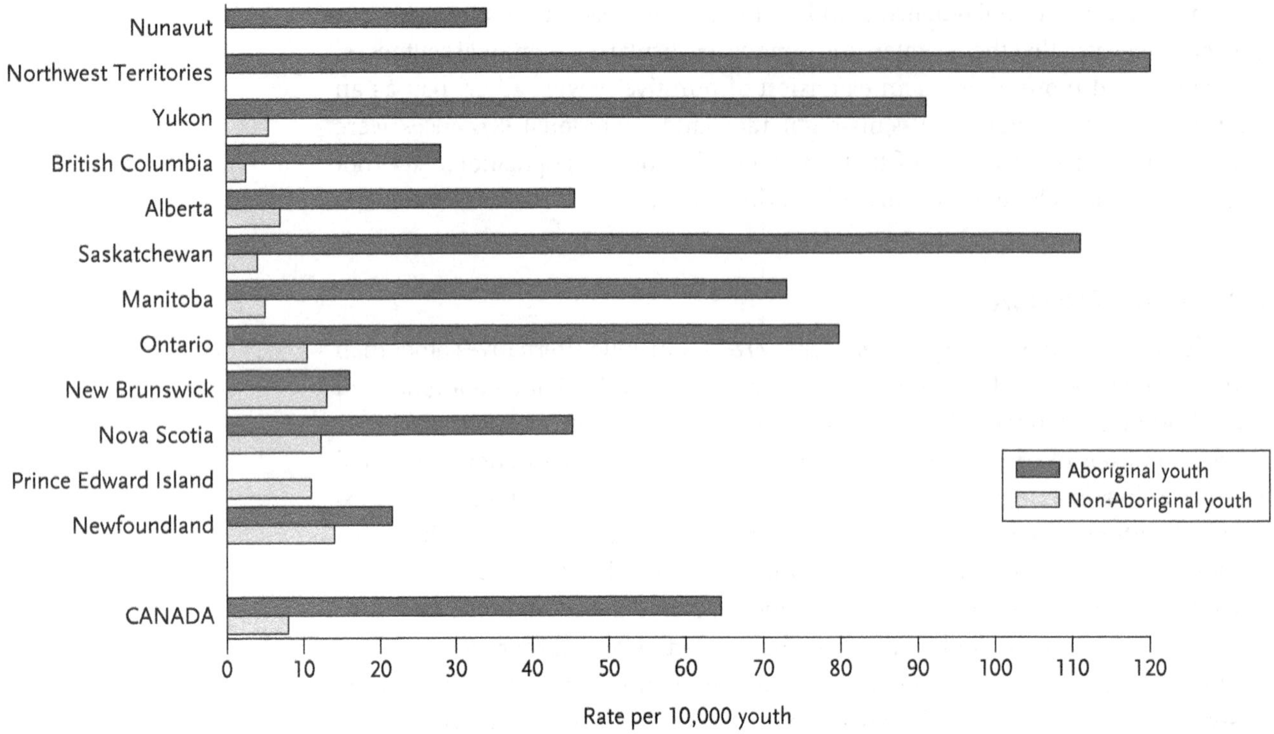

Source: Department of Justice Canada (2004). http://www.justice.gc.ca/eng/pi/rs/rep-rap/2004/yj2-jj2/p3.html.

number of Aboriginal youth are incarcerated for serious offences than are their non-Aboriginal counterparts. Aboriginal youth are also more likely than their non-Aboriginal counterparts to receive custodial sentences and to receive longer periods of probation. In a 2009 study, it was found that 22 percent of youth gang members in Canada are Aboriginal (Totten, 2009).

Without intervention, these youth will make their way into the adult system. To combat this, family group conferencing is available to all youth, particularly Aboriginal youth. It is a process by which the youth and members of his or her family, a youth advocate, a police officer, a social worker, and other community members meet to decide what types of intervention are available to the youth and what strategies can assist him or her to become a productive member of the community. Family group conferencing can take place pre-charge or post-charge. Unfortunately, family support is often unavailable for Aboriginal youth due to estrangement or family dysfunction, and often there is no youth advocate, particularly for those who are homeless.

In the one-day snapshot of youth in custody in 2001 reported by the Department of Justice Canada, it was found that only 23 percent of youth in custody were living on a reserve directly prior to admission; however, 65 percent of youth in custody spent the majority of their time on the reserve in the two years prior to their incarceration. Only 17 percent of the alleged offences that brought the youth into custody happened on-reserve and 58 percent happened in a city. These statistics indicate the need for youth crime prevention strategies directed at Aboriginal youth both on- and off-reserve (see Figures 12.9 and 12.10).

Figure 12.8   Ethnic Origins Reported by Street Youth

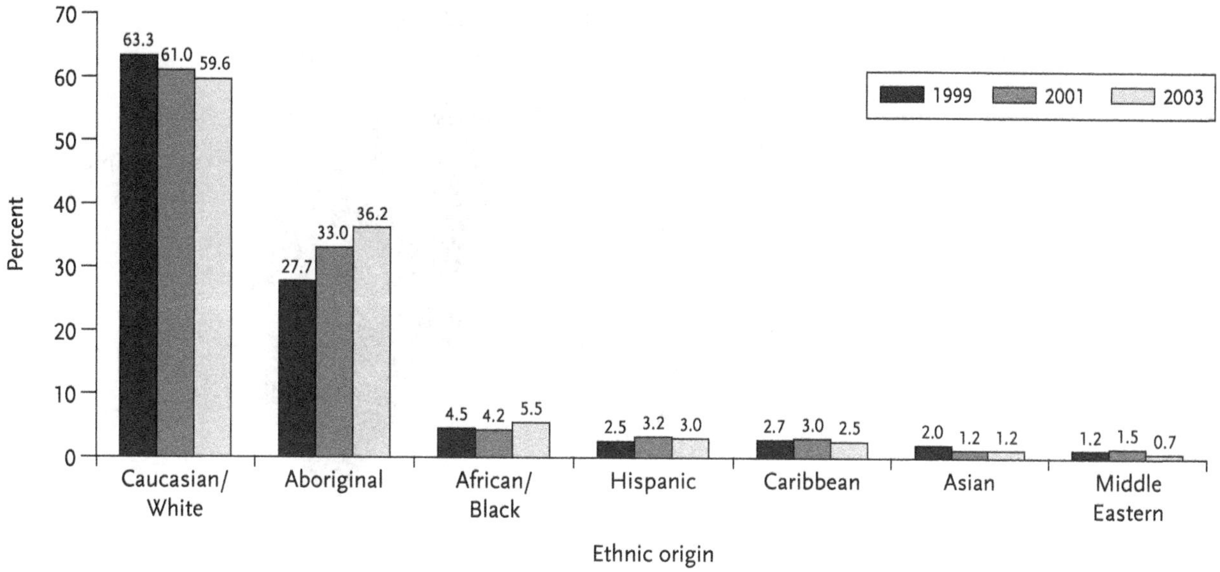

Source: Public Health Agency of Canada (2006, p. 8). http://www.phac-aspc.gc.ca/std-mts/reports_06/pdf/street_youth_e.pdf.

Corrections and Conditional Release Act

Amendments to the *Corrections and Conditional Release Act*, including ss. 79 to 84, which recognize the needs of Aboriginal offenders, provide for early release considerations by parole boards. This would reduce the cost of incarceration, but the processes must be in place within the community to assist the offender in successful readjustment. Considering the high rate of recidivism for Aboriginal offenders, this has not been an area of strength for our corrections system. Efforts to partner with Aboriginal communities and to allow their input into the release process are currently under way.

Recent revisions to the *Corrections and Conditional Release Act* include s. 81, which provides for the transfer of a First Nations offender from a correctional facility to a First Nations community in a non-institutional setting where supervision, treatment, and programming are provided under the 24-hour supervision of community members for the term of sentence. Other types of arrangements can also be made under this section; an offender may be transferred to a spiritual or healing lodge, or a treatment facility in an urban centre.

Section 84 of the Act gives First Nations communities the opportunity to participate in an offender's release plan once he or she is out of custody and on parole. The release plan balances the needs of the community with the needs of the offender. Successful reintegration is the primary goal for all parties: the victim, the offender, and the community.

First Nations community involvement in justice issues marks the beginning of mainstream Canada's devolution of control over these matters where Aboriginal people are concerned. However, it is only a beginning. The communities require funds to compensate members for the work these new responsibilities involve.

Figure 12.9   Location of Offence

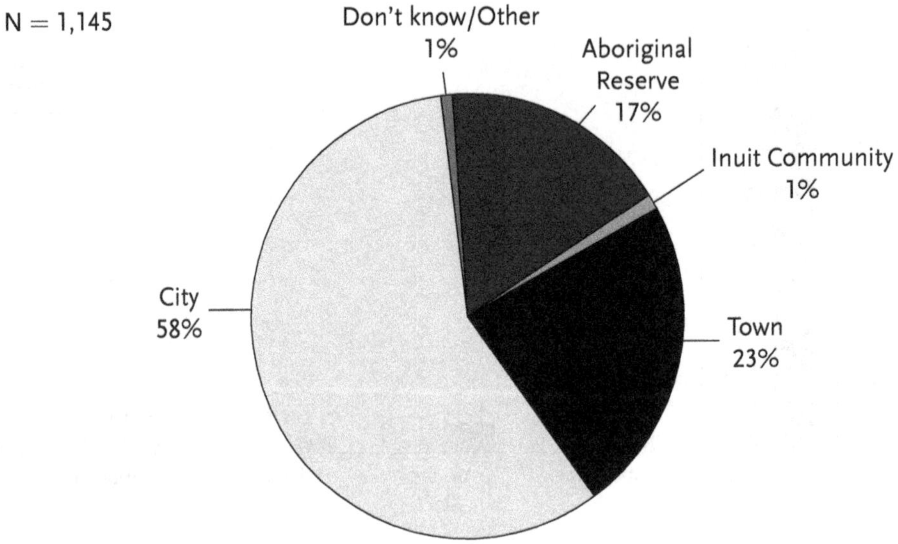

N = 1,145

Source: Department of Justice Canada (2001). http://www.justice.gc.ca/eng/pi/rs/rep-rap/2001/yj1-jj1/p2_6.html.

Culturally Appropriate Programs in Custody

CSC's Strategic Plan for Aboriginal Corrections involves providing culturally appropriate rehabilitation programs to Aboriginal people in custody. Under s. 80 of the *Corrections and Conditional Release Act*, CSC is required to provide programs designed to address the particular needs of Aboriginal offenders. This section authorizes the Solicitor General to enter into agreements with Aboriginal communities to provide services to offenders, such as traditional healers and elders. Furthermore, it mandates the establishment of a national Aboriginal advisory committee to advise CSC on how best to provide services to Aboriginal inmates.

This is an important initiative for Aboriginal inmates, since the chaplaincy program funded by CSC and other counselling programs are ill-equipped to deal with Aboriginal experiences. Furthermore, some evidence supports the fact that exposure to Aboriginal spirituality and connection to culture has been effective in the healing and rehabilitation of Aboriginal offenders. In the Cawsey Report, which was studied by RCAP, Justice Cawsey noted that "Everything that has worked for Aboriginal people has come from Aboriginal people" (RCAP, 1996a).

In its quest for appropriate initiatives for Aboriginal offenders, CSC (2011) has had to acknowledge the particularities of the Aboriginal population in the criminal justice system and recognize that, compared with the average non-Aboriginal offender, the Aboriginal offender

- is younger;
- is more likely to have served a previous youth or adult sentence;
- is incarcerated more often for a violent offence;
- is at a higher risk of being placed in increased security institutions, which limits access to rehabilitative programs;

Figure 12.10   Pre-Custody Location of Accused

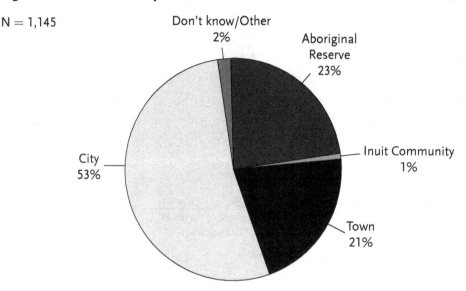

N = 1,145

Source: Department of Justice Canada (2002). http://www.justice.gc.ca/eng/pi/rs/rep-rap/2001/yj1-jj1/p2_6.html.

- is more likely to have gang affiliations;
- more often has increased health problems, including fetal alcohol disorders and mental health issues; and
- has a higher need rating when first admitted to custody.

With regard to needs, CSC assesses the needs of people who are admitted to custody in the following categories: employment, marital/family relationships, social interaction, substance abuse, community functioning, personal/emotional, and attitude. Because the presence of these needs (which are said to occur when assessed as medium or high) is correlated with a greater risk of re-offending, they represent areas in an offender's life that must be improved to increase the chances that the offender will be successfully reintegrated into his or her community. Currently, Saskatchewan and CSC collect data regarding offenders' needs (see Figure 12.11). In data collected for 2007–8, Aboriginal adults admitted into custody had a higher number of needs on average than non-Aboriginals, in all areas of assessment (Perrault, 2009).

Table 12.2 compares the proportion of Aboriginal and non-Aboriginal offenders in Saskatchewan and federal institutions that demonstrate a particular need. The figures may go some way to explaining the representation of Aboriginal offenders in custody; they suggest that the risk of recidivism—that is, the risk of returning to a correctional facility—may be higher for Aboriginal offenders.

In addition to the fact that, compared with non-Aboriginal offenders, a higher proportion of Aboriginal offenders demonstrate needs, Aboriginal offenders more often score as high risk (41 percent, compared with 22 percent among non-Aboriginal inmates) on the Reintegration Potential Reassessment Scales (RPRS). According to measures of "low potential for integration," the non-Aboriginal population has a 36 percent rating, whereas the Aboriginal population has a 69 percent rating. It

Figure 12.11 Average Number of Needs by Aboriginal Identity, 2007–8

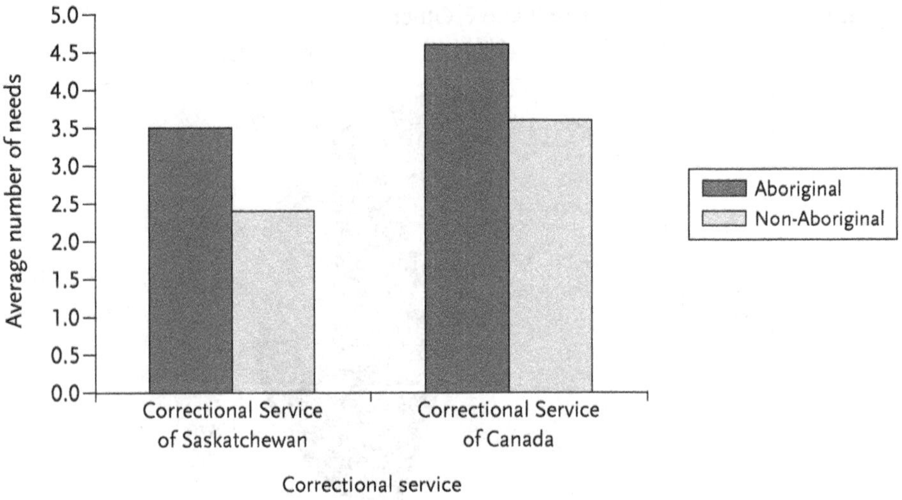

Source: Perrault (2009, July). http://www.statcan.gc.ca/pub/85-002-x/2009003/article/10903-eng.htm.

has been a priority of CSC to assess the risk-scoring process for bias against Aboriginal people in custody. Because of the risk ratings, Aboriginal inmates are paroled later than non-Aboriginal inmates, and less often complete sentences under community supervision. Aboriginal inmates are more likely to be denied applications for full parole (24 percent, compared with 5 percent for their non-Aboriginal counterparts). Lastly, Aboriginal inmates are more likely to waive parole application because of incomplete programs in custody (Mann, 2009).

New initiatives from CSC include

- rehabilitation programs intended specifically for Aboriginal people,
- increasing offenders' links to Aboriginal communities, and
- having Aboriginal elders available to those in the institutions.

These initiatives have been undertaken in close consultation with Aboriginal people and communities. CSC opened its first Aboriginal healing lodge, Okimaw Ohci, for women in 1995, in southern Saskatchewan. One of the many reasons for the creation of the lodge was to help these women stay connected to their communities rather than alienate them from their family and community for the long term by transferring their custody to Ontario. The lodges were a success; the recidivism rate for women completing their sentences in them decreased, which led to the opening of four healing lodges for male Aboriginal offenders.

EXERCISE 3

As a class, read Appendix 12.3, which discusses the Pê Sâkâstêw Healing Lodge, established by CSC in Hobbema. How does the information further your understanding of the crisis in Hobbema and some of the steps that can be taken to address it?

Table 12.2   Proportion of Aboriginal and Non-Aboriginal Adults Admitted to Custody and Assessed as Having Needs, by the Type of Need, Saskatchewan and Correctional Service of Canada, 2007–8

Type of need	Saskatchewan Correctional Service		Correctional Service of Canada	
	Aboriginal	Non-Aboriginal	Aboriginal	Non-Aboriginal
	percent			
Employment	63	33	73	49
Marital/family relationships	48	33	51	32
Social interaction	76	51	72	61
Substance abuse	81	58	82	67
Community functioning	..	..	39	27
Personal or emotional	10	8	82	72
Attitude	71	52	58	55
Average number of needs	3.5	2.4	4.6	3.6

Note: Represents individuals who were assessed as having either medium or high needs. For those who were admitted more than one time during the fiscal year 2007/2008, information is based on the most recent admission.

Source: Perrault (2009, July). http://www.statcan.gc.ca/pub/85-002-x/2009003/article/10903/tbl/t8-eng.htm.

As in regular CSC institutions, Aboriginal offenders in healing lodges receive counselling and are taught reintegration strategies in preparation for release. However, the counselling in healing lodges has a strong spiritual component. This, together with the focus on reconnection to family and community, appears to reduce the incidence of recidivism.

In regular institutions, there are a number of programs specifically intended for Aboriginal inmates, including one called "In Search of Your Warrior" that is aimed at reducing serious violence. A recent review of this program (CSC, 2005) showed that offenders who completed the program were 19 percent less likely to be readmitted to custody. CSC seems to be making some progress in its rehabilitation focus for Aboriginal offenders, but there is still much work to be done and key resources are still lacking in many areas. For example, some institutions (Mann, 2009, p. 25) report that they do not have the services of an elder for extended periods of time, and the burnout of elders and spiritual advisers—due to lack of recruitment, retention, and operational requirements—means that the way in which services are delivered in practice is not in line with what was originally envisioned. The incarceration rate of Aboriginal people in Canada has increased in the past few years, and considering the social conditions and the demographics of the Aboriginal population in Canada, the rate of incarceration can only increase if the criminal justice system and CSC do not make considerable efforts.

CONCLUSION

Among the proposals of Monture-Angus (2000), in her discussion of Aboriginal overrepresentation in the Canadian criminal justice system, is the creation of a separate but government-funded justice system for Aboriginal people. Aboriginal people should be responsible for their own populations and for addressing crime in their communities, empowered to find solutions independent of government interference. The mainstream government does not readily relinquish control of its criminal justice system, however. Current measures to accommodate the existing system to Aboriginal people are not moving fast enough for those experiencing the negative effects of crime in First Nations communities or those who are languishing in prison. Colonial structures with an indigenous flair, though cost-effective, are not enough.

Aboriginal efforts to create new programs for treatment of offenders and community are often hindered by lack of funding. The federal government should provide such funding wherever possible. But where there is a shortfall in federal funding for Aboriginal initiatives, these communities could try to finance those efforts themselves. This would give them more autonomy and creative independence in community problem solving. As long as the federal government is funding justice initiatives in Canada for Aboriginal peoples, there cannot be complete independence. A separate, Aboriginal-run justice system will ultimately require the economic independence of Aboriginal nations. This will also bring freedom from marginalization and poverty, the root causes of crime.

Legislative reforms in justice have shown some positive results but are not the only answer to the problem of Aboriginal overrepresentation in the criminal justice system. First Nations communities in Canada are diverse, complex, and various in their needs. Aboriginal people need to be leading the way in areas that are fundamental to their well-being. Up to this point, mainstream Canada has led the way. This is paternalism. Aboriginal people in Canada, working on all fronts to improve their situation, need a strong partnership with the Canadian government, but one in which the government is willing to follow their lead.

KEY TERMS

indigenization
paternalism
recidivism
systemic discrimination

REFERENCES

Aboriginal Justice Implementation Commission (AJIC). (1991). *Report of the Aboriginal Justice Inquiry of Manitoba* (Vol. 1). Winnipeg: Statutory Publications. http://www.ajic.mb.ca/volumel/toc.html.

Bittle, S., Quann, N., Hattem, T., & Muise, D. (2002, March). *A one-day snapshot of Aboriginal youth in custody across Canada.* Ottawa: Department of Justice Canada, Youth Justice Research. http://www.justice.gc.ca/eng/pi/rs/rep-rap/2001/yj1-jj1/yj1.pdf.

Bushie, B. (1999, August 7). *Community holistic circle healing.* International Institute for Restorative Practices. http://www.iirp.edu/article_detail.php?article_id=NDc0.

CBC News. (2004, July 2). Starlight tours. CBC News in Depth: Aboriginal Canadians. *CBC.ca.* http://www.cbc.ca/news/background/aboriginals/starlighttours.html.

CBC News. (2008, November). A community fights gangs and guns. *CBC News in Review,* 31–43. http://newsinreview.cbclearning.ca/wp-content/uploads/2008/12/nov-08-gangs.pdf.

Correctional Service Canada. (2005). The "In Search of Your Warrior" program for Aboriginal offenders: A preliminary evaluation. http://www.csc-scc.gc.ca/text/rsrch/reports/r172/r172-eng.shtml.

Correctional Service Canada. (2011). *Strategic plan for Aboriginal corrections: Innovation, learning, and adjustment 2006-07 to 2010-11.* Ottawa: Correctional Service Canada. http://www.csc-scc.gc.ca/text/prgrm/abinit/documents/spac06_e.pdf.

Cummins, B.D., & Steckley, J.L. (2003). *Aboriginal policing: A Canadian perspective.* Toronto: Pearson Education.

Department of Justice Canada. (2002). A one-day snapshot of Aboriginal youth in custody across Canada. Research and Statistics Division. http://www.justice.gc.ca/eng/pi/rs/rep-rap/2001/yj1-jj1/p2_6.html.

Department of Justice Canada. (2004). A one-day snapshot of Aboriginal youth in custody across Canada: Phase II. http://www.justice.gc.ca/eng/pi/rs/rep-rap/2004/yj2-jj2/p3.html.

Edmonton Public Library. (2010). Infofile detail—incarceration: Correctional institutions—costs. http://www.epl.ca/infofile-detail?subject_detail=Incarceration.

Fitzgerald, R., & Carrington, P.J. (2008). The neighbourhood context of urban Aboriginal crime. *Canadian Journal of Criminology and Criminal Justice, 50*(5), 523–557.

Fournier, S., & Crey, E. (1997). *Stolen from our embrace: The abduction of First Nations children and the restoration of Aboriginal communities.* Vancouver: Douglas & McIntyre.

Frideres, J.S., & Gadacz, R.R. (2005). *Aboriginal peoples in Canada: Contemporary conflicts* (7th ed.). Toronto: Pearson.

Gladue, R v. (1999). [1999] 1 SCR 688.

LaPrairie, C. (2002). Aboriginal overrepresentation in the criminal justice system: A tale of nine cities. *Canadian Journal of Criminology, 44*(2), 181–208.

Mann, M.M. (2009). *Good intentions, disappointing results: A progress report on federal Aboriginal corrections.* Office of the Correctional Investigator. http://www.oci-bec.gc.ca/rpt/oth-aut/oth-aut20091113-eng.aspx.

McGillivray, A., & Comaskey, B. (1999). *Black eyes all of the time: Intimate violence, Aboriginal women, and the justice system.* Toronto: University of Toronto Press.

Monture-Angus, A.P. (2000). Lessons in decolonization: Aboriginal overrepresentation in the Canadian criminal justice system. In D. Long & O.P. Dickason (Eds.), *Visions of the Heart: Canadian Aboriginal issues*. Toronto: Harcourt Canada.

Offman, C. (2008, April 15). Hobbema, Alberta: A town in a "state of crisis." *National Post*. http://www.nationalpost.com/most_popular/story.html?id=447948.

Perrault, S. (2009, July). The incarceration of Aboriginal people in adult correctional services. *Juristat*. http://www.statcan.gc.ca/pub/85-002-x/2009003/article/10903-eng.htm#a14.

Perrault, S. (2011). Violent victimization of Aboriginal people in the Canadian provinces, 2009. *Juristat*. http://www.statcan.gc.ca/pub/85-002-x/2011001/article/11415-eng.pdf.

Public Health Agency of Canada. (2006, March). Street youth in Canada. *Findings from Enhanced Surveillance of Canadian Street Youth, 1999–2003*. http://www.phac-aspc.gc.ca/std-mts/reports_06/pdf/street_youth_e.pdf.

Roach, K., & Rudin, J. (2000). Gladue: The judicial and political reception of a promising decision. *Canadian Journal of Criminology, 42*(3), 355–388.

Royal Canadian Mounted Police. (2011). Aboriginal people and the RCMP. http://www.rcmp-grc.gc.ca/recruiting-recrutement/aboriginal-autochtone/aboriginal-autochtone-eng.htm.

Royal Commission on Aboriginal Peoples (RCAP). (1996a). *Bridging the cultural divide: A report on Aboriginal people and criminal justice in Canada*. Ottawa: Supply and Services Canada.

Royal Commission on Aboriginal Peoples (RCAP). (1996b). *Highlights from the Report of the Royal Commission on Aboriginal Peoples*. Ottawa: Supply and Services Canada.

Royal Commission on the Donald Marshall, Jr., Prosecution. (1989). *Commissioners' report, findings and recommendations* (Vol. 1). Halifax: Province of Nova Scotia. http://aboriginallegal.ca/docs/hill_factum.htm.

Sangster, J. (1999, March). Criminalizing the colonized: Ontario Native women confront the criminal justice system, 1920-1960. *Canadian Historical Review, 80*(1), 32–60.

Shkilnyk, A. (1985). *A poison stronger than love: The destruction of an Ojibwa community*. New Haven, CT: Yale University Press.

Statistics Canada. (2006). 2006 census: Aboriginal Peoples in Canada in 2006: Inuit, Métis and First Nations, 2006 census: Findings. http://www12.statcan.ca/census-recensement/2006/as-sa/97-558/index-eng.cfm.

Statistics Canada. (2010a, Fall). Adult correctional services in Canada. *Juristat*. http://www.statcan.gc.ca/pub/85-002-x/2010003/article/11353-eng.htm#a8.

Statistics Canada. (2010b, September 28). General social survey—victimization. *The Daily*. http://www.statcan.gc.ca/daily-quotidien/100928/dq100928a-eng.htm.

Stone, L. (2009, November 14). Aboriginal inmate numbers still too high, report says. *Times Colonist.* http://www2.canada.com/victoriatimescolonist/news/story.html?id=1d4c16ec-7afd-40ad-8ca2-05989dae8036.

Thatcher, R. (2004). *Fighting firewater fictions: Moving beyond the disease model of alcohol in First Nations.* Toronto: University of Toronto Press.

Totten, M. (2009, March). *Preventing Aboriginal youth gang involvement in Canada: A gendered approach.* Paper prepared for Aboriginal policy research conference, Ottawa. http://www.nwac.ca/sites/default/files/reports/TottenAPRCGangGenderpaperFeb2609.pdf.

Trevethan, S., Auger, S., & Moore, J.-P. (2001). *The effect of family disruption on Aboriginal and non-Aboriginal inmates.* Ottawa: Correctional Service Canada. http://www.csc-scc.gc.ca/text/rsrch/reports/r113/r113-eng.shtml#Anchor-Figur-32166.

Wagamese, R. (1996). *The terrible summer: The national newspaper award-winning writing of Richard Wagamese.* Toronto: Warwick.

Whitehead, P.C., & Hayes, J.J. (1998). *The insanity of alcohol: Social problems in Canadian First Nations communities.* Toronto: Canadian Scholars' Press.

Wood, D.S. (2008). *Alcohol and violence in Nunavut: A comparison of wet and dry communities.* Washington: Canada Research Showcase. http://www.darrylwood.com/NunavutAlcoholViolence.pdf.

REVIEW QUESTIONS

TRUE OR FALSE?

_____ 1. Statistics show that most incarcerated Aboriginal offenders come from reserves.

_____ 2. The incarceration level of Aboriginal people in relation to non-Aboriginal people is declining, indicating that the justice system is adequately addressing the problem of Aboriginal overrepresentation.

_____ 3. Aboriginal people are more frequently victims of crime than are other Canadians.

_____ 4. Mary Ellen Turpel says in the 1996 report of the Royal Commission on Aboriginal Peoples that an exclusive pre-colonial Aboriginal justice system can successfully be resurrected in today's society.

_____ 5. The 1998 Royal Commission on the Donald Marshall, Jr., Prosecution concluded that Donald Marshall Jr.'s status as an Aboriginal person contributed to his false conviction for murder.

_____ 6. In 1991, the Manitoba Aboriginal Justice Inquiry found that more than half the inmates of Manitoba's jails were Aboriginal.

_____ 7. Alternative sentencing measures reflect Aboriginal values and therefore are only available to Aboriginal offenders.

_____ 8. Section 718.2(e) of the *Criminal Code* states that "all available sanctions other than imprisonment that are reasonable in the circumstances should be considered for only Aboriginal offenders."

_____ 9. To qualify for a sentencing circle, the accused must recognize his or her guilt and have a clear intention to rehabilitate.

_____ 10. The *Corrections and Conditional Release Act* has changed to allow First Nations communities to participate in an offender's release plan.

MULTIPLE CHOICE

1. Which of the following has not been a factor in Hobbema's descent into chaos?
   (a) unemployment
   (b) substance abuse
   (c) the erosion of Aboriginal traditions
   (d) lack of access to natural resources

2. Joan Sangster conducted a historical examination of the admission records at the Mercer Reformatory for women. She attributed the overrepresentation of Aboriginal women at the reformatory to three things. Which of the following is not one of those three?
   (a) material and social dislocation due to colonization
   (b) gender and race paternalism
   (c) the isolation of Aboriginal communities from the main cities
   (d) the cultural gap between indigenous ideas of justice and mainstream ideas of justice

3. The biological perspective of examining alcohol problems in Aboriginal communities was popular prior to 1970. This perspective relies on the belief that
   (a) problem drinking is a weakness of race and Aboriginal people have a genetic predisposition to alcoholism
   (b) all people have a predisposition to alcoholism; some people simply have more self-control
   (c) problem drinking is not race based but gender based
   (d) predispositions to alcoholism depend on the age of the drinker

4. The 1991 Report of the Aboriginal Justice Inquiry of Manitoba made several findings. Which of the following is not one of their conclusions?
   (a) Aboriginal offenders are more than twice as likely to be incarcerated as non-Aboriginal offenders are.
   (b) Lawyers spend less time with their Aboriginal clients than with their non-Aboriginal clients.
   (c) Aboriginal people spend more time in pre-trial detention than non-Aboriginal people.
   (d) Aboriginal offenders are more likely to have their sentences reduced.

5. Which of the following is the definition of *systemic discrimination* as it pertains to the justice system?

   (a) general flaws in the system

   (b) the enforcement of laws and policies that are inherently prejudicial to a group or culture

   (c) lack of attention to the needs of a specific group

   (d) a purposeful exclusion of a group from certain sentencing options

6. Most comprehensive studies of the criminal justice system in relation to Aboriginal people recommend

   (a) an autonomous indigenous system

   (b) a dependent indigenous system

   (c) healing circles

   (d) a system in which the Aboriginal system and the dominant system are interrelated

7. Which of the following is not a feature of Aboriginal traditional justice?

   (a) Laws are formulated by the community through tradition and consensus.

   (b) Traditional spirituality is the foundation of codes of behaviour.

   (c) Personal offences are seen as transgressions against the state.

   (d) Personal offences are seen as transgressions against the victim and the victim's family, and against the community when the peace is threatened.

8. Which of the following is the definition of race paternalism?

   (a) a system under which the dominant group takes authority to supply the needs and regulate the conduct of a minority group

   (b) an insistence that a group adopt the religion of the dominant culture

   (c) an institutionally approved form of racism

   (d) there is no such term

9. Gladue courts are

   (a) mostly in Toronto

   (b) courts where all Crown attorneys, defence counsel, and judges have received training in the concepts of Aboriginal justice

   (c) both (a) and (b)

   (d) courts where all Crown attorneys, defence counsel, and judges are Aboriginal

10. One of the aims of Aboriginal healing lodges is to

    (a) increase the recidivism rate of Aboriginal offenders

    (b) help Aboriginal offenders stay connected to their communities

    (c) formally address the issue of substance abuse

    (d) train Aboriginal people to become elders

APPENDIX 12.1

STARLIGHT TOURS

There are disturbing allegations that are poisoning relations between Saskatchewan's native communities and the Saskatoon police. They are quite astonishing. And if ever proven, they'd show natives are singled out for brutal treatment. The RCMP has been brought in to investigate the deaths of two native men found frozen, and the allegation of another that he was taken by police to the same out-of-the-way spot and simply left to find his way home.

February nights in Saskatoon can mean bone-chilling temperatures. Last month, the body of an Indian man was found near this power plant at the edge of town. Four days later, another discovery: another body found in the same area, frozen solid in this forest of powerlines. Lawrence Wegner was a half-blooded Cree Indian. He was found wearing jeans and a T-shirt.

"What would he be doing so far out of town with no jacket and no shoes? And what would anybody be doing that far out of town, period, in the middle of winter, you know?" one native man says.

Lawrence Wegner was last seen downtown on the streets. He was pounding on doors. Friends say he was high on cocaine. Around midnight, a passerby says he saw a man who looked like Wegner arguing with a police officer before being pushed into a cruiser.

"We used to call it a 'ride in the country' or a 'scenic tour.' A lot of friends I've had have been taken on scenic tours, you know," the man says.

They're also called "Starlight Tours": police driving drunk Indians out of town to walk home and sober up. The stories go back years. Some say it's an urban myth. And it might have stayed that way, except for one Indian man who came forward with a shocking charge, accusing police of dropping him in the same spot where the dead men were found. It was −22 C that night.

It all sounds familiar to Greg. He didn't want his face shown because he's afraid of police. He has a long criminal record, including theft, second degree murder—a charge that was later dropped. Greg says he's been on four starlight tours. Once he was driven 50 kilometres outside of Saskatoon.

"I asked them again, 'Where am I going? Where are you guys taking me?' They said 'Well if you're such a bad ass and you got a lot of steam, if you want to be a trouble maker,' he goes, 'you want to blow off steam.' He goes 'Well, you can blow steam out of town.' So we were driven—I was driven to the Borden bridge.

When I got to the Borden bridge, I was taken out of the car at the back; I'd been handcuffed all the way through the ride. I stood at the back and they took me out of the car. And they told me 'Well,' he says, 'This is how it is.' He says 'You can walk home.' And he said 'When you walk home,' he says, 'if we ever catch you again being a foul-mouthed little asshole, next time we'll drive you further or something else will happen,' he says. So the cuffs were taken off and they had driven away. And I ended up walking home. And it took me about seven hours to get home," Greg says.

"Why didn't you, you know, make a complaint?" Brass asks.

"If I'd launched a complaint, in my mind, it would never have went anywhere. It was just. It's the same thing: it's police investigating police; they're a brotherhood," Greg says.

There are stories like these all over town, but there are no records; no paper trial. Still, at a vigil to remember the dead men, suspicions are now openly traded that police may have deliberately left the Indians to fend for themselves in freezing temperatures. Those fears have only worsened the deep mistrust between police and the native community.

Saskatoon police chief Dave Scott suspended the two cops involved with the alleged drop-off. But he says nothing ties the officers to the deaths of the two men.

"Is this widespread? Are there reasons for me, as chief, to be concerned about the activities of our police officers. At this time, I have no indication of that," Scott says. "I would ask first that you have confidence in me as the chief of police and the leader of this police service, to ensure that a complete investigation will be done properly and I can assure you it will be."

But it was not enough to ease public fears. Five hours later, the whole thing was turned over to the RCMP. They've set up shop in a motel in what's become the largest investigation in the province's history. But restoring the reputation of the Saskatoon force will be a tough sell, especially to aboriginal youth.

Lyle also has had numerous run-ins with cops.

"It gets kind of frustrating you know," he says. "These people are supposed to be watching out for us and protecting us, to serve and protect. And they are out there just hiding behind their badges."

At 15, Lyle got caught stealing bikes. At 17, he says he was taken on a starlight tour: He was drunk, causing a ruckus; police picked him up. Lyle thought he was heading for the drunk tank. Instead, they headed out of town.

"One cop just turned around and he was talking to me, telling me like 'you're a tough guy; you think you're f****** tough.' And I was like 'No, I don't think I am tough. I am just going home. I am going home to go sleep.' And I thought I was going to get beat up by them. Like I started getting scared by that time. They pulled over to this driveway, and it was like driveway into a field. And the passenger cop got out and opened the door.

"And the other cop comes walking around and they got me out of the car. And the younger cop kind of shook me by my jacket. And then they told me like they were like 'You have 20 seconds.' And I was like '20 seconds for what?' And he says you see that field? And he is like run. Run into that field. I got really scared at that time. I didn't ask no questions—I just started running. I would rather have taken a beating then get dropped out there, like, you know. But you know I made it home. At least when you get a beating—I've had lots in my life and like I can take a beating and keep on ticking you know. And get up and walk away from it. Better to be swollen and alive than stiff and dead," Lyle says.

Sakej Henderson is a human rights lawyer who teaches at the Native Law Centre in Saskatoon. Henderson believes starlight tours grew out of police frustration at dealing with repeat offenders—and they weren't always sinister. Indians avoided jail. Police avoided a paper headache.

"It's been common knowledge in the profession, especially the defence bar, that this is what happens. These starlight tours are not new and they've been going on for a very long time. But there's very few times we have to bring it into court because of course when they drop them off, there's no charges laid usually," Henderson says.

"They know it's a solution to going to court—booking paperwork everything else they have to do. So they'll do the shortcut of dropping you off at the end of town or at a distance where you can walk back home and you know, cool off and collect yourself and let the alcohol wear off. Rather than just booking them and filling up the jail and taking all their time doing this stupid administrative paperwork. Well that becomes their normal thinking. But then they start crossing the line by getting a little more daring, or saying I'm going to make him take a longer walk or not paying enough attention to the weather and its changes on the prairies."

Jim Maddin was on the Saskatoon police force for 25 years. Now he sits on city council. "If somebody asked me does this happen—I couldn't look them in the eye and say absolutely no, it's never happened; never will happen. I couldn't say that," Maddin says. "General talk, discussion, locker room, coffee talk, what have you. Reference made to that. I've heard stories of people where this has happened to in other cities. Who's to say it didn't happen here? I can't say it didn't happen, but I can also say that I never observed it personally at all. And at no time when I was in charge of officers on the street, at no time was it ever brought to my attention."

Relations are tested nightly between police and Indians. Maddin says officers are tired of being blamed for the high number of native arrests.

"Officers, I think, can tend to get frustrated with it, sure because they don't tend to see the system actually contributing to the solution of the problem," Maddin says. "It's just a simple temporary fix to pick up the intoxicated person, get them out of the public view or off the public street until such time they're sobered up to better care for themselves and then release them back, only to repeat it again. Sometimes in a very short time—a matter of hours."

There were 2,000 arrests for drunkenness in Saskatoon last year—many on an infamous strip around the Barry and Albany Hotels. The action is testimony to more grim statistics. Natives are charged with half the crimes in the city, and over 70 per cent of inmates in the local prison are Indian. Aboriginals make up about 15 per cent of the population of Saskatoon. That's grist to the mill for the province's native leaders, who say the justice system discriminates against them. Now they've got something else, another case for the RCMP; a death that's resurfaced after 10 years. Another Indian found frozen on the outskirts of town.

Neil Stonechild's body was found in an empty lot at the north side of the city. It was −28 C the night before—one of the coldest of the year. Neil was 17 years old and on the run from a young offender's home with a warrant out for his arrest.

Neil's death was a frightening shock for his friend Jay. He says he immediately suspected foul play and he doesn't want his identity revealed. Jay says the two had been out partying when Jay called it quits and headed home alone. Then a police cruiser rolled up.

"The police stopped me and the first question was, is they asked me if I knew this guy," Jay says. "Neil was in the back of the police car with his face cut open, bleeding. And they asked me if I knew this guy and I said no. Why I said no is because I was on the run from the law and I didn't wanna be back in the police car with him, you know.

"And Neil was screaming and swearing at me and telling—he was saying 'Okay, help me man, these guys are gonna kill me.' He was swearing about a lot of different thing, but that's what struck out most in my mind is that he said that. And you know right at that moment it really scared me, because his face was cut open pretty good.

That was the last time he saw Neil alive. The frozen body was found five days later. The memory still bothers him. Jay says he made two reports to police, but nothing came of it. Police won't comment on the case now. At the time, police concluded Neil died of exposure—that he was heading to a nearby prison to turn himself in.

"That is so far-fetched, I just don't believe it. Neil was wanted by the police. He had more than a few drinks. And he was wanted by the police. And I didn't understand why they had let him go," Jay says.

Fred Gopher is chief of the Saulteaux Reserve near Saskatoon. He doesn't think the RCMP investigation will resolve much. Starlight tours are only part of the problem.

"Our own people have suffered enough. And I think the justice system has not done what it was supposed to do for our people," Gopher says. "I'd like to see some kind of solution with our people to be involved and look at the whole thing, look at the bigger picture. Why is our people overpopulating the incarceration institutions? Look at the employment factor on our reserve here—just 90 per cent on welfare. There is very little hope for our people. It's the whole system."

The scandal has hit the reserve hard. One of the dead men is buried there. And the man who alleges he was forced out by police at the power plant also has family here. Chief Gopher says it was difficult to persuade him to go public.

"'Well,' he says, 'nobody is going to believe him.' And I don't blame him for thinking that way. It will be just an allegation; he's just making it up. He's another drunken Indian. There's some good cops out there and I believe there's some cops that probably took advantage of the situation. Nobody's talking about it. Nobody's doing nothing about it."

"I think that the Saskatoon police service has, in fact, made some significant progress in dealing with aboriginal youth, especially through the efforts of the aboriginal relations officer that we have here," Maddin says. "Police have, in fact, been essentially reaching out to aboriginal youth to build better relationships, better bonds and a greater degree of trust."

That's something many Indians scoff at. Since the deaths of the two men, native leaders say they've received over 250 phone calls reporting similar stories across the province. Now they want a public inquiry to examine the entire justice system.

The two deaths have pushed race relations in the province to a critical point—and it could get worse. Resentment towards police is highest among aboriginal youth, the largest and fastest growing part of the population. Many get caught in a life on the street, on a collision course with police and prison, says Sakej Henderson.

"It's not gonna stop. That's what the over-incarceration figures tell us. If you're running about 60, 70 per cent of aboriginal inmates, they are gonna organize themselves into gangs. That's what they learn in jail, is that they have to unite. There may be two or three factions, but there are Indian gangs that are coming up and taking the place of family and protectors and political organizations for them," Henderson says.

"With a majority of our people as teenagers, we have all the problems of a teenage nation. But they're not real receptive to listening to us that are over 50 or so. That we didn't solve the problems; now they have to solve them."

"A dead Indian is just a good Indian to them, I guess. It's all I can figure," Lyle says.

For Lyle and others, all this talk about starlight tours has only led to more bitterness. And the worst part: so many saw it coming.

"I think with the two deaths, I think everyone saw themselves there," Henderson says. "I think we all saw ourselves complacent with this. We've all known about it, but now it's a crisis that's unfolded; that somehow the routine system has become a deadly system and there's now dead people in the field, and we have to find out why. And we have a whole backlog of cases that's never been solved, and now looks suspiciously similar to an alleged police drop off and we have to get to the bottom of it."

The RCMP won't say when its investigation will be completed, but there are many who aren't waiting.

Source: CBC News (2004, July 2). Starlight tours. CBC News in Depth: Aboriginal Canadians. *CBC.ca*. http://www.cbc.ca/news/background/aboriginals/ starlighttours.html.

APPENDIX 12.2

COMMUNITY HOLISTIC CIRCLE HEALING

INTRODUCTION

The area of Manitoba in which Hollow Water is located is one hundred fifty miles northeast of Winnipeg and has a combined population of approximately one thousand people. The people live in four neighbouring communities (Manigotogan, Aghaming and Seymourville which are Métis settlements, and Hollow Water is a status Indian Reserve).

In 1984, a Resource Team was formed to work on healing and development in these four communities. It was comprised of political leaders, service providers from all the agencies working in the area, and a strong base of community volunteers. In essence, the Resource Group had two vital functions. First, it was the core group of those people within the population who are on a healing journey themselves and are determined to help the rest of the people to undertake their own journeys, so that the communities will be safe and healthy for their children and grandchildren. Second, the Resource Group constituted the integrated program effort across all disciplines and sectors (such as education, politics, health, religion and economy) that is leading a sustained long-term community health development process.

The first disclosure of sexual abuse came in 1986. Before that time, no one talked about it. When Hollow Water people looked at their community before 1986, alcohol and drug abuse loomed large as a problem, as did unemployment and a need to reroute the education of their children in the cultural ways of their people. At that point there was no turning back. It became very clear that there had been a great deal of sexual abuse going on for many years, but that talking about it was taboo. Indeed, most of the members of the Resource Group had somehow been affected by it. They gradually discovered that as the blanket of alcohol abuse was removed, many of the people were holding on to acute anger, hurt and dysfunctional behaviour patterns that were related to sexual abuse or to some other violation that had been done to them in their past. It became increasingly clear that if the community was to ever succeed in the political and economic realms they had a lot of personal healing work to do.

What followed was a very active period of learning and healing. The Resource Group consulted with many groups across North America who were dealing with similar issues and by 1988 had set up their own training program called S.A.F.E. (Self-Awareness For Everyone), modelled after the New Directions Training being offered at that time by the community of Alkali Lake. This step allowed them to bring this type of training to as many of their community members who were willing to begin a journey of personal healing and development.

One of the by-products of the opening up of trust and communication produced by the personal growth training was a dramatic increase in the number of sexual abuse disclosures. The Resource Team soon realized that there was a fundamental conflict between what the justice system does with offenders and what the community needed to do. What was actually needed, they realized, was a new negotiated relationship with all the agencies who have a stake in dealing with sexual abuse cases, which are:

- child protection workers (if the victim is a child, which they most often are)
- police
- Crown attorney and judges
- mental health workers

Other primary stakeholders in the process needing a great deal of love, caring, and skilled attention include:

- the victim,
- the victim's family,
- the victimizer (or abuser),
- the victimizer's family, and
- other community members and community agencies affected by the abuse.

The new negotiated relationship would have to spell out a strict set of procedures about what to do at the time of disclosure and how a disclosure would be dealt with by the courts to allow for the healing process to take place. A basic system and agreements were worked out that have since been further developed and refined. This model was named Community Holistic Circle Healing (CHCH), and works basically as follows:

1. An intervention team consisting of representatives of CHCH, Child and Family Services, Band Constable conducts an initial investigation to find out what really happened. The victim's story is gently and lovingly recorded. The victim's safety and, as well, the presence of reliable and trusted people to support the victim through the crisis is ensured.

2. Once it has been determined (beyond reasonable doubt) that abuse has taken place, the abuser is confronted and charged. At this stage, the combined power of the law and the community are used to force the abuser to break through his or her own denial to admit to the abuse, and to agree

to participate in a healing process. The abuser's choices are a) to plead guilty and then to be sentenced to probation requiring full cooperation with the healing process, or b) to be abandoned to the courts, with jail as the probable outcome.

3. If the abuser agrees to the healing road, he or she then begins a three to five year journey, which ends in restitution and reconciliation between the abuser and the victim, the victim's family and the whole community. When an abuser commits him- or herself to the healing process, the CHCH team asks the court for a minimum of four months to assess the authenticity of the commitment. When abusers agree to take the healing option, they usually do so out of fear of going to jail. It is therefore important to determine whether or not they are actually ready to participate fully in the healing process. During the four-month period, abusers are asked to undergo a process of looking deeply into themselves and really breaking through the denial to admit to themselves and others what they have done and how their actions have hurt others. This process involves four circles.

The first series of circles is held in which the person is asked to share what they have done. Often they can only admit bits and pieces, and they try to avoid talking about the details. Gradually the abuser is able to admit everything, and is helped to feel the love and support of the circle. It is made clear that the goal of the healing process is to help the abuser to become a healthy and productive community member. During this time the abuser also must work with a sexual abuse counsellor once a week. This process also can involve psychologists or other helpers. They assess the abuser's willingness to fully engage in the healing process.

The second circle requires the abuser to bring his or her nuclear family together, to tell them what he or she has done, and to deal with the family's response. The third circle repeats the second circle process with the family of origin (i.e. parents, grandparents, aunts, uncles, etc.). The fourth circle is the sentencing circle. In this circle, abusers must tell the whole community (represented by whoever attends the circle) what they have done and what steps they have already taken on their healing journey. CHCH staff say that if a person goes through all of these steps, they are then convinced of his or her commitment to the healing process.

In all, the CHCH process for dealing with abusers has thirteen steps as follows:

1. Disclosures
2. Establish safety for the victim
3. Confront the victimizer
4. Support the spouse or parent of the victimizer
5. Support the families that are affected
6. A meeting between the Assessment Team and the RCMP
7. Circles with victimizers
8. Circles with the victim and the victimizer
9. Prepare the victim's family for the Sentencing Circle
10. Prepare the victimizer's family for the Sentencing Circle

11. A special gathering for the Sentencing Circle

12. A sentencing review

13. A cleansing ceremony

It is important to point out this model does not only focus on the abuser. Victims receive a great deal of care, love and skilled therapeutic attention in dealing with the trauma of their abuse. However, we believe that one of the unique features of Hollow Water CHCH model is the way it brings the Canadian legal system into the circle of the community in order to creatively use that system to help heal the community. Another feature of the CHCH model is a strong emphasis on the ownership of the abuse and the accountability required of abusers. This is a significant outcome in terms of the effectiveness of Aboriginal healing models and approaches.

Today Hollow Water enjoys a fairly high level of sobriety (around eighty percent) and they are actively dealing with the sexual abuse issue.

Source: Bushie, B. (1999, August 7). *Community holistic circle healing.* International Institute for Restorative Practices.
http://www.iirp.edu/article_detail.php?article_id=NDc0.

APPENDIX 12.3

A COMMUNITY FIGHTS GANGS AND GUNS

THE PÊ SÂKÂSTÊW HEALING LODGE

In an effort to address the need for a more culturally specific approach to helping Aboriginal Canadians rehabilitate after becoming involved in criminal behaviour, the Correctional Service of Canada (www.csc-scc.gc.ca) constructed eight healing lodges across the country, including the Pê Sâkâstêw Healing Lodge in Hobbema, Alberta. All of the healing lodges strive to embrace Aboriginal traditions in an effort to allow the inmates to reconnect with their roots and find a way out of the criminal justice system and back into society. The Pê Sâkâstêw Healing Lodge is a 40-bed, minimum-security facility that has been serving Aboriginal inmates since 1997.

Counselors at the Pê Sâkâstêw Healing Lodge find they are teaching many Aboriginal inmates their traditions for the first time. Most inmates arrive without a real knowledge of their social, historical, and spiritual roots. The teaching of traditions takes the form of practical participation in Aboriginal rituals in what has been called the "In Search of Your Warrior" (ISYW) program. Pê Sâkâstêw Program Director Sharon Bell explains the rationale behind the program: "ISYW was created to treat traumatic experiences, to heal the scars of abuse, to get rid of the blinding rage and anger that inmates carry deep inside. Some of them, for example, are suffering from the effect that residential schools have had on their lives or on their parents'—residential schools established by the Canadian government that in the past aimed to assimilate Aboriginal people into white society. The scars from abuse and the loss of identity can have a terrible impact on a human being. That is why some of them strongly feel the need to refocus on themselves, to get back in touch with their real selves, to be able to face the future with hope."

So Bell and her staff help inmates to participate in Aboriginal rituals like the cleansing ceremonies known as smudging. In a smudging ceremony, those gathered form a circle. Sweetgrass is burned and carried around the circle. All participants wash themselves in the smoke of the burning grass, drawing the smoke toward them with their hands. After the smudging, inmates take turns holding an eagle's feather and giving voice to their thoughts and feelings while everyone gathered listens intently. This is just one of 75 healing activities that inmates can take part in at the healing lodge.

There are six units in the Pê Sâkâstêw Healing Lodge. The units are designed to capture some of the main teachings of Aboriginal spirituality. Circular patterns represent influence, unity, and social interaction. If you were to fly over the lodge, each unit is shaped like an eagle, which symbolizes the embracing of life and the effort to ward off evil. The colours used on the outside of each unit represent the all-pervasive presence of the Creator, with red representing the east, yellow representing the south, blue representing the west and white representing the north.

Overall, the Pê Sâkâstêw Healing Lodge provides a unique approach to rehabilitation. It strives to embrace the ideals of Aboriginal spirituality and give the inmates a sense of their own traditions. While people working at the lodge recognize that the program is not a cure for the Aboriginal community's ills, it does bring hope to a few of the community members who need help the most.

Source: CBC News (2008, November). A community fights gangs and guns. *CBC News in Review*, 39. http://newsinreview.cbclearning.ca/wp-content/uploads/2008/12/nov-08-gangs.pdf.

Glossary

Aboriginal peoples' rights
the rights of Canada's Aboriginal peoples to preserve their culture, identity, customs, traditions, and languages, and to maintain any special rights that they have currently or may acquire in the future

acculturation
process of change in the cultural patterns of an ethnic group as a result of contact with other ethnic groups

agnostic
a person who believes it impossible to know God or to determine how the universe began

animism
the belief that non-human objects have souls that survive death

anti-racism training
training that addresses issues of racism and related systems of social oppression and that involves an action-oriented, educational, and political strategy for institutional and systemic change

assimilation
absorption of groups of different cultures into the main culture

assimilation ideology
ideology that expects people of diversity to relinquish their culture and linguistic identity and adopt the culture of the host state

assimilationist
intolerant of immigrants' heritage culture, demanding that they relinquish the culture and adopt the host culture

atheist
a person who professes no particular religion and does not believe in a higher power

authoritarianism
policy of demanding obedience to authority

bipolar disorder
a mood disorder, previously known as manic depression, that involves emotional swings between depression and mania

British North America Act
a statute enacted on March 29, 1867, by the British Parliament providing for the confederation of Canada

Canadian Charter of Rights and Freedoms
the part of the Canadian Constitution that protects the rights and freedoms that are deemed essential to maintaining a free and democratic society and a united country

Canadian Human Rights Act
the federal statute that prohibits discrimination based on race, national or ethnic origin, colour, age, sex, marital status, family status, disability, sexual orientation, or conviction for an offence for which a pardon has been granted

Canadian Human Rights Commission
the federal body responsible for investigating and adjudicating complaints concerning violations of the *Canadian Human Rights Act*

child abuse
physical and psychological abuse of children below the age of 14

child sexual abuse
the sexual exploitation of children under the age of 18

civic ideology
ideology that subscribes to multiculturalism ideology principles but does not support state funding to maintain and promote ethnocultural diversity

claims arising from Aboriginal title
claims based on the allegation that lands traditionally used and occupied by Aboriginal people were never surrendered to the Crown by Aboriginal people

claims arising from the surrender for sale of reserve land
claims occurring when First Nations seek compensation for, or the return of, land that had been surrendered to the Crown for sale for the benefit of the band

claims relating to the fulfillment of terms of treaties
claims that are usually a result of disagreement between the Crown and First Nations about the size and location of reserves set aside by treaties

community policing principles
principles that are associated with the police services approach and with the mandate of policing for and with communities

comprehensive land claims
claims to territory that are not covered by treaty or land cession agreements

constructive discrimination
a kind of discrimination that may not be obviously discriminatory and may seem based on a reasonable criterion, but that effectively excludes, restricts, or favours some people contrary to human rights laws

covenant chain
first agreement entered into between the Five Nations of the Iroquois and the British; a clear recognition by both sides that their political systems would remain separate even as their systems of trade and alliance bound them

cross-cultural training
training that prepares an individual for living in another country and for relating to people of diverse cultures in his or her own country

cultural awareness training
a formal, short-term program that prepares police to deal more effectively with cultural issues, either in general or in terms of a particular culture

cultural genocide
the deliberate and systematic destruction of the culture, tradition, language, and ways of being of a specific cultural group

culture
the patterns of behaviour and behavioural consequences that are shared and transmitted among members of a particular society

delusions
ideas that have no basis in reality; a common symptom of schizophrenia

democratic rights
rights to vote and to run in an election and the assurance that no government has the right to continue to hold power indefinitely without seeking a new mandate from the electorate

depression
a mood disorder characterized by extended periods of despair and hopelessness and a lack of interest in life

discrimination
a process by which a person is deprived of equal access to privileges and opportunities available to others because of prejudice

diversity
the variety of human qualities among different people and groups

diversity awareness training
training in how to be culturally competent so that the trainee can deal more effectively with diversity issues in all their forms

diversity competency
possessing the cultural knowledge and understanding to serve diverse communities effectively

diversity equity
a value according to which there are no superior or inferior cultural groups

elder abuse
the physical, sexual, emotional, or psychological abuse or neglect, or the financial exploitation, of an older person by a caregiver, staff member in an institution, or a criminal

employment equity
the principle, defined in Canadian law by the *Employment Equity Act*, according to which employers are required to increase the representation of women, people with disabilities, Aboriginal peoples, and visible minorities

equality rights
the rights of all Canadians, regardless of race, national or ethnic origin, colour, religion, sex, age, or mental or physical disability, to be equal before the law and to enjoy equal protection and benefit of the law

ethnic group
group of individuals with a shared sense of peoplehood based on presumed shared socio-cultural experiences and/or similar characteristics

ethnicity
the culture of origin with which an individual or group identifies within a multicultural context

ethnist ideology
ideology that expects people of diversity to assimilate, but the state defines which groups should assimilate and thus which ones are not rightful members of the state

exclusionary
intolerant of immigrants' heritage culture and of immigration in general

family violence
the different forms of abuse, mistreatment, or neglect that adults or children may experience in their intimate, kinship, extended, or dependent relationships

fiduciary responsibility
the legal or ethical responsibility to manage something, usually money or property, in trust for another person (or people) and act in their best interests

formication
a hallucinatory experience, sometimes undergone by cocaine users, that involves feeling that insects or snakes are crawling over or under one's skin

freedom from discrimination
the standard set out in part I of the Ontario *Human Rights Code*, granting freedom from discrimination with respect to services, goods, facilities, accommodation, contracts, employment, and vocational associations, and freedom from sexual solicitation in the workplace and by those in a position of power

fundamental freedoms
freedom of conscience and religion; freedom of thought, belief, opinion, and expression, including freedom of the press and other media of communication; freedom of peaceful assembly; and freedom of association

gender identity
a term that applies to people, mostly transgenderists and transsexuals, whose self-perception is in some way at variance with their birth-assigned gender; involves self-image, physical and biological appearance, behaviour, and gender-related conduct

gendered apartheid
a policy of segregation, followed in certain religions, based on a belief that women are inferior to men and constitute a subordinate class of human being

guiding spirits
personal spirits that are believed, by Aboriginal peoples, to protect individuals from bringing trouble to themselves or to their communities

hallucinations
delusional sensory experiences that may be disturbing to the person having them; a common symptom of schizophrenia

harassment
unwelcome comments or conduct toward another person

homelessness
the condition of having no fixed, regular, and adequate address

host community
comprises groups of people who have the power and influence to shape attitudes toward the remaining groups in society

Indian Act
a statute created in 1876 to consolidate all policies aimed at the administration of Indian populations in Canada and giving the federal government exclusive jurisdiction over Indians and reserves

Indian agent
a federal employee of Indian Affairs in charge of administration on reserves

Indian Residential Schools Settlement Agreement (IRSSA)
agreement by which Aboriginal people who could prove their attendance in the residential schools became eligible to receive a "common experience payment" (CEP)

indigenization
the incorporation of indigenous people into a social system, such as the justice system

integration
embrace of the host culture of settlement and continued maintenance of culture of origin

integrationist
supportive of immigrants' adopting features of the host culture while maintaining aspects of their heritage culture

intellectual disability
a condition characterized by significantly subaverage intelligence, significant limitation in adaptive functioning, and onset before the age of 18 years

Khalsa
the collective body of Sikhs who have undergone a baptism ceremony signifying dedication to the principles of Sikhism

kinesics
physical communication, including look and appearance, eye contact, facial expressions, posture, body movements, and touching

Koran
the holy text of Islam

legal rights
the basic legal protections granted to all Canadian citizens in their dealings with the state and justice system

mandatory arrest policy
a policy dictating that arrest must take place in family violence cases

mania
a mood disorder characterized by an emotional high, agitation, and impulsivity

marginalization
simultaneous rejection of the culture of origin and the host culture

mediative policy
a non-arrest police approach to family violence calls

mental illness
a group of disabilities marked by disturbances in thinking, feeling, and relating

misattribution
the misinterpretation of a message or behaviour; a common occurrence in cross-cultural communication

mobility rights
the freedom to enter, remain in, or leave the country, and to live and seek employment anywhere in Canada

monotheistic
a religion that worships a single god

mood disorders
mental disorders, including depression and bipolar disorder, that affect a person's mood

multicultural heritage
the unique and constitutionally enshrined character of Canadian society

multiculturalism
a policy relating to or designed for a combination of several distinct cultures

multiculturalism ideology
ideology that recognizes and supports people of diversity in maintaining or promoting their diversity, providing that their practices do not clash with the laws of the nation

official languages
English and French, as confirmed by the Charter, which guarantees that the federal government will serve members of the public in the official language of their choice

Ontario *Human Rights Code*
the Ontario statute that protects the dignity and worth of every person and provides for equal rights and opportunities without discrimination that is contrary to law

Ontario Human Rights Commission
the provincial body responsible for investigating and adjudicating complaints about violations of the Ontario *Human Rights Code*

Ontario *Police Services Act*
a statute requiring that the police services provided throughout Ontario will reflect the safeguards enshrined in the *Canadian Charter of Rights and Freedoms* and the Ontario *Human Rights Code*

paralanguage
the non-verbal features of speech, such as tone, loudness, speed, and the use of silence

paternalism
a system in which a dominant person or institution assumes authority for supplying the needs and regulating the conduct of those under its control

police force approach
the approach to policing that emphasizes the crime-control, enforcement aspect of the job, on the assumption that police need to be hard on crime

police services approach
the approach to policing that emphasizes the helpful, supportive aspect of the role, with a focus on problem solving, crime prevention, and partnership between police and communities

prejudice
an adverse judgment or opinion formed beforehand with little or no knowledge or experience or examination of the facts; a predetermined preference, idea, or bias

pro-arrest policy
a policy that favours arrest in family violence cases but leaves the decision to the discretion of the officers

proxemics
the conventions surrounding the physical distance between people

psychosis
a form of mental disturbance that involves a person's losing touch with reality

race
a classification based on ancestry or origin as indicated by physical characteristics

race relations training
training in how to deal more effectively with race-related issues, on the assumption that racism is a social disease that can be cured through education

recidivism
the process of relapsing into crime

refugee policy
humanitarian policy, based on the United Nations definition of a refugee, that assesses eligibility for entry to a country based on refugee status

reincarnation
the belief that the soul, after the body's death, comes back to life in a new form

religion
a spiritual belief system that addresses matters of ultimate reality, such as life and death, and instructs people in how to live

religious beliefs
tenets of particular faiths

religious practices
concrete expressions of religious beliefs

residential schools
church-run, government-funded residential schools for Aboriginal children designed to prepare them for life in white society

Royal Commission on Aboriginal Peoples (RCAP)
commission established in 1991 to investigate the issues facing Aboriginal people in Canada

Royal Proclamation of 1763
the cornerstone of Aboriginal land claims today; has been called the "Magna Carta of Indian Rights" and has been deemed by the courts to have the "force of a statute which has never been repealed"

schizophrenia
a serious mental illness marked by a breakdown in the connection between thoughts, feelings, and actions, and often accompanied by strong psychotic disturbances and delusions

scrip
a one-time payment issued to Métis to discharge treaty rights

segregationist
opposed to immigrants and other cultures, preferring that immigrants return to their countries of origin

seigniorial farms
a system in which a man, usually a soldier, was granted land in the name of France

separation
individual rejection of the host culture and maintenance of the culture of origin

settlement patterns
the variety of ways people physically establish themselves in a country, whether born there or as immigrants

sexual orientation
a person's settled sexual preference, whether heterosexual, gay or lesbian, or bisexual

Shabbath
Saturday, prescribed in Jewish law as the day of rest

Sixties Scoop
the practice of removing Aboriginal children from their communities and placing them in foster care or putting them up for adoption in non-Aboriginal homes

specific land claims
claims that relate to specific misdealings of the Crown with relation to land or resources

spousal abuse
violence or mistreatment suffered at the hands of a marital, common-law, or same-sex partner

stereotype
conventional, formulaic, and usually oversimplified conceptions that falsify reality through over-generalization and strip their subjects of individuality

substance-related disorders
mental disorders caused by substance dependence and abuse, and by substance withdrawal

suicide
a consequence of mood disorder, with suicidal mood disorder taking the possible forms of ideation, threat, gesture, attempt, and completed suicide

systemic discrimination

the enforcement of laws and the enforcement of policies that are inherently prejudicial to a group or culture

Tao

the energy source that flows through all life, according to Taoist belief

thought disorders

ideas and speech make sense to a schizophrenic person but not to others

treaty

an agreement between two states that has been formally concluded and ratified

values

standards or principles; ideas about the worth or importance of certain qualities, especially those accepted by a particular group

visible minority

individuals, other than Aboriginal peoples, who are non-Caucasian in race or non-white in colour

white machismo culture

a culture that values white skin colour, masculinity, and hierarchy while devaluing non-whites, women, and non-traditional sexual orientation

Index